Shaping a National Culture

The Philadelphia Experience, 1750–1800

EDITED BY

Catherine E. Hutchins

Henry Francis du Pont Winterthur Museum
Winterthur, Delaware

FIRST EDITION.

The text of this book is composed in Electra LH Regular

Library of Congress Cataloging-in-Publication Data

Shaping a national culture : the Philadelphia experience, 1750–1800 /
edited by Catherine E. Hutchins.—1st ed.

(Paper): ISBN 0-912724-27-7
(Cloth): ISBN 0-912724-30-7

1. Philadelphia (Pa.)—Civilization. I. Hutchins, Catherine E.

F158.44.S48 1994

974.8'11—dc20 94-22570

CIP

Contents

Contents

Preface

Catherine E. Hutchins

By 1750 Philadelphia, the capital of William Penn's colony of Pennsylvania, had become the largest and most influential city in British North America. During the ensuing decades it grew financially and politically, and by the 1770s and 1780s it was the center of the new nation. Pennsylvania's relatively central geographical position and Philadelphia's thriving mercantile economy allowed the populace to forge national and international ties. The city's cosmopolitan atmosphere encouraged a diversity of cultural and social activities, including the Quaker-led drive for the abolition of slavery and a widespread tolerance of free blacks. Thus Philadelphia proved to be fertile ground for the seeds of nationalism. Then in the waning years of the century, the city seemingly moved away from the opportunity to lead the fledgling country and turned inward. Or so the collective wisdom goes.

The sixteen papers in this volume explore specific aspects of Philadelphia in the last half of the eighteenth century. The authors—historians, museum educators and curators, and material culture specialists—were chosen because they bring very different perspectives and techniques to the study of written and artifactual records. Their analyses of social, economic, religious, and aesthetic developments test and quite often refute long-held assumptions about the quality of life in Philadelphia—political, economic, religious, and cultural. What we learn most emphatically is that Philadelphia was far from a placid, unified city in this half-century. Debates stretched across economic, social, and political lines, and the effects of the debates ranged from enervation to energization. Social and economic divisions extended in many directions, changing from issue to issue and year to year. The discrepancies that the historians and the culturalists illuminate in their analyses of Philadelphia provide answers, but they also raise a host of new questions. Only by using techniques and methods drawn from both historical and cultural disciplines can we reach a more holistic understanding of culture, Philadelphia, and the move toward nationalism that began in the latter part of the eighteenth century.

Double Vision

The Philadelphia Cityscape and Perceptions of It

Beth A. Twiss-Garrity

The cityscape of Philadelphia between 1750 and 1800 presented visitors with a changing face built on an unchanging grid system of streets. For many reasons, ranging from the city plan itself to the city's positions as one of the largest in the British Empire and as the political center of the colonies and early United States for most of the fifty-year period, people who lived outside Philadelphia endowed the city and its landscape with symbolic intent. Their descriptions and evaluations of the cityscape, consequently, were prejudiced by their attitudes about the symbol. A reading of travelogues, diaries, and letters shows that the cityscape fell from unanimous favor before the American Revolution to a more limited appreciation after the war.

Previously historians of Philadelphia have tended to examine its political, economic, and social history rather than its landscape. Those who have dealt with the cityscape have concentrated on the story of the city's founding and the inception of its plan. Few have considered the cityscape as an entrée into the thoughts and attitudes of people living in the eighteenth century and how their attitudes affected the way they saw Philadelphia.[1] Travelogues, diaries, and letters offer a way to discover these attitudes and perceptions. Often used in the past as illustrations to an urban history text, these types of literature are a unique source of information for uncovering personal and cultural viewpoints.

Between 1750 and 1800 at least twenty-two travelogues, diaries, and letters written by nonresident Philadelphians described and judged the cityscape—one by a Latin American, two by Americans, and nineteen by Europeans, of whom thirteen were British.[2] The authors' reasons for writing varied from personal notes to letters for friends to publications. Some authors, therefore, may not only have been expressing personal opinion but incorporating what they thought their audience's needs or viewpoints were. While each travelogue, diary, or letter must be examined for any bias inherent in its creation, as a group they can be used to ascertain commonly held cultural ideas, to document the symbol of Philadelphia as expressed in its cityscape, and to chart the changing attitudes toward the city because of the symbol.

The one physical feature on which the writers focused during the fifty-year period was the city plan. It seemed to typify for them all that was good or bad about Philadelphia. While visiting Philadelphia in 1774, Lord Adam Gordon, an officer of the British military stationed in the West Indies, opined: "The city . . . is perhaps one of the wonders of the world, if you consider its size, the Number of Inhabitants, the regularity of its Streets, their great breadth and length, their cutting one another all at right Angles, their Spacious publick and private buildings, Quays, and Docks, . . . one will not hesitate to Call it the first Town in America, but one that bids fair to rival almost any in Europe." About forty years later British diplomat Sir Augustus John Foster complained: "There is nothing surely so unfavorable to architectural ornament as long lines of broad streets cutting each other at right angles! . . . How much more beautiful is a city where no such regularity prevails!"[3] As these quotations illustrate, attitudes toward the plan had altered, although the plan itself had not.

Surveyor Thomas Holme drew up the city plan in 1683 at the request of proprietor William Penn. Holme's plan accommodated Penn's ideas for the city, the geography of the area, and prior claims by earlier settlers. Penn wanted the city on land that was healthy and well drained and where the rivers were deep enough to allow ships to unload at river's edge. The city was to serve as a port for the agricultural backcountry, and all market and government facilities were to be located on a wharf stretching out into the river.[4]

When Holme arrived in Pennsylvania in 1683, he found that most unclaimed areas were too swampy to build a city on. He also recognized that Penn's plan for populating the colony with European emigrants seeking civil and religious freedom would encourage those land speculators among the initial settlers to subdivide promptly any large city lots into irregular plots. To prevent this, Holme drew on his knowledge and experience and designed a plan that reflected his idea of what a city should be.

During the third quarter of the seventeenth century, Holme had been involved in surveying English military towns in Ireland, towns based on the grid system used in military camps. These towns had a central square for market and government buildings, and wide streets intersecting at right angles created thoroughfares for moving goods and supplies. Holme also probably was aware of the 1609 grid plan of Thomas Phillips for Londonderry and the 1666 plan, which incorporated parks into a grid plan, put forth by Richard Newcourt for rebuilding London.

Holme's plan for Philadelphia was a rectangular grid in which the town spanned the two-mile east-west distance between the Delaware and Schuylkill rivers and stretched one mile north-south (fig. 1). The twenty north-south streets were numbered sequentially beginning at

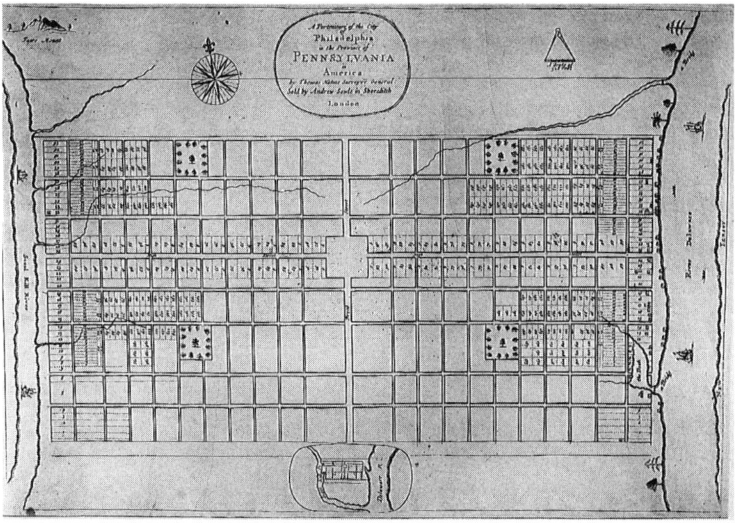

Figure 1. Thomas Holme, A *Portraiture of the City of Philadelphia in the Province of Pennsylvania in America*, London, 1683. Engraving on paper; H. 11 3/4", W. 17 3/4". (Library Company of Philadelphia.)

the Delaware River, and seven east-west streets were named after trees. Broad and High streets, the central axes, were to be 100 feet wide, wider than any street in London at the time. At their intersection Holme planned a ten-acre square for market and government buildings. In each of the four quadrants of the grid, Holme designated an eight-acre square for recreational use. Lots near the Delaware River and along main thoroughfares were large, while smaller half-acre lots were located along side streets. All structures were to be built in the center of each lot to retard the spread of fire, thus giving rise to the appellation "greene countrie towne."

Holme's plan served the city well, although settlement did not follow the anticipated pattern. During the next century the city developed along only the Delaware River rather than both rivers. By 1750 settlement ranged to Holme's northern and southern borders but extended west only to Seventh Street. It reached to Eighth Street by 1770, Ninth by 1800, and Broad by 1830. The slow physical expansion was accompanied by rapid population growth. Land developers subdivided even the half-acre lots and erected new structures for necessary housing and business. Alleys were cut through these blocks so that narrow lots could be carved out. Nonetheless, Holme's grid survived, its river-to-river configuration often illustrating maps long before the streets were laid out or lots sold (fig. 2).[5]

By 1750 the city built on the grid exhibited the mark of later inhabitants who "improved" its physical character in keeping with changes in technology and city planning. During the 1750s and 1760s, at the prompting of Benjamin Franklin, streets were paved with stone and brick sidewalks laid along them. Wooden gutters separated the two. Streetlights, water pumps, and wooden posts that prevented carriages and wagons from running up onto the sidewalk punctuated the streetscape at regular intervals (fig. 3).[6] Overall, throughout the eighteenth century Philadelphia presented the traveler with uniformity. Small wooden buildings and church spires punctuated blocks of two- and three-story red-brick row houses.

During the last decade of the eighteenth century, the new architectural designs of neoclassicism were introduced in the city in a few public buildings and palatial residential structures. Their marble facades with columned porticos created a new sort of streetscape with depth and shadowing compared to the flat facades of the brick row houses. Also in

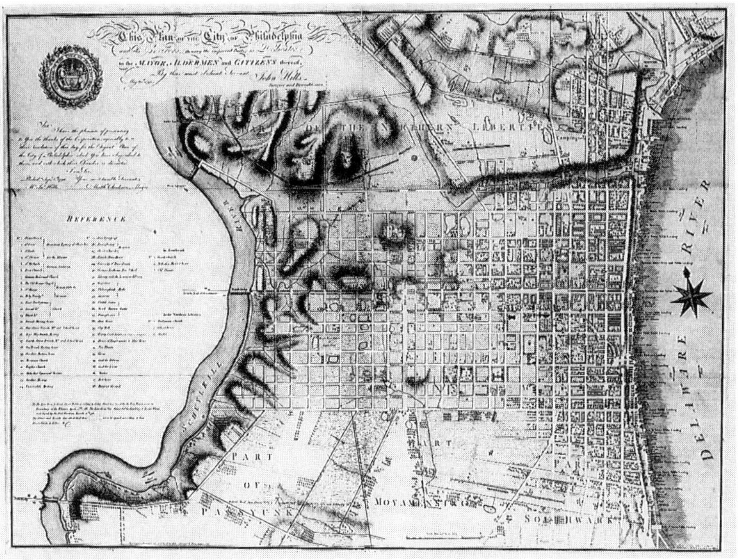

Figure 2. John Hills, *The Plan of the City of Philadelphia and Its Environs, Shewing the Improved Parts*, Philadelphia, 1796. Engraving on paper; H. 27″, W. 37″. (Library Company of Philadelphia.)

the 1790s one of the squares that Holme had intended as a park was developed as such. In 1794 the square in the southeastern quadrant that had served as a burial ground for paupers was finally redeveloped as a park. The northeastern square, however, continued to be used as a cemetery by the German Reformed Church until 1835, and the two western squares were in undeveloped areas well into the nineteenth century. The center square, planned to be a government center, was developed instead as the site of a water-pumping station.[7]

Beautification projects included the planting of trees to help establish parks and promenades. In 1785 British citizen Samuel Vaughan had the statehouse yard landscaped with trees and paths. While there had always been trees, particularly native sycamores, along the edges of some streets, in 1794 poplar trees were planted in the southeastern quadrant square and along streets near Delaware River (fig. 4).[8]

Visitors to Philadelphia often commented on the cityscape. Outsiders generally were more impressed with the city in the third quarter

Figure 3. William Birch and Son, *Arch Street, with the Second Presbyterian Church*, Philadelphia, 1799. Engraving on paper; H. 8 1/2", W. 11 1/4". (Library Company of Philadelphia.)

of the century than the fourth. In the earlier period they predicted a great future for the city and often compared it favorably with metropolitan centers in Europe. Swedish botanist Peter Kalm, who came through Philadelphia in 1750, typifies that response: "[The city's] fine appearance, good regulations, agreeable location, natural advantages, trade, riches and power are by no means inferior to those of any, even the most ancient towns in Europe."[9]

Travelers complimented the plan and the architecture as "regular" and "uniform." They often termed the public improvements, like paved and lighted streets, as progressive. As Rev. Andrew Burnaby of England put it: "The streets are laid out with great regularity in parallel lines, intersected by others at right angles, and handsomely built: on each side there is a pavement of broad stones for foot passengers; and in most of them a causeway in the middle for carriages. Upon dark nights it is well

Figure 4. William Birch and Thomas Birch, *High Street, from Ninth Street*, Philadelphia, 1799. Engraving on paper; H. 8 1/2", W. 11 1/4". (Library Company of Philadelphia.)

lighted, and watched by a patrol: there are many fair houses, and public edifices in it."[10]

During the last quarter of the century, attitudes toward the plan were changing. In 1788 French journalist and humanitarian Jean-Pierre Brissot de Warville exclaimed: "May God grant that these projected streets remain forever imaginary! If they should someday be lined with houses, it will be a misfortune for the charitable institutions, for Pennsylvania, for the whole of America." Visitors disparaged the grid plan and the architecture of the city as boringly regular. Robert Honyman, an English doctor who served both the English and American militaries, spoke for more than himself when he wrote in 1775, "I cannot see that extraordinary beauty & regularity in the streets and buildings that is so much boasted of."[11]

Although some visitors did applaud the new neoclassical buildings, in the last quarter of the century most spent more time commenting on the natural elements within the city than on the human-made elements that had earlier captivated the attention of travelers. Their interest in nature in the city seemed, on the surface, to be sparked by a great interest and concern with the weather. The heat and humidity of Philadelphia bothered most of them, affecting Charles Janson even more than the climate of Charleston, South Carolina.[12]

Before the relandscaping of the statehouse yard and the southeastern quadrant square in 1785 and 1794 respectively, travelers blamed the excessive heat on the lack of parks and trees and the overuse of brick as a building material. Marquis de Chastellux, visiting Philadelphia in the early 1780s, explained:

> The city of Philadelphia is not only at present destitute of public walks, but, in summer, the heat renders walking in the streets intolerably inconvenient; the houses and footpaths being generally of brick, are not even cooled until some hours after sunset. This extreme heat, and the abundance of excellent water, with which Philadelphia is supplied, occasion many accidents among the lower class of people, for it is no uncommon thing to see a labourer after quenching his thirst at a pump, drop down dead upon the spot, nor can the numerous examples of this kind every summer prevent them from frequently occurring; but it is to be observed, that if the heat be intense, the water is uncommonly cold.[13]

English actor John Bernard wrote in 1798, four years after the poplar-tree planting project, "Not only do trees, lining the streets of a town, conduce to health, . . . but there is something peculiarly beautiful in thus introducing the works of the Creator amid those of man, and establishing in the abode of traffic the groves sacred to meditation." The planting of trees, however, did not end the criticisms; travelers looked outside the city limits for relief from heat and for vistas. The banks of the Schuylkill, a recreational haven almost since the founding of Philadelphia, were a tourist attraction, the Delaware being "too low and lacking in the picturesque."[14]

The change in visitors' perceptions of the cityscape, occurring about the time of the Revolution, seemed more a change in attitude on their part than a reflection of the changes in the physical landscape, as illustrated by their desire to trek to the Schuylkill despite the addition of park space within the city proper. Visitors at century's end were more interested in viewing and experiencing "the picturesque" than in reveling in the regularity of the grid plan. The cityscape did change in the last quarter of the eighteenth century with the introduction of neoclassical architecture, the development of parks, and the planting of trees; all aspects of the popular taste that one might expect visitors to enjoy, visitors did not find these changes significant enough to offset the older elements of the cityscape.

The differing evaluations of the cityscape between visitors before and after the beginning of the war may be partially explained by their individual biographies, the date of their visit, and how these elements—who they were and when they visited—affected their view of Philadelphia (table 1). Before the Revolution all the writers were British except

TABLE 1. Visitors Writing on Philadelphia Cityscape, 1750–1800

Writer	Year(s) of visit	Nationality	Occupation	Reaction
James Birket	1750	English	merchant	liked
Peter Kalm	1750–51	Swedish	botanist	liked
Andrew Burnaby	1759–60	English	minister	mixed
Adam Gordon	1764–65	English	soldier	liked
John Adams	1774–80	American	statesman	liked
Thomas Jefferson	1774–1800	American	statesman	liked
Robert Honyman	1775	Scottish	physician	disliked
Patrick M'Robert	1775	Scottish	unknown	liked
Marquis de Chastellux	1780	French	officer	mixed
Abbé Robin	1781	French	chaplain	liked
George Grieve	1781–82	English	translator	liked
Francisco dal Verme	1783	Italian	aristocrat	mixed
Francisco de Miranda	1783–84	Latin American	officer	liked
Robert Hunter, Jr.	1785–86	Scottish	merchant	liked
Chateaubriand	1791	French	statesman	disliked
Charles William Janson	1793–1806	English	merchant	disliked
Henry Wansey	1794	English	clothier	disliked
Moreau de St. Méry	1794–98	French	lawyer	liked
John Bernard	1797–1811	English	actor	mixed
John Davis	1798	English	journalist	mixed
Brissot de Warville	1798	French	lawyer	mixed
Benjamin Henry Latrobe	1798–1807	English	architect	mixed

Kalm. They were fairly unanimous in their appreciation of Philadelphia, particularly its grid plan.

During and after the Revolution, visitors came from more countries. While half this set of fourteen writers were British, five were French. A closer look reveals that although some visitors continued to find favor with the Philadelphia cityscape, two-thirds expressed mixed reactions or total disdain. Of the British, those visitors who fell in the latter category tended to be merchants or professionals. Their dislike of the cityscape may have been influenced by the changed economic and political relationships between Britain and America because of the war. Visitors from other countries tended to be more mixed in their reactions to the cityscape too. While there are no prewar writings upon which to base a comparison, the visitors who came after 1775 and who were most supportive of the Revolution, such as Francisco de Miranda, Abbé Robin, and Moreau de St. Méry, had the more favorable opinions of the cityscape.

Responses to the landscape also may have been skewed by attitudes and values the visitors brought with them, including assumptions about the city itself. Many seemed to link Philadelphia with the late seventeenth- and early eighteenth-century ideals of rationalism and natural rights. For instance, before 1775 visitors generally did not evaluate the natural landscape but riveted their attention on the grid plan and the man-made improvements in the city. This vision was in keeping with landscape theories advanced between 1600 and 1740 in which emphasis was placed on human control and explicit order in the landscape. The colonial Irish towns built in Ulster between 1609 and 1613 and the city of Savannah, Georgia, laid out in 1733, are examples of this sort of ordering.[15] Philadelphia's plan was part of a tradition known to British citizens especially.

Further, Philadelphia was well known to Britons even before their visits because the Penns' promotional tracts usually included a sketch of the city plan. Throughout the eighteenth century, maps and other printed materials often included a cartouche in which the full city plan was illustrated. Consequently, visitors arrived with the image of the grid, fully built, in their heads, and this image may have shaped their perceptions of what they saw on the street. They were predisposed to like the plan and the order it stood for.[16]

About 1775 visitors began to look for different qualities in the landscape, such as picturesque views. This attitudinal change paralleled a change in landscape theory from the rational to the romantic. Two key elements of romanticism were the picturesque ideal and a theory of associations. *Picturesque* was defined as the ability to please the eye with variety in color or form and to present the viewer with an element of surprise through vistas and irregularity. The theory of associations asked designers to hark back to earlier times for design elements. By using a historical design element, the user not only created something picturesque but also could charge that object or landscape with the values associated with a historical period—for example, piety with Gothic design. Some of the earliest proponents of the romantic landscape were Englishmen like Sir William Temple, who published *Upon the Garden of Epicurus* in 1692, introducing the picturesque elements of Chinese garden design to the Western world.[17]

Philadelphia's grid plan was far from picturesque with its regular rhythm of straight, parallel streets. Post-1775 writers who focused on the physical aspects of Philadelphia's landscape, therefore, were disappointed. British merchants who may have found a different and difficult economic climate also may have been aware of the transformation occurring in the English countryside with the construction of naturalistic parks and romantic ruins.

Visitors who focused on the theory of associations, however, found Philadelphia to be rich in associations related to the ideology of the Revolution. Because they agreed with these values, they could admire the cityscape with its new improvements—city squares, tree-lined streets, and fashionable buildings. And since much of the ideology was built on the foundations of earlier English and French writers who believed in the rational ability of humans to know truth and govern themselves, the uniformity of Philadelphia's grid plan also was acceptable.[18]

All visitors then perceived the city as an embodiment of rationalism, melding the plan of the city to its image, but how they appraised the city depended on their attitudes toward rationalism. As the travelogue accounts and personal writings show, visitors to Philadelphia had double vision: they saw the city as it was, and they judged it against what they wished it to be. Changes to the physical landscape, or lack thereof, were less important in forming their evaluations of the city than were their attitudes toward landscape in general and American political ideology in particular. As landscape fashion moved from the rational to the romantic, Philadelphia's cityscape fell into disfavor except by those who could refocus their vision. They saw the city as a symbol of the war's ideals and thus could applaud the rational plan.[19]

Brissot de Warville, who visited the city in 1788 as part of a pilgrimage to the land of revolution, noted that Franklin, who himself had a hand in shaping the built cityscape, had said, "Any atheist in the world would be converted if he could see Philadelphia, a city in which everything is so much for the best." Most visitors earlier in the eighteenth century would have agreed wholeheartedly in the human extension of the hand of God. At the close of the century, however, more travelers would have sided with early romanticist Thomas Gray: "Not a torrent, not a cliff but is pregnant with religion and poetry. There are certain scenes that would awe an atheist into belief."[20] By 1800 Philadelphia's cityscape was not necessarily one of them.

---

[1] Urban histories traditionally have concentrated on the social, economic, and political developments rather than cityscapes; examples include Charles N. Glaab and A. Theodore Brown, *A History of Urban America* (New York: Macmillan Co., 1967); Alexander B. Callow, Jr., *American Urban History* . . . (2d ed.; New York: Oxford University Press, 1973); and Russell F. Weigley, ed., *Philadelphia: A Three-Hundred-Year History* (New York: W. W. Norton, 1982). Because of the well-documented development of Philadelphia's city plan, its history, although not its influence, is often discussed in urban history texts; two of the best are Sylvia Doughty Fries, *The Urban Idea in Colonial America* (Philadelphia: Temple University Press, 1977) and Anthony N. B. Garvan, "Proprietary Philadelphia as Artifact," in *The Historian and the City*, ed. Oscar Handlin and John Barchard (Cambridge: MIT Press and Harvard University Press, 1963), pp. 177–201. Both authors use William Penn's papers as primary sources.

[2] For data on the writers, see table 1. Residents of the city wrote few descriptive passages; the cityscape was merely the stage on which events of primary concern to them occurred. The difference between the number of accounts written by visitors and residents may have sprung from different motivations; travelers often came to see "something different"—the New World, the strange Indians, the unusual religious sect, the republic.

[3] Gordon quoted in *Travels in the American Colonies*, ed. Newton D. Mereness (New York: Macmillan Co., 1916), p. 410; [Augustus John Foster], *Jeffersonian America: Notes on the United States of America Collected in the Years 1805, 1806, 1807, and 1811 and 1812*, ed. Richard Beale Davis (San Marino, Calif.: Huntington Library, 1954), p. 259.

[4] History of the plan for Philadelphia and biographical data on Holme are drawn from Fries, *Urban Idea*; Garvan, "Proprietary Philadelphia"; and Hannah Benne Roach, "The Planting of Philadelphia: A Seventeenth-Century Real Estate Development," *Pennsylvania Magazine of History and Biography* 92, no. 1 (January 1968): 3–47.

[5] Martin P. Snyder, *City of Independence: Views of Philadelphia before 1800* (New York: Praeger Publishers, 1975), chap. 1 and particularly figs. 46, 47, 48, 138.

[6] *The Papers of Benjamin Franklin*, ed. Leonard W. Labaree, William B. Willcox, and Claude A. Lopez, 27 vols. to date (New Haven: Yale University Press, 1959–), 3:317, 14:304; Jean-Pierre Brissot de Warville, *New Travels in the United States of America Performed in 1788* (Dublin: P. Byrne, A. Grueber, W. McKenzie, 1792), p. 254.

[7] John M. Duncan, *Travels through Part of the United States and Canada in 1818 and 1819*, vol. 1 (Glasgow: Woodlaw and Cuninghame, 1823), pp. 187, 190; [Foster], *Jeffersonian America*, p. 260; *Franklin Papers*, 11:495; Richard J. Webster, *Philadelphia Preserved* (Philadelphia: Temple University Press, 1976), p. 106.

[8] Henry Wansey, *The Journal of an Excursion to the United States of North America in the Summer of 1794* (1796; reprint, New York: Johnson Reprint Corp., 1969), p. 131; Adolph B. Benson, ed., *The America of 1750: Peter Kalm's Travels in North America: The English Version of 1770*, 2 vols. (1934; reprint, New York: Dover Publications, 1966), 1:35; Charles William Janson, *The Stranger in America, 1793–1806*, ed. Carl S. Driver (New York: Press of the Pioneers, 1935), p. 184; *Moreau de St. Méry's American Journey [1793–1798]*, trans. and ed. Kenneth Roberts and Anna M. Roberts (Garden City, N.Y.: Doubleday, 1947), pp. 259–60, 344.

[9] Benson, *America of 1750*, 1:33.

[10] Charles N. Glaab, ed., *The American City: A Documentary History* (Homewood, Ill.: Dorsey Press, 1963), p. 20.

[11] Brissot de Warville, *New Travels*, p. 173; Philip Padelford, ed., *Colonial Panorama–1775: Dr. Robert Honyman's Journal for March and April* (San Marino, Calif.: Huntington Library, 1939), p. 19.

[12] Janson, *Stranger in America*, p. 187.

[13] Howard C. Rice, Jr., *Travels in North America in the Years 1780, 1781, and 1782 by the Marquis de Chastellux*, 2 vols. (Chapel Hill: University of North Carolina Press, 1963), 1:334.

[14] John Bernard, *Retrospections of America, 1797–1881*, ed. Mrs. Bayle Bernard (New York: Harper and Brothers, 1887), p. 63; Richard Switzer, trans., *Chateaubriand's Travels in America* (Lexington: University of Kentucky Press, 1969), p. 14.

[15] Good explanations of the rational approach to landscape are "The Chinese Origins of Romanticism" and "The Parallel of Deism as Classicism," in Arthur D. Lovejoy, *Essays in the History of Ideas* (Baltimore: Johns Hopkins University Press, 1948), pp. 78–98 and 99–135; Hugh C. Prince, "Georgian Landscape" in *Man Made the Land: Essays in English Historical Geography* . . . , ed. Alan R. J. Baker and J. B. Harley (Totowa, N.J.: Rowman and Littlefield, 1973), pp. 153–66; and Ronald Rees, "The Scenery Cult: Changing Landscape Tastes over Three Centuries," *Landscape* 19, no. 3 (May 1975): 39–47. Data on other city plans are from Fries, *Urban Idea*, pp. 28–89.

[16] Snyder, *City of Independence*, pp. 18–24, 39–41, 46, 60–63, 92, 98–104, 122, 166, 181, 185, 200, 203, 227, 272–73.

[17] For explanations of the romantic approach to landscape, see Lovejoy, *Essays*, pp. 99–135; Rees, "Scenery Cult," pp. 39–47; Hans Huth, *Nature and the American:*

Three Centuries of Changing Attitudes (Berkeley: University of California Press, 1957), pp. 10–27, 55–59; and Carroll L. V. Meeks, *The Railroad Station: An Architectural History* (New Haven: Yale University Press, 1956), p. 8.

[18] The grid plan of Philadelphia can be seen as a physical explication of Enlightenment ideas concerning immutable and knowable natural laws (e.g., mathematics and architecture) and the ability of educated persons to harness nature to their ends (e.g., overlaying a grid plan on unsettled terrain). For a short discussion of the effects of these ideas on the ideology of the Revolution, see E. James Ferguson, *The American Revolution: A General History, 1763–1790* (Homewood, Ill.: Dorsey Press, 1974), pp. 58–63. The impact of these ideas is explored in more detail by Garry Wills, *Inventing America: Jefferson's Declaration of Independence* (Garden City, N.Y.: Doubleday, 1978), pp. 93–110.

[19] A reading of 13 travelogues written between 1800 and 1850 showed that this trend continued.

[20] Brissot de Warville, *New Travels*, p. 199; Rees, "Scenery Cult," p. 42.

The Philadelphia Economic Elite at the End of the Eighteenth Century

Robert J. Gough

During the past twenty years the writing of American social history has been transformed by scholarly explorations of the working and living conditions of the masses of Americans. The results have been fruitful, but despite appeals to the contrary, there have been few complementary studies of the eighteenth century that focus systematically on the rich, wealthy, and powerful. These groups, indeed, often serve simply as ill-defined foils for the studies of lower strata. The common image of wealthy Philadelphians in the revolutionary period has been presented by Eric Foner: an "aristocracy" of "wealthy merchants" that "dominated the city's economic, political, and social life." This description is consistent with the image of wealthy Philadelphians in the twentieth century: a group of privileged descendants of colonial ancestors, with common ethnic and religious backgrounds, who share educational experiences, membership in prestigious private clubs, and residences in exclusive neighborhoods, and who control the public affairs of the city by overlapping business directorships and behind-the-scenes political manipulation.[1]

Over the years many individuals have assisted the author with this project. He especially acknowledges the help of Lee Benson, Deborah Mathias Gough, Jack D. Marietta, Whitman Ridgway, Jr., and Michael Zuckerman. None, of course, bear any responsibility for the results.

For the late eighteenth century, the experience of the so-called Republican Court, a circle of high-living Philadelphians moving around United States Senator William Bingham and his wife, Anne Willing Bingham, epitomized the social and economic stratification and aristocratic privilege thought to be characteristic of the city. The activity of men like Bingham, flush with wealth made during the Revolution, the weakening of the city's dominant dour Quaker ambience, and the arrival of the national capital from New York City in 1790 combined to encourage the wealthy to socialize at exclusive events, flaunt expensive clothing and furnishings, and benefit from policies initiated by friendly officials of the Washington and Adams administrations. As one contemporary wrote, "Certainly there never was in our country a series of such distinguished *reunions*. Brilliant balls, sumptuous dinners and constant receptions." Many of these events took place at Bingham's mansion on Spruce Street, described by an English traveler as "a magnificent house and gardens in the best English style, with elegant and even superb furniture."[2] The exclusive social and political activities at the Binghams' home became the object of criticism from Democratic-Republican opponents of the Adams administration.

Interpretations that see the Republican Court as typifying the lifestyle of wealthy Philadelphians, however, are incomplete. For one thing, the court included only some wealthy Philadelphians. Rich men such as John Nicholson were simply unwelcome. Dubious sexual morality, obnoxious personal characteristics, or simply being an arriviste kept some wealthy men out of the drawing rooms of the court circle. Many others avoided the circle by choice. Benjamin Rush, for one, eschewed it because of its Federalist orientation. Wealthy Quakers, in particular, spurned the opulence of the au courant court circle in favor of clothing and furnishings that were expensive but of a "plain style." Anna Rawle, daughter of a wealthy Quaker, wrote with distaste that "the greatest part of [Bingham's] wealth [was] acquired by the sale of some guinea negroes." "Many would feel disagreable sensations in using riches gained in that manner," she observed primly, "but every body's conscience is not equally tender alike." Still others were alienated by the moral tone of the Republican Court, exemplified by the vulgar language of its "queen," Anne Bingham, who in the words of Abigail Adams liked to "show more of the [bosom] than the decent Matron, or the modest woman." In this atmosphere, "the most truly respectable people," reported one newly arrived resident, "are least heard of." The long-established and politically well-connected Shippen family, for instance, felt alienated from "the gay folks about" them. And finally, personal temperament encouraged Thomas Willing, Tench Francis, Jr., George Harrison ("the leading man of fashion" in Philadelphia), and others simply to choose to minimize their social interactions with that part of the elite that pretended to social grandeur and exclusivity.[3]

The Republican Court was shallow and fragile. "With the exception of the foreign diplomats," commented one Portuguese visitor after being received by President John Adams, "all the rest breathed very little refinement or polished manners." The court attracted scorn from fellow Philadelphians. A critic mocked, "at a recent federal festival certain rules were posted up among one was 'That no segars shall be smoked during the evening' and the other 'That whoever breaks any of the furniture must pay for it.' " The imitation of English aristocratic models and simultaneous dependence—ironically—on French-inspired neoclassical designs in clothing and furniture made the court increasingly irrelevant in Philadelphia. As Samuel Breck, himself a rich Philadelphia Federalist, pointed out, the "pageantry" and ostentation of the Binghams was "contrary to the plain, unvarnished manners of the people." It was difficult, therefore, for most Philadelphians to see the court circle as distinctive and important; the members of the court, rather, tended to wind up looking silly, instead of deserving the subservience of the general public. With the recession of 1797, the removal of the national and state capitals from Philadelphia, and the death or departure of notables such as Bingham himself, the court circle quickly disappeared.[4]

SOCIAL CHARACTERISTICS OF THE ECONOMIC ELITE

Rich men in a city that was the cultural center of the nation and the location of its political capital certainly had access to power, patronage, and prestige. Why did social cohesion fail to develop among them? Answering this question requires gaining an understanding of some of the social characteristics of these wealthy men as a group. The present study is based on 345 men, approximately the richest 2.5 percent of the city's male population in 1800.[5] Despite their wealth, these men are not readily alike, and some of their social characteristics—the diversity in

TABLE 1. Ethnic Backgrounds in Philadelphia, 1800

	Economic elite (%)	Estimated entire population (%)
English	52	32–35
German	9	32–35
Scotch-Irish	9	18–20
Other	30	11–16

*N=345

Note: Economic elite based on projections from the 64% of the elite identified with certainty.

Source: Robert J. Gough, "Toward a Theory of Class and Social Conflict: A Social History of Wealthy Philadelphians, 1775 and 1800" (Ph.D. diss., University of Pennsylvania, 1977), pp. 183–88.

their social backgrounds, their relative lack of social distinctiveness from the rest of the city's population, and their failure to intermarry frequently—begin to explain the weak cohesion and short life of the Republican Court.

About 45 percent of the city's wealthy men in 1800 had been born in Philadelphia, about 30 percent elsewhere on the mainland of North America, and 25 percent overseas; in contrast, only 4 percent of the wealthy in Boston at the end of the eighteenth century had been born abroad.[6] Furthermore, while few among the Philadelphia rich had a rags-to-riches background, inherited wealth certainly did not characterize the group as a whole. Perhaps a third of the locally born, and more than half of those born elsewhere, did not have a rich father (defined as approximately the top 10 percent of the population). They were further fragmented by ethnic and religious differences. Approximately half of the wealthy were from English backgrounds (compared with a third of the city's entire population) and about half from the other nationalities that constituted two-thirds of the city's population. Germans, while not as numerous among the rich as they were in the entire population, were the second largest ethnic group (table 1).

Religiously, Episcopalians were most numerous among the elite by 1800, but with the allegiance of barely a third of the rich, Episcopalianism could not provide a model for wealthy Philadelphians the way Unitarianism did in Boston. In particular, the United Churches of

Christ Church and St. Peters, the oldest Episcopalian congregation in the city, has an ill-deserved reputation as elite-dominated: the wealthy were only 31 of 438 pew renters at Christ Church and 26 of 408 at St. Peters and only 40 percent of the combined churches' vestry.[7] Quakers were the next most numerous, but as time passed they were coming to make up a smaller percentage of the elite, just as their proportion of the city's entire population was declining. Correspondingly, while still underrepresented, Roman Catholics and Presbyterians were becoming more numerous among the elite, as they were also in overall population (table 2).

In sum, while the rich were not an exact cross section of the city's population, as a group their backgrounds did reflect the diversity of the city in which they had achieved economic success. These backgrounds, in turn, entangled them in the friendships, quarrels, and associational networks that fragmented all Philadelphians.[8]

There were many ways in which wealthy Philadelphians were socially indistinct from the rest of the city's population. For one thing, even with 68,000 residents, making it the largest city in the United States in 1800, preindustrial Philadelphia was not ecologically specialized; the

TABLE 2. Religious Identification in Philadelphia, 1800

	Economic elite (%)	Estimated entire population (%)
Episcopalian	34.2	10.5
Society of Friends	30.4	6.6
German Lutheran	0.7	12.6
German Reformed	0.3	8.0
Presbyterian	10.2	9.4
Roman Catholic	2.9	9.8
Other	7.7	5.1
Unchurched	0.3	37.0
Unknown**	14.1	—

*N = 345

**Most unknowns were presumably unchurched and have been placed in that category in the estimation for the entire population.

Source: Robert J. Gough, "Toward a Theory of Class and Social Conflict: A Social History of Wealthy Philadelphians, 1775 and 1800" (Ph.D. diss., University of Pennsylvania, 1977), pp. 188–93.

rich did not live by themselves in exclusive neighborhoods. All Philadelphians lived in a relatively promiscuous environment. Home and workplace were still almost always the same or nearby; there were no separate "residential" and "business" neighborhoods. Public areas were put to multiple use: in eighteenth-century Philadelphia crowds gathered on High Street in front of City Hall to cast election votes, hear itinerant preachers, or shop the market stalls that stood in the middle of the street. When visiting London, wealthy Philadelphians were impressed by the spatial differentiation evident in that city, in contrast to what they were familiar with at home.[9]

Although not evenly dispersed, the wealthy lived in every part of the city (table 3). Their homes were often flanked by those of citizens with more modest incomes, and their buildings were not architecturally distinctive from their neighbors'. For example, on the block of Water Street above Arch lived Samuel Shoemaker and Abel James, "very respectable residents, none more so in the city then," whose homes were among

TABLE 3. Distribution of Population by Ward, Philadelphia, 1800

	Economic elite* (%)	Entire population (%)
North	17.4	7.7
Dock	16.8	6.6
Middle	12.8	5.1
South	8.0	3.2
South Mulberry	7.6	10.6
New Market	7.3	10.6
Chestnut	5.2	1.7
Northern Liberties East	4.3	12.6
Southwark	4.3	13.3
Upper Delaware	4.0	2.4
Walnut	4.0	1.2
Northern Liberties West	3.4	12.9
North Mulberry	2.8	8.5
High Street	1.5	2.0
Lower Delaware	0.6	1.4

*N=328; outside city, 6; unknown, 11.

Source: County Tax Assessment Ledgers, Philadelphia County, 1800, Philadelphia City Archives (U.S. census data for 1800 are arranged by different boundaries).

those of "pump makers and coopers." Similarly, Henry Drinker and Henry Pratt, prominent merchants and next-door neighbors on North Front Street, to the immediate south had as neighbors a bricklayer, a tailor, a tobacconist, a milliner and mantua maker, and a mustard and chocolate maker. Elizabeth Drinker made matter-of-fact comments in her diary regarding these and other neighbors that indicated some disapproval but no surprise or disdain. She noted, for example, the behavior of "a molatto man," who rented a room next door to the Drinkers (as did five or six other "ordinary, noisy" families) and who publicly vomited while drunk. On the other hand, Abigail Adams, an outsider to Philadelphia, was sensitive to the status of her neighborhood: she expressed clear dissatisfaction with the noises, smells, and people she found around her home when living in Philadelphia in the 1790s as the wife of the vice-president of the United States.[10]

One reason why the economic elite did not develop distinctive neighborhoods was the tendency of even the wealthiest Philadelphians to rent rather than own their homes. Fluctuations in fortunes, conflicts among relatives, and the constant pressure of arrivistes seeking new homes often resulted in a house being occupied successively by numerous families, some wealthy and some not so wealthy. "This neighborhood is greatly altered," reported Anna Rawle in 1782; "except for one or two families we are amongst a new set of beings." Was it any wonder then that rich Philadelphians could not keep track of where one another lived? Ann Ridgely seemed disappointed, but not surprised, when she went to visit Mrs. James Bayard and found, on reaching the doorstep, that the house at Third and Walnut was no longer the Bayards' residence.[11]

Some of the new arrivals to the city became members of the 1800 economic elite. Thomas Pym Cope, a native of Lancaster, Pennsylvania, migrated to Philadelphia at age eighteen in 1786 and was apprenticed to his merchant uncle. By 1800 he was already among the wealthy and in the first few decades of the nineteenth century reached the very top of the economic elite. Like other newcomers, he found comfortable housing in the city in part because inheritance practices often resulted in the dispersion of real property rather than the transfer of an estate intact to an heir. An example of this involves the Shippen family. When his father died, Edward Shippen, Jr., a prominent member of the 1800 elite, inherited the elegant family home on Fourth Street jointly with his brother. Neither sibling could afford to buy the other's share of the property, so the home was sold and the cash proceeds divided.[12]

Country homes were modest structures reflecting their origins as retreats to escape the city's summer heat and do not deserve their twentieth-century designation as "mansions"; none approached the magnificence of the twenty- to forty-bedroom establishments that graced the English countryside. Furthermore, their ownership changed frequently. Of the thirty-nine best-known homes built before 1775, only eight remained continuously in the same family until 1820.[13]

The waning years of the eighteenth century were especially bad for Philadelphia owners of country homes. "Anybody who has long resided at Philadelphia especially," commented Sir Augustus John Foster, "must remember how often such houses changed hands." Sheriff's sales became common. In 1797 alone Samuel Penrose purchased Graeme Park, and William Bingham became owner of Lansdowne, once the residence of proprietor John Penn. Henry Pratt, a shopkeeper who became a wealthy merchant, took advantage of Robert Morris's bankruptcy to buy Lemon Hill in 1799. William Crammond, a recent immigrant who rose to wealth by land speculation in association with John Nicholson, also took advantage of Morris's problems to purchase the land on which he built neo-Gothic Sedgley. Crammond found himself bankrupt, and Sedgley passed at United States marshall's sale to Samuel Mifflin in 1806, and in 1812 James Cowles Fisher bought it at a private sale.[14]

Another dimension of civic life for the elite was participation in voluntary associations. But in Philadelphia the rich did not participate in a single association nor did a network of associations exist. To be sure, some voluntary associations attracted wealthy members; Schuylkill Fishing Company, for example, was described by a contemporary as consisting of the "most distinguished people of the colony." Yet no organization's membership came close to consisting entirely of the economic elite. Among the members of Schuylkill Fishing Company in 1800, just 37 percent were wealthy (although the nonwealthy members, of course, were not necessarily "poor").[15]

Furthermore, some associations encouraged interaction among members from different socioeconomic backgrounds. Libraries, for example, showed a pattern of consolidation and broad membership: in 1769 the Library Company of Philadelphia absorbed the Union Library

Company, a younger organization founded by artisans who desired lower membership fees and longer operating hours and which had in turn absorbed the Association Library Company. "Its advantages were not confined to the opulent," reported a foreign visitor. "The citizens of the middle and lower walks of life were equally partakers of them." The presence of the middling and lower sorts did not discourage wealthy Philadelphians from belonging to the Library Company; indeed, it was the commonest associational tie among members of the economic elite. In 1800, 120 of the wealthy were shareholders.[16]

A closer examination of voluntary association membership patterns also illuminates the divisions that existed among the rich. At Pennsylvania Hospital, for example, the managers were predominantly wealthy Quakers (five of the eight wealthy managers in 1800 were members of the Society of Friends); few Quakers, however, were elected to the American Philosophical Society. Wealthy Friends joined Union Fire Company and avoided Hand-in-Hand Fire Company, despite the overall more affluent membership of the Hand-in-Hand. Numerous societies strove to "revive and increase social intercourse and mutual attachments" among Philadelphians of particular ethnic backgrounds. These, too, divided the rich. In 1800 more than a third of the wealthy belonged to one of these eight or nine organizations. Since multiple memberships were extremely uncommon, however, this dispersed the wealthy and encouraged greater "social intercourse" with persons of more modest socioeconomic status. Socioeconomic backgrounds brought other pressures to bear on membership patterns. Rich men with inherited wealth tended to belong to such associations as the Hand-in-Hand Fire Company and the Schuylkill Fishing Company and not the Library Company, perhaps because their personal libraries were larger.[17]

Thus, the wealthy who joined voluntary associations had no single pattern of memberships, although there are some general trends. Non-Quakers often belonged to Hand-in-Hand Fire Company, American Philosophical Society, and the board of trustees of the University of Pennsylvania, organizations that represented public service or distinguished accomplishment. Few of these men also chose to join organizations that were more social in orientation. Those wealthy non-Quakers who were interested instead in pleasure were concentrated in Gloucester Fox Hunt, Mount Regale Fishing Company, Schuylkill Fishing Company, and St. Patrick's Society. William Tilghman, a prominent lawyer, belonged to each of the organizations in the first set. He, like most members of organizations that focused on public service or accomplishment, came from a high socioeconomic background—his father had served as secretary of the Proprietary Land Office. Merchant Richard Bache, on the other hand, belonged to Gloucester Fox Hunt, Mount Regale Fishing Company, and St. Patrick's Society but none of the organizations closely identified with public service and accomplishment. In contrast to Tilghman, Bache's economic position had been described as "not . . . worth anything" when he arrived in Philadelphia in the mid 1760s.[18]

Quakers generally had a different pattern of memberships. The Library Company and Pennsylvania Hospital were the central organizations of their network. The Welsh Society was the only ethnic association in which Quakers participated. Less central but still important to wealthy Quakers was the Abolition Society. Merchant Jesse Waln and "gentleman" Joseph P. Norris, for example, were members of prominent Quaker families who limited their membership to the four organizations just mentioned.

The wealthy had also joined another set of voluntary associations based on humanitarian interests: "There can scarce happen an instance of individual distress," wrote one foreign visitor, "for which a mode of advice, assistance or relief is not provided without resort to public begging." The Dispensary (an outpatient medical facility), the Humane Society (for rescuing "fallen" women), and the Sunday School Society were the core of this network. Most wealthy persons associated with this set of organizations, like Thomas Pym Cope, were Quakers; however, compared with the networks previously discussed, the wealthy members of the humanitarian network came from lower socioeconomic backgrounds.[19]

Educational practices and institutions did not foster cohesion among wealthy Philadelphians either. To begin with, secondary education in the city was limited in scope. Few adolescents of any rank attended school. Sectarian influence worked to keep enrollments down by blocking development of a comprehensive, publicly supported system of primary and secondary education. Quakers, Presbyterians, Episcopalians, and later both German Reformed and Lutheran denominations developed parallel school systems. Since these schools attracted students from a variety of socioeconomic backgrounds, the wealthy children who attended them had their religious distinctiveness reinforced rather than their economic status. Indeed, educational opportunities were so inadequate in 1800 that a group of Philadelphians proposed to establish a new academy because too many of their children had to go out of town for education.[20]

Higher education was largely restricted to the privileged in early America, but so few of the rich attended college, or at least the same college, that its influence in producing a special life-style among the wealthy was restricted. In business-oriented Philadelphia, the benefit of a classical education did not appeal to many who could afford it. And, of course, many of the wealthy of 1800 had not been in a position to afford collegiate education. Quakers, furthermore, formally proscribed higher education. Only 11 percent of the 1800 elite had attended college, and those that had done so had studied at a variety of institutions in Britain and the colonies, not a single college.

As a result, the University of Pennsylvania was not used by the wealthy as a place for their sons to socialize and develop a common life-style. In the thirty-six classes that entered between 1757 and 1800, only 5 percent of the known 436 matriculants in the university's college were wealthy Philadelphians, no more than a half dozen of whom were enrolled at the same time. Furthermore, these students did not receive special treatment from the trustees, faculty, or other students. In contrast to New England's colleges, the University of Pennsylvania faculty ranked students on the basis of achievement rather than social or economic status. The faculty believed that they were preparing students for the competitive struggle of adult life and stressed academic competition through class rank and prizes.[21]

Social cohesion among the wealthy was also inhibited by the relative infrequency of intermarriage among the rich. Only about 25 percent of the marriages of the children of the 1800 elite were to other wealthy persons or their children. One reason for this limited intermarriage (less frequent than might have been expected) was the declining value placed on marrying for wealth and an increasing value placed on affection between the spouses, as was coming to be the case throughout the nation. Even today, in traditional societies elders often warn against love as the basis for mate selection, especially among the higher socioeconomic strata. In late eighteenth-century Philadelphia, however, such prescriptions were weak and ineffective. Responding to the avuncular advice of Benjamin Franklin to use accounting techniques in considering marriage, Jonathan Williams declared sharply that before taking a wife a man "must fall in love and that seems to be as involuntary an act as falling into a well." Elizabeth Meredith expressed the view common among the wealthy after the Revolution when she explained regarding her daughter, "I am determined to avoid any influence in persuading her to place her affections where she has objections." Indeed, sometimes decisions by children left parents with no influence. Alexander Baring, a member of the 1800 elite, reported in regard to the marriage of William Jackson, another member of this elite, to Thomas Willing's daughter, "it is whispered in the court of scandals that family circumstances rendered the event necessary." Willing had opposed the match for several years but under the "circumstances" changed his position and acceded to the union. Elizabeth and Henry Drinker were shocked by the elopement of their daughter Molly and her marriage in a civil ceremony. Within three months, however, they were reconciled to the union.[22] As parents, they had little choice.

Religious ties also hindered marital integration of the elite. Denominations encouraged members to restrict their marriages to coreligionists. "In Philadelphia there are thirty-four different sects," commented one foreign visitor. "Individually they hate and despise one another," so everyone "refuses insofar as possible to become a member of the family of a different sectarian." There was, indeed, behavior that supported such conclusions. Quaker Thomas Fisher, for example, explained that he "could not attend with propriety" a celebration of the wedding of his son Joshua to Anglican Elizabeth Powel Francis, daughter of the wealthy Mr. and Mrs. Tench Francis, Jr. After 1763 Quakers, by now a minority in Pennsylvania, began to insist that Friends marry Friends—to little avail. However, wealthy Quakers remained more likely than most Quakers to marry within the faith. Of the eighty-six members of the 1800 elite who were raised as Quakers and about whom marriage information is known, sixty-three married in accordance with Quaker practice. For example, in discussing a sister of John Clifford, a member of the 1800 elite, Quakeress Ann Warder reported, "Elliston Perot had a mind for her but she refused him on account of not being in the Society." Perot joined the Society of Friends in 1786 and the following year married Sarah Sansom, daughter of Samuel Sansom II.[23] By maintaining a hold on many of the wealthy Quakers, religious norms regarding marriage impeded social cohesion among the rich.

Perhaps in part because of their limited social distinctiveness, rich Philadelphians, at least in the eyes of observers, were not dramatically different from the rest of the city's populace. Isaac Weld, for instance, was surprised to learn that the group of men he met at a local tavern were "eminent lawyers" and "judges." They were "so very plain, both in appearance and manners, that a stranger would not suspect that they were persons of the consequence which they really are." With perhaps only a little exaggeration, a German doctor who aided the United States in the Revolution concluded, "There is to be found as little distinction of rank among the inhabitants of Philadelphia as in any place in the world."[24]

Almost every visitor remarked on the relative lack of social distinctions based on economic characteristics. Johann Schoepf was impressed that "distinctions of rank among the feminine half [were] not striking as a result of any distinct costume." Gottlieb Mittelberger was shocked to find that "everyone [wore] a wig, the peasant as well as the gentleman." Other visitors reported that the citizens shared an ample diet and used the same vocabulary and diction. As a whole visitors interpreted wealth as an equalizing force in society: social distinctions that were based on this quality were fragile since wealth, in turn, was believed to be relatively accessible to everybody. "Riches make no positive material difference," concluded Schoepf, "because in this regard every man expects at one time or another to be on a footing with his rich neighbor."[25]

Given the amorphous nature of wealth-based distinctions, visitors who attempted to delineate the "class" structure of the city understandably mixed wealth with economic factors, such as occupation, and with noneconomic factors. The duc de la Rochefoucauld-Liancourt, for example, noted in the late 1790s, "fortunes and the nature of professions form different classes": a "first class" of merchants, lawyers, land owners, physicians, and the clergy; a "second class" of inferior merchants, farmers, and artisans; and a "third class" of "workers." He believed that a "small fortune" was sufficient to carry "men from one class to another." Ferdinand Bayard, who came to Philadelphia just a few years before la Rochefoucauld-Liancourt, also explicitly described a three-class structure but concluded "prestige" rather than wealth was the second dimension that interacted with occupation. In his scheme the first class comprised "carriage owners" with "coats of arms"; the second class consisted of merchants, lawyers, and doctors with no coaches; and the third class contained those individuals with "mechanical occupations." While la Rochefoucauld-Liancourt had reported that the classes he had identified "did not mix," Bayard wrote that his first two classes intermixed with each other but not with the third class. Both men observed that "Quakers live among themselves" and were an exception to the divisions they described.[26]

Noneconomic factors also played a major role in shaping the descriptions of the city's social structure. Henry Fearon pointed to differences in attitude as the basic distinction among social groups in Philadelphia. His "first class" displayed "pride" through their carriages, "elegant homes," and "superb furniture," in contrast to the "small and middling tradesmen" who "do not make much exertion, live easily, save no money, and appear to care neither about either the present or future." Observers also made distinctions among social groups based on family, background, pedigree, or length of residence in the city. In 1788 a magazine correspondent reported "several classes of company," which he labeled "the Cream, the New Milk, and the Canaille," and then added, "in private parties and in public meetings, the [social] distinctions . . . are accurately preserved." Finally, at least one visitor perceived the importance of race as a factor in the class structure of Philadelphia. Moreau de St. Méry, a fugitive French aristocrat who lived in the city for several years in the 1790s, explicitly outlined a three-"class" organization of society: "whites," "people of color," and "slaves."[27]

These comments reinforce the residents' perception that no single dimension, particularly wealth, determined social distinctions in Philadelphia at the end of the eighteenth century. Visitors were certainly confused, but the validity of their individual comments is not what is important; what is important is their multiplicity of views. Different dimensions struck different observers as important.

WHY WAS THE ECONOMIC ELITE NOT SOCIALLY DISTINCTIVE AND COHESIVE?

What was there about Philadelphia in 1800 that inhibited the rich from becoming an easily recognizable, socially cohesive group? The history of the city provides part of the answer. Different people, all in search of material advancement, had been attracted to Philadelphia by deeply rooted social practices. For one thing, toleration of diversity was an official principle indelibly planted in the city by William Penn. Opportunities for economic advancement were closely linked to Philadelphia's large, abundant hinterland. The establishment of the city as a profit-oriented land-development venture encouraged successful businessmen to display individualism and acquisitiveness. Consequently, conditions were ideal for a high level of social conflict among Philadelphia's residents, a conflict that the wealthy were unable to avoid.

The wealthy were unable to avoid the problems, to remain above or to control social and political patterns in the city, in part because their fortunes were neither fabulous nor secure. Visitors almost never commented favorably on the wealth of Philadelphians. George Washington expressed dissatisfaction with living in Robert Morris's house—by his own admission "the best single house in the city" in the 1790s—because "without addition it is inadequate to the commodious accommodation of my family." French aristocrat François-René de Chateaubriand found that "palace of the President of the United States," to be "a little house . . . resembling the neighboring houses." Probate records show that almost all the economic elite, while living comfortably to be sure, did not have fortunes large enough to support themselves without work (which endangered social cohesion because work involved them in business-related conflicts). Benjamin Rush, a member of the 1800 elite who by his own admission enjoyed the most lucrative medical practice in late eighteenth-century Philadelphia, estimated in 1784 that he possessed "an estate, which, if thrown into cash, would yield about 300-0-0 a year," less than the £500 per year estimated by historian Jackson T. Main as necessary to be "well-to-do" in colonial America.[28]

Even when income from employment is considered, most fortunes of the wealthy were not incredible. In 1800 it reportedly took an income of about $4,200 to support a family of six in a "genteel," not an "opulent," life-style, and Moses Levy, one of the most active lawyers in the city, whose tax assessment placed him in the upper quarter of the economic elite, had an income estimated at $6,000. Only about 5 percent of the 1800 elite lacked a gainful occupation. And at that time the city directory identified only seventeen members of the elite by the title "gentleman." This title could not have meant too much, for these men were not outstanding in possession of greater wealth, older lineage, or more social prestige within the elite. The most distinguished men in the city, in political, social, or economic achievements, were labeled by their actual occupations. Of the seventeen so-called gentlemen, at least ten had real occupations, including such seemingly nonprestigious vocations as boat builder, sea captain, cordwainer, and goldsmith. Benjamin Franklin was probably correct when in the early 1780s he observed that there were "very few rich enough to live idly upon their rents or income."[29]

There were perhaps a dozen men among the elite in the 1790s who could live such a life-style; in addition to Bingham, these were the scions of such well-known families as the Emlens, Pembertons, Morrises, Allens, Hamiltons, Stampers, Shippens, Merediths, and Willings. While impressive, their estates were paltry by the standards of the West Indies and southern mainland colonies and even more so by English standards, in which the largest fortunes were worth £700,000. When Richard Hockley, a top proprietary official and one of the wealthiest men in the province, died in 1774 leaving an estate worth £20,000, John Penn had to explain to his aunt Julianna in England that with that amount of property "in this country he might be called rich."[30]

The fortunes of wealthy Philadelphians, furthermore, were often unstable. There were few sinecures to support them, or indeed legal privileges of any sort. The 1776 state constitution required that public offices not be profitable to their incumbents. The legal system, furthermore, proscribed primogeniture. In conjunction with the rising valuation on affection within families, legal norms encouraged the rich to disperse their fortunes among their heirs. In Pennsylvania law, in contrast to that of Britain, all real as well as personal property of a deceased person could be attached for debt; in practice this meant that a landed estate was often dispersed if its wealthy holder had accumulated large debts.[31]

General economic patterns were most responsible for lost fortunes in late eighteenth-century Philadelphia. As historian Thomas Doerflinger has recently concluded, "Philadelphia traders, even the most successful, led demanding, nerve-racking lives in the tensely competitive, highly uncertain commercial climate of the Delaware Valley, and a large number of traders went bankrupt." Reliable information about prices and markets was scarce, institutional development to buffer economic cycles was limited, and the city's economy found itself at the mercy of economic cycles and disruptive warfare originating in Europe. No wonder that in the eighteenth century a merchant's activity was often referred to as "venturing." The depression of 1797 highlighted this vulnerability, and even Robert Morris found himself in debtor's prison, his country home sold at sheriff's auction—an unseemly action unknown in Britain. In the words of Elizabeth Meredith, the wife of one wealthy resident, "the great are ground little and the little great." Harrison Gray Otis, in town to attend Congress, reflected on the bankruptcy of Peter Blight, a member of the 1800 elite: "Overtrading and unbounded credit are the mischiefs, . . . and though I have thought or called myself rich, I would not exchange my property for that of many who talk of thousands and tens of thousands as if dollars were needles and pins."[32]

The economic environment encouraged the development of a set of values that emphasized individual acquisitiveness at the expense of social cohesion, which both natives and visitors noticed. "In Philadelphia, more than in any part of the world," reported la Rochefoucauld-Liancourt, attention is focused on "the accumulation of wealth; which passion is not diminished even by the possession of the greatest fortune." Amazed observers described wealthy Philadelphians as running almost any risk to increase their fortunes. In Philadelphia, "during the extreme heat few would voluntarily encounter the rays of the sun," wrote one visitor, "except in the pursuit of wealth," which encouraged them to "run every hazard." This contributed to a lack of social, personal, and residential attachments. "In Philadelphia," wrote de St. Méry, "everything is for sale, provided the owner is offered a tempting price. He will part with his house, his carriage, his horse, his dog—anything at all." "Among the rich class," Louis Auguste Félix Beaujour concluded scornfully, a man "lives only in himself, and for himself."[33]

Parents encouraged independence in their children, from fear that they would not succeed in a competitive society like that of Philadelphia if they became overly dependent on family largess. (Hence the atmosphere of the University of Pennsylvania.) William Allen, for one, worried because his son John did not "bustle in the world" enough, having acquired "the English taste for manners and customs." Family background carried limited weight in Philadelphia. "Rank of birth is not recognized," reported Schoepf. Elizabeth Powel identified the limited usefulness of family ties when she wrote, "The only claim to estimation on the score of Ancestry or in collateral relation is by emulating their virtues." By encouraging this "emulation," rather than employing threats, rich Philadelphians showed that, like Americans in general, they had shifted to child-raising practices that recognized offspring as independent, malleable individuals. George Logan, for example, urged his son to learn much by associating "with characters superior to [yourself] in virtue and good manners."[34]

Doerflinger argues, "divided along economic, ethnic, and religious lines, fragmented by extensive migration, and atomized by the competition of trade itself, Philadelphia's merchant community did not constitute a 'class,' an 'aristocracy,' or a cohesive social group of any other description." Although Doerflinger would hesitate to do so, perhaps his characterization can be extended to Philadelphia's entire economic elite in 1800, about half of whom were merchants.[35] The lawyers, craftsmen, and even the few rentiers who made up the rest of the elite were affected by the same socially, economically, and ideologically divisive forces that fragmented their counting-house colleagues.

THE HISTORICAL SIGNIFICANCE OF A SOCIALLY FRAGMENTED ECONOMIC ELITE

What were the consequences of the social fragmentation among the 1800 Philadelphia economic elite? I have suggested elsewhere that it inhibited the elite's ability to control public affairs and contributed to the highly conflictual and relatively democratic pattern of politics that developed in eighteenth-century Pennsylvania. Doerflinger has attributed Philadelphia's economic success at this time in part to the relative social openness and consequent constant reinvigoration of the merchant segment, at any rate, of the elite. Michael Zuckerman has argued that the city's ability to transform this economic success into national cultural leadership was encouraged by the stimulating, competitive atmosphere associated with an "incomplete" elite. On a national scale, Edmund Morgan has argued that the separation of social status from political officeholding, which was advanced by the financial and economic turmoil of the Revolution, changed political culture in the United States by diminishing deference and correspondingly bringing out egalitarian implications long inherent in Anglo-American ideas about popular sovereignty. This development encouraged the advent of professional politicians, dependent on "leadership" rather than deference for their success.[36]

From a theoretical perspective this social fragmentation among the rich suggests that economic factors, or at least the possession of wealth, were insufficient to create a socially cohesive group, a true upper "class." In the description of Karl Marx, for whom "manifold relations with one another" were requisite for individuals to form themselves into a "class," the wealthy were more like "potatoes in a sack" than a closely bonded group. Their experience also supports Max Weber's observation, "The rise of societal or even of communal action from a common class situation is by no means a universal phenomenon."[37] On the continuum of cohesive social groups, rich Philadelphians in 1800 were much farther from the cohesive end than most scholars have recognized. Not only could the rich have been more closely bonded hypothetically, but greater cohesiveness was actually displayed by the wealthy in Europe and elsewhere in the colonies. There was even greater cohesiveness displayed in Philadelphia by groups who were bound by noneconomic attributes, especially religion and ethnicity.

Rich Philadelphians at the end of the eighteenth century were both similar to and different from other groups of rich Americans. In part this was because they were enmeshed in a city with its own special qualities. But these were qualities that the rest of America was increasingly beginning to share as a national culture slowly began to develop.

Several scholars have recently described the gentry in revolutionary Virginia as in crisis. Rhys Isaac reports an unprecedented challenge to their social and political leadership from masses of Virginians increasingly alienated by their aristocratic life-style. Timothy Breen argues that the gentry faced a "cultural" crisis induced by a loss of self-confidence in their own independence brought on by an increasingly nagging debt to British merchants. Jan Lewis finds that after the Revolution the gentry was further disheartened by a deteriorating tobacco economy and an intensified concern about religion, which discouraged rather than consoled their spirits. During these years, as both Lewis and Daniel Blake Smith recount, the gentry began to adopt new family practices that stressed ties of affection and a diminished role for European aristocratic, hierarchical authority.[38]

Similarly, the revolutionary years shattered the fortunes of many wealthy Bostonians and highlighted the long-emerging limitations on economic growth in their region. In New York City the wartime dissolution of the Hudson River valley landed estates undercut the fortunes of many prominent families, and loyalism removed others from the state. Throughout revolutionary and early national America, as Jay Fliegelman argues, patriarchical coercive authority was under challenge by norms that emphasized independence by family members, a development with political and, although Fliegelman does not say so, economic implications.[39]

Groups of rich men of both old and new wealth emerged in these places and attained significant social cohesion that enabled them to exercise considerable power in all dimensions of society. This pattern appears in early nineteenth-century Boston, as Ronald Story identifies—interrelated Brahmins consolidated their economic power and increased their consciousness by dominating the cultural institutions of the city, especially Harvard.[40]

Wealthy Philadelphians reacted to many of the same developments with somewhat different results. In late eighteenth-century Philadelphia, as E. Digby Baltzell points out, the "class structure" remained that of "a highly mobile and heterogeneously plutocratic democracy." Philadelphia lacked the institutions and practices that aided the wealthy elsewhere to achieve a hegemonic position: it did not have the slavery of Virginia, the heritage of authoritarian political rule of New York City, or the religious and ethnic homogeneity of Boston. Consequently, as Harrison Gray Otis concluded with Yankee astuteness, in Philadelphia "Those who constitute the fashionable world are at best a mere oligarchy."[41]

Philadelphia in 1800 resembled what America was to become in the nineteenth century—mobile, prosperous, heterogeneous, archetypally capitalistic. In their social practices, the city's wealthy may also have anticipated the rest of America. C. Wright Mills traced the "social class" background of the "American business elite" downward toward "lower middle" and "lower" class origins beginning with the cohort of business leaders born between 1760 and 1789. Such a shift was already evident, however, among the Philadelphia economic elite in 1800, whose typical member was born in the middle of Mills's *preceding* cohort, whose members were born between 1730 and 1759. Why then did nineteenth-century elites in general not show the lack of social cohesion that this study has found among the rich in late eighteenth-century Philadelphia? Or perhaps they did, at least to a greater extent than some recent scholarship has led us to believe.[42]

What would the future hold for the members of the 1800 economic elite? Some of the conditions that encouraged both individual success stories and an overall lack of social cohesion among rich Philadelphians continued to be important in the nineteenth century. In general, however, Philadelphia became insular, less dynamic, less the place where a young man on the rise would choose to live. We do not know what these developments meant for social cohesion among the wealthy, hostility among the members of different economic strata in the city, or the city's history in general. But it is doubtful if they helped the wealthy Philadelphians of 1800 to entrench their fortunes and perpetuate family dynasties. If a cohesive upper class emerged in nineteenth-century Philadelphia, it was not based on the 1800 economic elite. There are perhaps only about thirty Philadelphia families today with a patriarch in the 1800 elite. Most of the titans of the 1800 elite established, at best, short-lived dynasties. William Bingham, the richest Philadelphian of 1800, and Stephen Girard, the member of the 1800 elite who subsequently succeeded Bingham as the wealthiest, left no heirs in the Quaker City. As most of the rich Philadelphians at the end of the eighteenth century understood, wealth in America is fleeting, and social ties that are meant to be lasting must be based on other characteristics.

---

[1] Eric Foner, *Tom Paine and Revolutionary America* (New York: Oxford University Press, 1976), p. 25. For similar discussions of the unity and power of the "gentry" or "aristocracy" in Philadelphia in the second half of the eighteenth century, see especially Gary B. Nash, *The Urban Crucible: Social Change, Political Consciousness, and the Origins of the American Revolution* (Cambridge: Harvard University Press, 1979); Richard G. Miller, *Philadelphia—Federalist City: A Study of Urban Politics, 1789–1801* (Port Washington, N.Y.: Kennikat Press, 1976); Carl Bridenbaugh and Jessica Bridenbaugh, *Rebels and Gentlemen: Philadelphia in the Age of Franklin* (New York: Reynal and Hitchcock, 1942), pp. 179–224; and Stephen Brobeck, "Revolutionary Change in Colonial Philadelphia: The Brief Life of the Proprietary Gentry," *William and Mary Quarterly*, 3d ser., 33, no. 3 (July 1976): 410–34. That a "highly self-conscious merchant elite with wide-ranging economic and political interests dominated" Philadelphia and "sought to control" the rest of the province is the conclusion of a review of the literature by Douglas Greenberg, "The Middle Colonies in Recent American Historiography, *William and Mary Quarterly*, 3d ser., 36, no. 3 (July 1979): 412. A widely known scholarly description of twentieth-century Philadelphia along these lines is E. Digby Baltzell, *Philadelphia Gentlemen: The Making of a National Upper Class* (Glencoe, Ill.: Free Press, 1958). The need for precisely determining the nature and function of elite groups in early America is pointed out by Jack P. Greene, "Uneasy Connection: An Analysis of the Preconditions of the American

Revolution," in *Essays on the American Revolution*, ed. James H. Hutson and Stephen Kurtz (Chapel Hill: University of North Carolina Press, 1973), pp. 35–36. More generally, while focusing primarily on Britain, the appropriateness of local and regional studies of class, especially prior to the twentieth century, is argued by Katherine A. Lynd, "The Use of Quantitative Data in the Historical Study of Social Classes," *Historical Methods* 17, no. 4 (Fall 1984): 230–37.

[2] Sophia Cadwalader, ed., *Recollections of Joshua Francis Fisher Written in 1864* (Boston: B. D. Updike, Merrymount Press, 1929), p. 202; Henry Wansey, *The Journal of an Excursion into the United States of North America in the Summer of 1794* (Salisbury, Eng.: J. Easton, 1796), p. 136. For details on the court, see Rufus Wilmot Griswold, *The Republican Court; or, American Society in the Days of Washington* (rev. ed.; New York: D. Appleton, 1855); Anne Hollingsworth Wharton, *Social Life in the Early Republic* (Philadelphia: J. B. Lippincott, 1902), pp. 27–56. A recent scholarly treatment can be found in Ethel Elise Rasmusson, "Capital on the Delaware: The Philadelphia Upper Class in Transition, 1789–1801" (Ph.D. diss., Brown University, 1962); and Ethel E. Rasmusson, "Democratic Environment—Aristocratic Aspiration," *Pennsylvania Magazine of History and Biography* 90, no. 2 (April 1966): 178–82.

[3] Anna Rawle to Rebecca (Mrs. Samuel) Shoemaker, November 4, 1780, Shoemaker Papers, Historical Society of Pennsylvania, Philadelphia (hereafter cited as HSP); Abigail Adams to Mrs. Cranch, March 18, 1800, as quoted in Rasmusson, "Capital on the Delaware," p. 82; unidentified traveler to David Humphreys, ca. 1790, as quoted in Griswold, *Republican Court*, p. 272; Randolph Shipley Klein, *Portrait of an Early American Family: The Shippens of Pennsylvania across Five Generations* (Philadelphia: University of Pennsylvania Press, 1975), p. 205; Robert D. Arbuckle, *Pennsylvania Speculator and Patriot: The Entrepreneurial John Nicholson, 1757–1800* (University Park: Pennsylvania State University Press, 1975), p. 155; Benjamin Rush, *Autobiography of Benjamin Rush*, ed. George Corner (Princeton: Princeton University Press, 1947), p. 95; Cadwalader, *Recollections of Fisher*, p. 185.

[4] Hipólito José de Costa diary, January 1, 1799, in Robert C. Smith, "A Portuguese Naturalist in Philadelphia, 1799," *Pennsylvania Magazine of History and Biography* 78, no. 1 (January 1954): 82; *Aurora*, January 18, 1799; *Recollections of Samuel Breck with Passages from His Notebooks*, ed. H. E. Scudder (Philadelphia: Porter and Coates, 1877), pp. 202–3; David L. Barquist, " 'The Honours of a Court' or 'the Severity of Virtue': Household Furnishings and Cultural Aspirations in Philadelphia," elsewhere in this volume; Beatrice B. Garvan, *Federal Philadelphia, 1785–1825: The Athens of the Western World* (Philadelphia: Philadelphia Museum of Art, 1987), pp. 54–65, 75. For contemporary dismissals of the court, see Jean-Pierre Brissot de Warville, *New Travels in the United States of America Performed in 1788* (Dublin: P. Byrne, A. Grueber, W. McKenzie, 1792), pp. 317–19; and Sarah Cadbury, "Extracts from the Diary of Ann Warder," *Pennsylvania Magazine of History and Biography* 18, no. 1 (1894): 52. On the disintegration of the court, see Rasmusson, "Capital on the Delaware," pp. 183ff.

[5] Selecting the upper 2.5% of the male population produced a group large enough to contain the interactions of an upper class and still be manageable for intensive study. As to the size of the "upper class" in eighteenth-century America, the group corresponds with the beliefs of Jackson T. Main, *The Social Structure of Revolutionary America* (Princeton: Princeton University Press, 1965), p. 161; and Gary B. Nash, "Urban Wealth and Poverty in Pre-Revolutionary America," *Journal of Interdisciplinary History* 6, no. 4 (July 1976): 554. The members of the elite were identified largely from county tax assessment ledgers, Philadelphia Co., 1800, Philadelphia

City Archives. In some wards where ledgers were missing for 1800, returns for surrounding years were used. Eleven men joined the elite by supplementary criteria, chiefly large personal property or western landholdings. For a complete identification of the wealthy, see Robert J. Gough, "Toward a Theory of Class and Social Conflict: A Social History of Wealthy Philadelphians, 1775 and 1800" (Ph.D. diss., University of Pennsylvania, 1977), pp. 644–48. Biographical information presented throughout this paper about these men was gathered from genealogical records, particularly at the Genealogical Society of Pennsylvania, Philadelphia; published biographies; collective biographies of prominent Philadelphians; local histories; city directories; newspaper obituaries; probate records; and census and related material. These are fully discussed in Gough, "Toward a Theory," pp. 644–45, 714–17, 729–35.

6 Robert Stanley Rich, "Politics and Pedigrees: The Wealthy Men of Boston, 1798–1852" (Ph.D. diss., University of California, Los Angeles, 1975), p. 51.

7 By 1800 more than 70% of rich Bostonians worshipped as Unitarians (Rich, "Politics," p. 277). For the United Churches, see William Montgomery, comp., "Pew Renters List of Christ Church, St. Peters, and St. James, 1775–1815," typescript, HSP. For examples of a different view, see Brobeck, "Revolutionary Change," p. 425; and Nash, *Urban Crucible*, p. 270. That in 1756 only about 15% of the members of Christ Church came from the highest 7% of the city's tax assessment is shown in Deborah Mathias Gough, "Pluralism, Politics, and Power Struggles: The Church of England in Colonial Philadelphia, 1683–1789" (Ph.D. diss., University of Pennsylvania, 1978), pp. 250–52.

8 For a different view regarding the distinctiveness of the elite, see Nash, *Urban Crucible*, p. 262; and Billy G. Smith, "Inequality in Late Colonial Philadelphia: A Note on Its Nature and Growth," *William and Mary Quarterly*, 3d ser., 41, no. 4 (October 1984): 643. The similarity in demographic characteristics between the elite and the rest of the city's population is described in Robert J. Gough, "The Significance of the Demographic Characteristics of Wealthy Philadelphians at the End of the Eighteenth Century," *Proceedings of the American Philosophical Society* 133, no. 2 (June 1989): 305–11.

9 James Mease, *Picture of Philadelphia . . .* (Philadelphia: B. and T. Kite, 1811), pp. 20–29. See also Thomas M. Doerflinger, *A Vigorous Spirit of Enterprise: Merchants and Economic Development in Revolutionary Philadelphia* (Chapel Hill: University of North Carolina Press, 1986), pp. 39–40. This pattern was normal in a preindustrial city (Gideon Sjoberg, *The Pre-Industrial City: Past and Present* [New York: Free Press, 1960], pp. 102–3). On comparisons with London, see Caspar Wistar to Thomas Wistar, July 3, 1787, Wistar Manuscripts, HSP; Edward Shippen, Jr., to Edward Shippen (of Lancaster), March 25, 1760, in Thomas Balch, ed., *Letters and Papers Relating Chiefly to the Provincial History of Pennsylvania* (Philadelphia: Crissy and Markley, 1885), pp. 173–74; and Charles N. Buck, *Memoirs of Charles N. Buck Interspersed with Private Anecdotes and Events of the Times from 1791 to 1841* (Philadelphia: Walnut House, 1941), p. 200.

10 Whitfield J. Bell, Jr., "Addenda to Watson's Annals of Philadelphia: Notes by Jacob Mordecai, 1836," *Pennsylvania Magazine of History and Biography* 98, no. 2 (April 1974): 139–40; Henry D. Biddle, ed., *Extracts from the Journal of Elizabeth Drinker from 1759 to 1807, A.D.* (Philadelphia: J. B. Lippincott Co., 1889), pp. 140, 155, 326; Elaine F. Crane, "The World of Elizabeth Drinker," *Pennsylvania Magazine of History and Biography* 107, no. 1 (January 1983): 21; *The Philadelphia Directory . . . 1801* (Philadelphia: William W. Woodward, 1801), p. 9; Rasmusson, "Capital on the Delaware," p. 46. That house types in urban neighborhoods did not vary by socio-

economic status in the eighteenth century is argued in Clifford Edward Clark, Jr., *The American Family Home, 1800–1960* (Chapel Hill: University of North Carolina Press, 1986), pp. 52, 191–92. For Philadelphia, Garvan concludes, "Buildings did not clearly reveal personal status" (Garvan, *Federal Philadelphia*, p. 15).

[11] Rawle to Shoemaker, February 6, 1782, Shoemaker Papers, HSP; Ann Ridgely to Ann (Mrs. Charles) Ridgely, February 24, 1799, in *The Ridgelys of Delaware and Their Circle: What Them Befell in Colonial and Federal Times; Letters, 1751–1890*, ed. Mabel Lloyd Ridgely (Portland, Maine: Anthoensen Press, 1949), p. 287. On the prevalency of renting, see Sharon V. Salinger and Charles Wetherell, "Wealth and Renting in Prerevolutionary Philadelphia," *Journal of American History* 71, no. 4 (March 1985): 826–40, esp. 831; Doerflinger, *Vigorous Spirit*, p. 131.

[12] Klein, *Portrait of an Early American Family*, pp. 206–7.

[13] These country homes can be identified from Harold Donaldson Eberlein and Cortlandt Van Dyke Hubbard, *Portrait of a Colonial City: Philadelphia, 1670–1838* (Philadelphia: J. B. Lippincott, 1939). By contrast, see G. E. Mingay, *English Landed Society in the Eighteenth Century* (Toronto: University of Toronto Press, 1963), pp. 214–15.

[14] Margaret Bailey Tinkcom, ed., "Caviar along the Potomac: Sir Augustus John Foster's 'Notes on the United States,' " *William and Mary Quarterly*, 3d ser., 8, no. 1 (January 1951): 68–107. On ownership of country homes, see Eberlein and Hubbard, *Portrait of a Colonial City*.

[15] *Burnaby's Travels through North America*, ed. Rufus Rockwell Wilson (3d ed.; New York: A. Wessels Co., 1904), pp. 97–98. On membership in the Schuylkill, see *History of the Schuylkill Fishing Company of the State in Schuylkill* (Philadelphia: By the company, 1889).

[16] John Melish, *Travels through the United States of America in the Years 1806 and 1807 and 1809, 1810, 1811*, 2 vols. (rev. enl. ed.; Philadelphia: By the author, 1815), 1:163; Dorothy F. Grimm, "A History of the Library Company of Philadelphia, 1731–1836" (Ph.D. diss., University of Pennsylvania, 1947), pp. 125–26. On membership in the Library Company, see "Chronological Record of the Names of the Members of the Library Company of Philadelphia," Library Company of Philadelphia.

[17] "Constitution and Rules Adopted by the Welsh Society," Welsh Society Minutes, 1748–1839, HSP.

[18] William Franklin to Benjamin Franklin, May [?], 1767, in *The Papers of Benjamin Franklin*, ed. Leonard W. Labaree, William B. Willcox, and Claude A. Lopez, 27 vols. to date (New Haven: Yale University Press, 1959–), 14:174–75. In 1797 a family friend admitted, "the Elder Branches of the Family were never Much Esteem'd" (Elizabeth [Mrs. Jonathan] Meredith to David Meredith, April 23, 1797, Meredith Papers, HSP.) See also Benjamin Franklin to Richard Bache, August 13, 1768, in *Franklin Papers*, 15:185–86.

[19] W[illiam] Winterbotham, *An Historical . . . View of the American United States*, 2 vols. (London: J. Ridgeway, 1795), 1:423. For the continuance of this pattern, see Allan M. Zachary, "Social Thought and the Philadelphia Leadership Community, 1800–1840" (Ph.D. diss., Northwestern University, 1974).

[20] James A. Mulhern, *A History of Secondary Education in Pennsylvania* (Lancaster, Pa.: Scientific Press, 1933), pp. 8–9, 163–64, 65–85, 246–47; Howard Charles Emmick, "The Role of the Church in the Development of Education in Pennsylvania, 1638–1834" (Ph.D. diss., University of Pittsburgh, 1959), pp. 52, 56–65, 120–28, 138–43, 157–60, 166–78, 181–83; *Gazette of the United States*, March 28, 1800. Similarly, education in New York City at this time was dominated by numerous "common

pay" schools with students from a wide range of socioeconomic backgrounds (Carl F. Kaestle, *The Evolution of an Urban School System: New York City, 1750–1850* [Cambridge: Harvard University Press, 1973], pp. 41–51). Quakers reportedly opposed public education since they were "unwilling to mingle their children with the children of other persuasions . . . or maintain their own schools at an exclusive expense while they would pay a general tax to those of the public" (François-Alexandre-Frédéric de la Rochefoucauld-Liancourt, *Travels through the United States of North America, the Country of the Iroquois and Upper Canada in the Years 1795, 1796, and 1797 . . .* , trans. H. Neuman, 2 vols. [London: R. Phillips, 1799], 1:387).

[21] Compiled from *Biographical Catalogue of the Matriculates of the College . . . (1749–1893)* (Philadelphia: University of Pennsylvania, 1894). Some nongraduates appear to have been omitted from this compilation. The variety of reasons why students came to the College of Philadelphia and the consequent motley nature of the student body are discussed in Ann Dexter Gordon, "The College of Philadelphia, 1749–1779: Impact of an Institution" (Ph.D. diss., University of Wisconsin—Madison, 1974), pp. 183, 186–87, 192–95, 289–90, and esp. pp. 135–36. For a different pattern in New England, see Clifford K. Shipton, "Ye Mystery of Ye Ages Solved; or, How Placing Worked at Colonial Harvard and Yale," *Harvard Alumni Bulletin* 52 (1954–55): 258–59, 262–63.

[22] Jonathan Williams, Jr., to Benjamin Franklin, April 13, 1779, as quoted in Claude-Anne Lopez and Eugenia W. Herbert, *The Private Franklin: The Man and His Family* (New York: W. W. Norton, 1975), p. 23; Meredith to Meredith, January 6, 1796, Meredith Papers, HSP; Alexander Baring to J. W. Hope, 1795, as quoted in Robert C. Alberts, *The Golden Voyage: The Life and Times of William Bingham, 1752–1806* (Boston: Houghton Mifflin Co., 1969), p. 26. For a detailed discussion of why marriage was infrequent among wealthy kin, see Robert J. Gough, "Close-Kin Marriage and Upper-Class Formation in Late Eighteenth-Century Philadelphia," *Journal of Family History* 14, no. 2 (Spring 1989): 119–36. In general, see Herman R. Lantz, "Romantic Love in the Pre-Modern Period: A Social Commentary," *Journal of Social History* 15, no. [3] (Spring 1982): 349–70; and Sjoberg, *Pre-Industrial City*, pp. 147–50, 153. For Philadelphia, see J. William Frost, *The Quaker Family in Colonial America: A Portrait of the Society of Friends* (New York: St. Martin's Press, 1973), pp. 167–68; and Judy Mann DiStefano, "A Concept of the Family in Colonial America: The Pembertons of Philadelphia" (Ph.D. diss., Ohio State University, 1970), pp. 21–61. For neighboring Germantown, see Stephanie Grauman Wolf, *Urban Village: Population, Community, and Family Structure in Germantown, Pennsylvania, 1683–1800* (Princeton: Princeton University Press, 1976), pp. 299–300. See also Richard Peters to William Smith, May 28, 1763, in *Pennsylvania Magazine of History and Biography* 10 (1886): 350–53; and Phineas Bond to John Cadwalader, April 13, 1779, Phineas Bond correspondence, Cadwalader Collection, HSP. For a discussion of how late eighteenth-century women used premarital pregnancy to undercut "paternal restraints" and express their "independence," see Robert A. Gross, *The Minutemen and Their World* (New York: Hill and Wang, 1976), pp. 100–101. Molly's elopement is covered in [Drinker], *Extracts from the Journal*, pp. 289–91. As early as 1766, John Penn ignored the objections of his uncle Thomas Penn and married Anne Allen, chief justice William Allen's daughter. Ironically, Thomas Penn opposed the union because he thought it might give the impression of wealthy officials consolidating their power—what was valued in England, it seemed, had to be avoided in Pennsylvania (Thomas Penn to John Penn, April 12, 1765, Private Correspondence, Penn Papers, HSP). John Penn had previously courted Andrew Hamilton's daughter,

who demonstrated the emerging independence of young people by rejecting Penn's proposals despite pressure to accept from her family (John Penn to Thomas Penn, October 13, 1765, Private Correspondence, and March 1, 1766, Official Correspondence, Penn Papers).

[23] *On the Threshold of Liberty: Journal of a Frenchman's Tour of the American Colonies in 1777*, trans. Edward D. Seeber (Bloomington: Indiana University Press, 1959), pp. 29–31; Thomas Fisher to [Tench Francis], undated draft, Joshua and Thomas Fisher Correspondence, HSP; Ann Warder, August 2, [1786], in Sarah Cadbury, "Extracts from the Diary of Mrs. Ann Warder," *Pennsylvania Magazine of History and Biography* 17 (1893): 460. On Quaker marriages, see Jack D. Marietta, *The Reformation of American Quakerism, 1748–1783* (Philadelphia: University of Pennsylvania Press, 1984), esp. pp. 51–55. For subgroups among the elite based on religion and marriage patterns, see Gough, "Close-Kin Marriages," pp. 121–27. For a good discussion of a situation in which boundaries between religiously based subgroups in a society are stronger at the elite than at the mass level, see Aren Lijphart, *The Politics of Accommodation: Pluralism and Democracy in the Netherlands* (Berkeley: University of California Press, 1968), pp. 59–77. Similarly, that identification with nationality increased as socioeconomic level increased in late nineteenth-century San Francisco was found by Peter R. Decker, *Fortunes and Failures: White-Collar Mobility in Nineteenth-Century San Francisco* (Cambridge: Harvard University Press, 1978), pp. 211–12.

[24] Isaac Weld, Jr., *Travels through the States of North America and the Provinces of Upper and Lower Canada during the Years 1795, 1796, and 1797*, 2 vols. (3d ed.; London: J. Stockdale, 1800), 1:102; Johann David Schoepf, *Travels in the Confederation*, trans. Alfred J. Morison, 2 vols. (Philadelphia: W. J. Campbell, 1911), 1:97–102.

[25] Schoepf, *Travels*, 1:97–102; *Gottlieb Mittelberger's Journey to Pennsylvania. . . (1750–1754)*, trans. Carl Theodore Eben (Philadelphia: J. Y. Jeanes, 1898), pp. 112, 117; Louis Auguste Félix Beaujour, *Sketch of the United States of North America, at the Commencement of the Nineteenth Century, from 1800–1810*, trans. and ed. William Walton, 2 vols. (London: J. Booth, 1814), 1:150; Weld, *Travels*, 1:26–30; Lord Adam Gordon, "Journal of an Officer's Travel in the Americas and the West Indies," in *Travels in the American Colonies*, ed. Newton Mereness (New York: Macmillan Co., 1916), p. 410; Edward Thornton to James B. Burges, October 13, 1791, as cited in S. W. Jackman, "A Young Englishman Reports on the New Nation: Edward Thornton to James Bland Burges, 1791–1793," *William and Mary Quarterly*, 3d ser., 18, no. 1 (January 1961): 92–93. On the importance of factors such as manners, dress, and speech in establishing socioeconomic distinctions in eighteenth-century Britain, see Anne Buck, *Dress in Eighteenth-Century England* (London: Holmes and Meier, 1979). On the rich as a mere plutocracy, distinguishable only by their money, see Beaujour, *Sketch*, 1:144; Chevalier de la Luzerne, as cited in John C. Miller, *Triumph of Freedom, 1775–1783* (Boston: Little, Brown, 1948), p. 651; and Ferdinand M. Bayard, *Travels of a Frenchman in Maryland and Virginia with a Description of Philadelphia and Baltimore in 1791 . . .*, trans. and ed. Ben C. McCary (Williamsburg, Va.: Privately published, 1950), p. 125.

[26] La Rochefoucauld-Liancourt, *Travels*, 2:386; Bayard, *Travels*, pp. 128–29. While not unaware of the different standards of living among different socioeconomic groups, Alice Jones points out that *consumption* was not as unequally distributed as was *wealth* in early America (Alice Hanson Jones, *The Wealth of a Nation to Be: The American Colonies on the Eve of the Revolution* [New York: Columbia University Press, 1980], p. 211).

[27] Henry Bradshaw Fearon, *Sketches of America: A Narrative of a Journey of Five Thousand Miles through the Eastern and Western States of America . . .* (London: Longman, Hurst, Rees, Orme, and Brown, 1818), p. 173; "The Thrifter," *Columbian* (1788), as quoted in J. Thomas Scharf and Thompson Westcott, *History of Philadelphia, 1609–1884*, 3 vols. (Philadelphia: L. H. Everts, 1884), 2:910; *Moreau de St. Méry's American Journey [1793–1798]*, trans. and ed. Kenneth Roberts and Anna M. Roberts (Garden City, N.Y.: Doubleday, 1947), p. 276 (de St. Méry also subdivided "whites" into free, servant, and indentured categories).

[28] George Washington to Tobias Lear, September 5, 1790, in *The Writings of George Washington . . . 1745–1799*, ed. John C. Fitzgerald, 39 vols. (Washington, D.C.: Government Printing Office, 1931–44), 31:254; *Chateaubriand's Travels in America*, trans. Richard Switzer (Lexington: University of Kentucky Press, 1969), p. 16. Chateaubriand may have invented his reported audience with Washington, but there is no reason to doubt that he at least saw the president's residence while in Philadelphia. On his income, see Benjamin Rush to Lady Jane Wishart Belsches, April 21, 1784, in Benjamin Rush, *Letters*, ed. L. H. Butterfield, 2 vols. (Princeton: Princeton University Press, 1951), 1:325. Income estimates for different ranks can be found in Jackson T. Main, *The Social Structure of Revolutionary America* (Princeton: Princeton University Press, 1965), pp. 116–22.

[29] Albert Gallatin to Thomas Jefferson, September 18, 1804, as quoted in Edwin Wolf 2nd and Maxwell Whiteman, *The History of the Jews of Philadelphia from Colonial Times to the Age of Jackson* (Philadelphia: Jewish Publication Society of America, 1957), p. 217; Benjamin Franklin, "Information to Those Who Would Remove to America," in *A Benjamin Franklin Reader*, ed. Nathan G. Goodman (New York: Thomas Y. Crowell Co., 1945), p. 346. The generous but not unreasonable estimate about living standards is by Joseph Nourse, receiver in the Treasury Department, and is reprinted in Ellis Paxson Oberholtzer, *Philadelphia: A History of the City and Its People . . .*, 4 vols. (Philadelphia: J. S. Clarke Publishing Co., 1912), 1:410. On the size of merchants' fortunes, see Doerflinger, *Vigorous Spirit*, pp. 126–34. For titles, see *The Philadelphia Directory . . . 1800* (Philadelphia: William W. Woodward, 1800). How Continental officers unsuccessfully tried to *use* their status as officers to become "gentlemen" is shown in Charles Royster, *A Revolutionary People at War: The Continental Army and American Character, 1775–1783* (Chapel Hill: University of North Carolina Press, 1980), pp. 93–95, 343–44.

[30] John Penn to Julianna Penn, December 5, 1774, Private Correspondence, Penn Papers, HSP; Richard S. Dunn, *Sugar and Slaves: The Rise of the Planter Class in the British West Indies, 1624–1713* (Chapel Hill: University of North Carolina Press, 1972), esp. pp. 268–70; Jackson T. Main, "The One Hundred," *William and Mary Quarterly*, 3d ser., 11, no. 3 (July 1954): 354–84; Richard Waterhouse, "The Development of Elite Culture in the Colonial American South: A Study of Charles Town, 1670–1770," *Australian Journal of Politics and History* 28, no. 3 (1982): 399. Good case studies of English fortunes can be found in Lawrence Stone, *Family and Fortune: Aristocratic Finance in the Sixteenth and Seventeenth Centuries* (Oxford, Eng.: Clarendon Press, 1973). See also Mingay, *English Landed Society*, pp. 1–62. For a similar comparison, see Doerflinger, *Vigorous Spirit*, p. 160.

[31] For a good discussion of the institutional factors that prevented "inequality and its characteristic system" from becoming "dominant" in eighteenth-century Boston, a much worse case for this sort of argument than Philadelphia, see G. B. Warden, "Inequality and Instability in Eighteenth-Century Boston: A Reappraisal," *Journal of Interdisciplinary History* 6, no. 4 (Spring 1976): 614–18. On estate transfers

at death, see Marylynn Salmon, "Equality or Submission? Feme Covert Status in Early Pennsylvania," in *Women of America: A History*, ed. Mary Beth Norton and Carol Berkin (Boston: Houghton Mifflin Co., 1979), pp. 106–8; G. B. Warden, "The Distribution of Property in Boston, 1692–1775," *Perspectives in American History* 10 (1976): 46.

[32] Doerflinger, *Vigorous Spirit*, p. 135; Meredith to Meredith, April 23, 1797, Meredith Papers, HSP; Harrison Gray Otis to Sally Otis, 1800, as quoted in Samuel Eliot Morison, *Harrison Gray Otis, 1765–1848: Urbane Federalist* (Boston: Houghton Mifflin Co., 1969), p. 139.

[33] La Rochefoucauld-Liancourt, *Travels*, 2:338; Charles William Janson, *The Stranger in America, 1793–1806*, ed. Carl S. Driver (New York: Press of the Pioneers, 1935), p. 118; *Moreau de St. Méry's Journey*, p. 270; Beaujour, *Sketch*, 1:145–46.

[34] William Allen to Thomas Penn, May 8, 1767, Official Correspondence, Penn Papers, HSP; Schōepf, *Travels*, 1:102; Elizabeth (Mrs. Samuel) Powel to unknown, May 23, 1807, Powel Collection, HSP; George Logan to Albanus Logan, February 8, 1803, Logan Papers, HSP.

[35] Doerflinger, *Vigorous Spirit*, p. 62. It has been incorrectly concluded that "merchants naturally predominated among the very rich" by Billy G. Smith, "Inequality in Late Colonial Philadelphia," p. 642; a similar undocumented assertion is made by Miller, *Philadelphia*, p. 14.

[36] Robert Gough, "Can a Rich Man Support Revolution? The Case of Philadelphia in 1776," *Pennsylvania History* 48, no. 3 (July 1981): 235–50; Doerflinger, *Vigorous Spirit*, esp. pp. 335–64; Michael Zuckerman, "Can Words Speak to Things? An Inconclusive Conclusion," elsewhere in this volume; Edmund S. Morgan, *Inventing the People: The Rise of Popular Sovereignty in England and America* (New York: W. W. Norton, 1988), pp. 292–95, 303–6. On the growing separation of wealth and officeholding in Philadelphia after the Revolution, see Gough, "Toward a Theory," pp. 504–10.

[37] Karl Marx, *The Eighteenth Brumaire of Louis Napoleon* (1852), reprinted in Karl Marx and Friedrich Engels, *Selected Works* . . . (New York: International Publishers, 1968), pp. 171–72; Max Weber, "Class, Status, and Party," in *From Max Weber: Essays in Sociology*, ed. and trans. H. H. Gerth and C. Wright Mills (1946; reprint, New York: Doubleday, 1959), pp. 181–83. On the use of the concept of social cohesion to establish economic and noneconomic social groups, see Lee Benson, "Marx's General and Middle-Range Theories of Social Conflict," in *Qualitative and Quantitative Social Research: Papers in Honor of Paul F. Lazarsfeld*, ed. Robert K. Merton, James S. Coleman, and Peter H. Rossi (New York: Free Press, 1979), pp. 189–209; and Lee Benson, "Group Cohesion and Social and Ideological Conflict," *American Behavioral Scientist* 16, no. 5 (May/June 1973): 741–68. The author attempts to explain this use of the concept of class in the context of the present study more fully in Gough, "Toward a Theory," pp. 99–112.

[38] Rhys Isaac, *The Transformation of Virginia, 1740–1790* (Chapel Hill: University of North Carolina Press, 1982); Timothy H. Breen, *Tobacco Culture: The Mentality of the Great Tidewater Planters on the Eve of the Revolution* (Princeton: Princeton University Press, 1985); Jan Lewis, *The Pursuit of Happiness: Family and Values in Jefferson's Virginia* (Cambridge, Eng.: Cambridge University Press, 1983); Daniel Blake Smith, *Inside the Great House: Planter Family Life in Eighteenth-Century Chesapeake Society* (Ithaca, N.Y.: Cornell University Press, 1980).

[39] Frederic Cople Jaher, *The Urban Establishment: Upper Strata in Boston, New York, Charleston, Chicago, and Los Angeles* (Urbana: University of Illinois Press,

1982), pp. 15–21, 171–75; Jay Fliegelman, *Prodigals and Pilgrims: The American Revolution against Patriarchal Authority, 1750–1800* (Cambridge, Eng.: Cambridge University Press, 1982).

[40] Ronald Story, *The Forging of an Aristocracy: Harvard and the Boston Upper Class, 1800–1870* (Middletown, Conn.: Wesleyan University Press, 1980).

[41] E. Digby Baltzell, *Puritan Boston and Quaker Philadelphia: Two Protestant Ethics and the Spirit of Class Authority and Leadership* (New York: Free Press, 1979), pp. 151–75; Otis to Otis, November 20, 1797, as quoted in Morison, *Harrison Gray Otis*, pp. 124–26. For discussions of how these differences between New York City and Philadelphia led to different experiences during the Revolution, see Nash, *Urban Crucible*, pp. 362–82; and Edward Countryman, *A People in Revolution: The American Revolution and Political Society in New York, 1760–1790* (Baltimore: Johns Hopkins University Press, 1981), pp. 163–69. For a more general description and explanation of differences between New York and Pennsylvania in the eighteenth century, see Robert J. Gough, "The Myth of the 'Middle Colonies': An Analysis of Regionalization in Early America," *Pennsylvania Magazine of History and Biography* 107, no. 3 (July 1983): 393–419.

[42] C. Wright Mills, "The American Business Elite: A Collective Portrait," *Journal of Economic History* 5, supp. (1945): 30. For contrasting details on the backgrounds of rich Philadelphians in 1775, see Gough, "Toward a Theory," p. 267. The "new men" in "every generation" of wealthy Philadelphians have been stressed in Baltzell, *Puritan Boston*, p. 212. For a view that stresses a tight-knit urban upper class in nineteenth-century America, see Edward Pessen, *Riches, Class, and Power before the Civil War* (Lexington, Mass.: D. C. Heath, 1972). A more varied and subtle view can be found in Jaher, *Urban Establishment*.

Class Relations, Political Economy, and Society in Philadelphia

Steve Rosswurm

Nearly every student of the American Revolution has concluded that it was more radical in Pennsylvania than in any other state. From Progressive to neo-Whig, historians have recognized the state's extensive social upheaval, agreeing that if the American Revolution shared any social aspects with the French Revolution, these were found there. A "genuine revolution," historian John Murrin argues, was needed to "sweep aside Quaker rule" and bring Pennsylvania into the independence camp.[1]

We now know a great deal about this revolution in Philadelphia. The precise reasons for it, however, are still obscure. Perhaps just as significant, there has been very little discussion of the role of the Revolution and the impact of its social upheaval on postwar class relations. In the period from 1750 to 1800 there was not just one battle—for "home rule"—and not even just two—for "home rule and who shall rule at home"—but rather a series of distinct but overlapping and interrelated struggles for power.[2] Those struggles were over whose vision of America would become reality, whose values would produce the institutions and laws that would govern the new country.

An Albert J. Beveridge Grant from the American Historical Association provided the basis for some research in this paper. The author thanks Susan Figliulo and Michael Meranze for comments on the original version.

I will do several things in this essay. First, I will briefly sketch the physiognomy of Philadelphia's ruling class ("the better sort") before the imperial crisis. Second, I will discuss its response to the crisis and how this established the framework within which developed the popular movement that produced Pennsylvania's revolution and the democratic constitution of 1776. Third, I will discuss the two very different kinds of "new men" who surfaced during these events and their ensuing political battles. The winners of that battle, the Robert Morris group, played critical national and local roles in the 1780s and the 1790s. Finally, I will discuss the demise of these men, the ascendancy of the Democratic-Republican coalition, and the return of the old ruling class.

THE PHYSIOGNOMY OF PHILADELPHIA'S RULING CLASS

After a settling-in period not unlike those in Virginia, Maryland, and other colonies, the immediate predecessors of Philadelphia's revolutionary era elite began establishing their fortunes and dominance. By the mid 1760s, if not before, several characteristics of Philadelphia's ruling class were evident.[3]

1. They had accumulated tremendous wealth through mercantile activity and buying and selling land (both in the city and in the countryside). Their estates were smaller than those of their European counterparts, but that is beside the point. Wealth in Philadelphia—whether measured by the distribution of taxable wealth, changing values of wealth left at death, or the distribution of income—was seriously maldistributed. That inequality deepened during the 1770s.[4] Joshua Emlen illustrates this point. Emlen, according to historian Robert J. Gough, was assessed for wealth in 1775 that placed him in the "top 1 percent" of all taxpayers. On his death in 1776, he left a personal estate of more than £1,750—cash, bonds, mortgages, plate, clothing, and house furnishings. He also owned at least fourteen rental properties in Philadelphia and probably received about £350 income in 1775 from his investments alone. By comparison, historian Billy Smith estimates that a laborer could hope to earn a maximum income of £60 per year.[5]

2. Wealth provided the means by which the ruling class set itself apart from and stood over most Philadelphians. The elite built elaborate, expensive urban mansions and country estates, employed servants for

household duties, and traveled in carriages. The elite dominated poor relief, city government, and provincial governmental posts.[6]

3. Religion and bases of political power divided the ruling class into two camps. Wealthy Anglicans were the mainstay of the Proprietary Party—a loose grouping centered on the Penn family and that family's interest in Pennsylvania—which was ensconced in the Colonial Council and other appointive governmental positions. The Quaker, or "popular interest," Party used the Assembly as its basis of power. Economic power was about evenly balanced between the two factions. Using a 1772 list of carriage owners as a sort of social register, we find that Quakers and Anglicans accounted for about 80 percent of the owners; the former owned about 43 percent of the carriages and the latter about 37 percent. Quakers held about 42 percent of the total measured shipping tonnage owned by this group, while Anglicans owned about 33 percent. The 6 top investors who were among this group of carriage holders owned their wharves and more than "seven percent of all tonnage purchased by Pennsylvania residents." Of the 6, 3 were Quakers, 2 were Anglicans, and 1 was a disowned Quaker.[7]

4. Pennsylvania's eighteenth-century political life was somewhat tranquil, both on its own terms and in comparison with other colonies. While some evidence from the 1720s on might be interpreted as an indication of popular participation in politics, it is instead an indication of the periodic efforts by those at the top to marshal support from those below. The Quaker and Proprietary parties contested elections beginning in the 1730s, but here, too, there was little genuine political participation and almost no initiatives from below.[8]

REVOLUTIONARY UPHEAVAL AND INDEPENDENCE

Philadelphia's ruling class responded to the imperial crisis in the same fashion as it had responded to previous crises. It opposed most of the new edicts that came out of London but did so cautiously and frightfully, concerned that the "middling" and "lower" sorts might become politically active. Thus, from 1765 to 1775, the city's "better sort" created the basis for its overthrow.

First came the Stamp Act crisis. The Quaker Party found itself advocating proprietary government at the precise time the British government was instituting an oppressive tax. The Proprietary Party exploited this by cautiously supporting popular protest against the Stamp Act. Further complicating the situation, the Quaker Party called upon its artisan supporters (fairly well off shipbuilding tradesmen) to protect the houses of both the Stamp Act Commissioner and Benjamin Franklin, Quaker Party member who supported the act.[9]

The Stamp Act was nullified in Philadelphia with almost no violence and relatively little crowd activity. Both sectors of the ruling class proudly claimed credit for the city's peacefulness and were pleased that the class hostility present in other cities' anti–Stamp Act activities barely surfaced in Philadelphia. As William Bradford explained to the New York Sons of Liberty, divisions among those Philadelphians actively engaged in politics precluded firmer action: "Our body in this City is not declared numerous as unfortunate dissentions in Provincial Politicks Keeps us rather a divided people."[10]

Philadelphia's peace was also undisrupted during the Townshend Duties crisis; however, two ancillary developments changed the balance of class forces in the city and established the necessary conditions for the internal revolution six years later. The merchants' general cautiousness in the battle against the new duties combined with the first official Quaker opposition to resistance activity to prompt the artisans to reassess their subordinate position in Philadelphia's political life.

Philadelphia merchants initially refused to support the Boston resolves for the formation of a nonimportation league but, under pressure from within and without the city, acquiesced and signed an agreement in February 1769. Some important Quaker merchants served on the committee appointed to oversee the agreement, but the *Charming Polly* incident led the Quaker meeting to reexamine its official attitude toward Friends' participation in committee work. (In July 1769 brewers refused to accept a cargo of malt, and a public meeting voted to brand anyone who took the goods as an "enemy to his Country"; the ship carrying the malt left port without unloading.) One month later, the Quaker meeting—or, more precisely, ruling-class Quakers within it—recommended that Friends withdraw from resistance activity because some participants "were incapable of judging prudently on a matter of so great importance." Once dry-goods traders, the most important of whom were Friends, had cleared their inventories and several colonies had resumed importation, merchants began campaigning to repeal the nonimportation agreement. Despite firm artisan or mechanic commitment to the policy, local merchants voted to end nonimportation in September 1770 in part because they feared mechanics would punish those who imported goods. The "lead of Affairs," one merchant noted, "here is (I think) now got too much out of the hands of the merchants."[11]

Artisan response to mercantile sabotage of the nonimportation agreement is critical to an understanding of the specificity of the city's revolution. Just a week after the merchants' decision, "Brother Chip" argued that artisans had accepted political subordination for so long that the ruling class had come to assume its right to govern. "Those Gentlemen make no Scruple to say, that the Mechanics (though by far the most numerous, especially, in this County) have no right . . . to *speak* or *think* for themselves." Mechanics had "an equal Right of electing or being elected," but if they lacked "the Liberty of nominating such Persons," their "Freedom of voting" was meaningless. Because artisans could best represent artisans, it was a great mistake "to elect Men of Enormous Estates" and thereby add "Power" to the "Wealth," making them "our Lords and Masters and us their most abject Slaves."[12]

Out of this ideological ferment came the artisans' organizational independence. In the 1770 Pennsylvania Assembly election, Philadelphia voters chose a tailor as a representative, and in 1772 artisans formed the Patriotic Society. Experience, "Publius" argued shortly afterward, had shown that corruption existed both in England and in America. The middling sort had to defend its liberties: "If ever your rights are preserved, it must be through the virtue and integrity of the middling sort of people, as farmers, tradesmen, &c. who despise venality, and best know the sweets of liberty."[13]

Philadelphia merchants, especially Quaker ones, had made a serious mistake that cost them dearly. Before 1769/70, few had questioned ruling-class authority. Much of the ruling class's ideological legitimacy had come from the congruence of its interests and those of the larger society. The Townshend Act developments, however, showed that mercantile self-interest could conflict with the public welfare and that Philadelphia traders would choose the former over the latter. A "Torrent of Corruption and self Interest," the Committee of Tradesmen argued, had defeated the efforts to continue nonimportation.[14] The delegitimization of ruling-class authority had begun.

How could the artisans do this? How did they establish themselves as an independent force with a strength that their counterparts in any other colonial city could not achieve? Among the many factors that surely accounted for artisan activity was the firmly established and widespread existence of petty commodity production. Between a third and a half of Philadelphia taxpayers in the late colonial period were "property-owner producer[s] of commodities" or "skilled craftsm[e]n owning [their] own tools but working for a contractor, as in the building trades." With few exceptions, this occurred in a paternalistic social setting and on a small scale, as few masters employed many free or unfree laborers. All artisans produced goods for sale in the marketplace, but most produced only for local markets and some only for orders given in advance. For most, the primary goal appears to have been, in the words of one, to "maintain himself & Family with decency" rather than the accumulation of capital.[15]

Petty commodity production provided at least some basis for independence of action. For those artisans who produced goods outside the shipping industry, the fortunes of which fluctuated with the vagaries of foreign trade, it furnished greater independence. For most artisans, it sustained something that was probably more important: a way to unite self-interest and public good. A program of home manufacturing had logically developed with the nonimportation campaign. Artisans argued that the best patriotic stand for colonial rights was to buy goods made in Philadelphia. The mercantile attack on nonimportation, then, was seen as unpatriotic, self-interested, and more important, an assault on home manufacturing and the artisans' developing sense of themselves as defenders of their country.[16]

From the context of ruling-class opposition to nonimportation and artisanal drive for independence came a popular party—mistakenly dubbed by some the "Presbyterian Party"—a coalition of artisans and radical lesser merchants and professionals. This popular party did battle with those advocating a more moderate resistance strategy; in extralegal elections held in November 1770, voters chose the mechanic ticket to oversee the Continental Association's nonimportation. Ruling-class merchants did not control this mechanic ticket as they had "every committee that the city had elected before"; the ticket included more artisans and was "less affluent" than previous committees.[17]

Philadelphia's better sort maintained a cautious attitude toward resistance into 1774. Some sporadically participated in committee work, and in response to the mechanics' electoral victory the Proprietary and Quaker factions began cooperating. In the Assembly political moderates and conservatives led by Joseph Galloway postponed discussion of instructions to its Continental Congress delegates, defeated efforts to raise a militia, and nearly put the Assembly on record in favor of sending another petition to the king. Moderates publicly criticized the Continental Association and Continental Congress, and a conservative faction established the *Mercury* to provide an organ of public opinion. Reacting too late with too little, this resurgence floundered when the king rejected Congress's petition and armed conflict began at Lexington and Concord.[18]

In January 1775 the Quaker meeting issued two epistles that firmly attacked the resistance movement and threatened to discipline Quakers who participated in it. The second epistle deeply angered resistance leaders because it condemned every "usurpation of power and authority, in opposition to the laws and government, and . . . all combinations, insurrections, conspiracies and illegal assemblies." Some in the meeting opposed this epistle, and this suggested to non-Quaker patriots, who already distrusted them, that ruling-class Friends had exercised privilege and power, not principles of conscience.[19]

Out of ruling-class intransigence came the refusal to adopt equitable rules to govern the militia, the internal revolution of 1775 and 1776, and the radically democratic constitution of 1776. This obstinacy raises two questions: Why did the Philadelphia ruling class fail to ride out the storm? Why did it contribute so mightily to making the question of "who shall rule at home" the issue in Pennsylvania?

It was possible for a sophisticated ruling class to direct the resistance movement and the struggle for independence toward somewhat moderate ends. Also, it was possible for a sophisticated elite to moderate the potentially radical implications of mobilization for armed combat with Britain. The elite of New York, facing perhaps as serious a threat of social upheaval, did just that from 1774 to 1776 and beyond. Maryland's ruling class, led by John Carroll, did so in 1777 and 1778. New York's gentry, as Robert R. Livingston commented, learned the "propriety of Swimming with a Stream" that was "impossible to stem"; it had to "yield to the torrent if [it] hoped to direct its course." This is exactly what the Pennsylvania elite, as Arthur St. Clair, a back-country aspirant to gentry status, realized, had not done: His friends had "taken an impolitic Part—generally Speaking tis both easiest and safest to swim with the Current, and Prudence teaches to submit to what cannot be prevented." Why had so many stood against the stream and seen "everything valuable . . . swept away"? Why did still others "become silent and inactive" in the "patient expectation" that the stream would "alter its course"?[20]

Timidity and cautiousness, besides obstinacy and a lack of political sophistication, characterized ruling-class response to both the resistance movement and independence. This cautiousness was true even of outright Tories who identified their political and economic interests with those of the British empire.[21]

That cautiousness came from several interrelated sources. First, the "better sort" had little experience in defending its class interests in open political battle, so it had developed neither the collective expertise to handle those below nor the personnel to impose its will. The Quaker Party, as historians Richard Ryerson and Alan Tully recently have shown, maintained power long after supposedly having relinquished it in 1756. The Proprietary Party never successfully challenged the dominance of the "Quaker oligarchy"; only outside political developments and demographics began to weaken its rule in the early 1770s. As Ryerson argues, the "deep and abiding stability of the legislature both arose from, and in turn protected and reinforced, a stable, orderly local political world." Quaker leaders "insulated Pennsylvania from the factional squabbles and imperial interventions suffered by other colonies . . . and from most political developments occurring outside its borders." For its part, the Proprietary Party controlled an abundance of appointed offices—many held multiple posts—and collected the appropriate fees.[22]

Second—and this is a natural consequence of the first point—the better sort had, indeed, come to assume their right to rule. As a Shippen noted, they had often "behaved as though they had a sort of fee simple" in government and "a right to dispose all places of honour & profit to such as pleased them."[23]

Third, the ruling class became increasingly insulated from the lower and middling sort in the 1750s and 1760s. While rich, middling, and poor often lived side by side in city neighborhoods, the wealthy set themselves apart from the poor by their houses, dress, and other outward signs of superiority, such as carriages. Members of the two ruling-class factions, particularly the various subgroups of each, increasingly intermarried and chose from within their ranks those individuals needed to fill social and political positions.[24]

A combination of points one, two, and three accounts for comments Charles Thomson, a key leader of the popular party, made in a letter to John Dickinson as he explained to Dickinson why it had been necessary to proclaim independence when Congress did. "From . . . the notions of honour, rank, & other courtly Ideas [I see] so eagerly embraced, I am fully persuaded, that had time been given for them to strike deeper roots, it would have been extremely difficult to have prepared men's minds for the good seed of liberty."[25]

Fourth, the ruling class misinterpreted the growing threat to its power. Some members feared that their colony would become another New England—that its "anarchy" would put Pennsylvania "on a level with some of the colonies to the Eastward." Some thought that New England resistance leaders were trying to impose tyrannical values on the colonies south of them. Others tried to use the generalized mistrust of New England as an organizing issue against independence.[26] None of these fears provided the "better sort" with the kind of assessment they needed to cope with the problems adequately.

Fifth, internal divisions, especially along religious lines, delayed the formation of a united class front against those below, and they hindered cooperation even when both factions began to recognize the threat that their common enemy posed.[27]

Sixth, Pennsylvania's better sort *did* face a serious threat to their rule by 1775—at least as real as in any other colony and probably more serious than in most. The gravity of the threat, however, largely had developed out of earlier timidity and shortsightedness. An outsider again saw the Pennsylvania situation more clearly than those on the scene: "They have been more apprehensive of evils than any others," as the Massachusetts member of the Continental Congress Elbridge Gerry put it, "and now they have the mortification to find that new measures for avoiding them have but served to increase them."[28]

John Dickinson's individual role in this failure was critical. Of the gentry, probably only he had the necessary stature with those below to help to chart a moderate revolution; he alone could have played the role in Pennsylvania that John Hancock, for example, performed in New England. Dickinson's commitment to firm resistance measures had begun to fade in 1774. In 1775 and 1776, his cautiousness turned into conservatism, and he supported sending yet another petition to the king. As late as April 1776, he still hoped that unsatisfactory negotiations with the peace commissioners would produce stronger elite support for independence. After April, a stubborn obstinacy and a "Spirit of Martyrdom" characterized his opposition to independence.[29]

Dickinson's failure was a personal one, but it had much larger implications. His decisions helped to call into question elite rule in Pennsylvania and, as Thomson realized, contributed to internal revolution: "I know the rectitude of your heart & the honest[y] & uprightness of your intentions; but still I cannot help regretting that through a perseverance which you were fully convinced was fruitless, you have thrown the affairs of this state into the hands of men totally unequal to them." Furthermore, mercantile defeat of nonimportation in 1770 had led the leaders of the popular party to adopt a cautious resistance strategy that emphasized unity over division and continuity over radical shifts.[30] Dickinson was central to this strategy, and its brief success convinced its proponents to continue to follow it long after it had lost all validity and long after Dickinson had played out his role. Moderate resistance leaders themselves thus contributed to the internal revolution.

None of these particularities of Pennsylvania elite rule automatically produced a radical movement below. Nor did opposition to independence or general ineptitude automatically create social upheaval. We can point to other colonies—New Jersey and North Carolina, for example—where the ruling class seemed equally unsuited to riding out the storm, yet a radical movement from below never developed or emerged stillborn. In Pennsylvania, however, such a movement produced the constitution of 1776 and the militant popular movement of the war years. In Pennsylvania, because the "better sort" (who tardily realized their "behavior had been too timorous and very impolitick") had not been "industrious" about independence, the people chose "governors among themselves."[31]

STRUGGLES OVER WHO SHALL RULE AT HOME

"Thus you can See," John Adams commented about Philadelphia's delegation to the Pennsylvania Constitutional Convention in 1776, "the Effect of Men of Fortune acting against the Sense of the People."[32] Adams was referring to the radical "new men" who came to power as leaders of the popular movement and replaced the Thomson group; however, the mistakes of the "Men of Fortune" had also thrown up a second group of new men: moderate/conservative patriots, who rose to economic prominence during the war years and continued their entrepreneurial climb in the 1780s and the 1790s.

As the prerevolutionary ruling class ran for cover, absorbed patriots' attacks, or quietly tried to continue supporting themselves and their families, the radical "new men" fought the moderate/conservative "new men" for political power. The former supported the democratic constitution of 1776, stern measures toward Tories, price fixing, paper money, and egalitarian militia burdens. Their leadership, for the most part, was drawn from the middling sort, and the militia, whose membership was largely of the lower sort, made up the remainder of the popular movement. The moderate/conservative new men struggled to overthrow the constitution of 1776, advocated an end to all price-fixing measures, opposed paper money, and wanted to diminish the role of the militia in Pennsylvania's war measures. Their leadership was drawn from two groups: wealthy Philadelphians who, in the main, had not been part of the older ruling class even if they had been connected with individual members of it; and men from middling ranks who were taking advantage of the expanded entrepreneurial opportunities that the war afforded. The prewar better sort, Tories, neutralists, and those increasingly disaffected by the war's exigencies provided the base for the moderates/conservatives.[33]

The moderates/conservatives decisively defeated the wartime popular movement in almost every contest. A merchant strike ended the price fixing, and at Fort Wilson on October 4, 1779, some radical middling sort leaders joined with moderates/conservatives to defeat radical militia men in a pitched battle that claimed lives on both sides. The conservatization of the Pennsylvania revolution began from that date, for the Fort Wilson episode split the popular movement; the radical middling sort offered little opposition to this conservatization—partly because it had come to recognize values shared with its erstwhile opponents and partly because it feared that decisive action would mean the mobilization of those below. By 1781 the Pennsylvania Assembly had repealed all price-fixing regulations and ended the embargo on the export of foodstuffs, abolished the legal tender provisions for paper money, halted the state's total reliance on the militia system for defense, and laid a heavy tax on property to finance the war effort.[34]

The vision of the lower sort—lesser artisans and wage laborers—of what America might become died at Fort Wilson and was buried with the subsequent conservatization of the Pennsylvania revolution. This group wanted an America in which egalitarianism ruled, in which the civil sphere and military spheres were unified, and in which it was morally unacceptable to exploit a scarcity of foodstuffs and to profit at the expense of consumers. But this version of America was not unique to the lower sort, for there were some in the middling sort who had espoused it also. Their advocacy of this program died as they realized the full implications of such an approach.

In a sense, the battle between the radical new men and the moderate/conservative new men was waged within the Anglican Christ Church. Thomas Doerflinger identifies the religious affiliation of many of his new men—the moderates/conservatives—as Anglican; among identifiable members of the radical Committee of Privates, which led the militia in 1775 and 1776, were also many Anglicans (as well as several ex-Anglicans). The radical new men achieved ascendancy in the late 1770s and moved to give the vestry more power; a decade later the moderate/conservative new men had vanquished the Committee of Privates new men and then dominated the vestry for the remainder of the period.[35]

Still other former members of the Committee of Privates worked quietly as individuals and in small groups to reshape specific Philadelphia institutions in light of American republicanism. Several were instrumental in reforms at the German Lutheran congregations of St. Michael's and Zion's; there they led the successful efforts of parishioners to gain more control over church affairs and drastically reduce the power of the old guard. One mason, as grand master, oversaw the Grand Lodge's declaration of independence from English Masonry in 1786. Still another joined other senior faculty at the University of Pennsylvania to upgrade its curriculum to entitle it "to the Name or Character of a University."[36]

But the future belonged, at least temporarily, to Doerflinger's new men. Some of these were "fortune builders," and others were "upwardly mobile staff officers." The revolution's disruption of normal trading patterns provided great opportunities, especially for the fortune builders, led by Robert Morris, who, in search of new sources of wealth, began diversifying their economic activities. Among their new endeavors were the tobacco, China, and westward trades; banking; securities; land speculation; and manufacturing. For the dozen years between 1776 and 1788, they cautiously explored these innovative avenues; after 1788, a "reckless, speculative environment" fueled their quest for wealth.[37]

This group of "new men" was the dynamic force in Philadelphia's "entrepreneurial efflorescence" for fifteen years following their triumph over radicalism and became an important element in the early nationalist movement. Convinced on the eve of the Constitution that the nation stood at a "crossroads," from which it could move either "to order and abundance" or to "weakness, chaos, and poverty," they provided key leadership and support for the Federalists and the Constitution. In short, they threatened to eclipse the battered prerevolutionary ruling class and establish hegemonic rule. Why they failed, both individually and as a class, is the focus of the remainder of this paper.[38]

These men were unsuccessful partly because of the inherent instability of merchant capital and partly because of the war-induced international trade fluctuations of the 1790s.[39] Yet there were deeper and more significant reasons for their failures.

First, this incipient ruling class mortgaged its future to Alexander Hamilton's political-economic program. That program was in its essence straightforward. Committed to what historian John R. Nelson, Jr., calls "stabilization," secretary of the treasury Alexander Hamilton worked at strengthening the new government and restoring fiscal responsibility both to resolve the ongoing crisis and to provide for a more orderly future. The funded debt, with its accompanying institutions and policies, was the key to Hamilton's program and was intended to create a "Repository of the Rights of the Wealthy."[40] A funded debt would restore the nation's credit and yoke the wealthy to the new government.

Hamilton was uninterested in promoting domestic manufacturing that would seriously compete with English exports. His very program demanded the subordination of American manufacturing to the import of British goods. About 90 percent of all imports, as historian Samuel Flagg Bemis has noted, came from England in the early 1790s, and almost all the government revenue needed to fund the debt came from duties collected on these imports. Anything that disrupted that trade would undermine Hamilton's stabilization program and adversely affect the wealthy who held the national debt. His "Report on Manufactures" did not—because it could not—provide the essential item for the development of American manufacturing: a protective tariff.[41]

Hamilton's program also entailed economic political dependence. Once the basic parameters of stabilization were institutionalized, all foreign policy had to take them into account. As Bemis noted concerning the source of funding of the debt, this "dominated the foreign policy" of the United States. Opposition to this policy threatened "public credit," Hamilton's program, and both the short- and long-range interests of merchants trading with England. The British consul in Philadelphia noted, in the midst of growing congressional support for commercial discrimination against Great Britain: "My Lord without one tried source of productive revenue except the import, [it] is at this time very problematical whether this plan of discrimination may not succeed which will completely cripple the revenue of the country and shake its credit."[42]

The Hamiltonian political-economic program to which Philadelphia's would-be ruling class tied its fortunes was neocolonialist. In its very success, then, came its undoing. Oppositionists criticized the Federalist program where it was the weakest: It ensured that America's independence would remain nominal, and it laid the basis for the reproduction of the worst of British values and culture in the United States. The suspicion that the separation from England had been more of a "revolution of *men* rather than *principles*" solidified, and by 1795 the pivotal political issue had become the nation's relationship with Britain and the federal government's role in that relationship. That issue, moreover, became inextricably linked to differing conceptions of what the United States was to be. Opponents of Hamiltonianism, therefore, often referred to the earlier battle against Britain in their polemical attacks on it.[43]

Philadelphians took the lead in this "domestic war for independence." The city's artisans, many of whom had remained politically active through the 1780s in the campaign for protection for home manufacturing, strongly supported the federal Constitution. This had required a merging of their interests and organizations with those of the merchants. (One is, indeed, hard pressed to find evidence of independent artisan political thinking and activity during the debate over the federal Constitution and the next several years.) By 1793, however, many artisans had ended their alliance with Federalism, and Philadelphia politics began to revolve around Hamilton's neocolonial program: "Old tories," the urban "fashionable circles," merchants "trading on British capital," and "paper men," according to Thomas Jefferson, opposed merchants who were "trading on their own capitals," artisans, and farmers. In 1793 and 1794, the latter grouping formed the Democratic Society of Pennsylvania, which vigorously opposed the excise taxes that were an integral part of Hamilton's program. It scored an immediate and impressive victory with the election to Congress of John Swanwick, an archetypical representative of the merchant wing of the Republican Party, and continued to contest Federalism for the remainder of the decade. It did not, however, win decisively until it had developed political machinery, defined issues, and mobilized most Philadelphia voters.[44]

Contrasting ideas of what America ought to be and become were embedded in the battle between Philadelphia's new men who remained in the Federalist camp and their opponents. Federalists espoused authority, hierarchy, deference, and privilege; England was both a symbol of the good society and a reality to be emulated. They adhered to, as historian Joyce Appleby argues, the "model of sober, ordered constitutional government committed to securing the maximum personal freedom consonant with the flawed nature of man." The Democratic-Republicans advocated equality of opportunity and political egalitarianism, and they looked to revolutionary France as a symbol and a model—"a vision of what a society of free men might be if the chains of customs and outworn creeds were cast off." Republicans spoke of the "Promise of Prosperity" in a "Vision of Classlessness."[45]

The struggle over the ratification of Jay's Treaty joined Federalist new men's commitment to neocolonialism and to their ideology. That also provides the second reason for their failure. They were willing to flex their economic and political influence in ways that the prerevolutionary ruling class was not: when necessary, they directly exerted their clientage power.

Jay's Treaty was a total Federalist victory; Jay "acquiesced in practice to the British System of maritime law." Philadelphia merchants were strongly protreaty. Over half the signatories of a supporting petition sent to President George Washington in August 1795 were merchants, about 10 percent were shopkeepers and grocers, and 5 percent gentlemen. Democratic-Republicans complained that the merchants used pressure to obtain many signatures; charges of intimidation increased following the victory of the protreaty state assembly ticket that October. As the House of Representatives vote on whether to appropriate money for the treaty's implementation neared, Federalists stepped up the pressure. Bank directors threatened to cut off discounts to customers, and, given the "general pinch for money," this was, James Madison argued, "like a Highway man with a pistol demanding the purse." Swanwick was offered the governorship if he supported the treaty (he refused), and F. A. Muhlenberg cast the deciding vote for the appropriation after William Sheafe threatened to refuse to allow his daughter Polly to marry Muhlenberg's son if he voted against it.[46]

Complaints of similar activity throughout the 1790s suggest that Federalists had no qualms about using crude tactics to ensure victories.[47] That there is no evidence of such behavior before the Revolution puts the actions of these men in a definite context: they lacked the legitimacy to rule without coercion. Moreover, coercion did not work for long. Two of the congressmen elected by Philadelphians in autumn 1796 were Republicans.

Furthermore, the life-style of these new men, who proudly displayed their wealth and engaged in the "etiquette of a court," set them apart from both those below and most of the old ruling class. William Maclay complained in 1790 that the "gloomy severity of the Quaker" had "proscribed all fashionable dress and amusement," but within several years the Morrises and the Binghams had become the center for ostentatious entertaining and conspicuous consumption of food and drink and had scandalized much of Philadelphia by their flaunting of almost every standard of propriety. William and Anne Bingham's house, an enlarged version of the duke of Manchester's London house, filled half a city block and stood as symbol of the new men. Imported furnishings from Europe filled its rooms, two fawns ran in the gardens, and a greenhouse furnished flowers year round. Robert Morris's "great marble palace," designed by Pierre Charles L'Enfant, was to occupy an entire city block. Its furnishings, too, came from Europe and included 5,000 "guineas' worth of mirrors." The life-styles of these two families were, as a contemporary understatedly put it, "not suited to our manners."[48]

Morris's inability to complete and live in the mansion brings us to the fourth reason for the failure of these new men: many collapsed economically in the 1790s. Morris's failure was merely the most spectacular;

we also may add, for example, those of John Nicholson, John Ross, and James Wilson. Others were "financially crippled": George Harrison, William White, and Thomas Fitzsimons. The fortunes of Doerflinger's "upwardly mobile staff officers" enjoyed a similar sort of track record.[49]

The spirit of Morris's solution to his ever-increasing debt—to intensify his land speculations, many in partnership with Nicholson—was found in other new men. John Chaloner, an "upwardly mobile" merchant and a former staff officer, had been a member of the Committee of Privates but had joined the conservative/moderate group of new men by 1779. Connected with many important entrepreneurs, Chaloner employed a variety of strategies to make money in the 1780s. In 1790 he became a state auctioneer in the wake of accusations of having mismanaged another firm's accounts. He died in massive debt in 1793, and creditors, who allowed his wife only the house and furnishings, battled with Pennsylvania in court for priority in payment.[50]

Most of these new men simply did not know when to stop. Some of their greed had to do with the speculative and quick-riches mania of the 1790s that extended far beyond Philadelphia but that was particularly intense there. In 1791 a Philadelphia newspaper noted the prevalence of "Sciptomania," and Jefferson remarked on the "rage for getting rich in a day." The "great gaming house" crashed that year but revived to fall again in 1792. Part of the speculative mania had to do with Hamilton's program, which provided irresistible opportunities for the very activity that threatened his stabilization program. Part had to do with how most new men made their money: fast and dirty by exploitation of their government positions and connections. They were among the many others who found clerks, surveyors, and probably even the surveyor general willing to help them in their land speculations. So they continuously sought to make the big score, working their connections with an optimism that in hindsight appears astoundingly short-sighted.[51]

Doerflinger has argued that the entrepreneurial activities of these new men contributed to the nation's economic development. Before assessing that claim we must define, as Doerflinger does not, "economic development." Within the terms of late eighteenth-century international political economy and of America's quest for political-economic independence—that is, within its actual context—economic development meant primarily the growth of manufacturing. Manufacturing was, as Nelson argues, a "necessary ingredient" to the creation of an "independent economy capable of assuring the political power to enforce commercial interests in territory and trade. In this respect manufacturing was synonymous with national independence." Thus, English "economic hegemony" in manufacturing and shipping was the "greatest threat" to America's independence.[52]

The activities of these new men look very different in light of this definition of economic development. They played the most significant role in the development and leadership of Pennsylvania's incorporated internal improvement companies in the 1790s. The Society for Promoting the Improvement of Internal Navigation, or, as contemporaries characterized it, Robert Morris's "canal junto," controlled the Schuylkill and Susquehanna Navigation Company, the Philadelphia and Lancaster Turnpike Company, the Delaware and Schuylkill Canal Company, and the Conwego Canal Company.[53] Yet only one of these ventures, the Philadelphia and Lancaster Turnpike Company, succeeded. Why?

First, while the stock of these companies initially was oversubscribed, investors did not complete payment for their stock. The goal seems to have been speculation, and speculators are notoriously impatient—Nicholson, for example, in 1798 still owed two canal companies for his shares. Second, these companies, as the directors of the Schuylkill and Susquehanna and the Delaware and Schuylkill argued, had to compete with other investment opportunities. Investors slighted them because of the "growing demands of capital" to finance the "increased domestic and foreign trade." When there was more money to be made elsewhere, investment went there. Third, Nicholson and others used the canal efforts as an interrelated part of larger money-making activities. Nicholson supplied stone for the two canal projects and used his shares as collateral for more land speculation. Although the chief engineer wanted to dig the canal in one place, the directors of the company decided "that the canal should pass through their estates" and were "deaf to every other proposal." Perceiving that the canal was being built on "the most difficult and circuitous plan, with little prospect of success," investors began holding back the remainder of the money due for their shares.[54]

The same dynamics typified other economic activities of these new men, especially investments in land and stock, where speculative profits were the only goal. It was also the case for Nicholson's manufacturing complex at Falls of Schuylkill, "one of many investment schemes he engineered to salvage failed land deals." A chronic shortage of cash to pay wage earners was perhaps the major reason for that complex's failure, but the shortage was relative, for Nicholson was simultaneously wheeling and dealing in other areas.[55]

These new men ought to be seen primarily as predators whose goal was to make money in any way possible. Their demise was part and parcel of their rise. Their willingness to take risks to make a profit—no matter how spectacularly innovative, no matter how indicative of an "entrepreneurial efflorescence"—lacked any larger goal in either a direct or an indirect sense and did not produce economic development. That economic development owed more to the infrastructure of merchant/commercial capitalism and petty commodity production.

The new men did help—although somewhat passively—by establishing the banks and insurance companies that played an important role in the mobilization of capital for more efficient transfer of commodities. Two important aspects, however, limited these new men's contribution. First, Democratic-Republican and old ruling-class merchants played a role in the establishment and day-to-day operations of these institutions. They were involved in the Bank of Pennsylvania, the Insurance Company of North America, and the Insurance Company of the State of Pennsylvania. Second, banks and insurance companies did not directly aid economic development. Banks did, as Doerflinger argues, speed the "movement of goods in and out of port" and reduced the amount of capital tied up in idle inventory," but they also lent money for only a short time—usually thirty or fewer days. Such terms were of negligible value for manufacturers. Marine insurance companies did aid in the home retention of capital that formerly had gone to English underwriters, but again the profits of these companies were not available for long-term loans to manufacturers.[56]

Merchant capital, even at a sophisticated and mature level of organization, did not directly aid manufacturing and provided the material basis for an elite whose power was predicated on the continued existence of Hamilton's neocolonial program and the United States subordination to the British Empire. The opportunity for handsome profits through investment in the banks and insurance companies also directly impeded investments in other areas. Adam Smith argued, "That part of the capital of any country which is employed in the carrying trade is altogether withdrawn from supporting the productive labour of that particular country to support that of some foreign country." Recent work in Europe and England points to a negative relationship between industrialization and merchant capital.[57]

Genuine economic development is most apparent in petty commodity production. Little work has been done on it, but the broad outlines are visible. As early as the 1760s and the 1770s, there was a breakdown of the system of unfree labor; a decline of apprenticeship; a dissolution of the bonds of paternalistic labor relations within the small shop; an uneven distribution of wealth within many trades; and an increasing supply of free labor. In the 1770s and the 1780s, the number of references to journeymen increased—some were in the transition to master status; others represented the growing number of permanent wage earners in each trade. Beginning with the 1786 journeymen printers' strike, there are continuing signs of an organizational distinction that separates journeymen and masters. There are also more strikes. In 1786 master cabinet- and chairmakers signed an agreement with their journeymen; in 1789 master cordwainers formed an organization, and their journeymen followed in 1790. In 1790 journeymen carpenters struck; in 1795 journeymen cabinet- and chairmakers struck, established a "Ware-Room" to sell their products, and urged journeymen to form an all-trades society. In 1799 journeymen cordwainers struck, as did journeymen printers. The number of strikes and the tempo of establishing journeymen trade societies increased after 1800.[58]

Although most Philadelphians worked in small shops well into the nineteenth century, the changes were very significant. In 1820, 3 percent of the work force labored in establishments with fewer than six people, yet the constant dollar amount of "industrial" exports increased 500 percent for the period 1800–1809 as compared with 1790–99. Attention to mere statistics also underestimates the political-economic significance of these changes. Artisans-turned-manufacturers in tobacco and sugar, as Roland Baumann has shown, led artisans and other opponents of Hamiltonian policy in the battle against the excise tax in 1794. This battle, Baumann demonstrates, laid the basis for the "Jeffersonian coalition."[59]

The city's artisans and artisans-turned-manufacturers increased output without a dramatic increase in the use of machinery or the introduction of new technology. In furniture making, for example, there was little use of machinery until the 1830s or 1840s; the same is true of shoemaking and tailoring. Yet we see increasing output and exports for all of them. Artisans and manufacturers achieved this by cheapening wages, increasing the division of labor, putting out, and introducing women's and children's labor. Accumulation and manufacturing preceded the advent of the factory.[60]

And what of the "old" ruling class? What was their relationship to these developments and battles? The Quaker gentry's continued inward retreat eventually led Friends back out into society on a mission of reform. Committed to abolition, prison reform, and other ameliorative activities, the Society of Friends largely remained outside the political battles of the 1790s. Individual members were active in the Federalist Party, and some took an interest in particular elections, but Quakerism per se remained a minor issue. Ensconced in important and solid social, economic, and cultural institutions, most of the Quaker elite, and as well some of their Anglican counterparts, continued an unspectacularly slow and steady pattern of economic activity. These men's very ploddingness and discipline provided them the basis for survival in the 1790s, when the spectacular "new men" challengers self-destructed.[61]

Philadelphia's old gentry, in the main, contributed only indirectly to the city's nineteenth-century industrialization. They were indifferent to the "developing textile industry," and only two of the thirty families that E. Digby Baltzell identifies as the elite had gone into manufacturing by about 1850. The gentry, moreover, became increasingly entrenched and insular. The Revolution, Benjamin Rush noted, ultimately had united the two "aristocracies." "They are now," he continued in a letter of 1813, "all powerful in all our monied institutions except one, in our Library Hospital, and University, and possess universal professional, mercantile, maritime, and mechanical patronage." By 1850 this insularity had deepened, as one observer wryly recorded. "There is no American city in which the system of exclusion is so rigidly observed as in Philadelphia. The ascent of a parvenu into the aristocratic circle is slow and difficult. There is a sort of holy alliance between its members to forbid all unauthorized approach. Claims are canvassed, and pretentions weighed; manners, fortune, tastes, habits, and descent undergo a rigid examination; and from the temper of the judges, the chances are that the final oscillation of the scale is unfavorable to the reception of the candidate."[62]

The gentry's aversion to the industrializing process and its increasing insularity contributed to the specificity of Philadelphia's history and economic development; both also contributed to the city's unique "matrix of accumulation." At the level of broadest generalization, two points stand out. First, the revolutionary struggle that produced both groups of "new men"—the radical and the moderate/conservative enterprisers—and the spectacular rise and fall of Doerflinger's new men helped to create the "proper Philadelphia" elite of the nineteenth century. Second, in ways that we are only now beginning to understand—and here Michael Meranze's work promises to be of signal importance—the conceptualization and the practice of social authority were reformulated and reconstituted on new grounds that had their origins in the particularities of Philadelphia's history.[63]

---

[1] John Murrin, "Political Development," in *Colonial British America: Essays in the New History of the Early Modern Era*, ed. Jack P. Greene and J. R. Pole (Baltimore: Johns Hopkins University Press, 1984), p. 440. For a discussion of the historiography of the Pennsylvania revolution, see Steven Rosswurm, *Arms, Country, and Class: The Philadelphia Militia and "Lower Sort" during the American Revolution, 1775–1783* (New Brunswick, N.J.: Rutgers University Press, 1987), pp. 3–6.

[2] Carl Lotus Becker, *The History of Political Parties in the Province of New York* (1909; reprint, Madison: University of Wisconsin Press, 1968), p. 22.

[3] Gary B. Nash, "The Early Merchants of Philadelphia: The Formation and Disintegration of a Founding Elite," in *The World of William Penn*, ed. Richard S. Dunn and Mary Maples Dunn (Philadelphia: University of Pennsylvania Press, 1986), pp. 337–62; Bernard Bailyn, "Politics and Social Structure in Virginia," in *Seventeenth-Century America: Essays in Colonial History*, ed. James Morton Smith (Chapel Hill: University of North Carolina Press, 1959), pp. 90–115; David W. Jordan, "Political Stability and the Emergence of a Native Elite in Maryland," in *The Chesapeake in the Seventeenth-Century*, ed. Thad W. Tate and David L. Ammerman (Chapel Hill: University of North Carolina Press, 1979), pp. 243–73. Although terms *elite*, *better sort*, and *ruling class* will be used interchangeably, the author's basic position is that *ruling class* accurately describes those at the top of Philadelphia society. The most sustained critiques of this position are offered in Robert Gough, "Toward a Theory of Class and Social Conflict: A Social History of Wealthy Philadelphians, 1775 and 1800" (Ph.D. diss., University of Pennsylvania, 1977); and Thomas Doerflinger, *A Vigorous Spirit of Enterprise: Merchants and Economic Development in Revolutionary Philadelphia* (Chapel Hill: University of North Carolina Press, 1986). The author remains unconvinced of these arguments even though both works contain much useful empirical data.

[4] Stephen J. Brobeck, "Changes in the Composition and Structure of Philadelphia Elite Groups" (Ph.D. diss., University of Pennsylvania, 1972), pp. 279–80, 317; Gough, "Toward a Theory," pp. 201–20; John J. McCusker, "The Pennsylvania Shipping Industry in the Eighteenth Century" (typescript, 1973), pp. 226, 229–30, 249–54, Historical Society of Pennsylvania, Philadelphia (hereafter cited as HSP); Gary B.

Nash, *The Urban Crucible: Social Change, Political Consciousness, and the American Revolution* (Cambridge: Harvard University Press, 1979), pp. 396–400; Billy G. Smith, "Struggles of the 'Lower Sort': The Lives of Philadelphia's Laboring People, 1750–1800" (Ph.D. diss., University of California, Los Angeles, 1981), pp. 146–57; Sharon Salinger and Charles Wetherell, "Wealth and Renting in Prerevolutionary Philadelphia," *Journal of American History* 71, no. 4 (March 1985), pp. 826–40; Billy G. Smith, "Inequality in Late Colonial Philadelphia: A Note on Its Nature and Growth," *William and Mary Quarterly*, 3d ser., 41, no. 4 (October 1984): 629–45; Rosswurm, *Arms, Country, and Class*, p. 259; Alice Hanson Jones, *Wealth of a Nation to Be: The American Colonies on the Eve of the Revolution* (New York: Columbia University, 1980), pp. 268, 272.

[5] Gough, "Toward a Theory," pp. 225–26; Smith, "Struggles of the 'Lower Sort'," p. 183.

[6] Nicholas B. Wainwright, *Colonial Grandeur in Philadelphia: The House and Furnishings of General John Cadwalader* (Philadelphia: Historical Society of Pennsylvania, 1964); Frederick B. Tolles, *Meeting House and Counting House: The Quaker Merchants of Colonial Philadelphia, 1682–1763* (New York: W. W. Norton, 1963), pp. 132–35; Carl Bridenbaugh and Jessica Bridenbaugh, *Rebels and Gentlemen: Philadelphia in the Age of Franklin* (New York: Oxford University Press, 1962), pp. 191–98; Margaret B. Tinkcom, "Cliveden: The Building of a Philadelphia Country Seat," *Pennsylvania Magazine of History and Biography* 88, no. 1 (January 1964): 3–36; Gough, "Toward a Theory," pp. 381–85; McCusker, "Pennsylvania Shipping," pp. 255–69; "Notes and Queries: An Account of Coaches," *Pennsylvania Magazine of History and Biography* 27, no. 3 (1903): 375; Robert F. Oaks, "Big Wheels in Philadelphia: Du Simitière's List of Carriage Owners," *Pennsylvania Magazine of History and Biography* 95, no. 3 (July 1971): 351–62; Sharon V. Salinger, "Colonial Labor in Transition: The Decline of Indentured Servitude in Late Eighteenth-Century Philadelphia," *Labor History* 22, no. 2 (Spring 1981): 188–89; Elaine F. Crane, "The World of Elizabeth Drinker," *Pennsylvania Magazine of History and Biography* 107, no. 1 (January 1983): 21–22; John K. Alexander, *Render Them Submissive: Responses to Poverty in Philadelphia, 1760–1800* (Amherst: University of Massachusetts Press, 1980), pp. 86, 92; Gary B. Nash, "Poverty and Poor Relief in Pre-Revolutionary Philadelphia," *William and Mary Quarterly*, 3d ser., 33, no. 1 (January 1976): 14, 15 n38; Gough, "Toward a Theory," p. 466.

[7] Gough, "Toward a Theory"; Doerflinger, *Vigorous Spirit*, pp. 58–62; Brobeck, "Changes in Composition"; McCusker, "Pennsylvania Shipping," pp. 262–65; Tolles, *Meeting House and Counting House*, p. 131 n60; Richard Alan Ryerson, *The Revolution Is Now Begun: The Radical Committees of Philadelphia, 1765–1776* (Philadelphia: University of Pennsylvania Press, 1978), pp. 279, 291.

[8] Nash, *Urban Crucible*; Alan Tully, *William Penn's Legacy: Politics and Social Structure in Provincial Pennsylvania, 1726–1755* (Baltimore: Johns Hopkins University Press, 1977); Alan Tully, "Quaker Party and Proprietary Policies: The Dynamics of Politics in Pre-Revolutionary Pennsylvania, 1730–1775," and Richard Alan Ryerson, "The Portrait of a Colonial Oligarchy: The Quaker Elite in the Pennsylvania Assembly, 1729–1776," in *Power and Status: Officeholding in Colonial America*, ed. Bruce C. Daniels (Middletown, Conn.: Wesleyan University Press, 1986), pp. 75–105 and 106–35.

[9] For the standard interpretation, see Edmund S. Morgan and Helen S. Morgan, *The Stamp Act Crisis* (rev. ed.; New York: Macmillan Co., 1967). For the basis of this account, see Steven J. Rosswurm, "Arms, Culture, and Class: The Philadel-

phia Militia and 'Lower Orders' in the American Revolution, 1765 to 1783" (Ph.D. diss., Northern Illinois University, 1979), pp. 63–78; and Rosswurm, *Arms, Country, and Class*, pp. 30–31.

[10] [William Bradford] to Sons of Liberty of New York, Philadelphia, February 15, 1766, Pennsylvania Nonimportation Agreements, 2, American Philosophical Society, Philadelphia.

[11] *Pennsylvania Gazette*, July 20, 1769; Quaker Meeting as quoted in Arthur Schlesinger, *The Colonial Merchants and the American Revolution* (1917; reprint, New York: Atheneum, 1968), p. 191; Clement Biddle to Thomas Richardson, July 24, 1770, Biddle Letterbook (1769–70), Am. 9180, HSP; Ryerson, *Revolution Is Now Begun*; Charles S. Olton, *Artisans for Independence: Philadelphia Mechanics and the American Revolution* (Syracuse, N.Y.: Syracuse University Press, 1975); Rosswurm, *Arms, Country, and Class*, pp. 39–42. The analysis of Quaker Meeting politics draws on Richard Bauman, *For the Reputation of Truth: Politics, Religion, and Conflict among the Pennsylvania Quakers, 1750–1800* (Baltimore: Johns Hopkins University Press, 1971). The author remains unconvinced by the criticisms of Bauman's analytical framework in Jack D. Marietta, *The Reformation of American Quakerism, 1748–1783* (Philadelphia: University of Pennsylvania Press, 1984).

[12] *Pennsylvania Chronicle*, September 27, 1770.

[13] *Pennsylvania Gazette*, August 19, 1772; "Publius," *Pennsylvania Chronicle*, September 5, 1772, as quoted in Olton, *Artisans for Independence*, p. 55.

[14] Committee of Tradesmen to Benjamin Franklin, November 1, 1771, *The Papers of Benjamin Franklin*, ed. Leonard W. Labaree, William B. Willcox, and Claude A. Lopez, 27 vols. to date (New Haven: Yale University Press, 1959–), 18:249.

[15] Eric Foner, *Tom Paine and Revolutionary America* (New York: Oxford University Press, 1976), pp. 28 n19, 29 n22. Petition of Hugh King, shipwright, December 29, 1775, microfilm, record group 27, reel 10, frame 183, Records of Pennsylvania Revolutionary Governments, 1775–90, Division of Archives and Manuscripts, Pennsylvania Historical and Museum Commission, Harrisburg. The discussion draws on Rosswurm, *Arms, Country, and Class*, pp. 14–16. Historians of America, especially of colonial America, have yet to integrate petty commodity production into their analyses. For the beginning of such work, see Ronald Schultz, "Thoughts among the People: Popular Thought, Radical Politics, and the Making of Philadelphia Working Class, 1765–1828" (Ph.D. diss., University of California, Los Angeles, 1985).

[16] The best discussion of the role of Philadelphia artisans during the revolutionary era is Olton, *Artisans for Independence*.

[17] James H. Hutson, *Pennsylvania Politics, 1746–1770: The Movement for Royal Government and Its Consequences* (Princeton: Princeton University Press, 1972), pp. 236–43; Ryerson, *Revolution Is Now Begun*, chap. 2, pp. 95, 180–95, esp. p. 180. For proponents of the ethnic-religious analysis besides Hutson, see Owen S. Ireland, "The Ethnic-Religious Dimension of Pennsylvania Politics, 1778–1779," *William and Mary Quarterly*, 3d ser., 30, no. 3 (July 1973): 423–48; Wayne L. Bockelman and Owen S. Ireland, "The Internal Revolution in Pennsylvania: An Ethnic-Religious Interpretation," *Pennsylvania History* 41, no. 2 (April 1974): 125–59; and Owen S. Ireland, "The Crux of Politics: Religion and Party in Pennsylvania, 1778–1789," *William and Mary Quarterly*, 3d ser., 42, no. 4 (October 1985): 453–75. This framework also is adopted by Gough, "Toward a Theory"; and Doerflinger, *Vigorous Spirit*. This analysis assumes that Quakers (and members of the Quaker Party), who most often complained about Presbyterians, accurately perceived what was going on around them; moreover, it ignores much evidence to the contrary. For a trenchantly critical

examination of this analysis for politics before the Revolution, see Alan W. Tully, "Ethnicity, Religion, and Politics in Early America," *Pennsylvania Magazine of History and Biography* 107, no. 4 (October 1983): 491–536; for more discussion, see Rosswurm, *Arms, Country, and Class*, pp. 5, 42 n154.

[18] Charles Thomson to William W. Drayton, n.d., *New-York Historical Society Collections* 11 (1878): 280–81; Joseph Galloway to Thomas Nickelson, July 1, 1774, November 1, 1774, letter to Nickelson, Joseph Galloway Papers, Library of Congress (hereafter cited as LC); Galloway to William Franklin, February 28, 1775, *Letters of Delegates to Congress*, ed. Paul Smith et al., 18 vols. to date (Washington, D.C.: Library of Congress, 1976–), 1:318–19; [February 25–March 1, 1775], Jonathan Potts Papers, LC. Stephen Collins to William Tudor, February 17, 1775, Collins letterbook (1771–75), LC; Galloway to Verplanck, February 14, 1775, "Some Letters of Joseph Galloway, 1774–1775," *Pennsylvania Magazine of History and Biography* 21, no. 4 (1897): 480–81; Joseph Reed to Charles Pettit, January 31, 1775, Joseph Reed Papers (microfilm, reel 1), New-York Historical Society; James and Drinker to Pigon and Booth, February 8, 1775, Philadelphia Tea Party (transcript), folder 3, HSP; "Transcripts of the Manuscript Books and Papers of the Commission of Enquiry into the Losses and Services of the American Loyalists . . . Audit Office Records . . . 1783–1790," 50:517 (hereafter cited as LoyTrans), New York Public Library; Ryerson, *Revolution Is Now Begun*, pp. 105–12.

[19] "An Epistle from the Meeting for Sufferings . . . the 5th Day of the First Month, 1775," Ab 1775–28, HSP; "The Testimony of the People Called Quakers," Ab 1775–29, HSP. See also Arthur J. Mekeel, *The Relation of the Quakers to the American Revolution* (Washington, D.C.: University Press of America, 1979), pp. 91–101; Bauman, *For the Reputation of Truth*, p. 148. For the opposition, see Samuel Sansom to James Pemberton, November 5, 1774, and Samuel Wetherill, Jr., to Pemberton, February 4, 1775, Pemberton Papers, 27:9, 67, HSP; William Bradford, Jr., to James Madison, January 4, 1774, William Bradford, Jr., letterbook, HSP; and Reed to Pettit, January 31, 1775, Joseph Reed Papers.

[20] Edward Countryman, *A People in Revolution and Political Society in New York, 1760–1790* (Baltimore: Johns Hopkins University Press, 1981); Ronald Hoffman, "The 'Disaffected' in the Revolutionary South," in *The American Revolution: Explorations in the History of American Radicalism*, ed. Alfred F. Young (DeKalb: Northern Illinois University Press, 1976), pp. 278–86; Robert K. Livingston to William Duer, June 12, 1777, as quoted in Alfred F. Young, *The Democratic-Republicans of New York: The Origins, 1763–1797* (Chapel Hill: University of North Carolina Press, 1967), p. 15; Arthur St. Clair to James Wilson, Tyconderoga, August 17, 1776, Gratz Collection, box 14, case 14, HSP; Edward Shippen to Jasper Yeates, Philadelphia, June 5, 1776, Greer Collection, HSP.

[21] Wallace Brown, *The King's Friends: The Composition and Motives of the American Loyalist Claimants* (Providence: Brown University, 1965), pp. 131, 137, 253; Robert Gough, "Can a Rich Man Favor Revolution? The Case of Philadelphia in 1776," *Pennsylvania History* 48, no. 3 (July 1981): 235–50; Thomas M. Doerflinger, "Philadelphia Merchants and the Logic of Moderation, 1760–1775," *William and Mary Quarterly*, 3d ser., 40, no. 2 (April 1983): 197–226.

[22] Ryerson, "Portrait of a Colonial Oligarchy," p. 134; Tully, "Quaker Party and Proprietary Policies." Several clauses in the 1776 Constitution were designed to end plural officeholding and take the profit out of officeholding. For an attack on the Proprietary Party on precisely these grounds, see *Pennsylvania Evening Post*, April 30, 1776.

[23] William Shippen to Edward Shippen, July 27, 1776, Shippen Papers, vol. 12, HSP.

[24] "Account of Coaches," p. 375; Oaks, "Big Wheels," pp. 351–63; Stephen J. Brobeck, "The Brief Life of the Proprietary Gentry," *William and Mary Quarterly*, 3d ser., 33, no. 3 (July 1976): 410–24; Brobeck, "Changes in Composition"; Randolph Shipley Klein, *Portrait of an Early American Family: The Shippens of Pennsylvania Across Five Generations* (Philadelphia: University of Pennsylvania Press, 1975), pp. 168–69, 171–72; Gough, "Toward a Theory," chaps. 5–11.

[25] Thomson to John Dickinson, August 16, 1776, Logan Papers, 8:78, HSP.

[26] Edward Shippen, Jr., to Yeates, Philadelphia, March 11, 1776, Shippen Papers, vol. 7, HSP; General Armstrong to Mrs. Armstrong, February 6, 1776, Armstrong Family Papers (transcripts), Force Collection, box 11, series 7E, LC; "For the Pennsylvania Evening Post," *Pennsylvania Evening Post*, June 1, 1776; Mary Frazer to Pensifor Frazer, August 27, 1776, as cited in "Some Extracts from the Papers of General Pensifor Frazer," *Pennsylvania Magazine of History and Biography* 31, no. 2 (1907): 136. On this point in general, see J. James Henderson, *Party Politics in the Continental Congress* (New York: McGraw-Hill Book Co., 1974), pp. 23, 51, 53, 76–77.

[27] These divisions are stressed in Gough, "Toward a Theory." For cooperation between the two factions, see Thomson to Drayton, *New-York Historical Society Collections* 11 (1878): 280–81; LoyTran, 50:442, New York Public Library.

[28] Elbridge Gerry to James Warren, Philadelphia, May 20, 1776, in C. Harvey Gardiner, ed., *A Study in Dissent: The Warren-Gerry Correspondence, 1776–1792* (Carbondale: Southern Illinois University Press, 1968), pp. 26–27.

[29] Bruce C. Daniels, "Patrician Leadership and the American Revolution in England: Four Case Studies," *Histoire Sociale—Social History* 9, no. 2 (Fall 1978): 375–89; Dickinson to Thomson, Elizabeth Town, August 7, 1776, Thomson Papers, vol. 1, LC. Dickinson's activities from 1774 to 1776 may be followed in Milton E. Flower, *John Dickinson: Conservative Revolutionary* (Charlottesville: University Press of Virginia, 1983).

[30] Thomson to Dickinson, Summerville, August 16, 1776; Thomson to Drayton, n.d., *New-York Historical Society Collections* 11 (1878): 274–86; Thomson to David Ramsay, November 4, 1786, in Paul H. Smith, ed., "Charles Thomson on Unity in the American Revolution," *Quarterly Journal of the Library of Congress* 28, no. 3 (July 1971): 163–71; Thomas Mifflin to Samuel Adams, May 21, 26, 1774, and Thomson to Adams, Philadelphia, June 3, 1774, Samuel Adams Papers (photostats), vol. 5, LC. For the strategy, see Thomson to Drayton, n.d., *New-York Historical Society Collections* 11 (1878): 274–86.

[31] Thomas L. Purvis, *Proprietors, Patronage, and Paper Money: Legislative Politics in New Jersey* (New Brunswick, N.J.: Rutgers University Press, 1986), pp. 232–54; A. Roger Ekirch, " 'Hungry as Hawks': The Social Bases of Political Leadership in Colonial North Carolina, 1729–1776," in *Power and Status*, pp. 136–45; Rosswurm, *Arms, Country, and Class*, chaps. 2, 3; "Extracts from the Diary of Dr. James Clitherall, 1776," *Pennsylvania Magazine of History and Biography* 22, no. 4 (1898): 469. On this issue more generally, see Jack P. Greene, "Independence, Improvement, and Authority: Toward a Framework for Understanding the Histories of the Southern Backcountry during the Era of the American Revolution," in *An Uncivil War: The Southern Backcountry during the American Revolution*, ed. Ronald Hoffman et al. (Charlottesville: University Press of Virginia, 1985), pp. 3–36.

[32] John Adams to Samuel Chase, July 9, 1776, *Letters of Delegates*, 4:414.

[33] These generalizations are drawn from Rosswurm, *Arms, Country, and Class*, pt. 2.

[34] Rosswurm, *Arms, Country, and Class*, pt. 3.

[35] Rosswurm, *Arms, Country, and Class*, pp. 260–61; Doerflinger, *Vigorous Spirit*, pp. 254–55. For the period 1761–1800, the United Congregations elected, on the average, 2.8 new men (those never elected before) each year to Christ Church vestry; from 1771 to 1780, however, the congregation elected an average of 4.6 new men per year. In 1774 and 1779, 13 new men were elected; in both years, the median and average taxable wealth of those holding vestry office dropped dramatically. The 1779 election brought into office the obscurest of the officeholders for the whole period. These generalizations draw from Records of Old Christ Church (microfilm), HSP.

[36] Henry Muhlenberg, March 24, 1779–June 5, 1780, *The Journals of Henry Melchior Muhlenberg*, trans. and ed. Theodore G. Tappert and John W. Robertson, 3 vols. (Philadelphia: Evangelical Lutheran Ministerium of Pennsylvania and Adjacent States, 1942–58), 3:225–323; Mason minutes, December 27, 1783, December 20, 1784, December 27, 1785, September 25, 1786, January 2, 1787, December 17, 1787, December 15, 1788, *Minutes and Proceedings of the Grand Lodge . . . of Free and Accepted Masons . . . in Pennsylvania*, vol. 1 (Philadelphia, 1894), pp. 68, 77, 87, 97, 105, 110, 119; John Ewing et al. to Reed, September 8, 1780, no. 443a, University of Pennsylvania Archives.

[37] Doerflinger, *Vigorous Spirit*, pts. 2, 3. A brief look at privateering is suggestive of how new men took advantage of new opportunities. If we look at the letters of marque issued in 1776 and 1777, we find that of the top four shareholders, only one is among John McCusker's top thirty investors in shipping during the colonial period. That person, Blair McClenachan, ranks twenty-fourth on McCusker's list; he held the fourth highest number of shares in the 1770s, Records of Pennsylvania Revolutionary Governments; McCusker, "Pennsylvania Shipping," pp. 229–30, 232.

[38] Doerflinger, *Vigorous Spirit*, pts. 2, 3.

[39] See, for example, Walter Buckingham Smith and Arthur Harrison Cole, *Fluctuations in American Business* (Cambridge: Harvard University Press, 1935); and John R. Nelson, Jr., *Liberty and Property: Political Economy and Policymaking in the New Nation, 1789–1812* (Baltimore: Johns Hopkins University Press, 1987), app. C.

[40] This discussion, unless otherwise noted, is from Nelson, *Liberty and Property*, chaps. 2–4. Similar arguments were made some years ago in William Appleman Williams, *The Contours of American History* (Chicago: Quadrangle Books, 1966), pp. 162–69. The phrase is from Hamilton's Constitutional Convention speech, quoted in Nelson, *Liberty and Property*, p. 27.

[41] Samuel Flagg Bemis, *Jay's Treaty: A Study in Commerce and Diplomacy* (New York: Macmillan Co., 1923), pp. 21–36. See also Joseph Charles, *The Origins of the American Party System* (New York: Harper and Row, 1961), pp. 13–19. The most recent discussion of the "Report on Manufactures" from this perspective, from which the author has drawn, is Nelson, *Liberty and Property*, chap. 3.

[42] Phineas Bond to Lord Granville, Philadelphia, March 10, 1794, in "Letters of Phineas Bond, British Consul at Philadelphia to the Foreign Office of Great Britain, 1790–1794," ed. J. Franklin Jameson, in *Annual Report of the American Historical Association for the Year 1897* (Washington, D.C.: Government Printing Office, 1898), pp. 544–45.

[43] An American Farmer [George Logan], *Letters Addressed to the Yeomanry of the United States, Containing Some Observations on Funding and Banking Systems*

(Philadelphia: Childs and Swaine, 1793), p. 7. Charles, *Origins of the Party System*, p. 6. Much of the current work on the 1790s takes this struggle into account but characterizes the worries of the opposition as, for example, "hysterical fears" (Lance Banning, *The Jeffersonian Persuasion: Evolution of a Party Ideology* [Ithaca, N.Y.: Cornell University Press, 1978], p. 127).

[44] Williams, *Contours of History*, p. 162; Olton, *Artisans for Independence*, chaps. 8, 9; George Bryan, "Account of the Adoption of the Constitution of 1787," George Bryan Papers, 1785–87, box 2, folder 4, HSP; John B. McMaster and Frederick D. Stone, eds., *Pennsylvania and the Federal Constitution, 1787–1788* (Lancaster: Historical Society of Pennsylvania, 1888); Herbert Storing, ed., *The Complete Anti-Federalist* (Chicago: University of Chicago Press, 1981), vol. 3; Merrill Jensen, ed., *The Documentary History of the Ratification of the Constitution*, vol. 2 (Madison: University of Wisconsin Press, 1976); Merrill Jensen and Robert A. Becker, eds., *The Documentary History of the First Federal Elections, 1788–1790*, vol. 1 (Madison: University of Wisconsin Press, 1976), pp. 227–429. Thomas Jefferson to Madison, May 12, 1793, in *The Writings of Thomas Jefferson*, ed. Paul L. Ford, 10 vols. (New York: G. P. Putnam's and Son, 1892–99), vol. 6, p. 251; Roland M. Baumann, "Philadelphia's Manufacturers and the Excise Tax of 1794: The Forging of the Jeffersonian Coalition," in *The Whiskey Rebellion: Past and Present Perspectives*, ed. Steven R. Boyd (Westport, Conn.: Greenwood Press, 1985), pp. 135–64; Roland M. Baumann, "John Swanwick: Spokesman for 'Merchant-Republicanism' in Philadelphia, 1790–1798," *Pennsylvania Magazine of History and Biography* 97, no. 2 (April 1973): 131–82. This is a theme in Richard G. Miller, *Philadelphia—Federalist City: A Study of Urban Politics, 1789–1801* (Port Washington, N.Y.: Kennikat Press, 1976). Voter turnout is in Miller, *Philadelphia*, p. 150; and Roland M. Baumann, "The Democratic-Republicans of Philadelphia: The Origins, 1776–1797" (Ph.D. diss., Pennsylvania State University, 1970), pp. 603–21.

[45] Joyce Appleby, *Capitalism and a New Social Order: The Republican Vision of the 1790s* (New York: New York University Press, 1984), p. 57. See also Richard Buel, Jr., *Securing the Revolution: Ideology in American Politics, 1789–1815* (Ithaca, N.Y.: Cornell University Press, 1974), pp. 85–90, 93–135, 230–31. For Republican ideology, see A. Farmer [George Logan], *Five Letters Addressed to the Yeomanry* (Philadelphia: Eleazer Oswald, 1792); [Logan], *Letters Addressed to the Yeomanry* (1793); George Logan, *An Address on the Natural and Social Order of the World as Intended to Produce Universal Good* (Philadelphia: Benjamin Franklin Bache, 1798); and Philip S. Foner, ed., *The Democratic-Republican Societies, 1790–1800: A Documentary Sourcebook of Constitutions, Declarations, Addresses, Resolutions, and Toasts* (Westport, Conn.: Greenwood Press, 1976), pp. 64–110. Roland Baumann's fine work on Philadelphia in the 1790s is essential for understanding this ideology.

[46] Bemis, *Jay's Treaty*, p. 267; "The Address of the Subscribers, Merchants and Traders of the City of Philadelphia," *American Remembrancer* (1796), 2:122–25 (Evans, 28389); Timothy Tickler, *The Philadelphia Jockey Club; or, Mercantile Influence Weighed, Consisting of Select Characters Taken from the Club of Addresses* (Philadelphia, 1795); Baumann, "Democratic-Republicans," pp. 522, 529. Madison to Jefferson, April 23, May 1, 1796, and *Aurora*, as quoted in Baumann, "Democratic-Republicans," p. 538; Baumann, "Swanwick," p. 171; Paul A. W. Wallace, *The Muhlenbergs of Pennsylvania* (Philadelphia: University of Pennsylvania Press, 1951), p. 287. For occupations of 268 of the 408 signers, see Edmund Hogan, *The Prospect of Philadelphia . . . Directory* (Philadelphia, 1795) (Billy G. Smith kindly provided a copy of the directory). Federalists also used these tactics in New York City (Young, *Democratic-Republicans*, p. 465).

[47] On the "Mercantile Interest['s]" retaliation on Clement Biddle for his activities around the Gideon Henfield case, see John Fenno to Joseph Ward, Philadelphia, August 24, 1793, typescript, Joseph Ward Papers, Chicago Historical Society; on the complaint about influence in the 1798 election, see Miller, *Federalist City*, p. 102; on numerous complaints about the election, see Schultz, "Thoughts among the People," p. 283. In 1810 Stephen Simpson argued that Federalists (during the previous decade) had received the votes of many "worthy tradesmen and mechanics" because of the "chain of connexion which exists between the merchant, the mechanic, and tradesmen, down to the laborer" (*Aurora*, September 21, 1810, as quoted in Schultz, "Thoughts among the People," pp. 342–43). Looking at returns on a ward basis reveals that those Philadelphia wards that were neither poor nor rich most often voted Republican in the 1790s (based on the wealth of those wards in 1798 as cited in Baumann, "Democratic-Republicans," p. 605). Miller, *Federalist City*. Although the ward ranked tenth in wealth, it produced the fourth highest number of Republican wins; the figures tend to support Simpson's arguments.

[48] Logan, *Letters* (1793), p. 24. *The Journal of William Maclay, United States Senator from Pennsylvania, 1789–1791* (1890; reprint, New York: F. Ungar Publishing Co., 1965), p. 331; Ethel E. Rasmusson, "Democratic Environment—Aristocratic Aspiration," *Pennsylvania Magazine of History and Biography* 90, no. 2 (April 1966): 155–82; Ethel Elise Rasmusson, "Capital on the Delaware: The Philadelphia Upper Class in Transition, 1789–1801" (Ph.D. diss., Brown University, 1962), pp. 66–103; Margaret L. Brown, "Mr. and Mrs. William Bingham of Philadelphia: Rulers of the Republican Court," *Pennsylvania Magazine of History and Biography* 61, no. 3 (July 1937): 286–324; Rasmusson, "Democratic Environment," pp. 166, 167; Ellis Paxson Oberholtzer, *Robert Morris: Patriot and Financier* (New York: Macmillan Co., 1903), pp. 297–99.

[49] Oberholtzer, *Robert Morris*, chaps. 9–11; Rasmusson, "Capital on the Delaware," pp. 189–92; Charles Page Smith, *James Wilson: Founding Father, 1742–1798* (Chapel Hill: University of North Carolina Press, 1956), chap. 25; Doerflinger, *Vigorous Spirit*, p. 247.

[50] Doerflinger, *Vigorous Spirit*, p. 233 n129; Rosswurm, *Arms, Country, and Class*, pp. 260–61. Chaloner's career may be followed in his papers at William Clements Library and HSP; see also *The Papers of Alexander Hamilton*, ed. Harold C. Syrett et al., 26 vols. (New York: Columbia University Press, 1961–79), vols. 2, 3. For the creditors' pressure to collect debts, see Theodore Hopkins to John Chaloner, Philadelphia, January 13, 1786, "Agreement of Mr. William Maccarty; Creditors, [1787?]," John Todd to Chaloner, June 20, 1792, and "Petition of George Meade and William Chance," February 9, 1788, Chaloner Papers, boxes 3–5, William Clements Library; Alexander Hamilton to Jeremiah Wadsworth, [New York, March 23, 1788], Philadelphia, March 12, 1791, *Hamilton Papers*, 4:624, 8:180. For his bankruptcy at death, see "We Whose Names . . . ," January 22, 1794, Chaloner Papers, box 4; Commonwealth v. Chaloner's Executors, Alexander J. Dallas, *Reports of Cases* . . . , 4 vols. (Philadelphia, 1793–1807), 3:500–502.

[51] *General Advertiser*, August 12, 1791; Jefferson to Edward Rutledge, Philadelphia, August 29, 1791, *Works of Thomas Jefferson*, ed. Paul L. Ford, 10 vols. (New York: G. P. Putnam's Sons, 1892–99), 5:376; *The Autobiography of Benjamin Rush: His "Travels through Life," together with his Commonplace Book for 1789–1813*, ed. George W. Corner (Princeton: Princeton University Press, 1948), p. 203; Nelson, *Liberty and Property*, pp. 34, 38. For the speculative mania more generally, see Charles Royster, *Light Horse Henry Lee and the Legacy of the American Revolution* (New

York: Alfred A. Knopf, 1981), pp. 66–83, 171–85; Douglas R. Littlefield, "The Potomac Company: A Misadventure in Financing an Early American Internal Improvement Company," *Business History Review* 58, no. 4 (Winter 1984): 562–85; and Joseph S. Davis, *Essays in the Earlier History of American Corporations* (Cambridge: Harvard University Press, 1917), vols. 1, 2. Norman B. Wilkinson, "Land Policy and Speculation in Pennsylvania, 1779–1800" (Ph.D. diss., University of Pennsylvania, 1958), chaps. 8–13; Robert D. Arbuckle, *Pennsylvania Speculator and Patriot: The Entrepreneurial John Nicholson, 1757–1800* (University Park: Pennsylvania State University Press, 1975), chaps. 10, 11.

[52] Doerflinger, *Vigorous Spirit*; Nelson, *Liberty and Property*, pp. 81–82.

[53] Davis, *Essays*, 2:149, 153; James T. Mitchell and Henry Flanders, comps., *Statutes at Large of Pennsylvania from 1682 to 1801*, 18 vols. (Harrisburg, Pa.: Harrisburg Publishing Co., 1896), 14:150–63, 279–94, 315–28, 400–404; J. Thomas Scharf and Thompson Westcott, *History of Philadelphia, 1609–1884*, 3 vols. (Philadelphia: L. H. Everts, 1884), 1:466; Schuylkill and Susquehanna Canal Company, *An Historical Account of the Rise, Progress and Present State of Canal Navigation in Pennsylvania* (2d ed.; Philadelphia: Zachariah Poulson, Jr., 1795), p. [ii].

[54] A Pennsylvanian [Mathew Carey], *Brief View of the System of Internal Improvement of the State of Pennsylvania* (Philadelphia: L. R. Bailey, 1831), pp. 3–4; Davis, *Essays*, 2:155; Schuylkill and Susquehannah Canal Company, *Historical Account*, p. 72; James Mease, *Picture of Philadelphia . . .* (Philadelphia: B. and T. Kite, 1811), p. 354; Arbuckle, *Pennsylvania Speculator and Patriot*, p. 157; François-Alexandre-Frédéric de la Rochefoucauld-Liancourt, *Travels through the United States of North America, the Country of the Iroquois and Upper Canada in the Years 1795, 1796, and 1797 . . .*, trans. H. Neuman, 2 vols. (London: R. Phillips, 1799), 1:15.

[55] Davis, *Essays*; Wilkinson, "Land Policy and Speculation in Pennsylvania"; Doerflinger, *Vigorous Spirit*, chap. 7. Cynthia J. Shelton, *The Mills of Manayunk: Industrialization and Social Conflict in the Philadelphia Region, 1787–1837* (Baltimore: Johns Hopkins University Press, 1986), p. 8, chap. 1. See also Arbuckle, *Pennsylvania Speculator and Patriot*.

[56] Baumann, "Swanwick," pp. 150–56; Rasmusson, "Capital on the Delaware," pp. 56–63; Mitchell and Flanders, *Statutes at Large*, 14:365–81, 15:41–48, 69–76; John A. Diemand, *"Insurance Company of North America": Protector of American Property since 1792* (New York: Newcomen Society in North America, 1953); Marquis James, *Biography of a Business, 1792–1942: Insurance Company of North America* (Indianapolis: Bobbs-Merrill, 1942); Doerflinger, *Vigorous Spirit*, pp. 303–10, quote at 309. Doerflinger argues that "substantial numbers of artisans and retailers" used the Bank of North America, but his analysis of the occupational composition of discounters at the Bank of North America for 1784/1785 and 1790/1791 does not support his claim for artisans. See also John Thom Holdsworth and Davis R. Dewey, *The First and Second Banks of the United States* (Washington, D.C.: Government Printing Office, 1910), pp. 63–64; Donald R. Adams, *Finance and Enterprise in Early America: A Study of Stephen Girard's Bank, 1812–1831* (Philadelphia: University of Pennsylvania Press, 1978), p. 2. For marine insurance before the incorporation movement of the 1790s, see Harrold E. Gillingham, *Marine Insurance in Philadelphia, 1721–1800* (Philadelphia: Patterson and White, 1933). For the investment patterns of the Insurance Company of North America, see James, *Biography of a Business*, pp. 53–55. Both insurance companies, moreover, were required to invest in the Bank of Pennsylvania (Baumann, "Swanwick," p. 156).

[57] Smith, *An Inquiry into the Nature and Causes of the Wealth of Nations* (New York: Random House, Modern Library Edition, 1937), p. 351; Charles P. Kindleberger, *Economic Response: Comparative Studies in Trade, Finance, and Growth* (Cambridge: Harvard University Press, 1978), chap. 5; François Crouzet, *The First Industrialists: The Problem of Origins* (Cambridge, Eng.: Cambridge University Press, 1985), pp. 99–102, 105–6, 126–43. For the dividends of the Insurance Company of North America, see James, *Biography of a Business*, pp. 29, 35, 53, 65. For merchant capital generally, see Elizabeth Fox-Genovese and Eugene D. Genovese, "The Janus Face of Merchant Capital," *Fruits of Merchant Capital: Slavery and Bourgeois Property in the Rise and Expansion of Capitalism* (New York: Oxford University Press, 1983), pp. 3–25; Gerald M. Sider, *Culture and Class in Anthropology and History: A Newfoundland Illustration* (Cambridge, Eng.: Cambridge University Press, 1986), pp. 34–38, 144–48; Smith, *Wealth of Nations*, pp. 341–55; Karl Marx, *Grundrisse: Foundations of the Critique of Political Economy* (Middlesex, Eng.: Penguin Books, 1973), pp. 856–61; and Karl Marx, *Capital: A Critical Analysis of Capitalist Production*, vol. 3 (New York: International Publishers, 1970), pp. 323–37. On merchant capital in American history, see the schematic but insightful comments of Bryan D. Palmer, "Social Formation and Class Formation in North America, 1800–1900," in *Proletarianization and Family History*, ed. David Levine (New York: Academic Press, 1984), pp. 234–54.

[58] Salinger, "Colonial Labor in Transition," pp. 165–91; Sharon V. Salinger, "Artisans, Journeymen, and the Transformation of Labor in Eighteenth-Century Philadelphia," *William and Mary Quarterly*, 3d ser., 40, no. 1 (January 1983): 62–84; Ian M. G. Quimby, "Apprenticeship in Colonial Philadelphia" (Master's thesis, University of Delaware, 1963); Rosswurm, "Arms, Culture, and Class," p. 17 table 2 (Index of Concentration for Occupations with Twenty or More Members, 1775); Rosswurm, *Arms, Country, and Class*, pp. 15–18. Because of their ambiguous and often transitory status, it is difficult to be precise about the number of journeymen. For the basis of the generalization in the text, see Rosswurm, *Arms, Country, and Class*, p. 17; Smith, "Struggles of the 'Lower Sort,'" pp. 113–14, 123, 171–73; and Tom W. Smith, "The Dawn of the Urban-Industrial Age: The Social Structure of Philadelphia, 1790–1830" (Ph.D. diss., University of Chicago, 1980), pp. 40–43. Henry P. Rosemont, "Benjamin Franklin and the Philadelphia Typographical Strikers of 1786," *Labor History* 22, no. 3 (Summer 1981): 398–429; John R. Commons et al., *A Documentary History of American Industrial Society*, 10 vols. (Cleveland: A. H. Clark Co., 1910–11), 3:127–29; Ian M. G. Quimby, "The Cordwainers Protest: A Crisis in Labor Relations," in *Winterthur Portfolio* 3, ed. Milo M. Naeve (Winterthur, Del.: Henry Francis du Pont Winterthur Museum, 1967), pp. 89, 90, 92; Charles F. Montgomery, *American Furniture: The Federal Period in the Henry Francis du Pont Winterthur Museum* (1966; reprint, New York: Bonanza Books, 1978), pp. 21–22; William A. Sullivan, *The Industrial Worker in Pennsylvania, 1800–1840* (Harrisburg: Pennsylvania Historical and Museum Commission, 1955), apps. A, B.

[59] Schultz, "Thoughts among the People," pp. 316–18; Smith, "Dawn of the Urban-Industrial Age," p. 44 table 15, p. 28 table 3; Bruce Laurie, *Working People of Philadelphia, 1800–1850* (Philadelphia: Temple University Press, 1980), chap. 1; Baumann, "Philadelphia's Manufacturers," pp. 141–45.

[60] Kathleen Matilda Catalano, "Cabinetmaking in Philadelphia, 1820–1840" (Master's thesis, University of Delaware, 1972), pp. 25–27; Montgomery, *American Furniture*, pp. 17–18; Commons, *Documentary History*, 3:59–248, 4:99–264. Schultz,

"Thoughts among the People," pp. 318–19; Philip B. Scranton, *Proprietary Capitalism: The Textile Manufacture at Philadelphia, 1800–1885* (New York: Cambridge University Press, 1983), chap. 4; Laurie, *Working People*, chap. 1. For the last point, see the introduction and case studies in Maxine Berg, Pat Hudson, and Michael Sonenscher, eds., *Manufacture in Town and Country before the Factory* (Cambridge, Eng.: Cambridge University Press, 1983); and Crouzet, *First Industrialists*. There is much to be learned from European work on proto-industrialization; see Peter Kriedte, Hans Medick, and Jürgen Schlumbohm, *Industrialization before Industrialization: Rural Industry in the Genesis of Capitalism* (New York: Cambridge University Press, 1981); Eighth International Economic History Congress, "A" *Themes* (Budapest, 1982). A good introduction is presented in Geoff Eley, "The Social History of Industrialization: 'Proto-Industry' and the Origins of Capitalism," *Economy and Society* 13, no. 4 (November 1984): 519–39.

[61] Marietta, *Reformation of American Quakerism*; Bauman, *For the Reputation of Truth*, pp. 175–78; Jean R. Soderlund, *Quakers and Slavery: A Divided Spirit* (Princeton: Princeton University Press, 1985); Michael Meranze, "Public Punishments, Reformative Incarceration, and Authority in Philadelphia, 1750–1835" (Ph.D. diss., University of California, Berkeley, 1987). Baumann, "Democratic-Republicans," pp. 86–87, 92, 174, 180, 182, 196, 199, 224, 334, 553, 568; McMaster and Stone, *Pennsylvania and the Federal Constitution*, 2:520–21; Miller, *Federalist City*, pp. 16, 99, 104, 106; Margaret Woodbury, *Public Opinion in Philadelphia* (Durham, N.C.: Seeman Prinkry, 1919), p. 124. The 1798 candidacy of Israel Israel and Jefferson's election apparently provoked much Quaker interest; see Drinker journal, October 11, November 4, 5, 1796, February 22, 23, 1798, in Henry D. Biddle, ed., *Extracts from the Journal of Elizabeth Drinker from 1759–1807, A.D.* (Philadelphia: J. B. Lippincott Co., 1889), pp. 292, 293, 317, 318. Rasmusson, "Capital on the Delaware," pp. 56, 60, 61–63, 173–78, chap. 5. See also Edward Shippen to Peggy Shippen, March 3, December 24, 1793, in Lewis Burd Walker, "Life of Margaret Shippen, Wife of Benedict Arnold," *Pennsylvania Magazine of History and Biography* 26, no. 1 (1902): 71–73, 76; Mease, *Picture of Philadelphia*, p. 54; Baumann, "Democratic-Republicans," p. 253.

[62] Scranton, *Proprietary Capitalism*, pp. 132–33; see also Diane Lindstrom, *Economic Development in the Philadelphia Region, 1810–1850* (New York: Columbia University Press, 1978), pp. 39–40. Benjamin Rush to John Adams, February 8, 1813, in Benjamin Rush, *Letters*, ed. Lyman Butterfield, 2 vols., Memoirs of the American Philosophical Society, vol. 30 (Princeton: Princeton University Press, 1951), 2:1182; Thomas Hamilton, *Men and Manners*, pp. 379–81, as quoted in Rasmusson, "Capital on the Delaware," p. 210. See also Rasmusson, "Capital on the Delaware," pp. 105, 143–44, 179; and Scranton, *Proprietary Capitalism*, pp. 90, 131.

[63] The "matrix of accumulation" concept is from Scranton, *Proprietary Capitalism*, pp. 3–11. Meranze, "Public Punishments"; Michael Meranze, introduction, in Benjamin Rush, *Essays: Literary, Moral, and Philosophical*, ed. Michael Meranze (Schenectady, N.Y.: Union College Press, 1988); Sider, *Culture and Class*, pp. 144–48; Rasmusson, "Capital on the Delaware," p. 65.

Black Family Life in Philadelphia from Slavery to Freedom

Billy G. Smith

During the past several decades, historians have joined the general public in scrutinizing the American family. Some modern observers have worried about the "deterioration" of contemporary family life, noting that families no longer either pray or stay together, that spouse and child abuse are rampant, that the power relationship between mates has shifted, and that casual intimacy outside marriage can lead to disease and death. Meanwhile, scholars have studied the evolution of American families, analyzing their size, structure, and composition on the one hand and the nature and ideals about interpersonal familial relations on the other. The character of black family life has particularly attracted the attention of historians, most of whom agree with Roger Bastide that in the New World, African Americans "hammered out a new cultural pattern of their own, shaping it in response to the demands of their new environment." Scholars consequently have focused on the ways in which enslaved and free African Americans defied and manipulated the power of their owners and the constraints of racist societies to create their own cultures.[1]

The author thanks Jean R. Soderlund, Gary B. Nash, Catherine Goetz, and Susan E. Klepp both for their critical comments and for generously sharing their research. He also appreciates the aid of Richard Wojtowicz in locating and helping to interpret the advertisements for runaway slaves and Patrick Caulfield for entering the information into the computer.

This essay will examine the successes and failures experienced by African American Philadelphians in their efforts to define their family lives and thereby fashion one vital aspect of their cultural well-being during the second half of the eighteenth century. Such a study should shed light not only on the specifics of family development among black Philadelphians but also on the more general shape of the emerging national culture. For, as a biracial and multiethnic urban society, Philadelphia represented the future paradigm of the new nation. Moreover, while slavery declined in the city during the postrevolutionary decades, free blacks constructed a new and vibrant community. The City of Brotherly Love—the center of Quaker humanitarianism and revolutionary egalitarian ideals—came to symbolize its name as many blacks and whites pursued the promise of racial equality and a harmonious society.[2]

The primary story of family life among black Philadelphians during this half century is one of struggle, survival, and eventually, a modicum of success in the face of enslavement and racism. Like all African Americans at that time, those in the City of Brotherly Love were, as anthropologist Sidney Mintz reminds us, "required to engineer styles of life that might be preserved in the face of terrible outrage . . . [for] the daily demands—to eat, to sleep, to love, to grow, to survive—do not become less imperious because their satisfaction is persistently thwarted by oppression."[3] While slavery in Philadelphia did thwart the family lives of its victims, severely limiting their opportunities to form lasting relationships, reside with their loved ones, raise their children, or even reproduce, among free blacks a community emerged, especially during the postrevolutionary decades, in which African Americans enjoyed greater chances to define and control their existence.

The number of slaves in Philadelphia rose and fell during the second half of the eighteenth century. The city contained approximately 800 enslaved residents in 1750. When the Seven Years' War curtailed the migration of European indentured servants and enticed many of those already in the colony to join the military, Philadelphians turned to blacks to solve their labor needs. Merchants, lawyers, taverners, craftsmen, and ship captains bought many of the several hundred slaves—some of them directly from Africa—who disembarked at the port each year during the late 1750s and early 1760s, and the number of slaves in the city increased to roughly 1,700. At the war's conclusion, unemployed veterans joined German and Scots-Irish redemptioners to renew the supply of white workers, and, as import duties on slaves increased, Philadelphians stopped buying black laborers. By the early 1770s, according to one observer, more slaves were exported than imported into the Pennsylvania capital. The number of unfree African Americans consequently dwindled to 1,375 by 1770 and to fewer than 700 by 1775. Pennsylvania's gradual emancipation law of 1780 spelled the eventual end of slavery; whites held 450 slaves when the legislation passed, 301 when the first federal census takers made their rounds, and only 55 at the century's close.[4]

Since Philadelphia's blacks lived in a "walking city" smaller than twenty square blocks, they undoubtedly enjoyed opportunities to socialize, form networks of friends, and establish sexual liaisons and families. No matter how hard they might try, masters could not completely control all aspects of slaves' lives. That numerous owners committed their bound laborers to a month in the workhouse for sneaking away for an evening with friends and lovers demonstrates the failure of their efforts. Thus, Lewis Farmer charged Philipina with "Having frequently gone out of the House after the Family had retired to Rest, [and] Remaining out during the Night in Company with disorderly Men"; P. B. Oram disciplined Edward for "going out at night and frequenting gaming houses"; and George Davis punished Amy for "absconding [from] him eight times" in a week.[5]

Indeed, whites complained throughout the century that slaves and free blacks gathered together far too frequently. In 1750, for example, county inhabitants protested to the Assembly about the crowds of blacks who celebrated New Year's. But socializing was not confined merely to holidays. Nearly four decades later the *Pennsylvania Gazette* warned its readers: "At the late city sessions a negro was tried and convicted for keeping a disorderly house; it appeared upon this occasion that the offender kept a place of resort for all the loose and idle characters of the city, whether whites, blacks or mulattoes; and that frequently in the night gentlemens servants would arrive there, mounted on their masters horses (for which the landlord had provided a stable in the neighbourhood) and indulge in riotous mirth and dancing till the dawn, when they posted again to their respective homes. These facts are laid before the public . . . as a hint to masters to watch the conduct of their servants."[6]

In carving out their own living space, slaves could take advantage of the large pool of potential partners in the city to form affective ties and even to marry and have children. Some carried on love affairs without their masters' knowledge. A few married in a Christian church with the full consent of their owners; sixty-seven slaves wed in Philadelphia's Anglican churches between 1765 and 1780. Masters in the surrounding countryside sometimes allowed their human property to marry, William Moraley, an indentured servant from England, observed, because it "makes them easier, and often prevents their running away." "Their Marriages," he continued,

> are diverting; for when the Day is appointed for the Solemnization, Notice is given to all the Negroes and their Wives to be ready. The Masters of the new Couple provide handsomely for the Entertainment of the Company. The Inhabitants generally grace the Nuptials with their presence, when all Sorts of the best Provisions are to be met with. They chuse some *Englishman* to read the Marriage Ceremony out of the Common Prayer Book; after which they sing and dance and drink till they get drunk. Then a Negro goes about the Company and collects Money for the Use of the Person who marry'd them, which is laid out in a Handkerchief, and presented to him.[7]

The records are silent about the marital customs of Philadelphia's slaves except for a brief comment by the Reverend Nicholas Collin of Gloria Dei Church. When he joined Joshua, a free black carpenter, and Eleonore Delancy in matrimony, he noted that "many Africans" were present. (All of them probably knew that the bride had lied about being free, but the rector did not. When he learned that she was a slave and did not have her master's permission, he voided the marriage.) While some slaves wed in the manner of whites, many others must have followed some variation of the common West African ritual of bride-right, wherein a man offered a present, and a woman, through her acceptance of the gift, became his wife.[8] That no record of such practices in Philadelphia exists may reflect only that blacks performed their ceremonies away from the prying eyes of whites.

Philadelphia's newspaper advertisements reveal the depth of emotional attachment within some slave families. Men and women occasionally risked whipping and other severe punishment simply to be with their mate. When Sam absconded, his master acknowledged that he "has a wife [in the city], a Negro . . . who it is thought secrets him." Dick jumped ship, his owner believed, to go "to Dover, as he has a Wife there." Stephen Carpenter advertised for an escaped "Negroe Woman, about 45 Years of Age" who he supposed was in Philadelphia where "she has a Husband, a Baker by Trade." Sue, another forty-five-year-old black woman, took refuge in Baltimore, "where she remained for some time, by the name of Free Poll." She may have married before being apprehended, for when she escaped again, her master warned, "She is now about Philadelphia, waiting for the return of her husband, as she calls him; a free Mulattoe, named Mark Stubbs, who sailed from Baltimore in a ship called the Enterprize. . . . She is a good cook, can wash and iron well; he is a butcher, and it is probable they may set up for themselves about the city."[9]

A few masters sympathized with the efforts of their slaves to maintain their marriages. John Reedle advertised a "Sober healthy young Negroe Wench for sale" but stipulated, "She will not be sold into the Country, because she is married, and it is thought improper to separate Man and Wife." When offering to sell his "Likely Negroe man, about 29 years of age," Lawrence Growden noted, "He has a wife in West Jersey, about two miles from Yeardley's ferry, and is very desirous of a master in that neighbourhood."[10]

Escapees sometimes sought out their parents, a few women carried small children while trying to elude their masters, and others relied on their siblings for aid and comfort. Declaring her intention "to see her mother this winter," twenty-year-old Nancy ran away from the Northern Liberties. Sambo, a seventeen-year-old slave in Chester County, presumably headed for the Pennsylvania capital, "as his mother lives in the city." Apparently trying to visit his father and mother in Maryland, Jack escaped twice within six months from his Philadelphia master. Phoebe carried her two-year-old child, and Maria took her four-year-old daughter. Andrew Lowrey thought Joe might seek refuge with his brother, a free black who worked in Philadelphia. Slaves sometimes fled to their family shortly after being separated by their master. Michael Hulings offered Hannah, a "hearty Negro Girl . . . this Country born" and "bred" in his family, for sale in 1765. Two months after a taverner a few miles from Philadelphia purchased Hannah, she eloped, running, her new master believed, either to her family in Philadelphia or to her brother and sister in Wilmington.[11]

The value that many slaves placed on their families is further evident in their efforts to preserve them. In 1762 the master of Absalom Jones sold his mother and six siblings and then moved with Jones to

Philadelphia. Eight years later, he and Mary, the slave of a neighbor, married and then borrowed money to purchase Mary's freedom, thereby bestowing the same status on their future children. After eight difficult years of working and saving, they paid off the debt, and it took another seven years to earn the money to buy Absalom's freedom. The gradual emancipation law of 1780 worked, ironically, to the detriment of some of the city's slaves. Masters not infrequently defied the law, selling their bondspeople out of state rather than manumitting them and, in the process, tore families apart. Numerous slaves sought aid from the Pennsylvania Abolition Society when their owners attempted to sell them away from their spouses and children. Anthony Benezet, a prominent Philadelphia abolitionist, averred that some slaves committed suicide rather than be separated from their loved ones. One, "having pressingly, on his knees, solicited a friend, without success, to prevent his being sent away to the southward" from his family, jumped from the deck of the ship into the Delaware River and drowned.[12]

A few blacks carried on the polygynous traditions of West Africa. Charles first eloped in 1782 and stayed away for nearly three years, "in which time he married two wives . . . by one of which he had three children." After a second escape, Charles's master expressed moral outrage: "I do apprehend he will reside chiefly . . . with his *plurality of wives* (notwithstanding it is against the laws of Moses and the United States)." Peter, "40 years of age, about 5 feet 6 or 7 inches high, square and well built, a little bow-legged, a smooth tongued artful fellow, a noted liar, a great villain, and fond of liquor," posed continual problems. Having periodically absconded "almost ever since he was 20 years of age; he has lived in New-Jersey . . . has been [on] a voyage or two to sea; has lived in Philadelphia, in Bucks county, and almost every part of Chester county." Peter apparently enjoyed an active love life in each of these places. In addition to his "Indian wife," he had "children by four black women, to all of whom he says he is lawfully married." His master was perplexed about which of his wives Peter "will apply to conceal him."[13]

Blacks occasionally became intimately involved with whites, although the legal penalties were severe. Interracial marriages were illegal, and any official who ignored the law was liable for a £100 fine. Whites cohabiting with free blacks could be fined £30 or sold as a servant for up to seven years; blacks could be enslaved for life. If caught fornicating together, blacks could be indentured as a servant for seven years, and whites could be whipped, imprisoned, or branded with the letter A. Offspring from such a union could be "put out to service" until their thirty-first birthday. Still, a handful of slaves absconded with their white lovers. "Negroe" Bob and servant girl Ann Broughton probably intended to "pass for Man and Wife." Thomas Bucher "took with him a white woman, which he says is his wife." During the revolutionary war, Maria, a "Mulattoe Woman Slave," left behind "her friends and children, [and] a good master and mistress" in Philadelphia in search of her "married white man, who is a soldier in the Continental service."[14]

The state abolished the miscegenation laws in 1780, but attitudes against such unions remained strong. At the end of the century many black and white couples—including "well-looking girls"—scandalized Reverend Collin by asking him to perform their wedding ceremonies. "Not willing to have blame from public opinion," Collin refused. One black man "came with a white woman, [and] said that he had a child with her which was dead, and was uneasy in his conscience for living in such a state," so the rector "referred him to the negro minister." On another occasion the intended bride "warmly pleaded her cause" as well, but Collin still declined. "Nevertheless," he lamented in his journal, "these frequent mixtures will soon force matrimonial sanction. What a particoloured race will soon make a great portion of the population of Philadelphia!"[15]

Even though many blacks struggled to create and sustain loving bonds with one another or even with whites, the nature of slavery in Philadelphia meant that the great majority of its bondspeople led fragmented family lives at best. While advertisements for runaways furnish many examples illustrating the strength of emotional attachments, the same notices suggest that the proportion of slaves with family ties was considerably smaller in Philadelphia than in the southern colonies. Between 1728 and 1790, advertisements for 1,033 fugitives appeared in the *Pennsylvania Gazette*; masters believed that only 1 percent of them sought to reunite with another family member. By comparison, 19 percent of black escapees advertised in newspapers in Virginia and Maryland tried to rejoin their loved ones.[16]

The demographic profile of Philadelphia's slaves likewise suggests that during the third quarter of the eighteenth century most failed to establish long-lasting relationships. One key indicator is the low birth rate. The best estimate is that the slaves' crude birth rates ranged around 22 per 1,000, between a third and a half of that of the city's whites.[17] This reproductive level was far below the mortality rate of blacks, in part explaining the precipitous decline in their number during the decade preceding the Revolution. The high proportion of adults among the city's slaves corroborates these findings and demonstrates that African Americans reproduced much more successfully in most other areas of mainland North America. Adults accounted for roughly 65 percent of slaves in eighteenth-century Philadelphia as compared with 50 percent in the lower western shore of Maryland and 40 percent in much of Virginia. Only in South Carolina during the height of slave importation did the imbalance between black adults and children resemble that in Philadelphia.[18]

This low fertility cannot be dismissed merely as an artifact of a skewed age or sex structure among slaves. Since owners preferred to purchase young adults whenever possible, proportionally more blacks than whites were in their child-producing years, making the low birth rates among slaves even more startling (table 1). In 1775, when the best records are available, fewer than 2 percent of slaves were infants, 12 percent were younger than ten years old, and 62 percent belonged in the sixteen-to-forty-five child-producing age brackets. In addition, because Philadelphia masters used both female slaves to care for their home and male

TABLE 1. Age Structure of Philadelphians

Group of people	Age -16 (%)	Age 16–45 (%)	Age 45+ (%)	Total (N)
Slaves in 1762, 1767, and 1770	27	59	14	156
Slaves in 1775	24	62	14	550
Slaves in 1780	29	58	13	78
White males in 1790	42	46	12	20,374
All whites in 1800	38	50	12	36,955

Sources: City Constables' Returns registering the ages of most slaves are available for Walnut Ward in 1762; Upper Delaware Ward in 1767; East Mulberry Ward in 1770; all ten city wards in 1775; and East Mulberry Ward, Middle Ward, and Walnut Ward in 1780. All are located in the Philadelphia City Archives, City Hall Annex. The first records that indicate the ages of whites are the federal censuses. The proportion of white males who were older than 45 in 1790 was assumed to be identical to the proportion older than 45 in 1800.

slaves to aid in their businesses, whites bought blacks of both sexes in fairly equal number. According to the prerevolutionary constables' returns, females accounted for 50 percent of all slaves. Based on the age and sex composition of slaves on the eve of the Revolution, each adult bondswoman may have borne, on average, one child every fifteen years, hardly a reflection of thriving families.[19]

Why was slave fertility so low? In part, blacks may have consciously controlled their own reproduction, deciding not to bring offspring into a society that would enslave them. They may have practiced birth control, abortion, infanticide, and child abandonment, although the evidence about these activities is scant. Philis left her three-year-old child at an inn, Lucy Low was jailed for killing her baby, and Jeremiah Goolin's mother gave him to the almshouse, although these could have been no more than isolated incidents. African customs might have played a more important role in maintaining low birth rates. Some of the city's slaves, especially those purchased during the Seven Years' War, disembarked from ships directly from Africa, and they would have been inclined to follow their old cultural mores. After giving birth, West African women generally abstained from sexual intercourse until their infant was weaned, a process that often took three years and, obviously, impaired their fertility.[20]

Masters discouraged their human property from bearing children as well. Philadelphia's slaves usually worked singly in their owner's home or small shop; most slaveholders had neither use for more than one bondsperson nor space for them to live except in back rooms and lofts in their cramped urban quarters. While farmers may have valued slave children because of their potential productive capacity, most urbanites viewed children as an extra expense and an added burden. "Indeed," one newspaper contributor commented, "in this city, negroes just born, are considered as an incumbrance only, and if humanity did not forbid it, they would be instantly given away." Newspaper advertisements illustrate the validity of this observation. John Johnston, a chandler, offered a "Healthy Negroe Woman, about 24 Years of Age; she is pretty far gone with Child, and sold for no other Fault, than that she breeds fast." Hugh McCullough described a "Likely young Negroe Wench, that can do any Kind of Family Business; sold for no Fault but breeding." Likewise, masters showed little hesitation in selling off girls and boys between six and twelve years of age.[21]

The inability of slaves to control their living arrangements contributed to their low fertility and the frailty of their family connections. Many Philadelphia masters conceived of slaves primarily as temporary labor rather than long-term investments. Moreover, since these owners often came from the middling classes, they did not possess the wherewithal of large planters to withstand short-term business cycles. The city's owners bought during good times and sold during bad ones. The urban market in human beings was brisk; nearly one of every five masters in the city in 1769 had not possessed a slave just two years earlier. In the same way that owners sold children away from their mothers, they showed little compunction about dividing up entire families, as in the following advertisement: "Two valuable Negroes, a Man and his Wife, both young and hearty, have had the Small-pox . . . sold for no Fault but Want of Employ. They have a fine promising Male Child, two Years old, that has had the Small-pox, likewise to be sold with them, if the Purchaser chooses." In March 1765 James Coultas offered a couple and their four children for sale; he must have sold the parents and infants because his subsequent advertisement noted that only the older boys were left. Indeed, the problem of slave families broken by the sale of their individual members attracted the attention of the legislature during and after the Revolution. Part of the justification offered for the gradual emancipation law of 1780 was the "unnatural separation and sale of husband and wife from each other and from their children." Eight years later the state restricted that "practice of separating which is too often exercised by the masters and mistresses of negro and mulatto slaves."[22]

The city's generally high mortality rate further undermined slave families, not only because black spouses, children, and parents died but also because the death of an owner meant that slaves would be dispersed as part of the estate. The integrity of black families was not a concern of Philadelphia's testators.[23] Bondspeople thus continually confronted the reality of imminent separation from those blacks with whom they had established personal ties.

Because the needs of masters rather than those of slaves determined the groupings in which unfree blacks were held, the great majority of Philadelphia's bondspeople did not cohabit with their loved ones. The tax lists of 1767 and 1772, the constables' returns for 1775, and the federal census of 1790 indicate that approximately a third of the slaves resided singly in their owners' homes; another third dwelled with one other slave at their master's residences; and the final third were held in groups of three or more (table 2). However, other records allow us to probe behind these numbers, revealing an even bleaker picture of the prospects that slave families might have resided together. Portions of three of the city's constables' returns taken between 1770 and 1780 register the age and sex of many slaves. Only 7 percent of adult slaves of the opposite sex shared living quarters, and the nature of their involvement, if any, is unstated and thus remains unknown. The age differences between slaves indicate that 23 percent of the ones who occupied the same domicile could have been related as a parent or child. The best estimate, then, is that a *maximum* of 30 percent of slaves lived with their relatives and loved ones at any point in time. Data from the inventories of estates corroborate these figures: 3 percent of women dwelled with men identified as their husbands, and 28 percent of women lived with their own children. This configuration differed dramatically from that in the South. On three large Maryland plantations during the years preceding the Revolution, for example, nearly half of all African Americans resided in two-parent households that included some children. On smaller Chesapeake farms, slightly more than half lived in either one- or two-parent families.[24]

The same demographic features that demonstrate the difficulties of slave family life suggest that free blacks in postrevolutionary Philadelphia enjoyed considerably greater success forming families and intimate personal relationships. Although constrained by racial discrimination

TABLE 2. Proportion of Black Philadelphians Sharing a Household

	Slaves				All blacks	
Number in household	1767 (%)	1772 (%)	1775 (%)	1790 (%)	1790 (%)	1800 (%)
1	33	39	32	33	22	19
2	30	29	38	27	17	21
3+	37	32	30	40	61	60
Total (N)	905	752	362	301	2,150	6,083

Sources: The tax lists of 1767 and 1772, which register slaves between 12 and 50 years of age only, and a sample of 50% of the City Constables' Returns for 1775, Philadelphia City Archives, City Hall Annex. The 1790 and 1800 figures are from the federal censuses. The 1767 figures are also presented in Gary B. Nash, "Slaves and Slaveowners in Colonial Philadelphia," *William and Mary Quarterly*, 3d ser., 30, no. 2 (April 1973): 237, 244.

and economic difficulties, most African Americans in the city during the 1780s and 1790s could define their private lives. Free blacks had never been very numerous during the colonial era; only 200 or 300 inhabited the city in 1775. But as emancipated and escaped slaves flocked to Philadelphia during and after the Revolution, the nonenslaved black population grew to roughly 1,000 by 1783, to 1,849 in 1790, then nearly tripled to 6,083 during the next decade.[25]

Many newly freed slaves married and started families shortly after they arrived in the Quaker City. Four times as many blacks wed in the city's churches during the 1780s than in the decade before the war; some were ex-slaves legalizing unions that had not been recognized under slavery, others were finally finding new partners among the increasing urban population of African Americans. Not surprisingly, since blacks had to delay marrying until their term of bondage was complete, most married at a later age than their white counterparts. In Gloria Dei, the church for which such records are available, the average age of black men and women on their wedding day was 27.5 and 26.0 respectively, as compared with 23.5 and 20.0 for their white counterparts.[26] Still, the average number of marriages was only a dozen annually, which was quite small.

Most free blacks ignored conventional rituals in white churches, choosing instead to follow another custom or simply to move in with one another. Thus, Ann Hayman lived with Philip Hayman for three years and even assumed his last name although they never took vows in a church. Having children out of official wedlock probably was not uncommon among black women. Elizabeth Thompson, a "single" woman, took refuge in the almshouse when she became pregnant; she had given birth to another child two years earlier. A black sailor impregnated Maria Harris, also unmarried. Cudjo Desire and Elizabeth Murray brought their sixteen-month-old infant to Gloria Dei Church when they decided to wed.[27]

Many African Americans moved to the Quaker City not only to escape slavery and the racial isolation of rural areas but also to join with other free blacks in a conscious attempt to create and enjoy their own community. Part of that endeavor entailed establishing viable family lives. The high fertility of Philadelphia's blacks after the Revolution testifies to their success. Their crude birth rates averaged about 45 per 1,000, slightly higher than that of the white population and more than twice the rates among slaves before the Revolution.[28]

Most free blacks succeeded in creating and maintaining family ties; about 80 percent of them resided with at least one other African American during the century's final decade (see table 2). But many continued to live under the supervision of whites: 50 percent dwelled in white households in 1790 and 64 percent a decade later. Both rising rents, which forced people to share their living arrangements, and the indenturing of hundreds of French West Indian slaves imported to Philadelphia accounted for the increase of blacks in white households. During this decade the vast majority of African Americans who lived on their own probably resided in family groups since 96 percent lived with at least two others of their race. Women headed these households in about 15 percent of these cases, approximately the same proportion as existed among whites. Still, by the end of the century, a majority of blacks lived in households controlled by whites—a few as slaves, more as servants, and most as boarders or domestics who occupied a room or a floor of a home. And nearly two-thirds of these in white households shared their quarters with at least one other black person. Even though the relationships among blacks in any of the households are not recorded, the statistical evidence strongly suggests the formation of black family units.[29]

Recreating the inner workings of black families from the extant records is nearly impossible. But the monetary problems common to most blacks undoubtedly helped to define familial life. To a far greater extent than among white families, black families constituted an economic partnership among all its members. While the men worked primarily as sailors and day laborers, women earned wages by cooking, cleaning homes, caring for children, and washing clothes for whites. Some parents, recently freed from slavery, found the task of providing for their offspring extremely difficult. One common solution, sometimes imposed on them by city authorities, was to bind out their children to other families. Thus, one-fourth of blacks living in white households in 1790 were indentured children.[30]

Several examples from the almshouse illustrate the fragility created by difficult financial circumstances. When their father fell ill and their mother, who worked as a domestic servant, could not care for them, Isaac and Samuel, aged three and five, entered the almshouse. Sarah Boardley and her small daughter, Ann, were given their freedom in Robert Thompson's will, whereupon she moved to Philadelphia and for two years "maintained herself and child in the line or business of a washerwoman." But on December 2, 1800, "much afflicted with pains through her limbs [so] that she cannot labour for her support," Sarah, "in a perishing condition," applied for aid. A week later Ann was indentured and Sarah discharged from the almshouse the following March. Harry Goolin deserted his wife and infant, Jeremiah, in 1798. Two years later Jeremiah's mother gave him to the almshouse clerk since she was "poor, and not able to support [him] and herself [and] having no other means to live but by hiring herself out at service as a Maid in a family which she could not do with the child." Jeremiah was bound eight months later. Not all quietly acquiesced to the forced separation from their children. Disregarding Isabella Johnson's objections, the Guardians of the Poor indentured her three-year-old in 1800 because Isabella was pregnant, abandoned by her husband, and destitute. Less than three months later Isabella recovered her child "by force," so the officials jailed her and bound the child to a farmer in Delaware, far from Isabella's reach.[31]

Other records reveal some of the more normal conditions in which many black families existed. At the end of the century, three black families and their boarders crowded into a few wooden structures along the wharves near the intersection of Front and Arch streets. In 1799 Samuel Saviel, his wife, and six children paid $75 annual rent for the two-story frame abode in which they had lived for the previous dozen years. Samuel had worked as a lime salesman, fruit dealer, huckster, and carter for the past three decades. Tinee Cranshaw and her children lived in a similar home next door; she sold lime and fruit for her livelihood, as had her husband, Caesar, before his death during the 1793 yellow-fever epidemic. That Joseph Santone, a French gentleman in the house beside Cranshaw's, owned one of the few slaves left in the city may have been a sore point for these black families.[32]

David Duncan headed a household of ten blacks in a three-story rental unit on the other side of Saviel and Cranshaw. Duncan worked both as a peddler and a sailor. He had married Phoebe Seymour, a huckster, two years earlier and with his two children moved in with her. In 1800 David pooled his funds with Robert Turner, a black laborer, to buy a plot of land near Turner's residence on the northwestern outskirts of the city. Several months later, setting out on an ocean voyage from which he would never return, Duncan made out his will to ensure that his property would be dispersed after his death according to his wishes. He left his entire estate to Phoebe, entrusting her to maintain and educate his children, and named as executors his wife and his friend John Exeter, a black carter. Thomas Shoemaker, a white merchant who owned a counting house across the street from the Duncans, appraised the estate, providing us with a view of the material home life of a more successful black family in the city. The value of their furnishings totaled slightly more than $100, the equivalent of a mariner's salary for four months. In the kitchen on the first floor Phoebe cooked meals and fed her family and lodgers. The Duncans spent most of their time in the room on the second story, where they kept a bureau, two mirrors, a small table, six chairs, a settee, and the family's two beds—one for Phoebe and David, the other for their three or four children. A set of china, a few wineglasses, a liquor case, and some books constituted the luxury items owned by the Duncans. Two or three boarders, or perhaps another family, occupied the third floor of the house. After David's death, Phoebe continued to peddle small items and rent space to lodgers; meanwhile, Jude Duncan, another huckster, moved in next door.[33]

In summary, slavery in Philadelphia severely limited the ability of most bondspeople to create or sustain loving relationships with one another. Even though slaves strove to establish and maintain viable families, they often failed, as indicated by their low fertility. While African customs may have influenced birth rates, the active resistance by masters, the sale of black children, and the rapid turnover in slave ownership also inhibited reproduction. Most important, the pattern of slaveholding prevented the great majority of slaves from living with spouses or in family groups. Blacks undoubtedly socialized with others in their predicament and taught one another the best ways to retain family ties under such adverse conditions, but that they produced so few children and were unsuccessful in keeping their families intact indicates that circumstances often were beyond their control.

As slavery gave way to freedom and blacks sought refuge in the postrevolutionary City of Brotherly Love, they enjoyed considerable success in establishing and maintaining families. While relatively few couples bothered to marry in white churches or before magistrates, a great many decided to live together and to reproduce. Establishing independent households and caring for their children posed serious financial problems to African Americans with few skills for many of the urban trades and who lived in a racist society that limited the available jobs. Still, free blacks employed a variety of adaptive strategies as men, women, and children strove to create and sustain meaningful family lives.

---

[1] Roger Bastide, *African Civilizations in the New World*, trans. Peter Green (New York: Harper and Row, 1971), pp. 23–24. The vast literature on the evolution of American families is synthesized in Robert V. Wells, *Revolution in Americans' Lives: A Demographic Perspective* . . . (Westport, Conn.: Greenwood Press, 1982); and Robert V. Wells, *Uncle Sam's Family* . . . (Albany: State University of New York Press, 1985). See also Michael Gordon, ed., *The American Family in Social-Historical Perspective* (2d ed.; New York: St. Martin's Press, 1978). Thirty years ago, Daniel P. Moynihan's assertions that slavery had destroyed African American families stimulated bitter debate. Many scholars, notably Herbert G. Gutman, challenged Moynihan's views, arguing that black Americans generally were able to overcome the oppression of slavery and racism to establish a viable and meaningful family existence. Many scholarly studies, too numerous to cite here, have supported Gutman's arguments. Daniel P. Moynihan, *The Negro Family in America: The Case for National Action* (Washington, D.C.: U.S. Department of Labor, 1965); Herbert G. Gutman, *The Black Family in Slavery and Freedom, 1750–1925* (New York: Pantheon Books, 1976).

[2] On the promise of postrevolutionary Philadelphia as a racially egalitarian urban society, see Gary B. Nash, *Forging Freedom: The Formation of Philadelphia's Black Community, 1720–1840* (Cambridge: Harvard University Press, 1988), pp. 2–7.

[3] Sidney W. Mintz and Richard Price, "An Anthropological Approach to the Study of Afro-American History" (1974), pp. 12–13, as quoted in Gutman, *Black Family*, p. 353.

[4] Anthony Benezet to Granville Sharp, February 18, 1772, Sharp letterbook, Library Company of Philadelphia. For the years before 1767, the numbers of slaves are estimated by multiplying the African American proportion of urban Philadelphia's total burials by the population. These estimates are in error if blacks died at significantly higher or lower rates than whites. Figures after 1767 are more reliable since they are tallied from various tax lists, constables' returns (virtual censuses taken by the city), and the federal censuses. The proportion of black burials and the number of slaves on the tax lists are in Gary B. Nash, "Slaves and Slaveowners in Colonial Philadelphia," *William and Mary Quarterly*, 3d ser., 30, no. 2 (April 1973): 231, 237. Population figures are from Billy G. Smith, "Death and Life in a Colonial Immigrant City: A Demographic Analysis of Philadelphia," *Journal of Economic History* 37, no. 4 (December 1977): 871. The author counted the number of slaves on the City Constables' Returns, 1775, Philadelphia City Archives, City Hall Annex (hereafter cited as PCA). The federal censuses of 1790 and 1800 provide data for slaves in those years; see *Return of the Whole Number of Persons within the Several Districts of the United States* . . . (Philadelphia: Childs and Swaine, 1791); and *Return of the Whole Number of Persons within the Several Districts of the United States* . . . (Washington, D.C.: House of Representatives, 1801). See also Jean R. Soderlund, "Black Importation and Migration into Southeastern Pennsylvania, 1682–1810," *Proceedings of the American Philosophical Society* 133, no. 2 (June 1989): 144–53; Darold D. Wax, "Negro Imports

into Pennsylvania, 1720–1766," *Pennsylvania History* 32, no. 4 (October 1965): 254–87; and Darold D. Wax, "Africans on the Delaware: The Pennsylvania Slave Trade, 1759–1765," *Pennsylvania History* 50, no. 1 (January 1983): 38–49.

[5] Such cases are scattered throughout the Vagrancy Dockets, PCA; Philipina appears on June 16, 1792, Edward on May 2, 1797, and Amy on February 9, 1793, in the 1790–97 volume.

[6] *Pennsylvania Gazette* (Philadelphia), August 8, 1787. The 1750 protest is noted by Jean R. Soderlund, "Black Women in Colonial Pennsylvania," *Pennsylvania Magazine of History and Biography* 107, no. 1 (January 1983): 55–56. Similar complaints about black gatherings in 1717, 1726, 1738, 1741, and 1751 are noted in Nash, *Forging Freedom*, p. 14.

[7] Susan E. Klepp and Billy G. Smith, eds., *The Infortunate: The Voyage and Adventures of William Moraley, an Indentured Servant* (University Park: Pennsylvania State University Press, 1992); this is one of the few descriptions of African American weddings in the region. The number of slave marriages is recorded in Jean R. Soderlund, *Quakers and Slavery: A Divided Spirit* (Princeton: Princeton University Press, 1985), p. 81; only 8 slave couples married in Christ Church or St. Peter's Church between 1727 and 1765.

[8] Marriage Records of Gloria Dei (Old Swedes') Church, May 2, 1801, Genealogical Society of Pennsylvania, Hall of Historical Society, Philadelphia. John Woolman noted that in Maryland and Virginia "negroes marry after their own way" (as cited in Gutman, *Black Family*, p. 348) but says nothing about the rituals of Philadelphia slaves.

[9] *Pennsylvania Gazette*, July 5, 1753, June 5, 1765, February 7, 1763, May 16, 1781. Most of the advertisements cited in this newspaper are reproduced in Billy G. Smith and Richard Wojtowicz, *Blacks Who Stole Themselves: Advertisements for Runaways in the Pennsylvania Gazette, 1728–1790* (Philadelphia: University of Pennsylvania Press, 1989).

[10] *Pennsylvania Gazette*, June 14, 1770, April 26, 1750. One master advertised a slave woman to be "sold for no other fault only she wants to be married, which does not suit the family she is in" (*Pennsylvania Chronicle* [Philadelphia], January 23, 1767).

[11] *Pennsylvania Gazette*, December 4, 1793, October 15, 1794, October 21, 1772, April 28, 1773, January 6, 1773, July 12, 1780, September 2, 1795. Advertisements for Hannah appeared in *Pennsylvania Gazette*, August 29, December 12, 1765.

[12] Jones cited and Benezet quoted in Nash, *Forging Freedom*, pp. 67–70. Many slaves who applied for aid to prevent being separated from their families are in the Papers of the Pennsylvania Abolition Society, Acting Committee, Minutes, 1789–97, AMS 412, Historical Society of Pennsylvania. The state legislature passed a law in 1788 designed to curb masters from selling their slaves out of state; James T. Mitchell and Henry Flanders, comps., *The Statutes at Large of Pennsylvania from 1682–1801*, 18 vols. (Harrisburg, 1896–1908), 13:52–56.

[13] *Pennsylvania Gazette*, September 21, 1785, April 13, 1796. The second advertisement is published in Richard Wojtowicz and Billy G. Smith, "Advertisements for Runaway Slaves, Indentured Servants, and Apprentices in the *Pennsylvania Gazette*, 1795–1796," *Pennsylvania History* 54, no. 1 (January 1987): 34–71. On the practices associated with polygyny in Africa, see Allan Kulikoff, "The Beginnings of the Afro-American Family in Maryland," in Gordon, *American Family*, p. 446.

[14] *Pennsylvania Gazette*, January 30, 1766, November 1, 1770, August 7, 1776. The law was enacted in 1726 (Mitchell and Flanders, *Statutes at Large*, 4:62–63). Ed-

ward Raymond Turner, *The Negro in Pennsylvania: Slavery—Servitude—Freedom, 1639–1861* (Washington, D.C.: American Historical Association, 1911), pp. 92, 112–13. Out of 1,033 slaves advertised as runaways in the *Pennsylvania Gazette* between 1728 and 1790, 10 were thought by their masters to have escaped with white lovers. See also the cases of interracial sex registered in the Vagrancy Dockets, 1790–97.

[15] Collin quoted in Susan E. Klepp and Billy G. Smith, "The Records of Gloria Dei Church: Marriages and 'Remarkable Occurrences,' 1794–1806," *Pennsylvania History* 53, no. 2 (April 1986): 129, 135–37, 139.

[16] Advertisements in the *Pennsylvania Gazette* indicate that 13 runaways likely sought refuge with relations; however, the probable destinations of only 295 slaves were offered. If the "unknown" objectives of the other 738 blacks are ignored, then masters believed that 4% of the fugitives attempted to join their loved ones. When only the 155 advertised slaves who lived in Philadelphia are considered, 6% of them tried to join their relations or friends. By comparison, masters suggested the destination of 599 of the 1,000 runaways advertised in Virginia. Adjusting for unknowns among Virginia notices, owners believed that 33% of fugitives ran to relatives. On runaways in Virginia and Maryland, see Gerald W. Mullin, *Flight and Rebellion: Slave Resistance in Eighteenth-Century Virginia* (London: Oxford University Press, 1972), pp. 108–9; and Gutman, *Black Family*, p. 344.

[17] Since the numbers of black births before 1783 were not recorded, it is necessary to use other evidence to estimate the crude birth rate of slaves. The ages of 784 slaves who lived in Walnut Ward in 1762, Upper Delaware Ward in 1767, East Mulberry Ward in 1770, ten city wards in 1775, and East Mulberry Ward, Middle Ward, and Walnut Ward in 1780 are registered in Constables' Returns, PCA. Of the 156 age-designated slaves on the 1762, 1767, and 1770 lists, only 3 were one year of age or younger, indicating a minimum birth rate of 19 per 1,000. Eight of the 550 slaves with recorded ages in 1775, and 2 of the 78 slaves with known ages in 1780 were aged one or less, suggesting a minimum birth rate of 15 per 1,000 in 1775 and 26 per 1,000 in 1780. This method of estimation appears to be quite reliable when applied to the white population for whom birth records survive; see Smith, "Death and Life," pp. 881–82. Klepp found that 33% of the children of Philadelphia's poorest inhabitants died before their first birthday. Applying this infant mortality rate to the above figures produces crude birth rates among slaves of 25 per 1,000 before 1770 and 21 per 1,000 in 1775 and 1780. On infant mortality rates, see Susan E. Klepp, "Social Class and Infant Mortality in Philadelphia, 1720–1830" (Paper presented at the Philadelphia Center for Early American Studies, 1981); and Smith, "Death and Life," p. 879. The baptismal records of the Anglican church, the only one to welcome black Philadelphians to baptism during the prerevolutionary period, support these figures. Only 50 infants belonging to slaves were baptized between 1767 and 1775, although the number of black bondspeople in the city averaged about 1,000 (Nash, "Slaves and Slave-owners," p. 239n). Yet the evidence about reproduction among Philadelphia's slaves is fragmentary and remains open to other interpretations. Higher birth rates were calculated by Susan E. Klepp, "Black Mortality in Early Philadelphia, 1722–1859" (Paper presented at the Annual Meeting of the Social Science History Association, 1988).

[18] Soderlund (*Quakers and Slavery*, p. 79) tabulated the ages of 955 slaves who appeared in probate inventories taken in Philadelphia between 1681 and 1780 and of 681 slaves from inventories taken in rural New Jersey and Pennsylvania during the same period. Children constituted 35% of the slave population in Philadelphia and 43% of slaves in rural areas. In 1780 slaves age 10 or younger accounted for 21% of Philadelphia's black bondspeople and 37% of those in Bucks County, Pa. (Nash,

Forging Freedom, p. 34). Blacks reproduced more successfully on the lower western shore of Maryland, where in the 1720s there were about 2 children for every adult woman (Russell R. Menard, "The Maryland Slave Population, 1658 to 1730: A Demographic Profile of Blacks in Four Counties," *William and Mary Quarterly*, 3d ser., 32, no. 1 [January 1975]: 29–54). Officials believed that there were 3 slave children for every 2 adults in Virginia on the eve of the Revolution (Mullin, *Flight and Rebellion*, p. 16). In 1726 66% of the slaves were adults in St. George's Parish, S.C.; only 29% were children in the entire colony in 1708 (Peter H. Wood, *Black Majority: Negroes in Colonial South Carolina through the Stono Rebellion* [New York: W. W. Norton, 1974], pp. 144, 161–64).

[19] Age structure was computed from the City Constables' Returns, 1775, PCA. The age and sex of 93 slaves are recorded on the 1770 returns for East Mulberry Ward and the 1775 returns for Chestnut and East Mulberry wards. Females constituted 51% of the 67 slaves in their child-producing years. Although the sex ratio of adult males and females was roughly equal between 1681 and 1780, in inventory records from 1750 to 1780, adult men outnumbered adult women 170 to 149 (Soderlund, *Quakers and Slavery*, p. 79; Soderlund, "Black Women," p. 54). Of 550 slaves whose ages are known in 1775, 338 were between sixteen and forty-five years old, and 8 were one year old or younger (Constables' Returns, 1775, PCA). Applying the infant mortality rate discussed in footnote 17, above, produces the estimate of 11 births within the previous year. If half of the slaves in their child-producing years were female, then 169 women gave birth to 11 children, meaning that 1 out of every 15 women bore a child that year.

[20] *Pennsylvania Gazette*, October 31, 1787; County Prison Sentence Docket, 1799, PCA; Daily Occurrence Docket, 1800, Guardians of the Poor, PCA. On African customs, see Menard, "Maryland Slave Population," p. 41. For similar practices among nineteenth-century slave mothers, see Eugene D. Genovese, *Roll, Jordan, Roll: The World the Slave Made* (New York: Vintage Books, 1976), pp. 498–99.

[21] "Another Letter to a Clergyman," *Pennsylvania Packet; or, The General Advertiser* (Philadelphia), January 1, 1780; *Pennsylvania Gazette*, August 4, October 24, 1765. On the working and living conditions of urban slaves, see Nash, "Slaves and Slaveowners," pp. 248–50; Soderlund, *Quakers and Slavery*, pp. 61–63; Berlin, "Time, Space, and the Evolution of Afro-American Society on British Mainland North America," *American Historical Review* 85, no. 1 (February 1980): 48. Young slaves were offered for sale in the *Pennsylvania Gazette*, January 16, February 13, March 19, December 6, 1750, January 17, 24, June 27, July 25, 1765, November 29, 1770, and June 28, 1775. See also Soderlund, *Quakers and Slavery*, pp. 79–80.

[22] *Pennsylvania Gazette*, July 12, 1775; Mitchell and Flanders, *Statutes at Large*, 10:68, 13:55. The urban market in slaves is discussed in Nash, "Slaves and Slaveowners," p. 243. See also the frequent selling of slaves indicated in the Papers of the Pennsylvania Abolition Society, Acting Committee, Minutes, 1784–88 and 1789–97, esp. entries for Susannah, May 27, 1784, and Hett, April 2, 1792. Coultas advertisements in *Pennsylvania Gazette*, March 21, April 25, 1765.

[23] On the high mortality rates in Philadelphia, see Smith, "Death and Life," pp. 863–89. In her reading of hundreds of Philadelphia wills, Soderlund did not find a single one that directed the executors to keep slave families together (Soderlund, *Quakers and Slavery*, p. 83n).

[24] The age and sex of slaves are identified in the following City Constables' Returns: East Mulberry Ward in 1770, Chestnut and East Mulberry wards in 1775, and Middle, Walnut, and East Mulberry wards in 1780, PCA. Of the 138 adults identified, 10 lived together; of the 190 slaves whose ages were indicated, 44 who lived together

could have been a parent or a child. The data from 955 probate inventories taken in the city between 1681 and 1780 was computed by Soderlund, *Quakers and Slavery*, pp. 81, 83. Slave families in Maryland are discussed in Kulikoff, "Beginnings," p. 456. For a somewhat different view, see Jean Buttenhoff Lee, "The Problem of Slave Community in the Eighteenth-Century Chesapeake," *William and Mary Quarterly*, 3d ser., 43, no. 3 (July 1986): 333–61.

[25] Nash, "Slaves and Slaveowners," p. 237; Gary B. Nash, "Forging Freedom: The Emancipation Experience in the Northern Seaport Cities, 1775–1820," in *Slavery and Freedom in the Age of the American Revolution*, ed. Ira Berlin and Ronald Hoffman (Charlottesville: University Press of Virginia, 1983), p. 5; Nash, *Forging Freedom*, p. 38; Susan E. Klepp, "The Demographic Characteristics of Philadelphia, 1788–1801: Zachariah Poulson's Bills of Mortality," *Pennsylvania History* 53, no. 3 (July 1986): 204. The federal censuses for 1790 and 1800 tabulate free blacks and slaves in urban Philadelphia.

[26] Between 1765 and 1779, 56 black couples, an average of about 4 per year, married in the city's churches; 84 couples, or approximately 12 annually, wed between 1779 and 1786. Soderlund, *Quakers and Slavery*, p. 81; Nash, *Forging Freedom*, pp. 75–76. The author thanks Klepp for the age data from Marriage Records of Gloria Dei Church, 1793–1805.

[27] Examination of Paupers, 1826–31, pp. 95–96, 29; 1822–25, p. 4, Guardians of the Poor, Philadelphia City Almshouse. The episodes described occurred early in the women's lives, specifically during the 1790s. Many other unmarried black women with children are recorded in the Daily Occurrence Docket, Guardians of the Poor, PCA; see Billy G. Smith and Cynthia Shelton, "The Daily Occurrence Docket of the Philadelphia Almshouse, 1800," *Pennsylvania History* 52, no. 2 (April 1985): 86–116. Marriage Records of Gloria Dei Church, November 22, 1800. Selections from these records are available in Klepp and Smith, "Records of Gloria Dei Church," pp. 125–51.

[28] Nash, *Forging Freedom*, pp. 72–73. Many African Americans migrated from the countryside to New York City for similar reasons; see Shane White, " 'We Dwell in Safety and Pursue Our Honest Callings': Free Blacks in New York City, 1783–1810," *Journal of American History* 75, no. 2 (September 1988): 448–51. While data are limited, it appears that neither the sex ratio nor the age structure among blacks could have accounted for the dramatic change in their birth rates from the colonial period to the last decades of the century. The burial statistics by gender suggest that males slightly outnumbered females during the 1780s and 1790s. That most African Americans during these decades were migrants probably skews their age structure toward people in their child-producing years; however, as stated earlier, the age structure of slaves before the Revolution may have been skewed in the same direction. Finally, the birth rates of blacks after the Revolution were below those of Catholics, a predominantly white immigrant group. On these topics, see Klepp, "Demographic Characteristics," pp. 204, 207, 217, 221.

[29] The author tabulated percentages from a count of a sample of 60% of households on the 1790 federal census and a sample of 50% of households on the 1800 federal census. Black women headed 17% and 12% of households in 1790 and 1800 respectively, compared with 13% and 15% of households headed by white women in those years. On rising rents during the 1790s, see Billy G. Smith, "The Material Lives of Laboring Philadelphians, 1750 to 1800," *William and Mary Quarterly*, 3d ser., 38, no. 2 (April 1981): 173. See also Nash, *Forging Freedom*, pp. 161–62; and White, "We Dwell in Safety," pp. 451–53.

[30] Nash, *Forging Freedom*, pp. 144–54. Occupations of blacks are given in Edmund Hogan, *The Prospect of Philadelphia and Check on the Next Directory* (Philadelphia: By the author, 1795).

[31] Isaac and Samuel appear in the Almshouse Census, 1807, Guardians of the Poor, PCA. The others are recorded in the Daily Occurrence Docket, Guardians of the Poor, PCA: Sarah and Ann, December 2, 8, 1800; Jeremiah, November 23, 1800, August 1801; Johnson and her daughter, August 16, November 3, 1800.

[32] These vignettes are created from information in *The Philadelphia Directory . . . 1785* (Philadelphia: Cornelius William Stafford, 1785); *The Philadelphia Directory . . . 1791* (Philadelphia: Cornelius William Stafford, 1791); Hogan, *Prospect of Philadelphia*; *The Philadelphia Directory . . . 1797* (Philadelphia: W. Woodward, 1797); *The Philadelphia Directory . . . 1816* (Philadelphia: J. Robinson, 1816); U.S. Bureau of the Census, *Heads of Families of the First Census of the United States Taken in the Year 1790: Pennsylvania* (Washington, D.C.: Government Printing Office, 1908); United States Direct Tax of 1798, Philadelphia, High Street Ward, 4, Form A, National Archives; and provincial tax lists, 1796 and 1798, PCA.

[33] These stories are reconstructed from County Probate Records, Wills and Inventories of Estate, 1800, no. 41, Registrar of Wills, Philadelphia City Hall Annex; Hogan, *Prospect of Philadelphia*; *The Philadelphia Directory . . . 1797*; *The Philadelphia Directory . . . 1801* (Philadelphia: W. Woodward, 1801); U.S. Census for 1810, Pennsylvania, City of Philadelphia, National Archives.

The Economy of Philadelphia and Its Hinterland

Mary McKinney Schweitzer

Philadelphia was the largest city in British North America in 1750 and the largest city in the new United States in 1800. It was the new nation's center of international trade, finance, manufacturing, and Enlightenment thought and, for a time, its political capital as well. The source of Philadelphia's size and prominence was the economic relationship between the city and the surrounding area, or hinterland, that it served. The region suffered some disruption during the political upheavals of the period; however, by the end of the century, it had returned to the economic patterns and relationships of the prewar period.

Philadelphia's rapid economic ascendance was due to the profitability in the hinterland of growing wheat for the overseas market. The exportation of flour abroad led to the development of a merchant community around which the city developed. At the same time, the nature of wheat production led to a fairly diversified hinterland economy, with economic growth and relatively well-distributed incomes. As a result, manufactured goods were in increasing demand in the hinterland, leading again to the expansion of the city as imported goods were unloaded and reexported. Philadelphia's growth experience duplicated that of

The data sets for Philadelphia in 1756 and 1790 were compiled in part through funding provided by the National Endowment for the Humanities through the Transformation Project of the Philadelphia Center for Early American Studies. Analysis of the data sets has also benefited from Villanova University Faculty Summer Research Grants.

Boston and New York, two other cities servicing wheat-exporting regions. However, Philadelphia had the added advantage in the eighteenth century of the sheer size of the region served by the city.[1]

Wheat production had profound implications for the size and nature of Philadelphia. First, wheat products were marketed abroad in a manner that required a collection and redistribution point on the American side of the Atlantic. Wheat was never sold abroad directly; it was always transformed into flour first. Thus the individual farmer dealt with a miller, never with the foreign purchaser. Similarly, the millers seldom dealt directly with the foreign market. If they had, they would have tended to export flour from the nearest port rather than shipping it to Philadelphia. Towns such as Bristol, New Castle, Burlington, and Chester would have been larger; Philadelphia would have been smaller. The key to Philadelphia's development was the early rise of a merchant class to mediate between the foreign market and the millers. Merchants were familiar with prices and market conditions in many ports, beginning with the West Indies in the 1680s and eventually adding southern Europe and New England by the end of the 1700s. Merchants also took on the responsibility of finding ships and filling up the return load. The city of Philadelphia thus developed around the community of merchant and seagoing activities that served the wheat-exporting hinterland.[2]

The importance of wheat production to the development of a merchant community in Pennsylvania, and thus to the emergence of a major port city, is clear when contrasting Pennsylvania's experience with that of the Chesapeake colonies just to the south. In the Chesapeake, plantation owners dealt directly with London merchants, bypassing any local merchant class. The London merchants organized the process of sending ships and filling return orders. Larger plantation owners often operated as middlemen for the smaller planters, but the whole process was controlled by the London side of the Atlantic. There was no need for information about markets because most of the tobacco had to pass through London before moving on to its final destination. So there was no need for a single site where merchants could share information and put together their "ventures." Despite population and income growth in the Chesapeake, no major cities emerged.[3]

The absence of a major city was not lost on the residents of the Chesapeake. There were several legislative efforts to create cities, but they all failed. Investors bought lots in the newly platted cities of Port Tobacco and Charlestown in Maryland, but the communities never developed beyond the level of crossroad towns. When a law was passed in 1747 in Maryland requiring the inspection of all tobacco before export, planters insisted on more than a dozen inspection sites so that they could continue to export tobacco from a site near their plantations. In contrast, Pennsylvania's flour-inspection law required merely three inspection sites, and only one—that in Philadelphia—was ever used. Much to the frustration of boosters in tobacco-growing Maryland, legislation could not create a city when trade did not flow from a central point. Much to the frustration of boosters in wheat-growing New Jersey and Delaware, their trade flowed to the central location of Philadelphia whether they wanted it to or not.[4]

Wheat production also had an impact on Philadelphia in its role as importer, manufacturer, and distributor of finished goods to the hinterland. By its nature, wheat farming was well suited to the needs and abilities of a family farm, and as a result the region was soon filled with middle-income families who were relatively prosperous and whose discretionary income rose each generation.

Wheat farming did not require a large year-round labor force. The optimal size of a wheat farm coincided precisely with the characteristics of a mature family: a middle-aged couple with teenage and young adult children at home. Delayed marriages kept children at home until their mid to late twenties, allowing their parents to reap at least a decade of full productivity. When family crops did not need attention, young men were free to sell their labor nearby and either keep or send home their earnings. Young men hired themselves out by the day to repair fences, build roads, or help with a neighbor's harvest. They could receive a weekly or monthly wage working at furnaces and forges nearby. Young women earned extra money making and marketing wool and linen yarn, stockings, butter, and cheese. These full-grown families maintained high levels of consumption at the same time they were able to save substantially. The successful farm family accumulated sufficient capital to settle each child on a farm: young men were given land and farm tools with which to start a new household; women were given livestock, household tools, and cash.[5]

Hired help was needed on farms that did not conform to this "optimal" size. A young couple with small children needed servants, either relatives or indentured immigrants, to round out the farm "family." So, too, did older couples whose children had left home. There were families that did not have enough children or who had the wrong mix of boys and girls. Finally, families beset by misfortune such as illness or death might need extra help.

At first servants did not form part of a different class, unlike slaves in the colonial south or wage earners in the next century. Most indentured servants were young, often teenagers. The law mandated they serve only until age eighteen (for girls) or twenty-one (for boys), and during that time they were to be taught the business of running a farm. Older immigrants also bound themselves out as servants, but their tenure seldom lasted longer than four years, during which they too learned local farming practices. At the end of their terms, these individuals could remain, contracting their labor by the day, week, month, or year, but most headed out to cheap land in Lancaster and Cumberland counties, in Virginia and North Carolina, or, eventually, in western Pennsylvania, Ohio, and Kentucky.

Wheat farming also encouraged diversification of the economy. Slack times when wheat did not have to be tended allowed farmers to include other crops and products. Pennsylvania farmers grew Indian corn and rye to augment wheat flour and provide cattle feed. Virtually every farmer had a flax patch, sending the seed for export and using the mature flax for course homespun cloth. A well-developed farm had meadowland cleared for cattle for both meat and dairy products, usually for home consumption but increasingly sold at market. Thus even in years when the wheat market languished, the farmers maintained other sources of income.[6]

Diversification extended into manufacturing as well as farming. Many farmers also practiced a craft on the side, which added yet another source of income. At midcentury in Chester County nearly half of all decedents with a recorded occupation listed a craft; the proportion might have been higher, as many who called themselves “yeoman” may have been practicing a trade on the side. Furthermore, those who termed themselves “artisans” died in possession of as much livestock and grain (both harvested and in the field) as did their contemporaries.[7]

The incomes earned in wheat farming and country artisan labor were high by the standards of the day. By the 1750s, the arduous process of capital formation was over for most farmers in southeastern Pennsylvania. Wills and inventories showed a marked increase in consumed items not only for older families but also for young couples, a sign that more couples were able to begin their families with an inheritance. The region was already experiencing a level of economic growth scholars have usually associated with the early nineteenth century: incomes for families with children increased annually at a rate between 0.9 and 1.65 percent a year. High and increasing incomes translated into demand for consumer goods—imports from England and domestically produced goods.[8]

Because of the relatively equitable distribution of income in Pennsylvania's hinterland, the types of imported goods that came through Pennsylvania tended to be items purchased for sale at retail rather than custom orders. This contributed to the city's growth because it encouraged the development of wholesale merchants in the city. Equitable incomes also led to demand for just the type of product that artisans in America produced. While the very wealthy continued to order products directly from England, and the poor could not afford much at all, the middling people, who abounded in Chester, Bucks, Lancaster, and Philadelphia counties, increasingly provided demand for American manufactures.

The nature of hinterland wheat farming would have led to the growth of Philadelphia as a sizable city. Philadelphia, however, rapidly grew to the largest of the eighteenth-century American cities, outstripping New York and Boston. The reason for this was the equally rapid growth of the wheat-producing hinterland for which Philadelphia served as the foreign trade center.

Pennsylvania's founding at the end of the seventeenth century coincided with the transition of West Indies producers to intense specialization. All available land and labor in the West Indies went to sugar production, making it necessary for the planters to purchase food from abroad for their slaves. Pennsylvania's early decades of prosperity were the direct result of the willingness of West Indies producers to pay high prices for imported foodstuffs, which in turn was a direct result of the willingness of Europeans to pay high prices for sugar. Pennsylvania's flour exports rose, as did those of New York, New Jersey, and New England. When the market for flour became saturated in the West Indies, Pennsylvania merchants first responded by asking their legislature to pass inspection laws that created a "brand" name for Pennsylvania flour (quite literally, as the name was "branded" on the flour barrel). Inspectors also graded the flour, with "Pennsylvania Super Fine" eventually winning an international reputation for quality. Next, the merchants turned to European markets, taking advantage of rising populations and increasing costs of food on the Continent. By the end of the 1700s, Pennsylvania flour was also being exported to neighboring New England.[9]

With each broadening of the demand for Pennsylvania flour came a rise in the price that Philadelphia merchants were willing to offer for Pennsylvania wheat. Millers reached out far into the distance for more regular sources of wheat. The area that had traditionally been a part of Philadelphia's hinterland was southeastern Pennsylvania, northern Delaware, and southern New Jersey. In the 1750s planters on the eastern shore of Maryland and in southern Delaware, where the land had never been appropriate to tobacco cultivation, began to switch to wheat. Shallops on the eastern shore carried the wheat to commercial millers close to Philadelphia, who then sent the flour to merchants in the city.[10]

At the same time as the northern Chesapeake began to convert to wheat production, the western fringe of Philadelphia's hinterland began to expand rapidly. Wheat farmers were willing to pay effectively high wages for labor—that is, indentured servants in the Philadelphia region were asked to give only four years of labor in exchange for their overseas passage. The apparent low cost of migrating coupled with the promise of available land attracted thousands from Ulster Ireland, Germany, and Switzerland to Pennsylvania. These immigrants, and the descendants of the original Delaware River valley settlers, quickly pushed settlement back into the Pennsylvania midsection. As early as 1730 settlement had reached the Cumberland Valley, which was as far west as Europeans could progress while the powerful Iroquois and their tribute nations controlled western Pennsylvania and New York. So settlers turned south, following and widening the main Indian trail until it became known as the "Great Wagon Road" to Philadelphia. Settlers quickly moved into western Maryland, the Shenandoah Valley of Virginia, the Great Valley of Virginia, and finally North Carolina's piedmont. Ignoring the danger from Indians, some moved into western Pennsylvania and the Ohio River valley beyond. Meanwhile, migrants from New England, New York, and New Jersey joined the flow, establishing settlements in northeastern Pennsylvania despite the possibility of Indian attack.[11]

All this new settlement greatly expanded the region that could be considered Philadelphia's hinterland. At some point, however, the cost of overland transportation became too great, and the farthest regions in the Carolinas and western Pennsylvania were effectively cut off both from the city and from international trade. The boundaries of what could be considered Philadelphia's hinterland were, nevertheless, very large, covering a geographic region consisting of Pennsylvania's northeast from the Lehigh Valley to the New York border; southern and western New Jersey, virtually all Delaware and Maryland's eastern shore, southeastern Pennsylvania, across the Susquehanna into central Pennsylvania, and south into western Maryland and the Shenandoah Valley of Virginia. Philadelphia was prosperous because of this hinterland, but the hinterland itself was prosperous because of the ties maintained to the international market through Philadelphia. Both the region and the city benefited from the relationship.

LONG-RUN CHANGE, 1750–1800

The economic relationships between Philadelphia and its hinterland, and between both and the outside world, remained active during the turbulent fifty years that took Philadelphia from leading city in the British colonies to temporary capital of a new nation. The city and the countryside grew substantially during the period, both in size and in complexity. At the same time, the region suffered disruption greater than at any time before or any time since.

The most obvious change in the relationship between Philadelphia and its hinterland between 1750 and 1800 was not qualitative, but rather quantitative: both Philadelphia and its surrounding countryside grew dramatically in size. The number of taxpayers listed in nearby Chester County doubled between 1754 and 1785, with virtually no new land left to develop. Areas on the city's far hinterland grew more substantially in population. The number of taxpayers assessed in Paxton Township along the Susquehanna rose from 164 in 1756 to 707 in 1782; historian Robert Mitchell estimates that the population of the upper Shenandoah increased fourfold during the second half of the 1700s. Thus the hinterland was growing in physical size and in population density. Correspondingly, Philadelphia also grew dramatically during this period. Population in the city and its suburbs grew from approximately 14,500 in 1750 to 43,500 in 1790, a threefold increase.[12]

There were also several shifts in the distribution of occupations within the city (see appendix). Occupationally, furniture, metals, leather, food, and cloth all declined in importance. In 1756, 36.4 percent of the populace who listed an occupation worked in these five industries. By 1790, in contrast, that proportion had dropped to 27.0—from about a third to only a quarter. The proportion reporting a specialized artisanal or manufacturing occupation rose very slightly: from about 3 to 4 percent. At the same time, the proportion of householders occupied in shipbuilding increased from 1.7 percent to 3.4 percent. The increase in specialized artisans and shipbuilders, however, was not large enough to offset completely the decline in the major artisan occupations. If all artisanal occupations are combined, the proportion still fell from 46.8 percent to 40.4 percent.[13]

While the proportion of householders reporting an artisanal occupation declined, the proportion of general laborers rose. In 1756, 5 percent of householders listed their occupation as laborer, in contrast to nearly 9 percent in 1790. A significant decline in the proportion of householders listed as practicing artisanal skills, combined with an increase in the number of general laborers, would support the contention that the city was moving from a traditional economy to a wage-based one. The difference might reflect discrepancies between both data sets: occupations were missing for 28 percent of householders in the 1754 data set, in contrast with only 17 percent in the 1790 data set.

At the same time, the number of "gentlemen" or "gentlewomen" increased dramatically. Only 9 men were referred to as gentlemen in 1756. In contrast, in 1790 there were 127 gentlemen and 109 gentlewomen listed, together accounting for 3.5 percent of total householders in the city.

Surprisingly, the proportion of householders identified as merchants declined, from 11 percent in 1756 to 9 percent in 1790. Some of those who called themselves gentlemen may have in fact been merchants, but even if all of them were merchants (and they were not) the proportion of merchants in 1790 would still have been lower than in 1756. At the same time, the proportion of shopkeepers rose, from 8.5 percent to 10.9 percent. An entirely new designation, grocer, accounted for about a third of the retailers, or about 3 percent of all householders. While the decline in the proportion of merchants and the increase in the proportion of shopkeepers is relatively small, it does confirm somewhat the merchants' complaints that they were losing control of trade to shopkeepers. The shopkeepers figure might also be higher if it could be determined how many of the women listed only as widows were also shopkeepers.

The proportion of residents listing a seagoing occupation, or, perhaps, the proportion of mariners who listed Philadelphia as their major residence, also declined. The percentage of householders listing themselves as mariners or sea captains dropped by half, from 8 to 4 percent. General trade also experienced a decline, with the proportion of residents listing those occupations falling from 6.3 percent to 4.2 percent.

Government became a major factor in city life during the period 1750 to 1800, as the city became the capital of the Confederation and then the temporary capital of the new nation. The tax lists of 1756 list virtually no government workers, probably because most people who held a government office listed themselves in some other capacity. By 1790, 2 percent of the occupants listed as their major occupation some form of government activity. As the 1790 list derives from the federal census, householders who lived in Philadelphia but maintained their primary residence elsewhere would not have been included, so the actual proportion was probably higher.

Even with all the activity brought into the city by the presence of the federal government, the proportion of inns, taverns, lodges, and other such establishments remained exactly the same as in 1754: 4.4 percent. Construction also remained stable, with 6.6 percent of residents listing an occupation in construction in 1756 and in 1790. The proportion of professionals rose slightly, however, from about 5 to 6 percent. The increase was not in lawyers or physicians, but rather in clerks, teachers, professors, and accountants.

The number of specialized occupations increased substantially between 1756 and 1790. In 1756 a merchant was a "merchant"; by 1790 he might be a lumber, flour, wine, iron, china, tea, or hardware merchant. Likewise, the "instrument maker" of 1756 became more specifically a maker of "mathematical," "obstetrical," or "musical" instruments in 1790. Also by 1790 there were specialists who made combs, cards, fans, pumps, engines, parchment, organs, pottery wheels, spinning wheels, "segars," and trunks. There were 4 residents who made Windsor chairs in 1790, and 3 made umbrellas, in contrast to 1 each in 1756. There were 41 coach and carriage makers where there had been only 1 in 1756. There were 15 woodworkers listed as cabinetmakers, where there were none in 1756, and there were 17 "hairdressers." There were 9 chocolate makers, 11 sugar refiners, 7 sugar bakers, 5 pastry cooks, 3 cake bakers, and 1 mustard maker. There was 1 hanging-paper manufacturer and 1 carpet manufacturer; there were 2 toy dealers, 1 china dealer, and 1 looking-glass dealer. The increasing specialization in occupations and trades represented the beginning of a trend that would continue until just before the Civil War.

One final significant change in Philadelphia between 1756 and 1790 was the increase in the number of woman-headed households. A woman was listed as the head in 1 out of every 8 households in Philadelphia in 1790, in contrast with less than 1 in 20 in 1750. Many of these women were labeled simply "widows," but a large number were identified with an occupation, including butcher. Women's occupations included 18 seamstresses, 10 nurses, 9 midwives, 9 mantuamakers, 7 milliners, and 2 fringe- and lacemakers. The contrast is also striking between the city and the countryside: in Chester County, for example, less than 4 percent of households were listed in 1785 as being headed by women.[14]

Meanwhile, the far hinterland was maturing into a commercial economy. Lancaster had developed into the largest inland town in the new nation and served as an internal entrepôt between the east and the backcountry. Iron production, already a major industry by 1750, continued to develop in the eastern mountain region of Pennsylvania. Cloth, hats, and rifles and other iron products were manufactured in Lancaster, Reading, Lebanon, Harrisburg, and across the Susquehanna in Carlisle. By the late 1700s, cattle drives to service Philadelphia's meat industry began far in the Carolinas. The economy of the near hinterland (southeastern Pennsylvania) increasingly concentrated on production of foodstuffs for the nascent urbanization in the countryside and for ever-growing Philadelphia, while continuing to produce wheat for export.[15]

The greatest economic change in both the city and the new hinterland, however, came not in the product market, but in the labor market. The period saw the beginnings, in both the city and the countryside, of a shift from a labor market organized around family labor and age relationships to one organized around wage labor. Through the period 1750 to 1800, there was a growth in the number of landless laborers. Swelling density led to continually rising land prices, making it more difficult for servants to purchase land. While large numbers continued to leave the region in search of cheap land elsewhere, increasingly there were workers who remained throughout their lives, forming the beginnings of a class dependent on wage labor. These changes in labor were similar to those occurring in the city, where increasingly, young men found themselves in the permanent role of wage laborers rather than apprentice artisans with any realistic expectation of reaching the position of master.[16]

DISRUPTION OF WAR

These long-term trends in Philadelphia's economy took place within the context of a series of major disruptions that occurred between 1750 and 1800. The city and its immediate hinterland faced the direct effects of the Revolution; the far hinterland suffered from both the Revolution and the French and Indian War. The French and Indian War led to the first real fighting on Pennsylvania soil since its establishment as a colony. During the Revolution, Philadelphia was physically occupied by the British; the immediate hinterland was devastated by the pillaging of both British and American armies. The far hinterland once again suffered from attack by a combination of Indian and European armies—this time British, rather than French. And the entire fifty-year period was characterized more by the disruption of international trade than the smooth continuation of it—trade patterns that had been established at the end of the 1600s were either disrupted or permanently shattered; new routes developed, and old ones died. By the 1770s Philadelphia was facing competition for supremacy as the American trading city.[17]

There were some who benefited from the disruptions and dislocations caused by war. Robert Morris was quick to respond to the need for supplies and quick to take advantage of the system by which supplies are acquired during wartime: by political, rather than pure market, means. The Shippen family used the needs of the British in the French and Indian War as an opportunity to improve the roads through their lands in

Lancaster and garner future trade. But most individuals who gained from the disruption did so in an indirect, rather than direct fashion. As historian Thomas Doerflinger has argued, merchants bereft of their usual markets sought new ones, such as the China trade, and eventually profited in spite of, rather than because of, war.[18]

Home manufactures benefited only temporarily from the war as well. Local artisans and small-time manufacturers were quick to see that patriotic nonimportation was virtually indistinguishable from protectionism of home manufactures and were quick to jump on the bandwagon. These were only temporary, however, because try as they might, the locals could not stem the flow of imports once the trade was resumed. If they had not found a method to produce that was cheaper than the imports, they did not last once the imports returned.[19]

When war was being waged elsewhere, Pennsylvania farmers benefited from the high prices awarded foodstuffs. These benefits, however, were unevenly distributed across families. At the same time that the price of foodstuffs was high, so was the price of labor due to the draft, and the drop in supply of indentured servants from Europe. Sectarian families still had some labor, as they refused to participate in the war effort, but they were taxed two to three times more than other families in deliberate retaliation. High prices for food did not necessarily translate into high incomes for local farmers.[20]

Some hinterland manufacturers prospered during this period. The iron industry in Pennsylvania supplied many of the cannon and shot used during the war. The area around Lancaster, Reading, and Lebanon benefited from the demand for their manufactured products, particularly the Pennsylvania (or Kentucky) rifle produced in Lancaster. The region had the added benefit of being too far east to suffer from Indian warfare and too far west to feel most of the ill effects of military occupation.[21]

On balance, the negative effects of the wartime disruptions probably outweighed the positive ones. The greatest cost, of course, was the actual physical destruction wrought by the war. There was substantial loss of life, and there were many who would return with their lives but not with their livelihoods—disabled in a society where physical labor was the key to prosperity. The far hinterland faced the effects of war first. Pennsylvania had a large, well-established, exposed border along territory controlled by the Iroquois tributaries. The political border between the European American and Native American nations ran in a line roughly along Blue Mountain from the New York border south, then across the Susquehanna to the north of well-settled areas in Carlisle and Bedford. Encroachment over the border had been occurring for some time, but the legal boundary remained. Much of the region had been settled and developed for a generation. York and Carlisle west of the Susquehanna had already grown to substantial size, and others were following suit. The Indian attacks of 1755 and 1756 were not against a frontier region newly hewn from the forest; they were attacks on a fairly well-developed society. During these battles of the French and Indian War, and again during Pontiac's War in 1763, the Pennsylvania populace took refuge farther east, so there was no great loss of life after the initial attacks. However, there was substantial destruction of property, with buildings, fences, and crops burned and animals slaughtered.[22]

The same area experienced another series of Indian attacks during the revolutionary war, this time led by the British. Attacks were frequent from 1777 until the defeat of the Iroquois in winter 1779/80. The most famous attack became known as the Wyoming Massacre, in the area near present-day Wilkes-Barre, Pennsylvania, which had been developed by settlers from Connecticut. Although women and children were spared, all the men that could be found were killed. Again there was substantial destruction of farm capital.[23]

In the Delaware valley the destruction of property was also great, although there was little threat to the lives of noncombatants. The areas of southern New Jersey and Delaware accessible by water from the Delaware River and the Delaware Bay were raided repeatedly by British privateers throughout the war. From summer 1777 to spring 1778, British and American armies marched through northern Delaware, southeastern Pennsylvania, and the Trenton-Burlington regions of New Jersey. From the Chesapeake Bay to Philadelphia, the British burned farms, slaughtered farm animals, took crops and seed corn, and even removed grindstones from the large commercial flour mills. The Americans did not burn buildings, but they took everything edible.[24]

What was the cost to the region of the destruction of all this capital? During the colonial period, Pennsylvania exported 38 percent of its wheat and beef products. In contrast, during the revolutionary war,

Pennsylvania was forced to import foodstuffs from Maryland and Virginia and eventually from New England. By the 1790s, however, Pennsylvania was again exporting substantial amounts of flour.[25]

The city of Philadelphia suffered during the occupation by the British in 1777/78, but most of the city's problems continued through 1780, caused by food shortages and currency inflation. There was some looting and destruction of property during the occupation, but apparently not as much as in either the far or the near hinterland. Tories prospered during the occupation; loyalists did not. The problems brought on by food shortages and inflation, in contrast, struck all the city's residents. The Pennsylvania legislature attempted to alleviate the situation by enacting an embargo on exports of wheat from Pennsylvania and by instituting price ceilings in Philadelphia: the plan backfired. Wilmington and Baltimore immediately made known their status as free ports, and what little wheat there was in the area soon left through neighboring states. Black-market prices in Philadelphia rose eightfold. The economic disaster in the city resulted in the fall of the radical Constitutional government in the state. The long-run consequences were perhaps even worse. Indirectly, the legislature's inability to resolve the city's economic problems led to the decision by the Continental Congress to relocate outside the city and may well have contributed to the later decision to place the new nation's capital in a site free of existing political jurisdictions.[26]

While the physical destruction brought on by war was probably the most dramatic effect of the political disruptions of the period, the breakdown in international trade was equally important to the region. For a brief period during the French and Indian War, West Indies ports were inaccessible to Philadelphia. After the war, trade would be increasingly disrupted, but for rather perverse reasons. The Delaware valley had always profited from participation in a substantial illicit trade to West Indian colonies of non-British nations. The British became determined to break up that trade, and to the extent they succeeded, another source of income for Pennsylvanians was lost. During the Revolution, the West Indian trade was again totally disrupted if not lost altogether. After the war, while the British trade was lost, the French opened up their colonies. While the effects of all these disruptions would seem to be substantial, it appears that the only serious losers here were merchants who were unwilling or unable to shift to a different market. Flour prices were hardly affected at all. Rising flour prices in Europe offset the problems in the West Indies, and during the war, although international trade was blocked, demand for foodstuffs ran high from both armies.[27]

A far more severe problem for both city and countryside than the disruption of international trade was the continuing inability of the Continental government to find a way to finance the war effort. Unable to raise enough funds from the independent state legislatures, the Continental Congress was finally forced to use inflation as a means to finance the war: print paper money, use it to pay for wartime purchases, and ignore the effects on the price levels. As has already been noted, this had disastrous consequences for Philadelphia: prices in the city rose higher than anywhere else on the continent.[28]

Hyperinflation, and the equally rapid deflation that followed, had other effects. The courts and the legislature were deluged with requests to redefine contracts in the face of all these changes in prices, and it took about five years to straighten it out. The resulting distaste for paper money may have cost the Pennsylvania economy in the 1790s when money was tight in the countryside and the legislature had no power to increase it.[29]

In the long run, however, few of the wartime disruptions had any permanent effect on the economy of Philadelphia and its hinterland. Long-run trends that had been in process since the mid 1700s continued in spite of, rather than because of, the war. The mixed manufacturing-farming economy of Pennsylvania was not substantially different in nature in 1800 than in 1750. There were several major centers of manufacture in the countryside, although still on an artisan level, by 1750. Coventry Forge, an iron-producing company town, characterized by wage labor and market relationships, was already in its second generation by 1750. Labor relationships in the countryside were characterized more by wage labor than by indentured servitude in 1800, but both wage labor and indentured servitude existed in 1750 and in 1800. Economic trends well in place by 1750 were perhaps disrupted by the war but were continuing by 1800. Ironically, if the war had any effects at all on development, it was probably not to serve as a catalyst, as has often been hypothesized, but rather to retard development for perhaps as much as fifty years. The region's economy, as Henry Drinker noted, was "stript and drained."[30]

There were some shifts in trade that resulted from the war and remained so afterward, but it is likely that they would have occurred anyway. The immediate rechanneling of the grain export trade from Philadelphia to Baltimore and Wilmington was clearly due to Philadelphia's grain embargo and other high charges in the port; however, from 1750 to 1800 the role of both cities as grain exporters seems only to continue a trend already in process. Philadelphia had benefited for a long time from having the major transportation routes into Greater Pennsylvania; as soon as other roads were cut to closer ports, it was inevitable that the city would lose most of the bulk trade. The import trade, however, continued to come through Philadelphia.[31]

The Revolution solidified political trends that had been in the making from 1750. Before 1750 the colony had been fairly unified in its perception of the proper economic goals for the commonwealth. When the hinterland was near Philadelphia, it was easier to perceive interests of the city and the countryside as one and the same. The major divisions in government in Pennsylvania before 1750 occurred between local and proprietary interests, or perhaps along religious or ethnic lines. Unlike New York or Albany, Philadelphia did not request special economic favors from the legislature; consequently, there was little animosity between urban and rural representatives. Major economic policies such as flour inspection and money creation were welcomed both in the countryside and in the city.[32]

Politics became more complicated in the second half of the century, however. During the French and Indian War, the city and the near hinterland had little sympathy for the defense needs of the far hinterland. After the Revolution, the goals of economic development no longer seemed as clear as they once did. In the city, development meant private banking; in the country, it meant the land bank and state-issued paper notes. Early in the century it was clear that the state capital had to be at Philadelphia to develop the city; by the end of the century demand was stronger to bring the state capital within closer reach of the western part of the state, first at Lancaster then later at Harrisburg. The question of development of trade routes to the Ohio River split the state as well, although Pennsylvania was successful in the construction of the nation's first turnpike west. Such an adversarial relationship between the city and the legislature had existed for a long time in the other large states, but it represented a major shift for Pennsylvania.[33]

Independence from Great Britain and the establishment of a new nation ironically left Pennsylvania with less direct control over economic policy than before. Before 1750 Pennsylvania had controlled major economic policies such as regulation of trade and money creation; after the ratification of the Constitution, these matters were no longer in the hands of the Pennsylvania legislature. The brutal reaction of the national government to the Whiskey Rebellion stands in stark contrast to the way the Pennsylvania legislature handled such incidents in the past.

Any student of eighteenth-century Philadelphia must finally face the shadow of the future: the city's promise was not fulfilled in the next century. New York superseded Philadelphia and eventually became a city of an entirely different category. Although Philadelphia continued to grow, it was unable to keep pace with New York.[34] Could Philadelphia have escaped this fate? Was the loss a consequence of poor judgment on the part of the legislature or complacency on the part of the city's merchant class? Or was it inevitable that Philadelphia's southern hinterland would eventually find an outlet for their produce closer to the sea and that New York would benefit from a growing hinterland in the early 1800s? Between 1750 and 1800, despite war and political upheaval, the most important factor in Philadelphia's prominence remained the prosperity and size of its hinterland. Therein lies any clues that the period has to offer to the decades that followed.

---

[1] A succinct analysis of the relationship between hinterland and city in colonial America can be found in Jacob M. Price, "Economic Function and the Growth of American Port Towns in the Eighteenth Century," in *Perspectives in American History* 8 (1974), pp. 128–88. The standard works on the development of Philadelphia's hinterland during this time period include James T. Lemon, *The Best Poor Man's Country: A Geographical Study of Early Southeastern Pennsylvania* (Baltimore: Johns Hopkins University Press, 1972). See also Diane Lindstrom, *Economic Development in the Philadelphia Region, 1810–1850* (New York: Columbia University Press, 1978); and Mary M. Schweitzer, *Custom and Contract: Household, Government, and the Economy in Colonial Pennsylvania* (New York: Columbia University Press, 1987).

[2] Thomas M. Doerflinger, *A Vigorous Spirit of Enterprise: Merchants and Economic Development in Revolutionary Philadelphia* (Chapel Hill: University of North Carolina Press, 1986), chap. 2; Richard Pares, *Yankees and Creoles: The Trade between North America and the West Indies before the American Revolution* (Cambridge: Harvard University Press, 1956), chaps. 1, 2; Arthur L. Jensen, *The Maritime Commerce of Colonial Philadelphia* (Madison: University of Wisconsin Press, 1963), chap. 2; Lemon, *Best Poor Man's Country*, pp. 42–43, 123–30; Price, "Economic Function," pp. 150–56.

[3] Price, "Economic Function," pp. 129–30, 163–69; Lemon, *Best Poor Man's Country*, p. 127.

[4] Schweitzer, *Custom and Contract*, chap. 6; Mary M. Schweitzer, "Economic Regulation and the Colonial Economy: The Maryland Tobacco Inspection Act of 1747," *Journal of Economic History* 40, no. 3 (September 1980): 551–69; Lemon, *Best Poor Man's Country*, p. 127.

[5] Mary M. Schweitzer, "Wage Labor and Community in Colonial Pennsylvania" (Paper presented at the annual meeting of the Organization of American Historians, St. Louis, April 8, 1989); Schweitzer, *Custom and Contract*, chap. 1.

[6] Lemon, *Best Poor Man's Country*, chaps. 6, 7; Schweitzer, *Custom and Contract*, chap. 2.

[7] Lemon, *Best Poor Man's Country*, chaps. 6, 7; Schweitzer, *Custom and Contract*, chap. 2.

[8] Schweitzer, *Custom and Contract*, p. 84; Lemon, *Best Poor Man's Country*, p. 223.

[9] Schweitzer, *Custom and Contract*, chap. 6; Lemon, *Best Poor Man's Country*, p. 125; Doerflinger, *Vigorous Spirit*, pp. 70–73; David Klingaman, "The Significance of Grain in the Development of the Tobacco Colonies," *Journal of Economic History* 29, no. 2 (June 1969): 268–78.

[10] David E. Dauer, "The Expansion of Philadelphia's Business System into the Chesapeake" (Paper presented at the annual convention of the American Historical Association, San Francisco, December 30, 1981); Klingaman, "Significance of Grain," pp. 268–78.

[11] Dauer, "Expansion"; Robert D. Mitchell, *Commercialism and Frontier: Perspectives on the Early Shenandoah Valley* (Charlottesville: University Press of Virginia, 1976), pp. 16, 35–36, 54. The best short description of the settlement of "Greater Pennsylvania" is Carl Bridenbaugh, *Myths and Realities: Societies of the Colonial South* (Baton Rouge: Louisiana State University Press, 1952), pp. 123–30.

[12] Chester County Tax List, 1754, Chester County Archives, West Chester, Pa.; Chester County Assessment, 1785, reprinted in William Henry Egle, ed., *Pennsylvania Archives*, 3d ser., 12 (1897): 665–823; George W. Franz, *Paxton: A Study of Community Structure and Mobility in the Colonial Pennsylvania Backcountry* (New York: Garland Publishing, 1989), p. 246; Mitchell, *Commercialism and Frontier*, p. 103; Billy Smith, *The "Lower Sort": Philadelphia's Laboring People, 1750–1800* (Ithaca, N.Y.: Cornell University Press, 1990), p. 206. For an in-depth description of the data for Philadelphia in 1790, see Mary M. Schweitzer, "The Spatial Organization of Federalist Philadelphia, 1790," *Journal of Interdisciplinary History* 24, no. 1 (Summer 1993): 31–57, esp. pp. 53–55.

[13] This and the following paragraphs concerning occupational distribution in Philadelphia are drawn from an ongoing study using a data set constructed by the author. The 1756 data are from the Philadelphia Tax List, 1756, Philadelphia City Archives (hereafter cited as PCA). The 1790 data represent a compilation of three sources: the Federal Census of 1790 for the city of Philadelphia, Southwark, and the Northern Liberties; the Philadelphia City Directory of 1791, at the Historical Society of Pennsylvania, Philadelphia; the Philadelphia City and County Tax Lists, 1789, PCA. All the residents listed in the Philadelphia Tax List of 1754 and the Federal Census of 1790 have been included in the data sets. See also Schweitzer, "Federalist Philadelphia."

[14] Chester County Assessment, 1785.

[15] Lemon, *Best Poor Man's Country*, pp. 182, 197.

[16] Lucy Simler and Paul Clemens have calculated the shift to a "cottager" class in Chester County, over the period 1750 to 1820. The number of "inmates," essen-

tially married or widowed landless workers, rose in the tax lists from 183 to 1,557 between 1750 and 1800, from about 4.5 inmates per 100 households to 20 inmates per 100 households. Paul G. E. Clemens and Lucy Simler, "Rural Labor and the Farm Household in Chester County, Pennsylvania, 1750–1820," in *Work and Labor in Early America*, ed. Stephen Innes (Chapel Hill: University of North Carolina Press, 1988), p. 115. For changes occurring in the labor market in the city of Philadelphia, see Smith, *Lower Sort*, esp. 144–47.

[17] The several studies of Pennsylvania's economy do not all agree on short-run trends. One problem is a general lack of data. There are good data on commodity prices but little on annual income levels in the countryside or the city. Much of the analysis of short-run trends has thus been based on the movement of commodity prices in Philadelphia, descriptions of the economy in merchant's letterbooks, and advertisements and bankruptcy announcements in the Philadelphia newspapers. Both Marc Egnal and William Sachs have tried to estimate "business cycles" for the period; however, in the eighteenth century the bulk of the population was relatively unaffected by the type of business cycles that afflicted merchants. Using crop prices to estimate prosperity or decline for farmers is not always helpful either, because total income for farmers depends on whether there was a bumper crop or a crop failure that year. And, as Doerflinger has noted, hard times for one industry may not have meant problems in another. Finally, when looking at prices one must keep in mind that they are "relative prices." As Doerflinger notes, "When everything is 'going up,' nothing is going up in real terms" (*Vigorous Spirit*, pp. 178–79, 200). Taking all the evidence thus far available, one must conclude that at best the economy stagnated between 1760 and 1790. Some farmers, some merchants, and some manufactures prospered, but they were offset by many who did not. Lemon notes there were few major innovations in either industry or agriculture, immigration virtually ceased, internal migration slowed, the formation of towns came to a temporary halt, and there were several years during the period where imports and exports came to a virtual halt (*Best Poor Man's Country*, pp. 224–26). For further discussion of short-run economic trends between 1750 and 1800, see William S. Sachs, "The Business Outlook in the Northern Colonies, 1750–1775" (Ph.D. diss., Columbia University, 1957); Marc M. Egnal, "The Pennsylvania Economy, 1748–1762: An Analysis of Short-Run Fluctuations in the Context of Long-Run Changes in the Atlantic Trading Community" (Ph.D. diss., University of Wisconsin, 1974); Doerflinger, *Vigorous Spirit*, chaps. 4, 5; and Lemon, *Best Poor Man's Country*, chap. 8. Billy Smith constructed a cost-of-living index to use with evidence on contemporary wages to conclude that the period of the Seven Years' War was generally prosperous, as were the 1790s. The early 1760s and 1780s represented depression years for most Philadelphians (Smith, *Lower Sort*, chap. 4).

[18] Randolph Shipley Klein, *Portrait of an Early American Family: The Shippens of Pennsylvania across Five Generations* (Philadelphia: University of Pennsylvania Press, 1975); Doerflinger, *Vigorous Spirit*, pp. 146–56, chap. 7; E. James Ferguson, *The Power of the Purse: A History of American Public Finance.* For an in-depth description of the data for Philadelphia in 1790, see Mary M. Schweitzer, "The Spatial Organization of Federalist Philadelphia, 1790," *Journal of Interdisciplinary History* 24, no. 1 (Summer 1993): 31–57, esp. pp. 53–55. (Chapel Hill: University of North Carolina Press, 1961), pp. 77–78.

[19] Eric Foner, *Tom Paine and Revolutionary America* (New York: Oxford University Press, 1976), pp. 59–62; Mary McKinney Schweitzer, "A New Look at Economic Causes of the Constitution: Monetary and Trade Policy in Maryland, Pennsylvania, and Virginia," *Social Science Journal* 26, no. 1 (1989): 15–26.

[20] The high taxation of "nonjurors" (those who would not swear support for the war effort) continued for several years after the war. As an anonymous contributor to the *Pennsylvania Gazette* wrote in January 1785: "It is well known that the Quakers and mononists [Mennonites] were formerly some of the best farmers in Pennsylvania. These people, from having their cattle, horses, farming utensils, etc., so often taken from them for taxes, have sensibly declined as farmers. . . . To this we may ascribe the great decay of the exports from our city, which in the articles of wheat and flour alone, do not amount to more than one-third what they were before the war. Thus we see how materially the agriculture and commerce of the state are affected by the test law [requiring that residents swear or affirm support of the revolutionary government]."

[21] Doerflinger, *Vigorous Spirit*, pp. 227–30; Lemon, *Best Poor Man's Country*, p. 139.

[22] There has been a great amount of research on the costs to the South of the Civil War but comparatively little on the costs of the Revolution. While the destruction in Pennsylvania was not as great as in Sherman's march to the sea, it was substantial. Economic historians have concluded that the negative growth of the wartime destruction kept the South in a backward economic state for decades. One has to wonder what similar effects negative growth had on Pennsylvania's own economic development. Much of the same analysis was suggested in George Rogers Taylor, "American Economic Growth before 1840: An Exploratory Essay," *Journal of Economic History* 24, no. 4 (December 1964): 427–44.

[23] There are many accounts of Indian warfare in Pennsylvania; a colorful description can be found in George P. Donehoo, *Pennsylvania: A History* (New York: Lewis Historical Co., 1926), pp. 662–795, 865–92, 976–96. For accounts of warfare from the perspective of the Indian nations, see Anthony F. C. Wallace, *King of the Delawares: Teedyuscung, 1700–1763* (Philadelphia: University of Pennsylvania Press, 1949); and C. A. Weslager, *The Delaware Indians: A History* (New Brunswick, N.J.: Rutgers University Press, 1972).

[24] Robert Middlekauff, *The Glorious Cause: The American Revolution, 1763–1789* (New York: Oxford University Press, 1982), pp. 285–86, 414–17, 535, 539, 541–44; John A. Munroe, *Federalist Delaware, 1775–1815* (Rutgers, N.J.: Rutgers University Press, 1954), p. 93.

[25] Mitchell, *Commercialism and Frontier*, p. 96; David Klingaman, "Food Surpluses and Deficits in the American Colonies, 1768–1772," *Journal of Economic History* 31, no. 3 (September 1971): 553–79; Doerflinger, *Vigorous Spirit*, pp. 203, 211, 227.

[26] Middlekauff, *Glorious Cause*, pp. 541–44; Robert L. Brunhouse, *The Counter-Revolution in Pennsylvania, 1776–1790* (Harrisburg: Pennsylvania Historical Commission, 1941), pp. 50–51, 70, 82–85; Anne Bezanson, *Prices and Inflation during the American Revolution: Pennsylvania, 1770–1790* (Philadelphia: University of Pennsylvania Press, 1951), p. 22.

[27] Mary Alice Hanna, *The Trade of the Delaware District before the Revolution* (Northampton, Mass.: Smith College Studies in History, 1917), pp. 267–73, 320–22; Alfred S. Martin, "The King's Customs: Philadelphia, 1763–1774," *William and Mary Quarterly*, 3d ser., 5, no. 2 (April 1948): 201–16; Doerflinger, *Vigorous Spirit*, pp. 175–78, 206–10; Bezanson, *Prices and Inflation*, p. 81.

[28] Ferguson, *Power of the Purse*, chap. 2; Bezanson, *Prices and Inflation*, p. 81.

[29] Mary M. Schweitzer, "State-Issued Currency and the Ratification of the U.S. Constitution," *Journal of Economic History* 99, no. 2 (June 1989): 311–22.

[30] Doerflinger, *Vigorous Enterprise*, p. 214. Another school of thought argues that forces unleashed by the Revolution hastened the transition from a traditional to a capitalist society; see Foner, *Tom Paine*, pp. 68–69. Doerflinger also argues that the Revolution set the stage for a more aggressive entrepreneurial class, although it was through a Schumpeterian clearing out of the less aggressive entrepreneurs rather than a major shift in the type of economy. However, the seeds of the nineteenth century could already be found in the mid eighteenth century; Schweitzer, *Custom and Contract*, chaps. 1, 2; and Schweitzer, "Wage Labor." The Revolution is virtually ignored in the analysis of the economic transition in the Delaware valley between 1750 and 1820 by Clemens and Simler, "Rural Labor," pp. 109–24. The critical turning point for Philadelphia is seen as 1810–40 by Lindstrom, *Economic Development*, p. 23. The changes in Philadelphia in the 1830s and 1840s, which were much more dramatic than any during the period 1750 to 1800, are described in Bruce Laurie, *Working People of Philadelphia, 1800–1850* (Philadelphia: Temple University Press, 1980), chap. 1.

[31] Price, "Economic Function," pp. 171–72.

[32] Schweitzer, *Custom and Contract*, chaps. 4, 6.

[33] Theodore Thayer, *Pennsylvania Politics and the Growth of Democracy, 1740–1776* (Harrisburg: Pennsylvania Historical and Museum Commission, 1953); Schweitzer, "State-Issued Currency"; Schweitzer, "New Look"; and Louis Hartz, *Economic Policy and Democratic Thought: Pennsylvania, 1776–1860* (Cambridge: Harvard University Press, 1948).

[34] Lindstrom, *Economic Development*, p. 32; Simeon J. Crowther, "Urban Growth in the Mid-Atlantic States, 1785–1850," *Journal of Economic History* 36, no. 3 (September 1987): 642–44.

Table 1. Occupations of Heads of Households

	Philadelphia 1756	Philadelphia, Northern Liberties, Southwark 1790
MISCELLANEOUS		
Laborer	78	612
Widow	62	317
Gentleman/gentlewoman	9	236
Spinster	-	65
Farmer/yeoman	2	20
Poor resident/invalid/pensioner	-	9
Sawyer	1	9
Corder	-	3
Inmate	2	-
Subtotal	154 (9.8%)	1,271 (18.2%)
PROFESSIONAL/SERVICE		
Teacher	13	98
Attorney	20	80
Physician/doctor	25	60
Clerk/scrivener/notary	10	58
Pharmacist/druggist	1	31
Minister/priest/sexton	9	29
Accountant	-	15
Professor	1	14
Nurse	-	10
Musician/actor	-	9
Surgeon/barber/bleeder	-	9
Midwife	-	5
Surveyor/draftsman	1	5
Dentist	-	3
Gardener	-	3
"Doctress"	-	1
Express rider	-	1
Picturemaker	-	1
Supervisor	-	1
Sweep	-	1
Writer	-	1
Subtotal	80 (5.1%)	435 (6.3%)

GOVERNMENT		
Miscellaneous city/state	1	47
Federal	-	40
Customs	-	17
State grain/lumber inspector	-	17
Watchman	-	9
Constable	-	8
Tax collector	-	6
Justice of the peace	-	5
Sheriff/subsheriff	-	3
Coroner	1	2
Crier	2	-
Subtotal	4 (0.3%)	154 (2.2%)
TRADE		
Nonspecific	174	448
Flour merchant/dealer	-	36
Lumber/board/stave merchant	-	32
Broker	-	17
Wine merchant/dealer	-	13
Iron merchant	-	11
China merchant	-	9
Wholesale grocer	-	9
Counting-house owner	-	8
Tea merchant	-	8
Bank of North America employee	-	5
Dealer	-	5
Hardware merchant	-	5
Insurance broker	-	5
Merchant taylor	-	5
Dealer/certificates	-	2
Dealer/public securities	-	2
Painter/oil merchant	-	2
Senior merchant	-	2
Vendue merchant/master	-	2
Exchange coffeehouse owner	-	1
Merchant manufacturing ash	-	1
Merchant, West Indies	-	1
Subtotal	174 (11.1%)	629 (9.0%)
SKILLED		
Printer	5	44
Coach- and carriagemaker	1	41
Chandler	10	25
Potter	1	23

Clock- and watchmaker	1	15
Bookbinder	1	13
Brushmaker	-	10
Watchmaker	1	10
Mill-stone maker	-	8
Combmaker	-	6
Cardmaker	1	5
Fanmaker	-	5
Pumpmaker	-	5
Clockmaker	1	4
Jeweler	-	4
Planemaker	2	4
Enginemaker	-	3
Parchmentmaker	-	3
Sievemaker	3	3
Soap boiler	3	3
Umbrellamaker	1	3
Paper stainer	-	2
Saddle-tree maker	-	2
Band-box maker	-	1
Button-mold maker	-	1
Canemaker	-	1
Chaisemaker	-	1
Copperplate printer	-	1
Engraver	-	1
Hair-powder manufacturer	-	1
Hanging-paper manufacturer	-	1
Ink, powder, and black-ball maker	-	1
Ivory turner	-	1
Limner	-	1
Mathematical-instrument maker	-	1
Mathematical- and obstetrical-instrument maker	-	1
Musical-instrument maker	-	1
Steamboat owner	-	1
Organmaker	-	1
Potter's-wheel maker	-	1
Reedmaker	1	1
Cigarmaker	-	1
Trunkmaker	-	1
Whalebone cutter	1	1
Wire-cage maker	1	1
Gluemaker	3	-
Instrumentmaker	2	-
Potashmaker	1	-

Whip- and canemaker	1	-
Wigmaker	1	-
Subtotal	42 (2.7%)	263 (3.8%)
LODGING/DRINK		
Innkeeper	6	101
Taverner	64	76
Boarding/lodging-house keeper	-	74
Housekeeper	-	38
Stable keeper	-	8
Beer-house keeper	-	6
Barkeeper	-	1
Mead-house keeper	-	1
Subtotal	70 (4.4%)	305 (4.4%)
RETAIL		
Grocer	-	271
Shopkeeper	94	261
Huckster	3	57
Barber	22	54
Tobacconist	13	48
Trader	-	18
Hairdresser	-	17
Stationer/bookseller	-	11
Lime seller	-	4
Storekeeper	-	4
Auctioneer	-	3
Vendue store master	-	3
Corn seller	-	2
Toy-shop keeper	-	2
Vendue crier	-	2
China-shop keeper/hatter	-	1
Haberdasher	-	1
Looking-glass storekeeper	-	1
Tinker	2	-
Subtotal	134 (8.5%)	760 (10.9%)
GENERAL		
Cooper	50	96
Porter	10	72
Carter	11	52
Cedar cooper	1	23
Shallop man/waterman	15	22
Peddlar	2	7
Wagon master/drayman	-	6

Ferry keeper/ferryman	-	5
Drover/cowherd	-	3
Coach owner/driver	-	2
Oysterman	-	2
Boatman	3	-
Flatman	6	-
Subtotal	98 (6.3%)	290 (4.2%)
WOOD/FURNITURE		
Joiner	38	81
Chairmaker	11	28
Wheelwright	5	22
Turner	5	16
Cabinetmaker	-	15
Upholsterer	2	7
Carver	1	5
Windsor-chair maker	1	4
Spinning-wheel maker	-	3
Board builder	-	1
Carver and gilder	-	1
Subtotal	63 (4.0%)	183 (2.6%)
METALS		
Blacksmith/smith	34	153
Ironmonger	2	34
Silversmith	12	25
Nailer/nailmaker	2	18
Tinsmith/tin man	4	16
Coppersmith	-	12
Blockmaker	6	11
Gunsmith	2	11
Brass founder/brazier	4	7
Whitesmith	-	6
Cutler	6	4
Goldsmith	3	4
Pewterer	2	4
Typefounder	-	3
White and blacksmith	-	2
File cutter	-	1
Silver plater	-	1
Steelmaker	1	1
Wiremaker	-	1
Founder	3	-
Subtotal	81 (5.1%)	314 (4.5%)

LEATHER		
Cordwainer/shoemaker	96	328
Skinner/tanner	24	66
Currier	-	24
Saddler/saddlemaker	13	23
Harnessmaker	1	13
Silk and stuff shoemaker	-	5
Lastmaker	5	3
Heelmaker	-	2
Chair trimmer/harnessmaker	-	1
Women's-shoe maker	-	1
Leatherworker	1	-
Saddle-tree maker	1	-
Subtotal	141 (9.0%)	466 (6.7%)
FOOD-RELATED		
Butcher	27	129
Baker	63	114
Biscuit baker	-	26
Brewer	5	21
Distiller	-	12
Sugar refiner	-	11
Chocolatemaker	-	9
Grazier	-	8
Sugar baker	-	7
Pastry cook	-	5
Loaf baker	-	4
Cake baker	-	3
Fishmonger	-	3
Liquor bottler	-	2
Milk woman/man	-	2
Bee-house keeper	-	1
Confectioner	-	1
Miller	5	1
Mustardmaker	-	1
Victualler	-	1
Jackmaker	13	-
Vintner	11	-
Chocolate grinder	3	-
Bolter	1	-
Subtotal	128 (8.1%)	361 (5.2%)
CLOTH/APPAREL		
Tailor	75	288
Hatter	33	81

Weaver	6	58
Breechesmaker	3	19
Seamstress	-	18
Stocking weaver	13	17
Mantuamaker	-	9
Dyer	4	9
Milliner	-	7
Starchmaker	-	7
Glover	2	5
Corder	-	4
Staymaker	8	4
Wool comber	1	3
Calico printer	-	2
Fringe- and lacemaker	-	2
Furrier	-	2
Bonnetmaker	2	1
Buckskin-breeches maker	-	1
Carpet manufacturer	-	1
Fuller	-	1
Collarmaker	1	-
Wool spinner	1	-
Subtotal	149 (9.5%)	539 (7.7%)
SHIPBUILDING		
Ship carpenter/joiner	5	88
Shipwright	6	40
Ropemaker	3	33
Boatbuilder	5	20
Ship chandler	-	17
Mastmaker	-	11
Caulker	-	10
Sailmaker	5	9
Rigger	2	8
Anchor smith	-	3
Ship painter	-	1
Subtotal	26 (1.7%)	240 (3.4%)
SEAGOING		
Mariner	68	145
Captain	58	127
Pilot	-	16
Mate	-	12
Stevedore	-	2
Subtotal	126 (8.0%)	302 (4.3%)

CONSTRUCTION		
Carpenter	58	253
Bricklayer	19	61
Painter	-	54
Brickmaker	7	22
Plasterer	10	23
Mason/stonecutter	4	21
Glazier	6	12
Wharf builder	-	4
Plumber	-	3
Shingle shaver	-	3
Millwright	-	2
Fencemaker	-	1
Paver	-	1
Well digger	-	1
Subtotal	104 (6.6%)	461 (6.6%)
TOTAL	1,574	6,973
Households with no occupations listed	612 (28.0%)	1,510 (17.8%)
Total households listed	2,186	8,483

Note: Many specific occupations are hidden under the general designations "laborer," "merchant," and "shopkeeper." Probably many mariners were merely called laborers in the census. Also, many of the widows were shopkeepers, but the census takers generally used "widow" as their occupational designation.

Sources: Philadelphia City Tax List, 1756, Philadelphia City Archives; Federal Census of 1790 for the city and county of Philadelphia; the Philadelphia City Directory of 1791, Historical Society of Pennyslvania; Philadelphia City and County Tax Lists, 1790, Philadelphia City Archives. All the residents listed in the Philadelphia City Tax List of 1756 and the Federal Census of 1790 for Philadelphia city, Southwark, and the Northern Liberties have been included in the data set. For information on the spatial distribution of occupations within the city of Philadelphia, Southwark, and the Northern Liberties, see Mary M. Schweitzer, "The Spatial Organization of Federalist Philadelphia, 1790," *Journal of Interdisciplinary History* 24, no. 1 (Summer 1993): 31–57.

The Quaker Vanguard
Philanthropy in Eighteenth-Century Philadelphia

Jean R. Soderlund

In 1712, soon after the bloody New York slave uprising shattered the confidence of slaveholders up and down the Atlantic seaboard, the Quaker-dominated Pennsylvania Assembly received two petitions concerning slaves. One was from William Southeby, a well-respected Philadelphia Friend who had moved to Pennsylvania from Maryland three decades earlier and had served on the Provincial Council and in other offices. His request for the "Enlargement," or general emancipation, of all slaves in the province was unprecedented. The legislators were concerned about the expansion of slavery in Pennsylvania, especially in light of the New York revolt, but in their minds freeing the blacks outright was not the answer. Indeed, many of the assemblymen owned slaves and looked forward to many years of service from them. The Assembly decided, "it is neither just nor convenient to set them at Liberty"; however, its members saw in the second petition, "sign'd by many Hands," a more moderate approach to curtail the slave trade, a way to slow the growth of slavery without hurting present owners. It laid a prohibitive duty of £20 (Pennsylvania currency) on each slave imported into Pennsylvania. This measure might have forestalled further importation had it been approved by the queen, but it was not. Subsequent laws lowered the duty on slaves, and both importation of blacks and the institution of slavery continued.[1]

The divergent petitions of 1712 represent well the divisions in early Pennsylvania over the question of slavery. William Penn's colony was the scene of a vigorous debate—a debate carried on almost entirely among Friends. A few Quakers opposed the institution absolutely and would use legislative fiat to bring about its demise. Southeby, for example, had witnessed the beginning of an influx of slaves to work the tobacco fields of Maryland before he settled in Pennsylvania and feared the same process would take place in the Quaker colony. Southeby and other abolitionists saw slavery as a contaminant of the "holy experiment." On the other hand, the majority of Friends were much less certain that slaveholding was wrong. Like European colonizers elsewhere in the New World, the founders of Pennsylvania were desperate for workers to build plantations and towns and to produce a marketable crop. Many bought slaves because they needed the labor and believed they could avoid offending God if they treated their slaves well. Most Friends, including the legislators of 1712, were more easily convinced that the slave trade violated Quaker doctrine—because it involved violence—than that they themselves sinned by employing black labor in their homes, shops, and farms. They, like other colonists in general, believed that their own property rights took precedence over any right of slaves to be free.

Although Southeby's appeal was the first such petition to reach the legislature, Quakers had been debating whether slavery was consistent with their beliefs for a quarter century. In 1688 four Germantown Friends, including brothers Derick and Abraham op den Graeff, Francis Daniel Pastorius, and Gerrit Hendricks, were the first to petition their meeting about slavery. They found it contemptible that a Quaker colony, established for liberty of conscience, should deny men and women "liberty of the body." Friends should consider the golden rule, to do unto others as you wish others to do to you, when separating wives from husbands and children from parents. They warned that Europeans had been shocked at reports "that the Quakers doe here handel men as they handel there cattle. And for that reason some have no mind or inclination to come hither." Pennsylvanians must stop robbing and stealing the bodies of men, women, and children, or surely the blacks would rise up "and handel their masters and mastresses as they did handel them before." Philadelphia Yearly Meeting took no action against slavery in response to this appeal.[2]

Indeed, for sixty-five years after the Germantown petition, Philadelphia Quakers debated among themselves their responsibility regarding slaves. Individuals like Southeby and several rural meetings argued that enslaving fellow humans was un-Christian; others, particularly those who were leaders both of Philadelphia Yearly Meeting and the Pennsylvania government, rejected the sinfulness of slavery and held on to their slaves. The most that Philadelphia Yearly Meeting would do before 1754 was to warn members not to participate in the slave trade or to buy imported slaves, but they placed no penalties on engaging in either of these activities.[3]

During the 1710s, 1720s, and 1730s a series of Quaker abolitionists spoke out against the scourge of slavery, seemingly with little effect. Southeby, for example, continued to protest even after he failed in 1712 to convince the Assembly to enact a law for general emancipation. In 1714, despairing of action by the Society of Friends or the Assembly to stop the slave trade, Southeby in an unpublished paper reproved Philadelphia Yearly Meeting for avoiding the issue with the excuse that London Friends would not ban the trade. He argued that the Pennsylvanians, who included so many "ministers and other ancient Friends," should "be exemplary to other places, and not take liberty to do things because others do them." A few years later, when the Yearly Meeting resisted a petition from Chester Quarterly Meeting against buying imported slaves, Southeby published several abolitionist papers (which have not survived) without Friends' permission. Philadelphia Monthly Meeting threatened him with disownment but apparently failed to follow through. At about the same time, an English Quaker, John Farmer, was disowned by Rhode Island Friends for demanding in print that all Quakers free their slaves. He appealed his disownment to Philadelphia Yearly Meeting, which upheld the New England meeting. In 1729 Philadelphia merchant Ralph Sandiford, an English immigrant who, had he wished, was wealthy enough to engage in the slave trade himself, rushed a pamphlet to press that reprimanded slaveholding Friends, the leaders of his meeting. He was greatly upset by the upswing in slave importation at that time—he could watch the slave auctions from his shop window—and published the tract even though the Quaker overseers of the press denied him permission. The Philadelphia meeting condemned him for his actions.[4]

The most exceptional abolitionist among Friends was Benjamin Lay, who with his wife, Sarah, emigrated from England to Barbados and, in 1731, to Philadelphia. He witnessed the barbaric conditions of slavery in Barbados, and when he discovered the institution entrenched in Pennsylvania as well, he started his crusade, using personal example and dramatic acts to portray the evil of the institution. Lay made his own clothes to avoid materials grown with slave labor and publicly smashed his wife's teacups to discourage use of slave-produced sugar. On one occasion during the 1730s he stood with one bare foot in snow outside a Quaker meeting to make those who owned slaves realize how badly they clothed their blacks in the winter. He also kidnapped a Quaker child to bring home to Friends the grief suffered by African families when their children were snatched by slave traders or when their owners separated parents from children. He even interrupted religious services of other denominations. The events that made leading Philadelphia Quakers lose patience altogether and repudiate him publicly were his publication of *All Slave-keepers, That Keep the Innocent in Bondage, Apostates* (1737), which bitterly denounced Friends, and his "bladder of blood" demonstration at the 1738 Yearly Meeting. At the meeting, Lay plunged a sword into a hollowed-out book that resembled a Bible and contained a bladder of red pokeberry juice, splattering those sitting nearby with "blood." His intention was to show Friends that they committed spiritual and physical violence by holding slaves, whether or not they treated them well and taught them Christian principles.[5]

The conservative Friends whom Lay confronted in 1738 were unmoved by his behavior. In the midst of a period of economic growth, Philadelphia Friends changed their stance only in the 1750s, when many circumstances combined to bring about a relatively rare occurrence in human history—the moral standards of an influential segment of society experienced a profound alteration. Whereas earlier, less-powerful individuals had assailed Quaker leaders for holding slaves, the weighty Friends themselves called for emancipation. And once influential Philadelphia swung to the abolitionists, other local meetings fell into line. In 1753 Philadelphia Yearly Meeting approved John Woolman's *Some Considerations on the Keeping of Negroes*, and in 1754 the meeting itself issued its *Epistle of Caution and Advice, Concerning the Buying and Keeping of Slaves*, which denounced slaveholding and instructed members to consider freeing their blacks. The meeting's epistle warned masters "to weigh the Cause of detaining them in Bondage," for if they kept slaves for financial reasons it was likely that "the Love of God and the Influence of the Holy Spirit" did not guide them in their daily lives and that their "Hearts [were] not sufficiently redeemed from the World." Four years later, in 1758, Philadelphia Yearly Meeting, led to a large extent by Philadelphians like Israel (Jr.), James, and John Pemberton, adopted a new rule of discipline that forbade Friends from buying, selling, or importing slaves. Although the Quaker meeting pulled back from banning slaveholding altogether and refrained from prohibiting slave ownership until 1776, the 1754 epistle and the 1758 rule together marked the Yearly Meeting's abolitionist stand.[6]

Why did this change take place in the 1750s? We can determine several reasons. First, by midcentury, many fewer leaders of the Yearly Meeting owned slaves (10 percent, compared with about 60 percent before 1730). Part of the reason for this was the greater availability of white labor from among the thousands of Europeans arriving in the colony. Between 1727 and 1754 about 58,000 Germans and 16,500 Irish came up the Delaware River, many of them settling in Philadelphia. To pay their passage many offered their labor as bound servants for three or more years; others worked as wage laborers to accumulate funds to establish their own shops or farms.[7]

Second, a half century of individual protests by abolitionists had made their mark even though they had failed to change the Yearly Meeting's policy at that time. Some Quakers had chosen to avoid buying slaves entirely. Since the 1720s, still others—including some of the leaders who resisted the abolitionists—had freed slaves in their wills. Two Quaker women, Patience Lloyd and Esther Shippen, widows of substantial officeholders, and Thomas Redman, a bricklayer, were apparently the first members of Philadelphia Monthly Meeting to heed in a practical manner the admonitions of the abolitionists. In the 1720s, Lloyd, widow of Thomas, an early Pennsylvania leader who had died thirty years before, freed the slave woman Ambo and her youngest daughter, Molly, but kept children Hannah and Sam in bondage. These young slaves she gave as bequests to her granddaughters. Shippen, whose husband, Edward, had held numerous posts including assemblyman and mayor of Philadelphia, directed in her will that her slave Moll should serve her sister-in-law for three years and then be freed. Redman specified that Negro James was to be freed after he served the widow for four years, eight months, and fifteen days from the signing of the will.[8]

Beginning in 1735, Quakers prominent in Philadelphia Yearly Meeting began freeing slaves in their wills. Isaac Norris, who had imported West Indian blacks as late as 1730 and was presiding clerk of the Yearly Meeting and an overseer of the press, which meant that he helped to decide what books could be published by Friends and had concluded that several abolitionist tracts should be suppressed, died in 1735. He had also been a long-time assemblyman and mayor of Philadelphia. Norris owned a house, lot, and wharf in Philadelphia and mills in Norriton Township, in addition to his Fairhill estate in the Northern Liberties. Norris freed his Native American slave Will within five years, providing that Will serve widow Mary Norris faithfully during that time. Norris mentioned no other slaves in his will, but his widow owned a black girl Dinah, whom she did not free when she died in 1748. As no inventory of Isaac Norris's estate exists, it is impossible to know if he owned additional slaves when he died. Possibly he did not, because he hoped that Will would be able to assist son Joseph at the mills in addition to serving Mary at Fairhill. Possibly Dinah replaced Will at Fairhill.[9]

When Samuel Preston died in 1743, he manumitted eleven slaves, comprising three generations of one family. Like Norris, Preston had helped to guide Philadelphia Yearly Meeting policy for many years: he had been treasurer since 1714, overseer of the press since 1717, and clerk and correspondent with London Yearly Meeting. Less important in politics than Norris, Preston served briefly as provincial councillor, assemblyman, and Philadelphia mayor. In his will Preston affirmed that he had already freed four of his slaves, husband and wife Ishmael and Judith, and Caesar and Cudgo, probably their sons, and that Ishmael and Judith had a child who was free-born. Still enslaved were their daughter Hagar, age twenty-five, and her two young sons. Preston indentured Hagar and one of her sons to Ishmael and Judith until age thirty. The other son Preston gave to his own grandson, also until the slave reached age thirty. His remaining blacks, a man Occo, a boy Ishmael, and two girls whose names were unspecified, all probably children of Judith and Ishmael, would be free at age thirty.[10]

The manumissions by first-rank Quaker leaders, who had previously agreed in meeting to censure Southeby, Lay, and other abolitionists for their antislavery activities, signify the turmoil in the minds of

Friends during the 1730s and 1740s. They felt discomfort with the institution. Apparently Norris and Preston recognized that slaveholding violated Quaker beliefs in nonviolence and the equality of all people in the sight of God but thought they needed the labor and eased their consciences with a moderate meeting policy against importation as they tried to silence antislavery critics who announced their hypocrisy to the world; then they freed their slaves in their wills. It is an uneven record on slavery, perhaps, but not a surprising one for such a complicated issue. Abolitionists in Philadelphia Yearly Meeting forced all Pennsylvania Quaker slaveholders to weigh the justice of their actions, well before masters of other religions had to make a similar choice.

Thus the first two factors leading to the 1750s antislavery reform among Friends were that fewer Quaker leaders owned slaves by the 1750s (which resulted from both religious commitment and ability to obtain white servants) and that early abolitionists had gradually convinced even some slave owners that slavery was wrong.

A third factor in the move to antislavery at midcentury was the tireless work of John Woolman and Anthony Benezet against slavery. Woolman, of Burlington Monthly Meeting in New Jersey, had been a successful tailor, shopkeeper, and farmer but had purposely cut back in his business activities in order to avoid the temptations of wealth and to devote time to ministry. He wrote several essays against slaveholding and took about thirty trips throughout the colonies, trying to convince Friends of the error of owning slaves. He had awakened to the evils of slavery around 1742, when at twenty-two years old and working in a Mount Holly shop, he wrote a bill of sale for a black woman, whom his employer had sold to an elderly Friend. Woolman regretted the act immediately and told both men that he "believed slavekeeping to be a practice inconsistent with the Christian religion." When subsequently asked to write another "instrument of slavery," Woolman refused. In 1746 he made his first journey to Maryland, Virginia, and Carolina, returning home full of remorse because he had eaten and "lodged free-cost with people who lived in ease on the hard labour of their slaves." He saw in the "southern provinces so many vices and corruptions increased by [the slave] trade and this way of life that it appeared to [him] as a dark gloominess hanging over the land."[11]

Soon after he returned from the South, Woolman wrote *Some Considerations on the Keeping of Negroes*, which was directed not only to the

Friends he had visited on his journey but to his neighbors in New Jersey and Pennsylvania as well. He did not submit the manuscript immediately to the Quaker overseers of the press because in 1746 fully two-thirds of that body owned slaves. In 1753, after the deaths of several slaveholding censors and their replacement by antislavery-minded Friends, Woolman requested permission to publish his tract. In the essay, published in 1754, he reminded readers that blacks had not forfeited "the natural right of freedom" and were equal to whites in God's eyes. He warned that slaveholders tested divine benevolence: "If we do not consider these things aright, but through a stupid indolence conceive views of interest separate from the general good of the great brotherhood, and in pursuance thereof treat our inferiors with rigour, to increase our wealth and gain riches for our children, what then shall we do when God riseth up; and when he visiteth, what shall we answer him?"[12]

Woolman was a gentle man who tried to press his case without creating bitterness among slave owners. He avoided dyes because they were produced by slave labor, and when he stayed in the houses of slaveholders, he refused to benefit from the services of blacks without reimbursing either the owner or the slave; at the same time, he insisted on paying the costs of publishing his second antislavery essay, *Considerations on Keeping Negroes: Part Second* (1762), instead of allowing the Yearly Meeting to underwrite them, because he felt that slave owners might resent having to contribute to printing the tract.[13]

Allied with Woolman in the drive against slavery was Benezet, who had begun serving on Yearly Meeting committees in 1747, just one year after Woolman, and was a new overseer of the press appointed in 1752. Benezet had been born in France in 1713 of Huguenot parents and with them escaped to England in 1715; sixteen years later they immigrated to Pennsylvania. He rejected a mercantile career, believing that a life seeking wealth was not his calling. Instead, he began teaching school in Germantown in 1739 and in 1742 became an instructor of poor children at the Friends' English School in Philadelphia. He chose schoolteaching knowing that his income would be small. His intention was to adhere strictly to the Quaker doctrine of plainness, and in fact he was considerably less affluent than most of his fellow reformers.[14]

In 1750 Benezet began holding free classes for black students at his home in the evenings while continuing to teach white children by day. He found that his black pupils were as capable as whites in both academic work and moral and religious instruction. He continued to teach free blacks and slaves on this informal basis for twenty years, until he convinced Philadelphia Monthly Meeting to open an "Africans' School" in 1770. The foundation on which he built all his labors—for abolition of slavery, justice for Native Americans and the poor, education, pacifism, and temperance—was his abhorrence of wealth: "The great rock against which our society has dashed" is "the love of the world & the deceitfulness of riches, the desire of amassing wealth."[15]

Soon after Woolman submitted his essay to the overseers of the press, Benezet laid a proposal to denounce slave trading before Philadelphia Monthly Meeting. This meeting referred the paper to the quarterly meeting, which in turn sent it to Philadelphia Yearly Meeting. Both Woolman and Benezet were now members of the inner circle that held sway over Yearly Meeting policy, and both attended the Yearly Meeting in 1754, which after revision issued Benezet's paper as *An Epistle of Caution and Advice, Concerning the Buying and Keeping of Slaves*. The tract was a stirring renunciation of slaveholding itself, not just importation, and marked acceptance by the Yearly Meeting leadership of abolitionist thought.[16]

Both Woolman and Benezet were effective lobbyists who were able to convince fellow Friends that slavery was wrong. Whereas earlier abolitionists like Lay had taken a more confrontational approach, Woolman and Benezet worked within the meeting structure, always aware of the society's stress on unity.

A fourth factor in the acceptance of abolitionism was the more general reform movement among Friends. In the 1750s Philadelphia Yearly Meeting underwent momentous changes, as reformers attempted to rid the society of laxity and corruption. A new generation of leaders took control, including Israel, James, and John Pemberton, sons of wealthy Philadelphia merchant Israel Pemberton, Sr.; Daniel Stanton, a Philadelphia joiner; and prosperous Chester County farmers John and George Churchman and William Brown. Joining them in their labors to enforce more rigorously the society's rules against marrying outside the faith and such worldly pursuits as gambling, shooting matches, and extravagant display were British Friends Mary Peisley, Catherine Payton, and Samuel Fothergill. The reformers interpreted the outbreak of the Seven Years' War as God's punishment for their waywardness and resolved to cleanse the society of sin. To do so, they believed that they must build a wall around the church, excluding those who married non-Friends or in other ways refused to adhere to the strict Quaker code.[17]

Woolman, Benezet, and other abolitionists, whose primary concern was the welfare of slaves, were able to hitch their campaign against perpetual bondage to this movement for reform. In the minds of Friends, war fulfilled the prophecies of Woolman, Benezet, and Lay. In 1756 John Churchman, an ardent reformer who, as far as we know, had not previously spoken against slavery, wrote in response to watching the bodies of slain frontier inhabitants carried through the streets: "How can this [calamity] be? Since this has been a land of peace, and as yet not much concerned in war; but as it were in a moment, my eyes turned to the case of the poor enslaved Negroes. And however light a matter they who have been concerned in it, may look upon the purchasing, selling, or keeping those oppressed people in slavery, it then appeared plain to me, that such were the partakers of iniquity." Abolitionism became part of the drive for purification. Friends who had little humanitarian concern for blacks took up antislavery ideology in the hope that purging the society of sin would pacify an angry God. The Quaker leadership embraced abolitionism as part of the crusade for moral revitalization.[18]

Thus Philadelphia Yearly Meeting in the 1750s was the first organized body to serve notice to its members that slavery was inconsistent with Christian practice and to prohibit members from importing, buying, and selling slaves. Although meetings did not begin disowning slaveholders for twenty years, in the interim they disciplined Friends who violated the rules against dealing in slaves and through these measures eroded the belief of slave owners that their way was justified. During the 1760s and 1770s increasing numbers of Quaker slaveholders freed their slaves; after 1776 they had to manumit their blacks or be disowned. By 1780 few still owned slaves.[19]

The irony of the story of Quakers and slavery, of course, is that when Friends had political control in Pennsylvania they resisted emancipation, but when they withdrew from power, first during the Seven Years' War and then during the Revolution, they embraced abolitionism. It was left to radical Presbyterians, primarily, to secure passage of the gradual abolition law of 1780, which required owners to register any slaves they wished to keep and freed all blacks born after March 1780 at age twenty-eight. Technically, this act freed no Pennsylvania slave until 1808, but in reality it ushered in a period during which Philadelphians of other faiths experienced the same conversion to abolitionism that Quakers had gone through before 1776. Quaker influence, revolutionary ideology, declining reliance on bound labor, and black resistance to slavery all contributed to the general movement away from black bondage—among Presbyterians, Episcopalians, members of other religions, and the unchurched. Whereas Philadelphians had almost 1,500 slaves in 1767, they owned just 55 by the turn of the century. In Pennsylvania as a whole, the number of slaves dropped from almost 7,000 in 1780 to 795 in 1810.[20]

Despite this rapid decline in slaveholding, among Friends first and then among others, the limitations of their commitment must be emphasized. Before 1770 almost all manumissions were by will, which meant that the slave owners benefited until their deaths from their slaves' labor, depriving only their heirs. In many cases, indeed, the slaves had to work even after their owner's death—until the decease of a widow, daughter, or son; in other cases the freed slaves had to pay a sum to the heirs, usually annually, to protect the estate against charges for support in later years. Slave children often had to serve the white family until maturity. For many blacks, freedom came only gradually. Some had to serve out terms of indentured servitude; others—although technically free—found it difficult to earn more than a subsistence. If they fell into debt, they indentured their children in order to make settlement and provide for the children's support. Slave owners sometimes paid freedom dues to the blacks whom they freed in order to give them something to start their new lives, but most free blacks in Pennsylvania experienced poverty and lived with the fear that they could be snatched by southern slave catchers at any time.

To help to protect blacks from reenslavement, secure manumissions for individuals, and work for the total abolition of slavery, Philadelphia Quakers organized the Pennsylvania Abolition Society (PAS). The group first had a brief existence in 1775, reorganized in 1784, and thereafter served as a catalyst for the destruction of slavery. Friends made up the majority of PAS activists, but they drew support from outside their meeting as well. Through the PAS, Quaker abolitionists assumed a new corporate identity and thereby eliminated the need to win the approbation of Philadelphia Yearly Meeting or local meetings before each antislavery thrust. As an autonomous body, the PAS vigorously pushed the

1780 gradual abolition act to its limits by suing for the freedom of individual blacks and repeatedly approached the legislature and courts to outlaw slavery.[21]

Close attention to antislavery reform, in which Friends took a leading role during the eighteenth century, has allowed us to examine the way in which Quaker reform impulses arose and grew. Until 1780 abolitionism represented their most sustained philanthropic effort on behalf of non-Friends; however, in the period after the Revolution, Quakers self-consciously expanded their concerns and immersed themselves in a variety of reforms. Young women set up the Friendly Band, the first female benevolent society, to help poor women. Friends involved themselves in prison reform, to eliminate the system by which prisoners had to pay for their own food and clothing, and worked against imprisonment for debt. Education of blacks—although it predated the Revolution and was not the special province of Friends because Anglicans had set up a school for blacks as early as the 1740s—remained an important concern.[22]

Examination of Quaker efforts in prison reform and education reveals patterns similar to what we have seen on abolition. The original impulse came from Quaker theology: individuals interpreted Quaker ideals in a way that demanded social change. Just as William Southeby and Benjamin Lay believed that the Quaker concept of equality of all people before God meant that slaves should be free, Friends' efforts to provide education for poor whites and blacks had the same basis, as did their drive for prison reform.

But careful analysis of the antislavery movement also shows how difficult it was for Quaker reformers to convince fellow members of their concern. And for this reason, when Friends embarked on their various reform efforts during and after the Revolution, they formed organizations outside the meeting. They took part, with like-minded people of other faiths, in philanthropic activities without having to win over everyone else in the Society of Friends to the idea that what they were doing was right. Education, poor relief, and prison reform had more support from the society than abolition in its early stages, but still individuals formed independent organizations rather than work directly through the meeting.

Thus the spark for Quaker involvement in reform came from their religion, but much of their early work—especially in abolition—was not approved by the Quaker meeting. Quakerism had within it two opposing forces: on the one hand, the justification for radical action that lay within the belief in universal equality; on the other, the requirement that Friends reach a sense of the meeting (or general agreement of what is God's will) before making any move. The Friends who spearheaded reform movements acted as individuals, not as representatives of their meeting, and they did so either in direct opposition to the will of their society or in the face of its belief that their concerns lay outside the purview of the meeting.

---

[1] *Pennsylvania Archives*, 8th ser., 8 vols. (Harrisburg, Pa.: Bureau of Publications, 1931–35), 2:1012–13; Kenneth L. Carroll, "William Southeby, Early Quaker Antislavery Writer," *Pennsylvania Magazine of History and Biography* 89, no. 4 (October 1965): 416–27; *The Papers of William Penn*, ed. Marianne S. Wokeck et al., vol. 3, *1685–1700* (Philadelphia: University of Pennsylvania Press, 1986), p. 110; Darold D. Wax, "The Negro Slave Trade in Colonial Pennsylvania" (Ph.D. diss., University of Washington, 1962), pp. 267–74.

[2] "Germantown Friends' Protest against Slavery, 1688," reprinted in J. William Frost, ed., *The Quaker Origins of Antislavery* (Norwood, Pa.: Norwood Editions, 1980), p. 69; Thomas E. Drake, *Quakers and Slavery in America* (New Haven: Yale University Press, 1950), pp. 11–20; Jean R. Soderlund, *Quakers and Slavery: A Divided Spirit* (Princeton: Princeton University Press, 1985), pp. 18–20.

[3] Drake, *Quakers and Slavery*, pp. 11–47; Soderlund, *Quakers and Slavery*, pp. 15–53.

[4] Southeby quoted in Drake, *Quakers and Slavery*, pp. 28, 24–33, 39–43; Soderlund, *Quakers and Slavery*, pp. 20–26.

[5] C. Brightwen Rowntree, "Benjamin Lay (1681–1759)," *Journal of the Friends' Historical Society* 33 (1936): 3–19; Roberts Vaux, *Memoirs of the Lives of Benjamin Lay and Ralph Sandiford, Two of the Earliest Public Advocates for the Emancipation of the Enslaved Africans* (Philadelphia, 1815), pp. 17, 25–28; Drake, *Quakers and Slavery*, pp. 43–47; David Brion Davis, *The Problem of Slavery in Western Culture* (Ithaca, N.Y.: Cornell University Press, 1966), pp. 321–23.

[6] The text of the epistle is in Philadelphia Yearly Meeting minutes, 14–19/9M/1754, Friends Historical Library of Swarthmore College, Swarthmore, Pa. Drake, *Quakers and Slavery*, pp. 48–62; Soderlund, *Quakers and Slavery*, pp. 26–31.

[7] Soderlund, *Quakers and Slavery*, p. 34; Marianne S. Wokeck, "A Tide of Alien Tongues: The Flow and Ebb of German Immigration to Pennsylvania, 1683–1776" (Ph.D. diss., Temple University, 1983), p. 111; Marianne S. Wokeck, "Irish Immigration to the Delaware Valley before the American Revolution" (Paper presented to the Philadelphia Center for Early American Studies seminar, October 1988, Philadelphia), p. 25a.

[8] Gary B. Nash and Jean R. Soderlund, *Freedom by Degrees: Emancipation in Pennsylvania and Its Aftermath* (New York: Oxford University Press, 1991), chap. 2; Philadelphia County Wills, book D, nos. 312, 326, 328, Register of Wills, Philadelphia.

[9] Darold D. Wax, "Quaker Merchants and the Slave Trade in Colonial Pennsylvania," *Pennsylvania Magazine of History and Biography* 86, no. 2 (April 1962): 149–52; Soderlund, *Quakers and Slavery*, pp. 37, 197–98; Philadelphia County Wills, book E, no. 412, book G, no. 239.

[10] Soderlund, *Quakers and Slavery*, pp. 38–39, 197–98; Philadelphia County Wills, book G, no. 41.

[11] *The Journal and Major Essays of John Woolman*, ed. Phillips P. Moulton (New York: Oxford University Press, 1971), pp. 32–33, 38.

[12] *Journal of Woolman*, pp. 204, 207, 44–45, 198–209; Soderlund, *Quakers and Slavery*, pp. 34–35.

[13] *Journal of Woolman*, pp. 32–47, 117–22; Drake, *Quakers and Slavery*, pp. 51–64.

[14] George S. Brookes, *Friend Anthony Benezet* (Philadelphia: University of Pennsylvania Press, 1937), pp. 12–30; Philadelphia Yearly Meeting minutes, 1746–54; Philadelphia tax assessment list, 1774, Historical Society of Pennsylvania.

[15] Quoted in Jack D. Marietta, *The Reformation of American Quakerism, 1748–1783* (Philadelphia: University of Pennsylvania Press, 1984), p. 100. Nancy Slocum Hornick, "Anthony Benezet and the Africans' School: Toward a Theory of Full Equality," *Pennsylvania Magazine of History and Biography* 99, no. 4 (October 1975): 399–421.

[16] Soderlund, *Quakers and Slavery*, p. 27; Philadelphia Yearly Meeting minutes, 14–19/9M/1754.

[17] Marietta, *Reformation*, pp. 32–96.

[18] *An Account of the Gospel Labours and Christian Experiences of that Faithful Minister of Christ, John Churchman* (Philadelphia, 1882), pp. 209–10, as quoted in Marietta, *Reformation*, p. 119. Soderlund, *Quakers and Slavery*, pp. 173–77; J. William Frost, "The Origins of the Quaker Crusade against Slavery: A Review of Recent Literature," *Quaker History* 67, no. 1 (Spring 1978): 56–58.

[19] Nash and Soderlund, *Freedom by Degrees*, chaps. 2, 3.

[20] Nash and Soderlund, *Freedom by Degrees*, chaps. 4, 5.

[21] Nash and Soderlund, *Freedom by Degrees*, chap. 4.

[22] The standard source on Quaker philanthropy is Sydney V. James, *A People among Peoples: Quaker Benevolence in Eighteenth-Century America* (Cambridge: Harvard University Press, 1963). See also Marietta, *Reformation*; Drake, *Quakers and Slavery*; and Margaret Hope Bacon, *Mothers of Feminism: The Story of Quaker Women in America* (San Francisco: Harper and Row, 1986).

Religion and Social Change
The Rise of the Methodists
Dee E. Andrews

In February 1786 Richard Allen, ex-slave and Methodist preacher, settled in Philadelphia. By any measure Allen had made an interesting choice of residence. Philadelphia was the premier city of the New Republic. The colonies' chief cultural center before the revolutionary war, the city continued as the capital of religious denominationalism and the enlightenment after the war. Numerous churches graced its neighborhoods, from the Greater Friends Meeting House, "Old Buttonwood" Presbyterian Church, and St. Michael's Lutheran Church in the north, to St. Paul's Anglican and St. Mary's Roman Catholic churches in midtown, and St. Peter's Anglican and the Third Presbyterian churches in the south. Christ Church, completed by the Anglicans on the eve of the war, dominated High Street. New buildings were planned for the American Philosophical Society, the Library Company, and the Pennsylvania Hospital. Together with the Statehouse, the "Whitehall" of the new United States, these structures endowed the cityscape with a cosmopolitan dimension missing from William Penn's seventeenth-century country capital.[1] At the birth of the New Republic, Philadelphia seemed to fulfill a happy enlightenment ideal: the art of nature working in harmony with the arts of humanity to create the perfect eighteenth-century town.

The author thanks Tony Fels and Catherine E. Hutchins for their insightful comments.

Research for this essay was supported partially by an American Philosophical Society Research Grant and a Summer Stipend from the National Endowment for the Humanities.

But Philadelphia was also a changing city. By the 1780s its social life was marked by contrasts. Merchants thrived on trade with the West Indies and Spain, and a middling class of shopkeepers and artisans prospered on the fruits of economic development; at the same time, the city's rising population after the war included many poor laborers, unemployed immigrants, and their families. As merchants and artisan-entrepreneurs experimented with primitive forms of factory production, lesser artisans and journeymen adjusted to an unfamiliar system of wage labor. The city's most imposing structure was neither a church nor a government office, but the poor, or "bettering," house. America's leading port contained the seeds of its own transformation into a diverse and powerful industrial city.[2]

These changes revealed that despite the appearance of orderly transition the Revolution produced more than a change in government in the colonies. The new republican order was indeed something new, one in which the perceived harmonies of colonial culture and society were replaced by a dynamic and at times jarring combination of democratic politics, ethnic and religious pluralism, and economic development. Increasingly visible as well were new religious sects and movements. Of these, the most visible and in the long run the most successful was the network of revivalists known both in Great Britain, their country of origin, and in the United States as the Methodists.

The Methodist movement was founded in 1739 by English clerics John Wesley and his brother Charles as a series of evangelical "united societies" in affiliation with the Church of England. In short time, the "connexion" was composed of itinerant preachers who officiated over revival meetings, prayer groups called "classes" within each society, and thousands of members subscribing to a free-will theology expressed in popular hymns and the set of clear and concise social values codified in John Wesley's "General Rules." While the English Methodists remained a part of the Anglican Church until Wesley's death in 1791, the Methodists' evangelizing challenged many aspects of the Anglican world view. The Anglicans celebrated an enduring hierarchy of an educated clergy exercising authority from the top down. The Methodists celebrated the communalism and egalitarianism of the revival meeting where preachers were former followers and followers potential preachers, and authority appeared in many guises. Anglicans were stereotypically sophisticated, worldly, and urbane. Methodists were austere, spiritually serious, and rustic. And while Anglicanism celebrated an ideal of church and state united under enlightened rulers, American Methodists pressed for a new order in which state and church operated in separate spheres, the one to govern society, the other to act as its moral guide.[3]

In light of these differences, the rise of the Methodists in Philadelphia is an instructive case study. In it one finds cultural tensions between the old church and the new that signify some of the important differences between the old colonial world and the new republican one. And as the eighteenth century drew to a close, the Methodists themselves were to discover that the social dynamics empowering their movement also had the capacity to divide it into its separate parts, each representing a different group in the Republic's leading city. Allen, his life experience shaped by the combined power of social and religious change, was an important actor in the events that ensued.

The Philadelphia Methodist Society was founded in 1768 as a small gathering of evangelicals affiliated with St. Paul's Anglican Church. The group met near the waterfront in a sailmaking loft on Dock Street. Its organizers originated from the city's middling class of artisans and tradesmen and their wives, including recent Irish immigrant James Emerson, shoemaker John Hood, blockmaker Robert Fitzgerald, and chandler Miles Pennington. Shopkeeper Lambert Wilmer and his wife, Mary, joined shortly thereafter, along with Edward Evans, another Irish immigrant and shoemaker who had lived with the Moravians under Count Zinzendorf, probably at Bethlehem, Pennsylvania, and served as a Moravian traveling preacher in the 1740s. By 1769 the group had moved to the "Pott House" in Loxley Court at Arch and Fourth streets. Among the new adherents here was Lucy Watson, mother of John Fanning Watson, Philadelphia's first chronicler.[4]

The spiritual leader of this group was Thomas Webb, a British infantry officer and veteran of the Seven Years' War. Webb preached in uniform, a patch over one eye to cover a wound received at the Battle of Montmorency, and he spoke in a visionary, prophesying style that prompted more than one observer to describe him as a religious enthusiast. He was, however, just a more colorful version of the itinerant preachers who had been working through the colonies since the Great

Awakening, his own informal "circuit" stretching from Jamaica, Long Island, to Baltimore County, Maryland. In the same year that the Philadelphia group was organized, Webb assisted the New York Methodists in building their own chapel. This endeavor led to a financial shortfall for the New York group that was brought to John Wesley's attention in England. Since the English "united societies" were still defraying the cost of their own exertions in chapel building, Wesley was able to fund the New York chapel only partially. He was more successful in raising his itinerants' interest in traveling in the colonies, and in 1769 he sent Richard Boardman and Joseph Pilmore, the first pair of a series of licensed preachers, to establish formal links between the American Methodists and the English connection.[5]

Boardman and Pilmore arrived at Gloucester Point, New Jersey, in October 1769 and concentrated their efforts in Philadelphia and New York. In Philadelphia they were able almost immediately to purchase the shell of a building that had been erected at Fourth above Sassafras (now Race) Street by a small German Reformed society. The chapel, called St. George's, lacked galleries, a pulpit, and even floorboards. Nevertheless, its unadorned condition suited the Methodist plain-style aesthetic and gave the Philadelphia society a potentially permanent home in the city. The itinerants appointed gifted singer John, or "Johnny," Hood as class leader to assist the members in spiritual exercises and hymn singing. In September 1770 they secured a new deed for the chapel, guaranteeing its use for Wesleyan preachers. In November they did the same for the New York chapel.[6]

In 1771 Wesley sent the next pair of preachers, Francis Asbury and Richard Wright, to the colonies. Asbury preached his first American sermon at St. George's on October 28, 1771. By June 1772 the Wesleyan missionaries had expanded their circuit to include the city and county of Baltimore. And in 1773 Thomas Rankin, Wesley's chief assistant, arrived in the colonies. Other Wesleyan missionaries traveled to North America at their own or a benefactor's expense. The new preachers began to recruit Americans into Wesley's connection of itinerants and led religious revivals up and down the Atlantic seaboard. By May 1775 the Wesleyans were already holding their third annual conference in Philadelphia. At this meeting Rankin stationed nineteen itinerants, English and American, on ten circuits from New York to the Carolinas. The colonies now had an official Methodist population of more than 3,000. Philadelphia served as the movement's unofficial headquarters, although its society, not entirely established in a city of well-established churches, remained relatively small with fewer than 200 members.[7]

The expansion of Methodism in Philadelphia, furthermore, and the labors of the missionaries on many of their circuits were shortly interrupted by escalating conflicts between the colonies and Britain. In 1775 the revolutionary war began in New England. Independence was declared a little more than a year later, and in September 1777 the British seized Philadelphia. During the occupation the Royal Cavalry took the opportunity to convert St. George's, with its street-level floor, into a riding school. The Methodist Society met in private houses and at the Baptist chapel at LaGrange Place and Second Street. The center of American Methodism moved to Baltimore.[8]

The revolutionary war, it turned out, signaled the beginning of portentous changes for religious institutions that far outweighed these temporary inconveniences. In the minds of many of its creators, the New Republic was a *novus ordo seclorum*, a new order for the ages whose future lay in fulfilling the curtailed promise of the ancient republics of Greece and Rome. American republican government was to be free from the corrupting influences of a monarchy and aristocracy, a standing army, and an established church. Under these circumstances, the role of religious institutions was transformed. Religion was recognized as the chief source of moral standards for the Republic, and the separation of church and state was sought to protect religious freedom from the state as much as political freedom from the church. Outside New England, however, the formal power of churches was greatly diminished. Religious influence was to be exercised informally within the realm of the churches rather than in association with the state governments. Consequently, religious allegiance was made wholly voluntary.[9]

In Pennsylvania disestablishment had been a practical part of the Quaker Commonwealth's social order since its founding. At the same time, the differences among denominations in Pennsylvania were accentuated by their efforts to adapt to new political conditions and to create their own versions of the New Jerusalem in a Christian Rome. For the Anglicans the transition required a unifying of contrary trends. William White, soon to be the new Protestant Episcopal bishop of Pennsylvania, embraced both the principles of the Revolution and the ideal of social hierarchy. Recognizing that the Anglican church would not achieve dominance in America and that Philadelphia was not destined to be the episcopal seat of the New Republic, he and other Anglican leaders, in particular William Smith, Provost of the College of Philadelphia, nonetheless believed that an Anglican education would continue to be the appropriate training for American rulers. The church would accommodate itself to separation of church and state by adapting the old distinction between temporal and spiritual realms to the new principle of independent spheres of civil and ecclesiastical government. This change was a radical one for the church, which had maintained historically that temporal and religious institutions were both under the Crown's authority. But the new formulation had the merit of reflecting the Anglican love of order and balance.[10]

For Methodists, the separation of religious and political spheres appeared at first to pose greater problems. In order to establish their own independent sphere, American Methodists needed to break ties with the Anglican Church in England and America and the Wesleyan connection. The Wesleyan preachers accomplished these objectives by adopting revolutionary rhetoric as their own and declaring independence from all three institutions. In December 1784 Francis Asbury, with Wesley's approval, convened a preachers' conference in Baltimore, at which the itinerants elected to form their own connection, which they called the Methodist Episcopal Church (MEC), and chose Asbury and another English preacher, Thomas Coke, as their bishops. Wesley bridled at the Americans' use of the title "bishop," but the leader of the English movement appeared to accept the founding of the new MEC as an inevitable result of the war. By remaking themselves into a new denomination, the preachers moved in the direction of all future churches in the United States.[11]

Asbury and the American itinerants were now in a stronger position to promote the goals of Wesley's reform movement. Primary among these was the conversion of participants in religious meetings. The mixing of secular and spiritual spheres in Anglican worship appeared as an increasingly disorderly form of religious instruction to those persuaded by Methodist preaching. During the war, Daniel Newton, a New England servant living in Philadelphia with Continental Congressman Artemus Ward, took the opportunity away from his relatively homogeneous native region to experience the remarkable variety of Sunday services held in the city, including one officiated at Christ Church by the Reverend William White. Here he observed a congregation more interested in worldly than otherworldly matters: "the noise and bustle of the great [and] the rich and the objects that [came] in my view took up my attention soo I did not hear but little of what he [White] read," Newton reported, "for he read his Sermon very fast." By contrast, a Methodist revival the same day, even in a hot and overcrowded private room, appeared to Newton the epitome of orderliness, focusing almost entirely as it did on the subjects of conversion and salvation: "the Preacher took his text . . . [from] these words of Christ—I am the door—his Prayer had apperated strongly on me it seeme to Come from his heart." Newton concluded: "I think my future state never lay on my mind soo before."[12]

The Methodists also continued to promote Wesley's teaching, derived from earlier pietistic movements and codified in the "General Rules," that the holy life was best expressed in the eschewal of worldly wealth and power. Methodists were to avoid "evil in every kind," especially blaspheming, drunkenness, fighting, and the wearing of ostentatious apparel—attributes, that is, of laboring-class culture or imitation of upper-class extravagance. They were to shun unethical or excessively risky business enterprises. And Methodists were also to do good works in the form of giving to the poor, caring for the sick and imprisoned, participating in divine worship and family prayer, and attending to the reading of scriptures and periodic fasting, this last injunction reflecting Wesley's own personal asceticism.[13]

Many Methodists viewed the American seaports, the Republic's chief economic and political centers, as less than ideal locations for the expansion of this austere evangelicalism. Bishop Asbury was especially wary of Pennsylvania's capital city. "O Philadelphia!" he lamented on one occasion, "I have had very little faith for that city." Here Asbury found a "general contempt of the Sabbath; the constant noise of carriages; . . . a perpetual disturbance of worshipping assemblies." Worse yet, the glory of the city hid the covetousness, religious indifference, and threat of mob violence that Asbury believed lay beneath its sophisticated veneer. In Philadelphia Asbury felt "shut up in Sodom." Far more to his liking were the agrarian hinterlands, where pious farmers, wives, children, and servants might practice their religious faith unimpeded by corrupting urban influences.[14]

For many middling- and laboring-class Americans, however, Philadelphia represented an escape from the old order: from engrossing landlords in Ireland, from paternal authority in the rural countryside, and especially from the most notorious of colonial institutions, slavery. Since an important Methodist ambition was to provide the religious means to social uplift for the poor and unchurched, these groups were the typical audience sought out by Philadelphia's Methodist preachers and lay leaders. Consequently, as the society attempted to fulfill its missionary mandate, the complexities of postwar social change, in particular the reordering of racial and social class relations, were played out in their church, producing not one, but two divides by the end of the century.

In many respects Richard Allen, the former slave, was a typical Methodist. Born on Benjamin Chew's Dover, Delaware, plantation, he was sold, while still a boy, with his family to a neighboring small planter named Stokeley Sturgis. Sturgis was a benevolent master, but financial difficulties forced the resale of the family with the exception of Allen, now seventeen years old, and his younger brother. The event appears to have triggered a spiritual crisis for the two boys who approached Sturgis around this time for permission to attend a local Methodist class meeting. Although an "unconverted man," Sturgis complied, as had many slaveholders in the area. Allen later recalled that slaves were among the Methodists' "greatest support" in Delaware, and they frequently worked overtime in their garden allotments to raise money for the Methodist preachers as well as themselves. Likewise, Allen and his brother initiated a self-imposed, Methodist-inspired work regimen to reverse the impression among many other slaveholders that religion made slaves "worse servants": "We always continued to keep our crops more forward than our neighbors," Allen recollected; "At length our master said he was convinced that religion made slaves better not worse, and often boasted of his slaves for their honesty and industry." Ultimately, Sturgis was prompted by the preaching of Freeborn Garrettson, an antislavery advocate and a Methodist itinerant, to offer Allen and his brother the opportunity to purchase their freedom for £60 in specie or $2,000 in Continental currency. Allen was manumitted officially on January 25, 1780, before his twentieth birthday. Three and a half years later he was able to pay his part of the manumission price in full from his earnings as an itinerant laborer.[15]

The anti-Methodist slaveholders in Delaware were right: religion had made Allen a worse servant. His association with the Methodists led directly to his freedom and the remarkable change in social status that followed. Combining day labor and small trading with preaching, Allen continued to travel through Delaware, New Jersey, Pennsylvania, and Maryland, subsidized in part by the Methodist Society in Baltimore where he was a member by 1785. He appears to have spoken to mixed audiences of whites and blacks alike. In winter 1786 he began working in the vicinity of Philadelphia, and in February, at the behest of the Methodist elder, the presiding senior preacher of the Philadelphia circuit, Allen moved into the city itself.[16]

Here he "soon saw a large field open in seeking and instructing [his] African brethren," few of whom attended the city's many churches. Allen quickly recognized the potential for what historian Gary Nash has described as the forging of a strong black community in Philadelphia. In the belief that a religious society was the best context for accomplishing this goal, Allen organized a black class in association with St. George's. He conceived the idea, furthermore, of a separate black Methodist congregation. This radical proposal was unprecedented in Philadelphia and was rejected summarily by the presiding elder.[17]

A year later Allen chose instead to join with other free blacks to found the Free African Society (FAS). Chartered as a mutual-aid organization for the support of the city's indigent black population, the FAS also aimed to bring blacks together to defend themselves against the sharper barbs of racism and, like the Methodists, to live "an orderly and sober life." As the Philadelphia society wrote to a similar group in Boston: "[Free blacks ought] to lay aside all superfluity of naughtiness, especially gaming and feasting. . . . [I]t is this practise of ours that enables our enemies to declare that we are not fit for freedom." By abandoning their slave identity and the attributes of laboring-class culture shared with lower-class whites, free blacks, the FAS argued, could stand on equal footing with other reform-minded citizens in Philadelphia. In addition, they would see the day when the "captivity [of the African race] shall cease, and buying and selling mankind have an end."[18]

Allen in the meantime continued to maintain his allegiance to the Philadelphia Methodist Society, now in the process of transition. According to John Fanning Watson, St. George's at the end of the war was "a dreary, cold-looking place," heated in winter by a leaky stovepipe from which "the smoke would frequently issue, and fill the house." The society had installed a new floor and erected a box pulpit, "a square thing not unlike a watch box, with the top sawed off," for the use of stationed preachers. The chapel soon saw the addition of a new pulpit and a "frame-step" altar similar to that at St. Paul's. Membership also rose substantially in the revivals of the 1780s. When it began to fall again at the end of the decade, Asbury persuaded a small group to accept appointment as trustees for incorporation. In 1790 construction began on a second chapel in Southwark on land supplied by shipbuilder John Petherbridge. Like the successful Fell's Point society in Baltimore, the new society at Ebenezer Chapel was in the heart of the mariners' district, a source of many Methodist converts.[19]

By 1791 Asbury's efforts paid off as the society experienced another upswing. In this year 290 Methodists were meeting in nine white and two black classes, one of them probably Allen's, an increase of more than 60 members from the previous year. Perhaps inspired by this rise in numbers or tired of their drafty quarters, the trustees now initiated a series of extensive renovations at St. George's. The first of these was the redesigning of the chapel's interior. In winter and spring 1792 Hugh Smith and Richard Moseley, carpenters and members, constructed galleries on opposite sides of the hall. The work entailed the addition of stairs, columns, friezework, and 538 feet of seating. By late May, Smith and Moseley had completed the additions "in a plane, neet, maner" as promised. The reconstructed interior was freshly painted in the fall. By December 1794 St. George's had improved sufficiently in appearance for John Poor, the principal of the Young Ladies' Academy, to choose it as the setting for his school's commencement, attended by members of Congress and "the principal Ladies and Gentlemen of the City."[20]

Philadelphia also regained some of the prominence among Methodists that it had lost to Baltimore during the revolutionary war. John Dickins moved the MEC book business to the city in the early 1790s. Another located preacher, Thomas Haskins, served as editor of Asbury's journals. By 1797 the general conference of the church recognized the credit worthiness of the Philadelphia members by appointing Haskins and eight other trustees as managers of the Chartered Fund, a pension plan for indigent preachers and their families.[21]

For other reasons the Philadelphia society was different from its prewar predecessor. Unlike the small, relatively homogeneous gathering of the early 1770s, the society was now racially and socially heterogeneous, including both wealthier members and poorer ones. The trustees were chiefly businessmen and professionals. Jacob Baker was a partner in the merchant firm Baker and Comegys on North Front Street. Josiah Lusby divided his time between shopkeeping and a medical practice on North Second Street. Samuel Harvey ran the wholesaling hardware firm Harvey and Worth on Front Street. John Hewson was increasingly renowned as an innovative calico printer. His wife, Zibia Smallwood Hewson, and four daughters, also Methodists, participated in an exhibit of textile printing in the July 1788 Federal Procession. Other leading members of the society were former itinerants now engaged in commerce. Dickins entered the book trade to support his work as the MEC book agent. Haskins had trained as a lawyer in Caroline County, Maryland, and taught at the Methodist academy, Cokesbury College. He now resided on Branch Street where he and his wife, Martha Potts of the Pennsylvania iron-foundry family, lived off the profits of his wholesale grocery business. Another located preacher, Daniel Ruff, opened a shoe warehouse on North Second Street, two doors from Lusby.[22]

Likewise at Ebenezer, founding member Robert Fitzgerald was now "a man of ample means." He was joined by James Doughty, a relatively new but also upwardly mobile member with an expanding shipwright and lumber business in Southwark. Together with John Hood, still a shoemaker, Lambert Wilmer, prospering as a flour merchant, and the society's trustees, these men represented the Methodist elite in Philadelphia, participating successfully in interstate trade and nascent forms of industrial production.[23]

By contrast, the other important offices of the society continued to be filled from the city's artisan ranks. Prominent among the class leaders was Hugh Smith, one of the builders of St. George's galleries. Smith was an ardent follower of Benjamin Abbott, a charismatic preacher and a common figure at St. George's in the 1790s. Other class leaders included shoemakers William Blair and John Dennis, cordwainers William Pigeon and Manley Smallwood, tailors Reiner Gilbert and Joseph Elton, and cabinetmaker Pennel Beale. Among the few leaders who were not artisans was Wilmer, who appears to have preferred the office of leader to trustee, and Henry Manley, a shoe dealer living on High Street. Trustees Hood and Doughty also served as class leaders; leaders Smith and Manley also served as trustees. Multiple officeholding was the exception, however, rather than the rule.[24]

The majority of the rest of the Philadelphia Methodist men, furthermore, like their class leaders, were shopkeepers and artisans or unskilled laborers. In 1794, the earliest year for which membership records survive, 354 men and women belonged to the society as a whole. Of the white men in the society, 23 percent of those whose occupations can be identified made their livings as shopkeepers and merchants of varying status; more than twice that proportion, 53 percent, were artisans. Approximately 40 percent of the comparable population in the city in 1798 were merchants, professionals, and government employees, and 42 percent were artisans; hence, the Methodist Society attracted fewer than the average number of merchants and more than the average number of mechanics and tradesmen. Two-thirds of the total number, furthermore, appear in neither the city directories nor tax assessments, indicating that most of Philadelphia's male Methodists were young, geographically mobile, or of the city's so-called "lower sort."[25]

Underlying the increasing social contrasts in the society was a remarkable mixture of men and women and of ethnic and racial groups. Although men dominated the church's offices, Mary Wilmer, Lambert's wife, led a female class in the mid 1790s. In 1794, 60 percent of the society's rank and file were female. Many, whether single or married, joined on their own, independent of their parents or husbands. In Philadelphia as elsewhere, men were frequently drawn to Methodism and participation in class meetings by the examples of their sisters, wives, and daughters. The greatest variety in the society appears in its ethnic groups. The majority of Philadelphia Methodists were Anglo-Americans, with names like Armstrong, Ash, Fuller, Gray, Johnson, Palmer, Parker, and Smith. But Scottish, Welsh, Irish, and German patronymics appear, including Brodie, Ferguson, and Ross; Jones and Williams; Doughty, Kelly, McFarlen, and McGee; Kramer, Shreider, and Weiss. And about an eighth of the members were black, bearing the surnames of liberated slaves: Barbary, Boss, Gibbs, Green, Lux, and Solomon.[26]

Thus, in many respects the Philadelphia Methodists were accomplishing their missionary goals in the early and mid 1790s. The popularity of their church attested to the power of Methodist preaching and the degree to which the "General Rules" served as a successful guide to daily living for one portion of the city's laboring folk. At the same time, as a part of a movement whose success depended on popular support rather than a secure hierarchy, like the Anglicans, or ethnic consensus, like many of Pennsylvania's German churches, the Methodists had to come to terms with their diversity and the bigger question: who controlled the movement in Philadelphia?

Tensions over the issue first emerged in a crisis between several of the trustees and the more prominent black members, Allen and other Methodists associated with the FAS. By the early 1790s, the FAS had undergone its own transformation. The founders, men of varying religious persuasions, had initially decided against a denominational affiliation for the society. By 1789, however, the influence of Quaker supporters and members was increasingly strong. When the society voted for a moment of silence at the commencement of meetings, Allen and others, apparently disappointed by the drift away from evangelicalism, left the group.[27]

Despite his departure, Allen continued to associate with like-minded Free Africans, in particular fellow black Methodists Absalom Jones, William White, and Dorus Jennings. In 1791 Allen was drawn back into FAS affairs when the society voted against the advice of the Friends but with the support of Benjamin Rush, a leading antislavery advocate, to build an independent or "union" African Church. In February 1792 the Free Africans purchased two lots for the church on Fifth Street below the Statehouse, and in March they began to circulate subscription papers to help defray the cost of construction.[28]

The preachers and trustees at St. George's, apparently fearing that the new union church would draw off part, perhaps most, of the African Methodists, greeted the Free Africans' move toward religious autonomy with little enthusiasm. At the same time, the behavior of the Methodist Society's leadership served only to confirm the Free Africans' argument in favor of a separate church. First, as the numbers of blacks in the society increased, they were segregated into separate sections within the chapel. Second, the raising of the galleries only accelerated the move toward separate seating. On or near the day that the renovated building reopened, probably in early June 1792, Allen, Jones, and several of the other Methodist Free Africans were directed by the church's sexton to sit in the new galleries, which they did willingly. In short time, however, they were forcibly interrupted in the middle of prayer by Manley and another trustee who insisted that they move to yet another section of the hall. Profoundly disturbed by this sudden display of white dominance, the FAS members walked out of the church. "This raised a great excitement and inquiry among the citizens," Allen noted, "in so much that I believe [the trustees] were ashamed of their conduct."[29]

Undeterred, in many respects compelled, by white opposition and the troubles at the Methodist Society, the FAS initiated construction on their church in March 1793 with the financial assistance of Welsh immigrant and entrepreneur John Nicholson, a Rush associate. At this point, the FAS also decided that their church would be best served by a denominational identity. The matter of religious affiliation was then put to a vote. According to Allen, only two members, Jones and he, favored the Methodists; the rest, including now former Methodists White and Jennings, favored the Protestant Episcopal Church. The completion of St. Thomas's, as the new African church was called, was delayed for another year by the yellow fever epidemic of 1793. It opened finally to a large congregation in July 1794 and applied shortly thereafter for association with the Protestant Episcopal Church. Absalom Jones, who had by this time also quit the Methodists, was ordained as the first minister.[30]

The choice of the Protestant Episcopal Church was not a surprising one. The Anglicans had long sought to convert blacks as part of their missionary goals in North America. The minister at the evangelically inclined St. Paul's, furthermore, was former Methodist itinerant Joseph Pilmore. Between 1789 and 1794, Pilmore officiated at the marriages of more than thirty black couples at St. Paul's, an indication of his high standing in the black community and the good will of the Anglicans in general.[31]

In the long run, however, the Anglican mission to blacks in the New Republic was undermined by the same problems that had hurt the church's mission in the colonies—namely, an emphasis on social duty and order that left unaddressed the larger question of how blacks were to cope with both slavery and freedom. The lengthy discourse delivered by Anglican minister Samuel Magaw at the inaugural ceremonies at St. Thomas's delineated this emphasis. "Remember your former condition," Magaw cautioned his audience. "Pride was not made for man, in any, even the highest stations in life; much less for persons who have just emerged from the lowest." According to the Anglicans, the new African Protestants were to abandon their pagan condition for suitable participation in Christian society. Religion's role was as an educating rather than transforming agent.[32]

By contrast, Methodist preaching, focusing on the egalitarian and life-changing experience of conversion, provided one means by which blacks could interpret and to some extent control their social experience, in particular the complexities of the transition from slavery to freedom. Allen believed that Methodism spoke to the condition of slaves and free blacks alike. "I was confident," he wrote, "that there was no religious sect or denomination would suit the capacity of the colored people as well as the Methodist; for the plain and simple gospel suits best for any people; for the unlearned can understand, and the learned are sure to understand." The Methodists were successful in raising a black following, Allen believed, because they had a "plain doctrine," and "a good discipline." Allen's strong antislavery convictions, indeed, were backed by the church's public antislavery position, spelled out in the MEC discipline of 1784. Although the church's policy was soon modified under pressure from slaveholding Methodists, many followers and listeners, like Allen's own former master, had freed at least some of their slaves on the basis of Methodist preaching.[33]

After the confrontation between the Free Africans and the trustees at St. George's, Allen engaged in an ongoing debate with presiding elder Robert McClaskey over the legitimacy of a separate black Methodist church. By spring 1794, with competition from St. Thomas's pending, Allen was finally able to persuade the preachers and the officers of the Philadelphia society of the utility of his idea. He and another former FAS member, John Morris, then met with other black Methodists to establish the guidelines for a congregation. The group moved an empty blacksmith's shop to a previously purchased site on Sixth Street near Southwark to serve as temporary quarters. The new African Methodist Episcopal chapel, called Bethel, opened on June 29, 1794. The trustees at Bethel accepted the discipline and authority of the MEC, including the presence of white itinerants and initially of white class leaders. At the same time, the "African" identity of the church was clear in its 1796 charter of incorporation. The church was to be run by a board of black trustees. Only "Africans and descendants of the African race" would be admitted as members. The white stationed preacher was to license black exhorters and local preachers, to defer to the opinion of black officers in the church's disciplinary affairs, and to recommend qualified candidates for ordination in the MEC. By contrast, the articles of association for St. Thomas's, drawn up in the same year, made no reference to race.[34]

Despite their original objections to these remarkable developments, the MEC and white Methodists in Philadelphia had soon to recognize two important points. One was the extent to which Bethel was fulfilling the Methodist goal of bringing the gospel to the poor. The other was that Bethel was the fastest-growing Methodist congregation in the city. The total number of members in the Philadelphia society rose steadily in the 1790s, from 432 in 1795, to 543 in 1797, to 622 in 1799. Bethel's first congregation included 32 adherents. Few of the blacks belonging to St. George's in spring 1794 joined Allen's maverick church, and Bethel's numbers compared poorly with St. Thomas's. Within a year, however, the black Methodist population in Philadelphia had begun a proportionately steadier rise than its parent church, from 121 members in 1795, to 163 in 1797, to 211 in 1799. Black members comprised 28 percent of the society in 1795, 30 percent in 1797, and 34 percent in 1799. The Methodists opened a second black chapel, called Zoar, in the Northern Liberties in 1796, but its adherents accounted for a small proportion of Philadelphia's African Methodists, most of whom were now attending worship at Bethel.[35]

By 1800 revivals were drawing listeners to *all* the Methodist churches in the city. In the following year, more than 250 new members joined the white chapels, raising the total number of adherents at St. George's and Ebenezer to 670 by spring 1801. The number of black Methodists, chiefly at Bethel, rose to 448. Altogether, more than 1,100 Methodists were now living in Philadelphia.[36]

Audiences were attracted to the Methodist churches for many reasons. Not the least of these was the hymn singing. According to Watson, Methodist hymns were sung in a "quicker and more animated style . . . than prevailed in the slower, heavier cadence of the other churches of the city." They emphasized typically the evangelical experience, often in words that encouraged a personal interpretation for listeners of the lower sort, white and black, as in these verses published in a Philadelphia hymnbook:

Come, ye sinners, poor and needy,
Weak and wounded, sick and sore,
Jesus stands ready to save you,
Full of pity, love, and pow'r
He is able,
He is willing, doubt no more.

Other attenders at the Methodist churches came to hear and sometimes to challenge the preachers visiting or stationed on the Philadelphia circuit. These ranged from Benjamin Abbott, Hugh Smith's mentor, a local preacher in the charismatic tradition, to the more reticent John Dickins, the MEC book agent until his death in the yellow fever epidemic of 1798; to his successor, Ezekiel Cooper, an antislavery advocate with literary ambitions whom Asbury chastised for his enjoyment of city life; to Asbury himself, now more than fifty years old, a relentless traveler and the single most important figure for the expansion and unity of American Methodism, which had grown now to comprise a network of circuits and societies stretching from New England to Georgia and Tennessee.[37]

Philadelphia Methodists continued to be a part of this expansive, inclusive denomination. The elite at the Philadelphia society, however, viewed the rising popularity of their church with some alarm. Twenty-five years removed from Thomas Webb's influence, they failed to see how the new converts' emotional, sometimes ecstatic, responses to revivals were guides to social improvement, particularly since revival behavior was so often class specific—that is, associated with groups who appeared not to be rising, such as poor artisans, mariners, day laborers, and blacks. Lucy Watson observed that Methodism at this time became "extravagant & noisy—by force of cherished animal spirits." Her son recalled that she tolerated the new members in a spirit of "meekness & patience."[38]

The wealthier members were also accustomed to running the Methodist society, from receiving and boarding itinerants at their homes, to subsidizing the MEC's book business, to arranging and in some cases paying for the extensive renovations at St. George's and the building of Ebenezer. The building at St. George's, furthermore, had continued after 1797, with the replacing of the roof, the raising of the church's sills, the laying of new curbstones, and the addition of delicate moldings and newels to the chapel's windows and banisters. At the end of the decade the church was still paying for these expenses with public subscriptions, Sunday and weekly class collections, and donations and loans made by individual members. Prominent among the latter were Thomas Haskins, Jacob Baker, and a new member, merchant Caleb North.[39]

By autumn 1800 it was apparent that all was not well at the society as its preachers, officers, and members became embroiled in their second crisis in eight years. The new conflict arose ostensibly over stationed preacher Lawrence McCombs's dismissal of several class leaders, namely, Hugh Smith, David Lake, and a new member, William Sturgis, who disagreed with the preacher over a minor incident. McCombs replaced the leaders with five new appointees, including North, none of whom had held the office before. The dismissed leaders, in keeping with the MEC discipline, turned to the presiding elder, Joseph Everett, for a judgment. In Everett's opinion the three petitioners had been removed unjustly from their offices. He promptly reappointed Smith, Lake, and Sturgis. When McCombs, described later as a man with "a taste for polemic theology," refused to comply with the decision, Everett replaced him with a new stationed preacher, Richard Sneath.[40]

The society then rapidly disintegrated into two contending factions, the one supporting McCombs's action and the other Everett's decision. Mediating between the two groups was Ezekiel Cooper, the new book agent. Cooper attempted to resolve the groups' differences. He soon discovered, however, that the quarrel was over more than the rules in the MEC discipline. He reluctantly but sharply characterized the two factions as distinct social interests, the "wealthy and respectable" on the one hand and those they called the "poor and ignorant" on the other.[41]

On preacher McCombs's side were the "wealthy" party comprised of Thomas Haskins, newly located preacher Charles Cavender, founding members Lambert Wilmer and John Hood, Jacob Baker, John Hewson, and Samuel Harvey at St. George's and James Doughty at the Ebenezer chapel. Opposing McCombs were the "poor," including Hugh Smith and David Lake, and the class leaders now appointed to office by Sneath, among them Manley Smallwood, William Pigeon, and John Petherbridge. The dispute, the cause of which was now long forgotten, became, in Cooper's words, a conflict over which side was to be supported, "wealth and worldly respectability on the one side, or the majority on the other?" Worse yet in Cooper's opinion, the wealthy party "endeavored to make it be believed that [the winter revival] was a delusion."[42]

By spring 1801 Haskins and Cavender's group had made up their minds about their place in the ever-growing Methodist movement. When their early June appeal to the annual conference of preachers in Philadelphia fell on deaf ears, they prepared hastily but resolutely to leave not only St. George's but also the MEC. Haskins wrote to the new stationed itinerants with indignant emphases, declining reappointment as a local preacher: "For me to *exercise* any Official function in the Methodist Churches in *Philadelphia in the present Situation of its affairs*," he explained, "would be repugnant to those feelings, as well as a violation of that sense of propriety & duty which ought to activate every upright honest Man, *Sacrifices* which your enlightened & feeling hearts cannot expect me to make." A few days later he and his aggrieved associates resigned their memberships.[43]

To make up for the loss of the chapel building they had been renovating for so many years, the seceding group secured for their use part of the Academy of Philadelphia a block and a half south of St. George's. The new church was comprised of the socially prominent members of the Philadelphia society, including Wilmer and Hood, who had been Methodists for more than thirty years. Joining them were merchants and entrepreneurs Doughty, Hewson, North, and Haskins, thirty-two other men, and forty-four women. In August they held their own small conference to found the so-called Academy Church, which they characterized optimistically as part of a new connection of Methodist "United Societies." Addressing their main grievance in their new constitution, the group provided that the "private members" of the church were empowered to admit new congregants. The church's trustees and longstanding members were to make all the major decisions.[44]

In short, the Academy Church abandoned the missionary goals of the Methodist movement in which a brotherhood of preachers labored for the conversion and social betterment of their followers. Still subscribing to this effort were the many adherents remaining at the Philadelphia society, now a church of small artisans, shopkeepers, and unskilled laborers. Two-thirds of the society, nearly 400 in number, were women. The group was led by stationed preacher Ezekiel Cooper and the remaining trustees, namely, Hugh Smith, David Lake, John Dennis, and Alexander Cook. Smith continued to serve as the in-house carpenter for the society. Cook, a chandler living next door to St. George's, supplied the chapel with its lighting. Lake and Dennis, both shoemakers, belonged to an occupational group represented heavily among city-dwelling Methodists. Together with Cooper, these trustees counteracted the impression, widely held among the Academy group and many preachers, that their "poverty, . . . want of skill in management, [and] . . . small influence among those who were able to contribute to [their] relief" would lead to the mortgaging of the chapel building. By November 1801 they had begun to pay off the society's substantial debts.[45]

Remaining also were the African Methodists at Bethel and Zoar. The "African" chapels were linked in another way with the "poor" party at St. George's. Smith and Lake had been leaders of several black classes before the founding of Bethel. William Sturgis, the third leader contesting McCombs's authority, was a class leader at Zoar. Signifying the importance of geographical mobility and ties between whites and blacks in the Methodist movement, Sturgis was from the Methodist branch of the Delaware family that had once owned Richard Allen.[46]

Slavery, wrote Allen in his memoir, "is a bitter pill." In the early nineteenth century it became the main divisive issue in the Methodist movement, quickly overshadowing crises at local churches.[47] But the events in Philadelphia explain in part why divisions in the church came about. In short, the more expansive the Methodist movement became the more likely it was to experience the same racial and social strains as the nation itself and at the same time to reflect the potentially democratic forces set loose by the revolutionary war.

Beginning as a small group of evangelicals in connection with John Wesley, the Philadelphia Methodists had gone on to survive the war, successfully adapting to the requirements of separation of church and state and offering a clear alternative to the colonial churches. Much of their success rested on the appeal of Methodist ideology, supported by a missionary system of traveling preachers. The itinerants promoted especially the belief that religious experience was a prerequisite for social happiness, a conviction that was to have a lasting impact on antebellum America.

Different Methodists, however, interpreted this belief in different ways. For African Methodists conversion represented the route to ethnic solidarity. For merchants and artisan-entrepreneurs, who by chance and choice of occupation were able to reap the benefits of Philadelphia's booming economy, it was the way to wealth. And for the remaining middling and laboring classes, like the African Methodists, the connection between religious experience and social betterment was the route to stability in an unstable working world. In the revival meeting religious experience was the reward to the "poor and needy" who were also rigorous believers.

By 1800 a new dimension had been added to Philadelphia's already rich religious landscape. The Methodists had transformed St. George's into a graceful chapel in a city of graceful chapels. Their society was composed of four thriving congregations of more than 1,000 members, white and black. The main African chapel soon became a leading influence on race relations. From obscure beginnings the Methodist church had become one of Philadelphia's most important cultural institutions.

---

[1] Henry F. May, *The Enlightenment in America* (Oxford and New York: Oxford University Press, 1976), pp. 197–222; J. Thomas Scharf and Thompson Westcott, *History of Philadelphia, 1609–1884*, 3 vols. (Philadelphia: L. H. Everts, 1884), 2:1229–1449; Beatrice B. Garvan, *Federal Philadelphia, 1785–1825: The Athens of the Western World* (Philadelphia: Philadelphia Museum of Art, 1987); Richard G. Miller, "The Federal City, 1783–1800," in *Philadelphia: A Three-Hundred Year History*, ed. Russell F. Weigley (New York: W. W. Norton, 1982), pp. 172–75.

[2] Thomas M. Doerflinger, *A Vigorous Spirit of Enterprise: Merchants and Economic Development in Revolutionary Philadelphia* (Chapel Hill: University of North Carolina Press, 1986), pp. 107–16; Gary B. Nash, *The Urban Crucible: Social Change, Political Consciousness, and the Origins of the American Revolution* (Cambridge: Harvard University Press, 1979), chap. 12; Gary B. Nash, "Forging Freedom: The Emancipation Experience in the Northern Seaports, 1775–1820," in *Race, Class, and Politics: Essays on American Colonial and Revolutionary Society* (Urbana: University of Illinois Press, 1986), pp. 283–321; Scharf and Westcott, *History of Philadelphia*, 3:2228–34; Julius Rubin, "Urban Growth and Regional Development," in *The Growth of the Seaport Cities, 1790–1825*, ed. David T. Gilchrist (Charlottesville: University Press of Virginia, 1967), pp. 3–21.

[3] Anthony Armstrong, *The Church of England, the Methodists, and Society, 1700–1850* (Totowa, N.J.: Rowman and Littlefield, 1973), pp. 59–61; Rupert E. Davies, Introduction to John Wesley, *The Works*, vol. 9, *The Methodist Societies: History, Nature, and Design* (Nashville: Abingdon Press, 1989), pp. 1–29. The contrast between the Anglicans and their other evangelical competitors, the Baptists, is described in Rhys Isaac, *The Transformation of Virginia, 1740–1790* (Chapel Hill: University of North Carolina Press, 1982), esp. pp. 161–205. See also May, *Enlightenment*, pp. 66–87; Patricia U. Bonomi, *Under the Cope of Heaven: Religion, Society, and Politics in Colonial America* (New York and Oxford: Oxford University Press, 1986), pp. 41–61.

[4] Frank Baker, *From Wesley to Asbury: Studies in Early American Methodism* (Durham, N.C.: Duke University Press, 1976), pp. 33–34; John Lednum, *A History of the Rise of Methodism in America* (Philadelphia: By the author, 1859), pp. 41–48; Frank Baker, "Edward Evans, Founding Philadelphia Methodist," *Methodist History* 14, no. 1 (October 1975): 56–69; Abraham Ritter, *History of the Moravian Church in Philadelphia* (Philadelphia: Hayes and Zell, 1857), pp. 42, 70–71. John Fanning

Watson, Preface to Lucy Watson, "Experience and Incidents in the Life of Mrs. Watson," [n.d.], Lucy Fanning Watson Papers, Joseph Downs Collection of Manuscripts and Printed Ephemera, Winterthur Library, Winterthur, Del.

[5] Another Wesleyan lay preacher, Robert Strawbridge, traveled mainly in Maryland; see Baker, *From Wesley to Asbury*, pp. 53–57, 73–85. Frank Baker, "Early American Methodism: A Key Document," *Methodist History* 8, no. 2 (January 1965): 3–15.

[6] Joseph Pilmore, *The Journal of Joseph Pilmore, Methodist Itinerant*, ed. Frederick E. Maser and Howard T. Maag (Philadelphia: Message Publishing Co., 1969), pp. 27–28; Lednum, *History of the Rise*, pp. 45–46; John Fanning Watson, *Annals of Philadelphia and Pennsylvania in the Olden Time*, 2 vols. (Philadelphia: Whiting and Thomas, 1856), 1:456–58; St. George's Methodist Episcopal Church deeds, June 14, September 11, 1770, photostats, Church Records, Old St. George's Historical Society, Philadelphia (hereafter cited as OSGHS); J. B. Wakeley, *Lost Chapters Recovered from the Early History of American Methodism* (New York: Carlton and Porter, 1858), pp. 58–63.

[7] Baker, *From Wesley to Asbury*, pp. 90–98; Methodist Episcopal Church, *Minutes of the Methodist Conferences, Annually Held in America from 1773 to 1794, Inclusive* (Philadelphia: Henry Tuckniss, 1795), p. 14; Francis Asbury, *The Journal and Letters*, ed. Elmer T. Clark, Manning Potts, and Jacob S. Payton, vol. 1 (Nashville: Abingdon Press, 1958), p. 7n.

[8] Watson, *Annals*, 1:456; *History of Ebenezer Methodist Episcopal Church of Southwark, Philadelphia* (Philadelphia: J. B. Lippincott Co., 1890), p. 14. On the war years, see Harry M. Tinkcom, "The Revolutionary City, 1765–1783," in Weigley, *Philadelphia*, pp. 109–54. The preachers' conference moved to Baltimore in 1776. See Methodist Episcopal Church, *Minutes . . . 1773 to 1794*, p. 18.

[9] Bernard Bailyn, *The Ideological Origins of the American Revolution* (Cambridge: Harvard University Press, Belknap Press, 1967), pp. 246–72; Gordon S. Wood, *The Creation of the American Republic, 1776–1787* (Chapel Hill: University of North Carolina Press, 1969), pp. 48–53; Sydney E. Ahlstrom, *A Religious History of the American People* (New Haven: Yale University Press, 1972), pp. 368–79.

[10] J. William Frost, "Pennsylvania Institutes Religious Liberty, 1682–1860," *Pennsylvania Magazine of History and Biography* 112, no. 3 (July 1988): 323–38; May, *Enlightenment*, pp. 204–5; Frederick V. Mills, Sr., *Bishops by Ballot: An Eighteenth-Century Ecclesiastical Revolution* (New York: Oxford University Press, 1978), pp. 288–307; John Frederick Woolverton, *Colonial Anglicanism in North America* (Detroit: Wayne State University Press, 1984), pp. 30, 207–19.

[11] Baker, *From Wesley to Asbury*, pp. 100–131, 162–82; John Wesley, *The Letters*, ed. John Telford, vol. 8 (London: Epworth Press, 1931), pp. 90–91; Methodist Episcopal Church, *Minutes of Several Conversations between the Rev. Thomas Coke, LL.D., the Rev. Francis Asbury and Others . . . in the Year 1784* (1785; reprint, Rutland, Vt.: Academy Books, 1979).

[12] November 5, 1780, Daniel Newton, notebook 1780–81, New-York Historical Society. The author thanks Steven Rosswurm for this valuable source.

[13] John Wesley, "The Nature, Design, and General Rules," in Wesley, *Works*, 9:69–73.

[14] Asbury, *Journal and Letters*, 2:132, 300.

[15] Richard Allen, *The Life Experience and Gospel Labours . . .* (Nashville: Abingdon Press, 1960), pp. 29–30, 16, 17; Gary B. Nash, "New Light on Richard Allen: The Early Years of Freedom," *William and Mary Quarterly*, 3d ser., 46, no. 2 (April

1989): 334–36 (Allen's freedom certificate is reproduced on p. 338). For a recent account of Allen's life and times, see Barbara Clark Smith, *After the Revolution: The Smithsonian History of Everyday Life in the Eighteenth Century* (New York: Pantheon Books and National Museum of American History, 1985), pp. 136–86. At the time of his death in 1787, Sturgis still owned a black woman and three children (Stockley Sturgis inventory, May 17, 1787, Kent Co. Wills, vol. A49, pp. 109–10, Hall of Records, Dover, Del.).

[16] Allen, *Life Experience*, pp. 17–23.

[17] Allen, *Life Experience*, pp. 23–25; Gary B. Nash, *Forging Freedom: The Formation of Philadelphia's Black Community, 1720–1840* (Cambridge: Harvard University Press, 1988), p. 7.

[18] Free African Society, "Minutes," in *Annals of the First African Church*, ed. William Douglass (Philadelphia: King and Baird, 1862), pp. 15, 31–32.

[19] Watson, *Annals*, 1:456. See account for St. George's in Thomas Armat ledger, April 12, 1781, Armat Section, Loudoun Papers, Historical Society of Pennsylvania, Philadelphia (hereafter cited as HSP). The new altar and pulpit are described in Fred Pierce Corson, "St. George's Church: The Cradle of American Methodism," in *Historic Philadelphia: From the Founding until the Early Nineteenth Century . . .* , Transactions of the American Philosophical Society, n.s., 43, pt. 1 (1953; reprint, Philadelphia: By the society, 1980), p. 232. Methodist Episcopal Church, *Minutes . . . 1773 to 1794*, pp. 61–146; St. George's Methodist Episcopal Church, Appointment of Trustees, November 7, 1789, Church Records, OSGHS; St. George's Methodist Episcopal Church, *An Act of Incorporating the Methodist Episcopal Church . . . in the City of Philadelphia* (Philadelphia: W. W. Woodward, 1789); *History of Ebenezer*, pp. 24–40.

[20] *The Prospect of Philadelphia . . . 1796*, pt. 1 (Philadelphia: John Turner, 1796), p. 45; Methodist Episcopal Church, *Minutes . . . 1773 to 1794*, pp. 145–46, 159–60; St. George's Methodist Episcopal Church, Register of Class Leaders, 1791, in Blotter, April 25, 1787–April 17, 1795, and Various Accounts: estimate for building galleries, January 21, 1792, sundry disbursements for the galleries in the church, April 25–September 4, 1792; carpenter work done by Moseley and Smith, May 28, 1792, account and receipt of the painting, October 9, 1792, Church Records, OSGHS.

[21] St. George's Methodist Episcopal Church, Report on Book Fund, 1792, Church Records, OSGHS; Asbury, *Journal and Letters*, 3:212–17; Methodist Episcopal Church, *Articles of Association of the Trustees of the Fund for the Relief and Support of . . . Ministers and Preachers of the Methodist Episcopal Church* (Philadelphia: Henry Tuckniss, 1797), p. 4.

[22] St. George's Methodist Episcopal Church, Membership Registers, ca. 1794, 1795, "The Names of the Officers and Members of the Methodist Church in Philadelphia," ca. 1794–1814, Church Records, OSGHS; *The Philadelphia Directory . . . 1791* (Philadelphia: James and Johnson, 1791); *The Philadelphia Directory . . . 1793* (Philadelphia: T. Dobson, 1793); *The Prospect of Philadelphia . . . 1795* (Philadelphia: Francis and Robert Bailey, 1795); *History of Ebenezer*, p. 27; Samuel Harvey business papers, 1797–1829, Samuel Harvey Papers, HSP. On Hewson, see *The Concise Encyclopedia of American Antiques*, ed. Helen Comstock, s.v. "Cotton Printing." On Haskins, see Douglas R. Chandler, "A New Church in a New Nation, 1784–1800," in *Those Incredible Methodists: A History of the Baltimore Conference of the United Methodist Church*, ed. Gordon Pratt Baker (Baltimore: Baltimore Conference, 1972), pp. 63, 67; and Asbury, *Journal and Letters*, 3:140n. The occupation of a fourth located itinerant, Richard Tolliff, is unidentified.

[23] St. George's Methodist Episcopal Church, Membership Register, ca. 1794; *Prospect . . . 1795; History of Ebenezer*, pp. 27, 44. James Doughty's occupation is identified in Philadelphia County Tax Assessments, Southwark East, 1796 and 1799, Philadelphia City Archives.

[24] St. George's Methodist Episcopal Church, Register of Class Leaders, 1791, and Membership Register, ca. 1794; occupations are identified in *Philadelphia Directory . . . 1791, Philadelphia Directory . . . 1793*, and *Prospect . . . 1795*. On Smith and Abbott, see Hugh Smith to Ezekiel Cooper, October 7, 1801, in Benjamin Abbott, *The Experience and Gospel Labours of the Rev. Benjamin Abbott* (Philadelphia: Solomon W. Conrad, 1801), pp. 237–39.

[25] Doris Elisabett Andrews, "Popular Religion and the Revolution in the Middle Atlantic Ports: The Rise of the Methodists, 1770–1800" (Ph.D. diss., University of Pennsylvania, 1986), table 4; Billy G. Smith, *The "Lower Sort": Philadelphia's Laboring People, 1750–1800* (Ithaca, N.Y.: Cornell University Press, 1990), app. C, p. 214.

[26] Andrews, "Popular Religion," table 1, pp. 187–88, table 2; St. George's Methodist Episcopal Church, Membership Register, ca. 1794–1801. See profiles of American Methodist women in Abel Stevens, *The Women of Methodism: Its Three Foundresses . . .* (New York: Carlton and Porter, 1866).

[27] Free African Society, "Minutes," pp. 21–23. Two recent accounts of the founding of the African churches in Philadelphia are Julie Winch, *Philadelphia's Black Elite: Activism, Accommodation, and the Struggle for Autonomy, 1787–1848* (Philadelphia: Temple University Press, 1988), pp. 4–25; and Nash, *Forging Freedom*, pp. 100–133.

[28] Free African Society, "Minutes," pp. 43–46; Winch, *Philadelphia's Black Elite*, pp. 9–11; Nash, *Forging Freedom*, pp. 112–18.

[29] Allen, *Life Experience*, pp. 25–26.

[30] Allen, *Life Experience*, pp. 28–29; Nash, *Forging Freedom*, pp. 116–33; St. Thomas's African Church, Recommendation of Absalom Jones as Candidate for Orders, and Register of Members up to 1794, in *Annals of the First African Church*, pp. 100–101, 107–10.

[31] C. E. Pierre, "The Work of the Society for the Propagation of the Gospel in Foreign Parts among the Negroes in the Colonies," *Journal of Negro History* 1 (1916): 349–60; Nash, *Forging Freedom*, pp. 112–13.

[32] Samuel Magaw, "A Discourse Delivered July 17th, 1794, in the African Church of the City of Philadelphia," in *Annals of the First African Church*, pp. 80–81.

[33] Allen, *Life Experience*, p. 29; Methodist Episcopal Church, *Minutes of Several Conversations . . . 1784*, p. 14; Albert J. Raboteau, "The Slave Church in the Era of the American Revolution," in *Slavery and Freedom in the Age of the American Revolution*, ed. Ira Berlin and Ronald Hoffman (Urbana: University of Illinois Press, 1986), pp. 197–200.

[34] African Methodist Episcopal Church, *Articles of Association of the African Methodist Episcopal Church* (1799; reprint, Philadelphia: John Ormrod, n.d.), pp. 6–10. The articles also placed Bethel's property under the legal control of St. George's, a drawback that prompted further conflicts between Allen and the MEC preachers; see Nash, *Forging Freedom*, pp. 195–99; and Charles H. Wesley, *Richard Allen: Apostle of Freedom* (1935; reprint, Washington, D.C.: Associated Publishers, 1969), pp. 77–81. See also Allen, *Life Experience*, pp. 26–31. The first class lists for the African Methodist Episcopal Church are reprinted in Dee Andrews, "The African Methodists of Philadelphia, 1794–1802," *Pennsylvania Magazine of History and Bi-*

ography 108, no. 4 (October 1984): 483–86. St. Thomas's African Episcopal Church, *Act of Incorporation, Causes and Motives, of the African Episcopal Church of Philadelphia* (Whitehall, Pa., 1810).

[35] Methodist Episcopal Church, *Minutes of the Methodist Conferences, Annually Held in America, from 1773 to 1813, Inclusive* (New York: Daniel Hitt and Thomas Ware, 1813), pp. 154–56, 190–93, 223–26; Andrews, "African Methodists," pp. 479, 483–86. Bethel also eventually surpassed St. Thomas's in size and influence; see Winch, *Philadelphia's Black Elite*, pp. 11–12.

[36] Methodist Episcopal Church, *Minutes . . . 1773 to 1813*, pp. 243, 262; membership register, 1801, St. George's Episcopal Church, OSGHS.

[37] Watson, *Annals*, 1:456–59; *A Pocket Hymn-Book, Designed as a Constant Companion for the Pious, Collected from Various Authors* (13th ed.; Philadelphia: Parry Hall and John Dickins, 1791), pp. 210–11; Benjamin Abbott, *The Experience and Gospel Labours of the Rev. Benjamin Abbott . . .* (Philadelphia: Solomon W. Conrad, 1801); Ezekiel Cooper, *A Funeral Discourse, on the Death of that Eminent Man the Late Reverend John Dickins* (Philadelphia: H. Maxwell, 1799); George A. Phoebus, comp., *Beams of Light on Early Methodism in America: Chiefly Drawn from . . . the Rev. Ezekiel Cooper* (New York: Phillips and Hunt; Cincinnati: Cranston and Stowe, 1887); Asbury, *Journal and Letters*, 1:ix–xiv, 3:132–33.

[38] Watson, Preface to Watson, "Experience and Incidents."

[39] St. George's Methodist Episcopal Church, Various Accounts: subscriptions for new roof, January 20, 1797, May 15, 1798; "Repairing Fund to Sundries," 1800; repairing fund, January 30–September 23, 1800; with James Pearson (surveyor), March 14–June 9, 1800; with William Roney, April 9–July 16, 1800; entries April 1800–February 1801, receipt book, 1795–1801, Church Records, OSGHS. North's occupation is identified in Caleb North, Election Speech, 1819, Society Collection, HSP.

[40] Phoebus, *Beams of Light*, pp. 288–89; William B. Sprague, *Annals of the American Pulpit . . .*, vol. 7, *Annals of the American Methodist Pulpit* (New York: Robert Carter and Brothers, 1861), p. 213. For discussion of the disciplinary issues involved, see Dee Andrews, "The People and the Preachers at St. George's: An Anatomy of a Methodist Schism," in *Rethinking Methodist History: A Bicentennial Historical Consultation*, ed. Russell E. Richey and Kenneth E. Rowe (Nashville: Kingswood Books, 1985), pp. 125–33. Names here and below appear in St. George's Methodist Episcopal Church, Membership Registers, 1800–1801, Church Records, OSGHS.

[41] Phoebus, *Beams of Light*, p. 290.

[42] Cooper quoted in Phoebus, *Beams of Light*, pp. 287–88; St. George's Methodist Episcopal Church, appointments January 23, 1801, Membership Registers, 1800–1801, Church Records, OSGHS.

[43] Haskins to Messrs. Swain and Coate, June 8, 1801, Conference Records, OSGHS; Lambert Wilmer et al., to the Methodist Connection in the City of Philadelphia, June 12, 1801, Ezekiel Cooper Papers, United Library, Garrett Evangelical-Seabury Western Theological Seminaries, Evanston, Ill.

[44] Academy Church, "[Constitution for the] United Societies 1801," and Membership Register, 1801, in "Register of the Names of Official and Private Members of the Methodist Society Meeting at the College," 1801–11, Church Records, OSGHS.

[45] Phoebus, *Beams of Light*, pp. 290–91; St. George's Methodist Episcopal Church, Membership Register, 1801, receipt book, 1795–1806, "Monies Received for the Church by E. Cooper and Paid over to the Committee for the Dividend to

Creditors," November 3, 1801, Church Records, OSGHS; Andrews, "Popular Religion," table 4; *The Philadelphia Directory . . . 1800* (Philadelphia: William W. Woodward, 1800).

[46] St. George's Methodist Episcopal Church, Membership Register, 1800, Church Records, OSGHS. Two other Sturgises, Stockley and Jonathan, appear as members at St. George's (St. George's Methodist Episcopal Church, Membership Register, 1801, Church Records, OSGHS). Stockley is identified as a laborer in *The Philadelphia Directory . . . 1802* (Philadelphia: William W. Woodward, 1802) and hence is unlikely to have been Stockley Sturgis's son, who inherited Sturgis's Delaware estate (Stockley Sturgis will, April 26, 1787, Kent County Wills, vol. A49, pp. 109–10). Jonathan Sturgis is identified as "from Wilmington," and his marriage is recorded November 22, 1791, Asbury Methodist Episcopal Church, Wilmington Marriages, 1788–1954, Hall of Records, Dover, Del.

[47] Allen, *Life Experience*, p. 18; Donald G. Mathews, *Slavery and Methodism: A Chapter in American Morality* (Princeton: Princeton University Press, 1965).

Torah, Trade, and Kinship

Edwin Wolf 2nd

Torah, trade, and kinship created for the American Jews of the eighteenth century a network of trust and communication. The network originated in Amsterdam and London, spread first to the West Indies, and then involved the mainland cities. Mutual assistance made ritual observances possible; business was conducted with dependable and frequently related coreligionists; marriages cemented the bonds of faith and commerce.

By 1800 the Jewish population of the United States was still so small—a fraction of 1 percent of the total—that it exerted no influence by weight of numbers on the vast non-Jewish majority. While there were some well-to-do Jewish merchants, no one had outstanding wealth, and the Jewish community as a whole had no appreciable financial impact on the economy. No eighteenth-century Philadelphia Jews held any elective or appointive governmental offices; they were barred from them during most of the century by a test oath. They did take part in economic, military, and civic life, but they participated as individuals except on very rare occasions, as for instance, the 1783 petition seeking the striking of the test oath in the state constitution and the address of several congregations, including that of Philadelphia, to George Washington on his assumption of the presidency.[1]

A Jewish congregation came into existence as soon as there were ten adult males to join in a religious service. In New Amsterdam such a gathering, or minyan, was possible in 1654, and by the end of the seventeenth century the Jewish community of New York was well organized. In Philadelphia enough Jews had settled in the city by the 1740s to conduct services. At first there was no formal administration. It took some decades of influx and consolidation before Kahal Kodesh (Holy Congregation) Mikveh Israel formally came into being.[2]

The only quasi minister, a communal employee, was a hazan who chanted the service, and only a mature community could afford one. There was no ordained rabbi in British America in the eighteenth century, and as with the Quakers, Catholics, and Anglicans in colonial times, no national authoritative person or synod. Jews, again as the Quakers, tried to settle disagreements within the group rather than in courts of law. A few men, moderately well versed in the interpretation of religious law, were looked to for opinions, but serious controversial matters had to be referred to European rabbis for decision. The individual Jewish congregations policed the religious observance of their members, as did the Quakers, but their only punishments were exclusion from religious services and the withdrawal of ritual privileges, such as marriage ceremonies and burials.

There were more single Jewish males than females, a characteristic of many immigrant groups. As a consequence, conversion or intermarriage with non-Jews occurred. Isaac Miranda, the first Jew to settle in the city, was called by James Logan (who was happy to buy his Hebrew books), "an apostate Jew or fashionable Christian." David Franks, who arrived in town in 1738, ten years later married Margaret Evans, and all their children were baptized at Christ Church. A very distant relative, Isaac Franks, a revolutionary war veteran who rented his Germantown house to Washington during the yellow-fever epidemic of 1793, also wed out of the faith, although his sister was married to synagogue leader Hyam Salomon. Even religious Mathias Bush's son Solomon, also an old soldier who had been wounded at Brandywine, married a Christian woman and ordered in his will that he be interred in the Friends burial ground.[3] There were others.

In Philadelphia, with but few exceptions, the eighteenth-century Jews were of Ashkenazic, or central European, origin, but the community from the beginning settled into a Sephardic, or Mediterranean, manner of worship. Like the Church of England to other Protestant sects, Sephardism was held to be more socially desirable. Nathan Levy, the founder of continuing Judaism in the city, and his partner David Franks, both born of Ashkenazic parentage in New York, had been members of the Sephardic Congregation Shearith Israel. In a new country, one started at the top, so even later Yiddish-speaking arrivals, such as

Barnard and Michael Gratz, happily became "Portuguese," as the Sephardic ritual was known.

There was in the American colonies long a shortage of ritual objects, chiefly Torah scrolls and their appurtenances. When there was movement in 1761 toward more structured religious life, Philadelphians borrowed a Torah scroll from the New Yorkers for the High Holy Day services to which came Joseph Simon from Lancaster, Pennsylvania, and Meyer Josephson from Reading, Pennsylvania. For decades Philadelphia remained a religious magnet for the surrounding towns where the convocation of a minyan was frequently difficult. However, the earliest surviving documentary record of Mikveh Israel, as the Philadelphia congregation was eventually named, is of 1773, an agreement by Barnard and Michael Gratz, Henry and Levy Marks, Solomon Marache and Levi Solomon "to support our holy worship and establish it on a more solid foundation."[4]

As the Jewish population increased, a synagogue had been opened in Cherry Alley between Third and Fourth streets in summer 1771. The announcement of the first services there appeared in the local German newspaper, not extraordinary in view of the relationship of Yiddish to German. It may have been at the time of this formalization that a constitution for the congregation was drafted, written in Yiddish but based on the Sephardic organizational pattern of New York's Shearith Israel. In 1771 Barnard Gratz asked his English friend Michael Samson to pay for a Torah scroll imported for the Philadelphians' permanent use and for some tefillin that had been sent from London. Shortly thereafter Michael Gratz received from New York a silver *yod* (pointer) and a pair of *rimonim* (crowns) for the Torah made by master silversmith Myer Myers.[5]

There was a shortage, too, of men qualified to perform religious rites. Although practiced laymen could perform the ceremonies required if need be, an experienced *mohel* (circumciser) and *shochet* (ritual slaughterer to provide kosher meat) were functionaries whom established Jewish communities sought. Abraham Isaac Abrahams of New York was both mohel and shochet. In 1767 he went to Newport to circumcise the brothers and nephews of Aaron Lopez, Marranos, or secret Jews, who had just arrived from religiously intolerant Portugal. Barnard Itzhak Jacobs, a shopkeeper of Heidelberg, Lancaster County, doubled as a circuit-riding mohel in eastern Pennsylvania many years in the second half of the eighteenth century. Before the Methodist circuit riders covered the same territory, Jacobs went on horseback through Pennsylvania to perform the covenant of Abraham wherever a Jewish boy was born.[6]

In his role as shochet Abrahams provided a certificate assuring the Jews of Barbados that meat that Michael Gratz shipped to them was kosher. Some families had their own private butcher or did their own killing. It was not until 1776 that triple-role Abraham Levy was hired by the Philadelphia community to slaughter, chant services in the synagogue, and "Teach Six Children the Art of Reading Hebrew."[7]

Philadelphians had no hazan until Gershom Mendes Seixas came as a refugee in 1780. He had officiated in New York and after the British occupation of that city fled with Shearith Israel's ritual property to Stratford, Connecticut, and when threatened there, down to Philadelphia. Noting that many sons of Tories were Whigs, Benjamin Rush observed, "so were the Jews in all the States." As a result, most of the Jews from British-occupied New York, Charleston, and Savannah sought asylum for some years in Philadelphia, thereby for a time vastly enlarging the local congregation and strengthening trade and family ties. Seixas and the others returned home after the peace treaty of 1783, leaving the Philadelphians with a synagogue too large for them, debts that construction had incurred, and a new hazan, Jacob Raphael Cohen.[8]

Consultation was sometimes international. A London rabbi asked Hyam Salomon, best known as the official broker for Robert Morris's Office of Finance, to help settle a claim that originated in Poland against a Virginia Jew; it was settled by a *beth din* (traditional Jewish court) in Philadelphia. A beth din in London was appealed to in a controversial case concerning the request of Moses Nathans to have his non-Jewish mistress converted and to be permitted to marry her according to Jewish law. And an Amsterdam rabbi was asked in Yiddish what to do about Mordecai Moses Mordecai who took it upon himself to perform a mixed marriage ceremony and later, contrary to the orders of the congregation, ritually prepare for burial the corpse of Benjamin Moses Clava, who had been wed to a Christian. The answers of the European authorities have not survived. In 1789 the religiously skilled Manuel Josephson of Philadelphia in a detailed letter chided Moses Seixas of Newport because knowledge of Hebrew was at such a low ebb in that city that the Torah portion was being read from a printed text with vowels instead of from a manuscript scroll without them.[9] The ties of religion were strong among the small independent Jewish congregations, but there was no central governing body in America.

Tsedaka (philanthropy) has always been an integral part of Jewish life. Jews expected to take care of their own. In America, first as individuals and then through their congregations, they cared for the local needy and participated with the Jews of other cities in helping wayfaring strangers and answering the requests of Palestinian towns. From London in 1761 came an appeal for emergency funds to help the inhabitants of Safed in Palestine when an earthquake partially destroyed the city. From the same land in 1763 money was requested for the congregation in Hebron, and seven years later the Jews of that Palestinian town made another plea that resulted in the earliest records of a national Palestine appeal. New York raised £32.1.6, Newport £25.12.0, and Philadelphia £13.10.0. The *Pennsylvania Packet* of August 16, 1788, carried an item reporting that two Jews had come from Hebron by way of Jamaica seeking funds to liberate some of their brethren from Turkish slavery. It ended by urging Christians also to contribute.[10]

In 1768 one Jacob Musqueto of St. Eustatia was sent from Shearith Israel in New York to Michael Gratz with a request that he "Collect Sufficient among the Yahudim [Jews] at Phila. as would defray the Expence" of getting Musqueto passage to Barbados. After the Revolution Mikveh Israel formed a special philanthropic arm, Ezrath Orechim, or Society for Destitute Strangers. From it a young French Jew sought clothing. Two Poles were sent on to New York by private subscription because there was not enough money in the society's treasury, but it did pay for Mordecai Moses's passage to Charleston. And when two Jews arrived on the eve of Yom Kippur as bond servants on a ship from Hamburg, money was sought to redeem them beyond the capacity of Ezrath Orechim. A plea from Congregation Nidche Israel of Barbados was answered by members of Mikveh Israel.[11] Some Philadelphians maintained membership in New York's Shearith Israel, and erstwhile refugees from New York, Charleston, and Savannah continued to support the Philadelphia congregation.

The ties with other American cities were made fast by marriages that took place during the period of exile. Philip Moses from Charleston wooed and won Sarah Machado, the step-daughter of merchant Israel Jacobs, long a resident of Philadelphia. Earlier, Jacobs's wife's sister Rebecca had become the wife of Jonas Phillips by whom she had twenty-one children, some of whom played major roles in Philadelphia and nationally. Benjamin Rush attended and described the wedding of Phillips's daughter Rachel to Michael Levy of Virginia. And when Moses Sheftall of Savannah was studying medicine under Rush, he met Elkalah Bush, daughter of Mathias, and in 1792 married her.[12]

When Mikveh Israel needed funds for its new synagogue building in 1782, the congregation instructed its president to write, soliciting help from the Jews of Surinam, several West Indies cities, Newport, and Lancaster. Pointing out that the synagogue had been built to take care of a congregation swollen by those who had been "obliged to leave on account of their Attachment to American Measures" and who had since gone home, "the good People of the Hebrew Society in the City of Philadelphia, commonly call'd Israelites," also appealed to their non-Jewish fellow citizens. The appeal, dated April 30, 1788, prefaced a subscription form. In an unusual ecumenical response, Benjamin Franklin signed up for £5. For varying amounts, he was joined by Attorney General William Bradford; Thomas Fitzsimons, the leading Catholic layman of the city and one of the drafters of the Constitution; scientist-astronomer David Rittenhouse; Secretary Charles Biddle of the Supreme Executive Council of Pennsylvania; Thomas McKean, a signer of the Declaration and later governor of the state; sculptor William Rush; Peter Muhlenberg, war hero and leader of the German community; and others.[13]

While the Jews of Philadelphia, comparatively few in number, were not the promoters of social and civic organizations, some belonged to and supported them. David Franks and Sampson Levy, before his lapse from Judaism, were among the first members of the Assembly Ball, and the former also belonged to the exclusive Mount Regale Fishing Club. As early as 1762 tailor Levy Marks was elevated to the Third Degree in Philadelphia's Masonic Lodge No. 2, and Michael Gratz was raised to the sublime Degree of Master Mason in New York's St. John's Lodge in 1764. A short-lived Sublime Lodge of Perfection in Philadelphia was composed only of Jews with Col. Solomon Bush as Grand Master and Isaac Da Costa, Simon Nathan, Benjamin Seixas, and Hyam Salomon, among others, as members.[14]

Aaron Levy, who founded the town of Aaronsburg in central Pennsylvania, gave the Reformed Church there land and its sacramental plate. He had invested heavily in land. Childless in his advanced age, he turned all of it over to Michael Gratz's sons Simon and Hyman in return for an annuity. By will he left various members of that family a quantity of silver, including the massive tankard by Peter Getz of Lancaster now in the Rosenbach Museum. David Franks and Aaron Levy were members of the Library Company of Philadelphia. Although Nathan Levy was not, it was reported that he played violin very well and left a good library of standard English works, as well as twenty-two Hebrew and eight Spanish Hebrew books. From 1760, when David Judah, late of Wilmington, and David Salisbury Franks of Germantown were registered in the College of Philadelphia, until 1795, when future lawyer Zalegman Phillips graduated from its successor University of Pennsylvania, a handful of Jews attended the local college. Mathias Bush and Barnard Gratz were early contributors to the Pennsylvania Hospital. Physician David de Isaac Cohen Nassy from Surinam was a major supporter of a mild regime at the Bush Hill hospital during the yellow-fever epidemic of 1793. After the Pennsylvania Society for Promoting the Abolition of Slavery was reconstituted in 1787, a number of Jews who never held slaves and more, like Benjamin Rush and others who had owned them but saw the light, joined and formally manumitted their slaves. Even Nassy, whose ancestors built a colony based on slave labor, was moved to free his two personal servants.[15]

Trade and religion, frequently intertwined with marriage, were main strands of the Jewish network. Moses Levy and David Franks established the first substantial Jewish mercantile house in Philadelphia. Franks's mother was the sister of his partner Levy, and after 1754 Franks's partner was Levy's younger brother Isaac. Two of Franks's brothers, Naphtali and Moses, went to England to work with an uncle there, and the latter's London connections were helpful in getting David Franks and his father, Jacob, appointed contractors to the British army during the French and Indian War. The ad hoc supply firm of Plumsted and Franks suffered from Braddock's defeat in 1755, but when Maj. George Washington marched again three years later he ordered from Franks some supplies for his Virginia troops, and for himself two saddles, a letter case, "a pair of light shoeboots, round toes, without linings, and jockey tops made of thin, english calf-skin," a trunk, and some china. Another example of the international connection of the firm of Levy and Franks is the letter of Franklin's partner David Hall to London publisher-bookseller William Strahan. Sending him a bill of exchange on some Scots of Ayr, Hall told Strahan that, were it refused, he should "apply to Mr. Isaac Levy Merchant in London who will pay for Levy and Franks."[16]

Barnard Gratz, born in Upper Silesia, had received his mercantile training under a cousin, Solomon Henry, in London. When he came to Philadelphia in 1754, Gratz began his American career in Franks's counting house. It was just then that Pennsylvanians who were engaged in the Western trade, including Franks and Joseph Simon of Lancaster, lost all their goods when French and Indian attacks ignited the frontier. With trading resumed, in 1760 Gratz wrote to Simon about a shipment of sugar and wampum and inquired about money owed him by a Virginia regiment for supplies. This was Gratz's introduction to the opening of the West. The Simon connection gave the Philadelphians a western outpost and was strengthened by marriage ties. Simon had wed the niece of New Yorker Samuel Myers Cohen. Cohen's daughter Richea married Barnard Gratz, daughter Elkalah married silversmith Myer Myers, and daughter Rachel married Mathias Bush, Nathan Levy's successor as leader of the Philadelphia religious community. Furthermore, Cohen's nephew Solomon Myers Cohen wed Simon's daughter Belle, and his niece Elkalah wed New York hazan Gershom Seixas.[17]

When Barnard Gratz's brother Michael arrived, he also began his American career clerking for Franks. Soon the brothers formed their own partnership and by the mid 1760s were among the leading Jewish merchants of the city. Their connection with Franks and his partners in the Indian trade, William Trent and Lancaster-based Simon and his son-in-law Levy Andrew Levy, remained close. Michael Gratz wed Simon's daughter Miriam and thereby became Levy's brother-in-law and a brother-in-law of Solomon Etting of York, Pennsylvania; of Levy Phillips, who moved from Lancaster to Philadelphia and became a postwar pillar of Mikveh Israel; and of Solomon Myers Cohen, later a New York refugee. It was in 1769 when Michael and Mirriam married that the superb Chippendale high chest of drawers, now at Winterthur, was made for the newlyweds.[18]

Suddenly the frontier blazed again. In 1763 Franks wrote to Michael Gratz: "The Indians have begun a war near the Forts; killed and taken several people and traders, and Levy is a prisoner." The traders and the merchants who had let them have merchandise on credit lost vast sums. One of these was Indian trader George Croghan, who had a substantial shipment of "Sundries for the Use of Indians" sent him at Fort Pitt by Simon, Levy, and Company in 1765. The subsequent attempt by the "Suffering Traders" of 1754 and 1763 to obtain compensation led to the cession by the Indians of vast tracts of land that involved Franks, Simon, Levy, the Gratzes, and eventually Benjamin Franklin, his son William, and several English noblemen in complicated negotiations on both sides of the Atlantic. On behalf of one of the groups with questionable title to vague acres of land, the United Companies of Illinois and Wabash, signer of the Declaration of Independence George Ross as chairman and Barnard Gratz as secretary signed a proposal in 1779 for the settlement of a town at the junction of the Ohio and Wabash rivers.[19] By taking over land for debts, notably from Croghan, the Gratzes became owners of tens of thousands of acres in western New York and what is now Kentucky and Illinois and opened up those areas to settlement.

The Gratzes, like others, carried on trade throughout the colonies and formed ad hoc partnerships with both coreligionists and non-Jewish merchants. Their correspondence indicates, however, that they found it easier to unbutton with fellow Jews and speak of personal matters. When Barnard told his cousin Henry in London that he was setting up for himself and had sent to Moses Franks there for a cargo, the letter was in Yiddish.[20]

Barnard Gratz engaged in a partnership with Benjamin Moses Clava of Gloucester, New Jersey. Isaac DeLyon of Savannah sent Gratz rice and deer skins and ordered fish, gingerbread, and apples. Meyer Josephson of Reading, writing in Yiddish, inquired of Michael Gratz about the possibility of obtaining a black female slave or a white indentured maidservant. When the merchants of Philadelphia drew up and signed a nonimportation agreement during the Stamp Act crisis, nine Jews joined them. Michael Gratz bought the ship *Rising Sun*, later fitted out by him as a privateer during the Revolution, from the Jewish firm of Hays and Polock of Newport. After the war he sought financial information about some Charleston businessmen from Isaac DaCosta, Jr., who had been a war refugee in Philadelphia.[21]

As with non-Jewish Philadelphia merchants, notably the Quakers, West Indian trade played a substantial role in their business transactions. A loose association of the Gratzes with Elias and Isaac Rodriguez

Miranda of Curaçao sent liquor and groceries south and specie north, including in 1765 a large sum through Daniel and Moses Gomez of New York. "Provitions is in great Damand," an amanuensis wrote the next year for the Portuguese-speaking Mirandas, who appended a list of prices current for commodities. Business was also conducted by the firm of Miranda and Gratz as far north as Canada with Jews and non-Jews alike. One of the latter in Montreal heard that the Gratzes had "Destillet a Sort of English Brandy from Corn" and asked that four pipes be sent him. This is the earliest known reference to bourbon.[22]

Communication with the islands was often indirect. Jacob Melhado of Jamaica asked Michael Gratz to forward a letter to his brother in St. Eustatia, "As I find it very Inconvenient to Convey Letters from this place to Any of the Windward Island[s]." Other Philadelphia merchants had similar connections. One is particularly noteworthy. In July 1776, by way of St. Eustatia, Jonas Phillips of Philadelphia suggested to his Amsterdam relative Gumpel Samson that trade in Dutch goods, although dangerous, would be lucrative. Enclosed in the letter written in Yiddish was a copy of the first printing of the Declaration of Independence. The ship carrying it was intercepted by the British; the letter was deemed to be in code, and it and the broadside ended up in the Public Records Office in London. Later Haym Salomon sent a large sum of money to his family in Poland through the offices of Samson.[23] As Quakers found it more comfortable to deal with other Quakers, so Jews felt more confident doing business with fellow Jews.

Like Catholics and Anglicans and unlike Quakers and Methodists, Jews required ritual objects for the performance of their religion. It was also imperative that males be circumcised, by a professional mohel if available, and it was only slightly less important that the meat they ate was kosher. These religious necessities bound the small American Jewish communities together. Trade followed, or indeed may have preceded, the give-and-take of religious life. While Jews freely did business with non-Jews, their closest ties were with coreligionists. Part of trade network was the result of family connections—and they were extensive—for like Catholics and Quakers, intermarriage was contrary to a religious way of life. The result was that the web of Torah, trade, and kinship promoted the practice of Judaism, fostered trade, and increased the Jewish population.

[1] Morris U. Schappes, *A Documentary History of the Jews of the United States, 1654–1875* (New York: Citadel Press, 1950), pp. 63–66, 82–83; Jacob Rader Marcus, *American Jewry Documents Eighteenth Century* (Cincinnati: Hebrew Union College Press, 1959), pp. 167–70.

[2] Jacob Rader Marcus, *Early American Jewry*, vol. 1 (Philadelphia: Jewish Publication Society of America, 1951), pp. 24–33, 48; Edwin Wolf 2nd and Maxwell Whiteman, *The History of the Jews of Philadelphia from Colonial Times to the Age of Jackson* (Philadelphia: Jewish Publication Society, 1957), p. 32.

[3] Wolf and Whiteman, *History*, pp. 18–19; "Abigail Evans Franks' Bible," *American Jewish Historical Quarterly* 58 (1968): 137–38; Wolf and Whiteman, *History*, pp. 429, 158. Franks was known as "Colonel" by virtue of a militia appointment late in the century. Why Franks's name was left out of the public denomination of the house when its only claim to fame was under Franks's ownership is pondered in Edwin Wolf 2nd, "Why Not Call It the Deshler-Franks-Morris House?" *Germantown Crier* 33, no. 4 (Fall 1981): 80–81.

[4] Wolf and Whiteman, *History*, pp. 41, 60–61.

[5] *Pennsylvanische Staatsbote* (Philadelphia), July 30, 1771; Marcus, *Early American Jewry*, 1:94–96; Barnard Gratz to Michael Samson, October 15, 1771, Etting manuscripts, Historical Society of Pennsylvania, Philadelphia; Wolf and Whiteman, *History*, p. 59.

[6] Marcus, *Early American Jewry*, 1:90–91.

[7] Wolf and Whiteman, *History*, pp. 49, 48. There is also a blank form for meat sent to Curaçao, ca. 1767, McAllister manuscripts, Library Company of Philadelphia (hereafter cited as LCP). Articles of Agreement between Michael Gratz and Abraham and Ezekiel Levy, June 18, 1776, Gratz Papers, Henry Joseph Collection, American Jewish Archives, Watham, Mass.; Marcus, *Early American Jewry*, 1:104–5.

[8] Benjamin Rush, Commonplace Book, p. 77, LCP; Wolf and Whiteman, *History*, pp. 122–24.

[9] Wolf and Whiteman, *History*, pp. 133–34; Congregation Mikveh Israel to Congregation Shagnar a Shamaim of London, August 7, 1793, Mikveh Israel Archives, Philadelphia; Marcus, *Early American Jewry*, 1:188–89; Manuel Josephson and Joseph Wolf Carpeles to Rabbi Saul Lowenstamm of Amsterdam, March 20, 1785, Mikveh Israel Archives; Wolf and Whiteman, *History*, pp. 128–31; Marcus, *Early American Jewry*, 1:138–41; Manuel Josephson to Moses Seixas, February 4, 1790, Lyons Collection, American Jewish Historical Society, Watham, Mass.

[10] Wolf and Whiteman, *History*, pp. 55–56; printed circulars addressed to Michael Gratz, Sulzberger manuscripts, American Jewish Historical Society; *Pennsylvania Packet* cited in Wolf and Whiteman, *History*, p. 138.

[11] K. K. Shearith Israel, Minute Book, May 16, 1768, Lyons Collection; Wolf and Whiteman, *History*, pp. 136, 137.

[12] Wolf and Whiteman, *History*, pp. 198–99, 127–28.

[13] Subscription List, April 30, 1788, Mikveh Israel Archives; K. K. Mikveh Israel, Minute Book, June 30, August 18, 1782, Mikveh Israel Archives; Wolf and Whiteman, *History*, pp. 119, 143–44.

[14] Wolf and Whiteman, *History*, p. 33; Julius F. Sachse, *Old Masonic Lodges of Pennsylvania* (Philadelphia, 1912), p. 75; Certificate of Michael Gratz, April 25, 1764, Wolf Collection, LCP; Wolf and Whiteman, *History*, pp. 155–56.

[15] *The Annual Report of the Library Company of Philadelphia for the Year 1980* (Philadelphia, 1981), pp. 25–26; Library Company of Philadelphia, Minute Book, 1:168, Archives, LCP; Wolf and Whiteman, *History*, p. 314; Administration Papers,

no. 58, Book F, 527, Register of Wills, Philadelphia; Marcus, *Early American Jewry*, 1:8–10; Wolf and Whiteman, *History*, p. 42; Henry Samuel Morais, *The Jews of Philadelphia* (Philadelphia: Levytype Co., 1894), p. 431; Wolf and Whiteman, *History*, pp. 42, 193–94, 190–92.

[16] Washington to David Franks, May 1, 1758, in *Writings of George Washington*, ed. John C. Fitzpatrick, vol. 2 (Washington, D.C.: Government Printing Office, 1931–44), p. 190; David Hall to William Strahan, April 28, 1751, Hall letterbook, American Philosophical Society, Philadelphia; Malcolm B. Stern, *Americans of Jewish Descent: A Compendium of Genealogy* (Cincinnati: Hebrew Union College Press, 1960), p. 109; Marcus, *Early American Jewry*, 1:374–80.

[17] Wolf and Whiteman, *History*, pp. 36–37, 66; Barnard Gratz to Joseph Simon, April 3, 1760, McAllister manuscripts; Stern, *Americans of Jewish Descent*, p. 160.

[18] Stern, *Americans of Jewish Descent*, p. 194; William Vincent Byars, *B. and M. Gratz, Merchants in Philadelphia, 1754–1798* (Jefferson City, Mo.: Hugh Stephens Printing Co., 1916), p. 35; Joseph Downs, *American Furniture: Queen Anne and Chippendale Periods in the Henry Francis du Pont Winterthur Museum* (New York: Macmillan Co., 1952), no. 198.

[19] Franks to Michael Gratz, June 12, 1763, and George Croghan, Invoice of Goods from Simon, Levy, and Co., March 23, 1765, McAllister manuscripts; Wolf and Whiteman, *History*, p. 68, pl. 11, 65–75; Carl Van Doren, *Benjamin Franklin* (New York: Viking Press, 1938), pp. 364–67; Schappes, *Documentary History*, pp. 42–44; United Companies of Illinois and Wabash, Proposals and Terms, March 6, 1779, Wolf Papers; *Annual Report of the Library Company*, pp. 24–25.

[20] Barnard Gratz to Solomon Henry, November 20, 1758, translation, Etting Papers, Historical Society of Pennsylvania; Byars, *B. and M. Gratz*, p. 36.

[21] Wolf and Whiteman, *History*, p. 37; Isaac DeLyon to Barnard Gratz, September 24, 1760, McAllister manuscripts; Meyer Josephson to Michael Gratz, July 25, 1762, Henry Joseph Collection, American Jewish Archives; Marcus, *Early American Jewry*, 1:358–60; Schappes, *Documentary History*, pp. 38–40; Wolf and Whiteman, *History*, p. 58; Isaac DaCosta, Jr., to Michael Gratz, February 2, 1784, Etting Papers, Historical Society of Pennsylvania.

[22] E. and I. Rodriguez Miranda to B. and M. Gratz, September 1, 1766, L. S. Hayne to Miranda and Gratz, June 22, 1765, McAllister manuscripts; Wolf and Whiteman, *History*, p. 46; Byars, *B. and M. Gratz*, pp. 75–76.

[24] Jacob Melhado to Michael Gratz, July 17, 1771, McAllister manuscripts; Wolf and Whiteman, *History*, pp. 80, 134.

The Library Company of Philadelphia

America's First Philosophical Society

George F. Frick

The Library Company of Philadelphia has had the longest continuous history of all the many institutions founded by Benjamin Franklin. Now in a period of renaissance as a center of scholarship in rare books and Americana, its modern energy resembles that of the ambitious young men, "then chiefly Artificers," who bought those works for their own edification and advancement in the eighteenth century. But the Company was, in its early years, much more than a repository of books; it was also a place for the study of experimental philosophy and of natural history. The Library Company of Philadelphia was the first real scientific society in America, certainly the earliest to have a lengthy existence as such.[1]

Increase Mather's philosophical society, begun in 1683 in Boston, preceded the Library Company by nearly a half century, but Mather's coterie of philosophers apparently met for no more than four years before succumbing to the "Calamitous Times" that were the lot of Massachusetts Bay in the period following the revocation of its charter in 1684. Boston produced no other scientific societies during the late seventeenth and early eighteenth centuries, after which time cultural leadership tended to shift to Philadelphia. The medical society that William Douglass founded in the New England metropolis in 1736 was contemporary with the scientific activities of the Library Company but was exclusively medical in its interests.[2]

In Philadelphia, Franklin's Junto was concerned with scientific matters and preceded the establishment of the Library Company by three years. The Junto, which was parent to the Library Company, was the source of much of the experimental activity of its offspring. In this respect, it is difficult to tell where one began and the other left off, largely because the Junto has remained so anonymous. We know that this club, with and without its founder, continued to meet into the 1760s, through the most productive scientific period of the Library Company. But apart from some of its papers published in Franklin's *Pennsylvania Gazette* in the 1730s, some scattered references to it in his autobiography, and occasional mention of it in his correspondence, there is little existing evidence of its activities. All except one of the original members of the Junto were among the first subscribers to the Library Company, and most new participants in the club were members of the Company.[3] It is possible then to think of the library as an extension of the Junto and to credit the one with what may have been the accomplishments of the other.

The Library Company's accomplishments, like much of history, cannot be packaged neatly in a fifty-year bundle. Many of those who founded the Company in 1731 were scientific amateurs. By midcentury their interests had matured to the point where they could provide a scientific core for Philadelphia and even for British America, and the principal founder stood on the verge of international reputation. The library's first two decades, then, were germane to what followed.

The scientific concerns of the Library Company were shown first in their books, which in turn helped to mold those interests. This was true from the time of the first order that the Company placed in London in 1732. The list that Franklin and his Junto friends, assisted by Pennsylvania's first great bibliophile, James Logan, sent to their member Thomas Hopkinson included at least 11 works dealing with natural philosophy, natural history, and mathematics out of a total of just over 45 titles. Some Hopkinson found to be "out of print or Dear," but he, along with Thomas Cadwalader and Peter Collinson, who thus began his career of tutelage to the Company, chose others in their places. The final list on these topics contained 13 books, including gifts from Collinson, in the shipment of 47.[4]

At least two of the books selected by the Company for their first purchase indicate the early interest of Franklin and his associates in experimental Newtonianism and foreshadow the course that they would take:

W. J. Gravesande's *Mathematical Elements of Natural Philosophy Confirmed by Experiments; or, An Introduction to Sir Isaac Newton's Philosophy* (London, 1731) and the translation by Peter Shaw and Ephraim Chambers of the unauthorized edition of Hermann Boerhaave's *Chemistry* (London, 1727). These were books that strove to teach experimentalism to a nonmathematical public.[5] They were ordered not to decorate a gentleman's shelves but because rising artificers considered them to be useful to their purposes. They are in the library today, with *Chemistry*, at least, showing signs of considerable use.

Collinson, Quaker mercer of London, who subsequently became a great scientific entrepreneur, sought to give direction to his new friends in Pennsylvania. Collinson became involved with the Library Company because the bill of exchange that was sent to London with Hopkinson was drawn on him by his correspondent, Robert Grace. For nearly thirty years he served as unpaid book buyer and unsolicited adviser to the Company. Collinson began this relationship with gifts of a "Curious Print of an Orrery"; Henry Pemberton's *View of Sir Isaac Newton's Philosophy* (London, 1728), among the most important popularizations of Newtonian science; and Philip Miller's *Gardener's Dictionary* (London, 1731), popular and useful for plant identification (particularly for those whose Latin was weak). Collinson considered the last, along with a few others, quite sufficient for the botanical correspondents he sought to encourage in America.[6]

Collinson's passion for natural history was, if we ignore for a moment the cabinets of natural curiosities that the library acquired at an early date, pursued less ardently by the Company than was natural philosophy. This is not surprising. English natural history was in a stage of collection, as was its offspring in the American colonies. At a time in which natural history was dominated by taxonomy, the English, after the deaths of great seventeenth-century systematists John Ray and Robert Morison, were notably unsystematic. Botany, zoology, and their related fields must have seemed much less exciting than the physical sciences that felt the full impact of the Newtonian revolution.

Some early members of the Library Company were interested in natural history. Both ironmaster Robert Grace and merchant Hugh Roberts seem to have had botanical or horticultural avocations, although they accomplished little in this area. Joseph Breintnall, first secretary to the Company, scrivener, and a man of some literary pretensions, also had an interest in natural history. He was even able to combine his hobbies in a rhymed description, botanically recognizable, of a wild raspberry that his Junto and library colleague Nicholas Scull found surveying in the "Oley Valley." Breintnall's principal botanical effort lay in leaf prints made by inking both sides of leaves and pressing them between sheets of paper, an imaginative, if unoriginal, solution to the problem of transporting plants, one that provided a copy for sender and receiver. (It lost utility, though, with the spread of the Linnaean system, which emphasized the details of the flower.) Breintnall also dabbled in zoology. When Collinson sent the library a copy of Sir Hans Sloane's experiments refuting the supposed ability of rattlesnakes to charm their prey, Breintnall responded with naive, hearsay accounts that denied Sloane's thesis. In spite of Collinson's assurance to the contrary, Breintnall's letter was not well received by the Royal Society. Breintnall also kept meteorological records that were detailed but unquantitative—good examples of an inexact discipline in a prescientific era. In natural philosophy, Breintnall joined Franklin in experiments on the absorption of heat by color inspired by a reading of Boerhaave. None of these activities was either important or original, but Breintnall displayed the spirit of inquiry that characterized Franklin's circle and the founders of the Library Company. He recalled, "I was not its first projector, but no man has been more active in forwarding its interest."[7] With others of like mind, Breintnall helped to give it direction toward scientific inquiry.

Logan and John Bartram were undoubtedly better naturalists than was Breintnall; both were also connected with the Library Company. But while they were a part of its environment, their role in it has sometimes been overemphasized. Logan, whose work with the fertilization of Indian corn places him in the forefront of American experimental botanists in the first half of the eighteenth century, acted as tutor and friend to the library during its early years and was an honorary member. Those experiments, his principal efforts in natural history, were completed within a few years of the Company's founding.[8] His own library at his Germantown home was one of the great colonial collections, and he had little need of the infant subscription library.

Bartram, like Logan, experimented with plant fertilization but was preeminently a plant collector, and he also had a far different relationship with the Company. If Collinson was Bartram's creator, then the Library Company shared in the creation. The two men's correspondence began in 1733 through Breintnall's offices. The Collinson-Bartram exchange, as well as Breintnall's own communication with the generous English patron of American science, was an outgrowth of Breintnall's duties as secretary to the Library Company and of the circumstances that first tied Collinson to the library. While Breintnall lived, Collinson's letters to Bartram were sent through him, and after Breintnall's death, the Londoner's parcels continued to come in the library trunks. Finally, in 1759, when the directors complained too vehemently about the trouble involved in these shipments, they were the cause of Collinson's refusal to act further as their London agent.[9] In the meantime, Breintnall and the Library Company had helped to introduce Bartram to English and European gardeners and botanists and made him (after Logan, perhaps, and before Franklin had earned his reputation) Philadelphia's best-known scientific figure.

Bartram found the Library Company of relatively little use. When he asked Collinson for botanical books, his benefactor replied that the Library Company had Miller's *Dictionary* and John Parkinson's *Theatrum Botanicum* (London, 1656) and would surely let their neighbor use them. Bartram was not happy with this and was even less satisfied when, within a few years, he saw the great botanical libraries of Logan and William Byrd and even that of Gov. Lewis Morris of New Jersey. Not until 1743, after he made a major beginning toward the Company's cabinet of curiosities with his gift of "Stones in which were Shells and Impressions of Shell fish," and after Collinson requested it, was Bartram named an honorary member of the Library Company. By this time his own library was so much improved that he would not have joined had he been required to pay £6 for a share plus yearly dues.[10]

In order to accomplish anything in natural history or natural philosophy, the Library Company needed room and equipment, as Breintnall recognized clearly. Talking with Thomas Penn in 1737, he envisioned a lot for the library on which there would "be room for a few Trees under which contemplative persons may walk or sit." It should have a building of two stories, the room above for books and the "Room below not to be partitioned but kept free to walk and converse" and to be used for "Instruction and Entertainment by Lectures." Penn suggested that the Company cultivate a collection of curious plants. The botanical garden did not materialize because the lot on Chestnut Street that the proprietor granted the Company in 1738 was too far removed from the center of town and especially because the Company lacked the means or the absolute need to build there until the Company's scientific momentum was spent. Breintnall's hopes for a lecture hall were soon realized, however. In April 1740 the library left the house on Pewter Platter Alley, rented from Grace, for the more commodious west wing of the new State House.[11]

By the time of their removal, the Company had acquired a small collection of experimental apparatus. In 1739 John Penn had sent them "an Air-Pump with some other things to shew the nature and power of the Air" (fig. 1). The pump and Thomas Penn's lot were not unexpected.

Figure 1. John Harrison, air pump case, 1739. (Library Company of Philadelphia.)

Franklin, Breintnall, and the directors in Philadelphia and Collinson in London had hinted for proprietary patronage almost since the beginning of the library. With the pump, Penn sent Samuel Jenkins, a young gentleman skilled in natural philosophy, who presented the Company with their first philosophical demonstration. He instructed the directors in the use of the pump on May 8 and displayed many experiments on it during summer 1739. Apparently, members of the Library Company began to use the pump themselves, for, although Jenkins had repaired some of the valves, during the course of the next year, Hopkinson and Philip Syng presented bills for further repairs and modifications of the apparatus. During the next decade, the minutes were dotted with orders to Collinson to replace broken vessels for the pump. As early as 1742, after "the Directors had some Conversation about several of the Glass Implements belonging to the Air pump, which were lately broken, but no Person present knew by whom," the librarian returned the keys to the pump, and his responsibility for it, in a fit of disgust.[12]

Having both room and equipment, the Company was by 1740 ready to undertake more formal activity in experimental philosophy under the guidance of a series of lecturers. During the next twelve years, their quarters in the State House provided the principal platform for experiments in Philadelphia. Along with published popularizations of the new science, they provided insights into Newtonian experimentalism for an untrained public.

The first of these lecturers, Isaac Greenwood, was the best qualified experimentalist in America, having studied in London under the premier practitioner of that art, J. T. Desaguiliers. Greenwood was well qualified in all respects save his intemperance, which had caused his dismissal as first Hollis Professor of Mathematics and Natural and Experimental Philosophy at Harvard. On May 28, 1740, Franklin secured permission for Greenwood to use the air pump and one of the Company's rooms for a "Course of Philosophical Lectures and Experiments" early in June.[13]

Four years later, Archibald Spencer, Edinburgh-trained physician and an early intercolonial scientific lecturer, visited Philadelphia and used the library rooms for two (perhaps three) courses of experimental philosophy. Spencer's demonstrations, as seen from the accounts of those who attended them, were fairly complete summaries of the physical sciences as known in the early eighteenth century. Spencer, the "Dr.

Spence" of the *Autobiography*, whose apparatus Franklin later bought, did not give the first impetus to the electrical experiments made by Franklin and his associates in the Library Company. His demonstrations of electrical fire were at a stage removed from that at which Franklin, with Collinson's aid, began, but they increased the knowledge of the experimental method by Franklin's circle and other Philadelphians.[14] Spencer contributed further to the function of the Library Company as an institution for scientific education.

That function did not end with him. In December 1750, David James Dove, English-born schoolmaster and polemicist, advertised still another course of lectures, encompassing physics, pneumatics, hydrostatics, optics, geography, and astronomy, the last "explained and illustrated by a curious large Orrerey." This ambitious series was again held in the library chambers. When appointed English master at the Academy of Philadelphia, Dove sold his apparatus to Lewis Evans, Philadelphia mapmaker, who repeated similar lectures in New York, Charles Town, and the West Indies.[15]

In April 1751, Ebenezer Kinnersley, Baptist minister, Franklin's principal collaborator in electricity, and the most durable of the colonial scientific itinerants, began a "Course of Experiments on the Newly-Discovered Electrical Fire" in the library, which he repeated in September 1752. Then, after his succession to Dove's post at the academy, Kinnersley transferred his public lectures to his new place of employment.[16] As the academy (established 1751) and the College of Philadelphia (established 1755) acquired their own apparatuses, there was less need for the library to act as a patron of scientific education.

Quite apart from the formal demonstrations, the Library Company increasingly assumed the characteristics of a scientific society during the 1740s. Collinson recognized this potential and tried to encourage it. As early as 1739, when Bartram first suggested the formation of a philosophical society in Philadelphia, Collinson replied: "As to the Society that thee Hints att, Had you a Sett of Learned, Well Qualified Members to Sett out with, It might Draw your Neighbors to Correspond with you. Your Library Company I take to be an essay towards Such a Society. But to Draw Learned Strangers to you, to teach Sciences, requires Salaries and good Encouragement; and this will require the Publick as well as proprietary assistance, which can't be at present complied with, Considering the Infancy of your colony." Collinson had a firmer grasp of

Philadelphia realities than did his correspondents there. The Philosophical Society, its first resident members also being from the scientifically inclined members of the Library Company, was active for less than a year. It was not revived until after the formation of the rival American Society for Promoting and Propagating Useful Knowledge more than twenty years later in Philadelphia.[17] The Library Company continued to be Philadelphia's real philosophical society until the late 1760s.

The stock of apparatuses belonging to the Company continued to increase during the period. Thomas Penn sent a double microscope and a camera obscura in 1741, a "handsome pair of Globes" in 1743, an electrical machine in 1747 (well after Franklin had begun his experiments), and a reflecting telescope in 1748. These benefactions constituted a respectable collection but did not satisfy members of the Company. In 1745 they had Collinson buy them a solar microscope and a "polished concave" (presumably simple) microscope and asked him to inquire about the prices of orreries, although they did not acquire one. Sometime before 1757 they also obtained a "Hydrostatical Ballance" to measure specific gravity. These were all important acquisitions, but the most significant piece received by the Library Company was also the simplest: a glass tube that Collinson sent them in 1745 along with an "Account of the new German Experiments in Electricity . . . and some directions for using it, so as to repeat those experiments." The German experiments were recounted in a bad translation published by *Gentleman's Magazine* in March of that year of a review by Albrecht Haller of German works on electricity in the *Bibliothèque raissonnée* of Amsterdam. Although the Company subscribed to that magazine, Collinson probably sent them a separate copy, as he had to Cadwallader Colden in New York.[18]

It was characteristic of Collinson to transmit things that excited him almost immediately. In 1735 he broadcast copies of Sloane's experiments with the purported fascinating power of the rattlesnake and in 1743 distributed to many of his curious correspondents copies of the microscopal discoveries concerning the nature of polyps by Abraham Trembley and others. The Library Company had been among the first to receive both of these. Once the "Virtuosi of Europe" were "taken up in Electrical Experiments," it seems likely that Collinson put his friends in the Library Company on these as promptly.[19]

The story of these experiments has been told often and well, beginning with Franklin himself, so that it does not need to be retold here.

Franklin, Kinnersley, Hopkinson, and Syng developed the single fluid theory of electricity, elucidated the doctrine of points (and of lightning rods), and confirmed the electrical nature of lightning. The most important scientific discoveries made in colonial America were the work of members of the Library Company, using its apparatuses and working, in a real sense, under its sponsorship. Franklin's *Experiments and Observations on Electricity* (London, 1751) stood as a kind of surrogate "philosophical transactions" in publicizing the Philadelphia findings, while Kinnersley personally spread the doctrine in his long-continued lecture tours of colonial cities.

These experiments in the late 1740s and early 1750s were the most important scientific accomplishments of the Library Company, although it continued to conduct experiments throughout the eighteenth and even into the nineteenth century. Its place in the scientific life of Philadelphia changed as new institutions developed to arouse the interests and absorb the energies of its philosophically minded citizens. The Academy and the College of Philadelphia have already been mentioned in this connection. In 1766 Charles Thomson, schoolmaster turned merchant, revived the Young Junto. That group, modeled on Franklin's old club, soon called itself the American Society for Promoting and Propagating Useful Knowledge and took as its exemplar the practical concerns of the Society of Arts of London. By the end of 1767, Thomas Bond had resurrected the moribund American Philosophical Society, which patterned itself on the Royal Society of London. With the merger of the two new organizations late in 1768, Philadelphia was given an active society dedicated to the promotion of science and the practical arts. The Library Company no longer needed to act as a philosophical society, although its interest in science continued. The changes they brought, however, were those of a total expansion of scientific effort. These Philadelphia institutions had interlocking directorates and overlapping memberships, so that they can be viewed as manifestations of specialization within a single, widening circle. The leaders of both the American Society and the Philosophical Society were also active members of the Library Company.[20]

Even with the establishment of competing collections, the apparatuses owned by the Library Company were used and continued to grow in number. In 1776 the directors purchased, among other things, "a Barometer, Cylinder Thermometer, Hydrometer, a Sextant," and some unspecified optical paraphernalia. By 1785 the Company had three solar microscopes, one of which they sold the next year. These and the other microscopes belonging to the library were used sufficiently to need repair. Owen Biddle, instrument maker and scientific amateur, who wished to use them in 1765, found that some were "a little out of order" and promised to mend them; even with this generous gesture, he had to give a note for £10 as security. Similarly, one was left with David Rittenhouse for repairs in 1787, and he too wanted to use it and was required to post bond. Franklin ensured that the electrical machine that Thomas Penn had sent in 1747 was kept in order, repairing it himself in 1763.[21]

Penn's reflecting telescope had a much longer, useful life. It was repaired as late as 1819 and in 1827 was still considered too valuable to lend for student use. Throughout the eighteenth century this instrument played an important role in Philadelphia astronomy, being used by many Philadelphians who were interested in that science. Nicholas Scull, mapmaker and surveyor, borrowed it in 1757 for the purpose of fixing the longitude of the city, and he may have used it in his surveying activities as well. Although the loan was for four months, Scull finally returned the instrument more than two years later and reported that it was unfit for use. While this condition may have been due to improper storage and to Scull's handling of the telescope, it is more likely that hard use since its arrival in 1748 had caused the deterioration. Probably Thomas Godfrey, glazier, mathematician, and inventor of the mariner's quadrant, had made use of it. William Parsons, sometime librarian, surveyor, and, like both Scull and Godfrey, an original member of the Junto, seems to have made observations with this instrument. Probably also Franklin and his philosophical associates readied the telescope to view the transit of Mercury in 1753, a project that was unsuccessful due to clouds. In 1761 the instrument was sent to Franklin in England to have repairs made. He brought it back to Philadelphia in 1762, and thereafter greater care was taken to see that it should not again rust.[22]

The telescope was soon put to use. Early in 1764 Francis Alison, vice-provost of the College of Philadelphia, joined his former pupil and fellow Presbyterian minister, John Ewing, and John Lukens, surveyor general of Pennsylvania, who borrowed it for use in connection with the establishment of the Pennsylvania-Maryland boundaries by Charles Mason and Jeremiah Dixon. Five years later Lukens joined Biddle in requesting use of the instrument so that Biddle might take it to Cape Henlopen as a part of the American Philosophical Society's effort to view the transit of Venus. This occasion of the greatest scientific cooperation in the eighteenth century was also the first important activity of the Philosophical Society and made the society known to the savants of Europe. The directors of the Library Company not only cooperated with the society in this undertaking but also, at their own expense, had Biddle affix a micrometer to the instrument so that it might be raised and lowered readily. The expedition to the cape and possibly additional uses of the instrument resulted in still more expense for the Company. Twice during the early seventies the directors sent the telescope to David Rittenhouse for repair and modification.[23]

Probably it was well that the transit occurred when it did, for not many years later the directors might have been much less willing to aid the Philosophical Society. In 1784 they jointly petitioned the Pennsylvania House of Representatives for building lots on the State House Square, maintaining, "the Buildings thus commodiously situated will have a Tendency to bring together and unite Gentlemen of science." Those gentlemen then quarreled over which should have the Fifth Street side of the square and the advantage of being nearer to the center of town. The society, as the site of Philosophical Hall affirms, won the battle. This struggle, when added to the resentment resulting from the conflict between the College of Philadelphia and the University of the State of Pennsylvania, may have been a factor in causing the directors to refuse the university (then housed in Philosophical Hall) the use of the library's apparatus in 1789.[24]

While the philosophical apparatus owned by the Library Company was significant in advancing the cause of science in Philadelphia, other cabinets and displays had nearly as much significance. From the 1740s, the Library Company had a museum, probably the first such collection in British America that was open to the public. The Company, although it was a private society, was open for the use of others, even though nonmembers could not borrow books. The holdings included curiosities of all kinds—natural, antiquarian, ethnological, and artistic—but were principally centered in the area of natural history. While it is difficult to date the beginnings of the collections, they probably originated in Bartram's gift of Pennsylvania fossils in 1742. This was a small beginning, but it was sufficient to impress Peter Kalm, Carolus Linnaeus's protégé, when he was given use of the library during his visit to America some six years later. By November 1749 the library also displayed another of its early wonders, a snake skin 12 feet long and 16 inches across.[25]

The largest and, for a time, the most important addition to the natural history collections was made in 1763 when, after almost three years of negotiation, the Company granted one of its shares to Matthew Clarkson, mapmaker, in return for "a curious and valuable Assortment of Fossils . . . disposed in a Cabinet in methodical order." These "fossils," including earths, ores, and minerals, had originally been assembled by merchant Samuel Hazard. The specimens were largely American in origin but contained some English and European samples for comparison.[26]

The collection was not immediately usable. Clarkson was dilatory in sending a catalogue, and, when he did, it seems to have been inadequate. Franklin and Thomson tried to put the specimens in order, "being wrapped in Paper which is liable to wear and the Numbers on them to be defaced," but contented themselves with putting a lock on the cabinet. In 1765 a committee completed "an exact list numerical and Alphabetical of the Collection." The materials were now easily accessible and were, in a scientific sense, the best the library had. In 1775 Thomas Paine was sufficiently excited by Hazard's collection to write an essay for his *Pennsylvania Magazine* extolling the practical virtues of the study of earths and minerals and urging that the American Philosophical Society undertake a sort of geological survey. Johann David Schoepf, a German physician, was less impressed by it in 1783, at which time the cabinet was bereft of the names of specimens or where they had been found.[27]

Many other natural curiosities flowed into the library. They were not always noted in the Minute Books, but the records of the last third of the eighteenth century give a good idea of the wide-ranging commerce of the port on the Delaware and also of the breadth of interest of her citizens. A "GarFish," yellow coral of Hispaniola, a "marine substance" taken off Turk's Island, an ostrich egg, a chicken with four legs, a "curious double Sea Cocoa-Nut that drives ashore on the Coast of Corrondal," and many similar treasures were presented by its citizens. During those same years, Philadelphia was frequently the seat of the Continental Congress and later of the Congress of the United States. The Library Company was open to delegates and members and served as a kind of Library of Congress, which helped to elicit gifts from gentlemen of other states. For example, Alexander Moultrie, attorney general of South Carolina, sent a "Scorpion and Santipee" (centipede) in

1781. The library already possessed a scorpion preserved in a bottle of spirits with some snakes.[28]

Occasionally the library actively sought such items; it apparently never refused them. Certainly the directors were caught up in the excitement over the discovery of mastodon bones in the Ohio River valley after the end of hostilities in the Seven Years' War. They were not alone in this. Collinson and his circle in England felt the same enthusiasm. When the officers of the Company heard of the "elephant" teeth (possibly from Bartram to whom Col. Henry Bouquet had written concerning the find), they appointed a committee to wait on Bouquet to get an account of the skeletons of these wonderful animals. The account, if it was given, was never entered in the minutes. Much later, in 1783, the company did acquire some bones from Isaac Craig, who presented "a petrified thigh bone of an uncommon animal with two Teeth and a Tusk." When Jean-Pierre Brissot de Warville, member of the Académie des Sciences, visited Philadelphia in 1788, he found these relics the most curious of all of those housed in the library. Probably they were, for in 1832, when interest in the museum declined, among the items that the Academy of Natural Sciences saw fit to "borrow" were the leg bone of a mammoth and two molars of a mastodon. The thigh had been traded to Charles Willson Peale in 1801 for one of his two famous reconstructions of the "great American Incognitum."[29]

The Company's cabinet was not confined to natural history. Almost from the beginning the library was a repository for Native American and other ethnological artifacts: clothing, arrowheads, spears, and utensils. Some of these items were kept (out of sheer necessity) for only a short time. After many complaints, the librarian in 1760 reported, "several Skins in the form of Indian Dresses in a room adjacent to the library grew offensive and troublesome." He received permission to dispose of those overripe habiliments.[30]

These items were not confined to gifts from Indian traders or to ax heads uncovered by Chester County plowmen, although these were the most numerous. The Company was proudest of a group of Eskimo dresses and utensils, which were the principal returns of expeditions in 1753 and 1754 by the Northwest Company in search of a northerly route to the Orient. In a sense, these were a repayment. The organizers of the expeditions included many Library Company members, and maps and books of the Company played a part in the promotion of these ambitious Philadelphia undertakings.[31]

The Company's cabinets also held items from more distant cultures. In 1786 company member Joseph Poyntell presented several pieces of cloth made by the "Otaheite Indians" and other Tahitian rarities collected during Capt. James Cooke's second voyage around the world. In the same year also, Franklin, among others, donated Chinese curiosities that reflected the newly begun American commerce with the Orient.[32]

All of these, along with the holdings of coins and medals and such hard-to-classify items as the hand of an Egyptian mummy sent by expatriate Pennsylvanian Benjamin West in 1767, constituted quite a respectable museum. Even before the Revolution, the collections of apparatuses and natural curiosities so taxed the space available in the State House that they were an important factor in causing the Company's removal to the second floor of Carpenter's Hall in 1772.[33]

Their next move, in 1790, to their own building on Fifth Street was more the consequence of a doubling of the rent by the Carpenter's Company than of an immediate lack of space. Library Hall provided room on its second floor for the Library Company's apparatuses and curiosities. Apparently those curiosities still had an audience in the last two decades of the eighteenth century. On June 11, 1782, the directors, prompted perhaps by the advertisement only a few days earlier for Pierre Eugène du Simitière's American Museum, finally set aside two special hours a week to view the collection "when proper application is made."[34]

The appearance of du Simitière's proprietary exhibition points up that the Library Company had competitors for the attention of scientifically inclined Philadelphians. Even before that time, the Philosophical Society had begun its own collections, which resembled those of the Company, and the Pennsylvania Hospital had developed an anatomical cabinet, which was opened in 1762 and which far excelled the library's meager holdings in that area. Even more significant, in 1786 Peale opened his museum, which would be housed for much of its existence across Fifth Street in Philosophical Hall or in the State House.[35] The Library Company seems to have welcomed and assisted Peale; but his far more ambitious natural history collections soon made their holdings seem meager and even irrelevant.

By 1802, when Peale removed his collections to the State House, much of Philadelphia's scientific energy also passed across Fifth Street to that museum, which served a nearly national function, or to the American Philosophical Society. The Library Company's instruments were used well into the new century, and its museum remained intact until the 1830s and 1840s, when finally it was lent and sold to make room for a growing collection of books.[36] It retained its scientific books and continued to buy them, even as its members looked elsewhere to satisfy other scientific needs. The Company had always been primarily a library and now increasingly devoted its resources to that end.

Franklin called his first foundation "The Mother of All the North American Subscription Libraries," and certainly it provided the model for many that were founded in the eighteenth century. That model included scientific activity. Its Philadelphia neighbor, the Union Library Company, acquired scientific apparatuses, provided a hall for lectures, and gave room to the Young Junto and the American Society, all before it merged with its "mother" in 1769. The Charles Town Library Society, one of whose founders was Peter Timothy, son of the Library Company's first librarian, followed a similar pattern. It also advertised philosophical lectures and in 1773 established a public natural history collection, the forerunner of the Charleston Museum.[37] These instances may be multiplied but cannot measure the extent to which other subscription libraries mimicked the behavior of the Library Company or whether bookish eighteenth-century men simply acted in simi-lar ways. It is certain, however, that the Library Company's example guided its Philadelphia "children" and affected the interests of its more distant offspring.

Above all, the Library Company had been tutor and encourager of Philadelphia's scientific interests in those critical years when the city on the Delaware was the North American metropolis. It brought some Philadelphians to the attention of a wider scientific community, its philosophical collections constituted the first American natural history museum, and it assisted in the development of competing but supplementary scientific institutions.[38] The Company began the second half of the eighteenth century in the midst of the Philadelphia Electrical experiments that helped to fix the terms of discourse for electrical science for years to come. It strengthened American pride, even if it did not set the course of American science. In quieter, less spectacular ways, however, the Library Company of Philadelphia helped to establish the place of science in an emerging national culture.

[1] "Artificers" scarcely fits some of the founders like Robert Grace and Thomas Hopkinson but is justified by Franklin's recollection when he composed the inscription for the cornerstone of Library Hall still in the possession of the Library Company. The Library Company as a scientific society has been dealt with in part in Dorothy Grimm, "Franklin's Scientific Institution," *Pennsylvania History* 23, no. 4 (October 1956): 437–62.

[2] Otho T. Beall, Jr., "Cotton Mather's Early 'Curiosa Americana,'" *William and Mary Quarterly*, 3d ser., 18, no. 3 (July 1961): 360–72; Kenneth Silverman, *The Life and Times of Cotton Mather* (New York: Harper and Row, 1984), pp. 244–49; Brooke Hindle, *The Pursuit of Science in Revolutionary America* (Chapel Hill: University of North Carolina Press, 1956), p. 61.

[3] The declining years of the Junto are covered well in the correspondence of Hugh Roberts with Franklin; see particularly Roberts to Franklin, June 1, 1758, May 15, 1760, October 12, 1765, *The Papers of Benjamin Franklin*, ed. Leonard W. Labaree, William B. Willcox, and Claude A. Lopez, 27 vols. to date (New Haven: Yale University Press, 1959–), 8:81–85, 9:113–16, 12:312–14.

[4] Library Company of Philadelphia, Minutes Book, 1:12, Archives, Library Company of Philadelphia (hereafter cited as LCP); Austin K. Gray, *Benjamin Franklin's Library . . .* (New York: Macmillan Co., 1937), pp. 9–10. For the company's early scientific books, see Edwin Wolf 2nd, "The First Books and Printed Catalogues of the Library Company of Philadelphia," *Pennsylvania Magazine of History and Biography* 78, no. 1 (January 1954): 41–55.

[5] I. Bernard Cohen, *Franklin and Newton . . .* , Memoirs of the American Philosophical Society, vol. 43 (Philadelphia: By the society, 1956), pp. 209–14, 234–43.

[6] Peter Collinson to John Bartram, January 20, 1734/35, London, in *Memorials of John Bartram and Humphry Marshall . . .* , ed. William Darlington (Philadelphia: Lindsay and Blackiston, 1849), pp. 59–62.

[7] Joseph Breintnall to Collinson, [November 1737, with postscript dated November 26, Philadelphia], Smith manuscripts, 1:164, LCP. For Grace, see Collinson to Breintnall, August 30, 1737, London, manuscript Ch. A, 3.84, Boston Public Library. For Roberts, see Franklin to Jared Eliot, September 12, 1751, Philadelphia, *Franklin Papers*, 4:192–95. Breintnall's poem, about what is probably *Rubus odoratus* L., "On the Lately Discover'd Wild Raspberries," du Simitière Scraps (fn. 26, LCP), has been published in Kenneth Silverman, ed., *Colonial American Poetry* (New York: Hafner Publishing Co., 1968), pp. 375–76. For a reproduction of one of Breintnall's sheets, see Edwin Wolf 2nd and Marie Elena Korey, eds., *Quarter of a Millenium: The Library Company of Philadelphia, 1731–1981 . . .* (Philadelphia: Library Company of Philadelphia, 1981), p. 16. Breintnall to Collinson, February 17, 1736/37, Journal Book of the Royal Society, 16:44–46, Royal Society of London Library. A second letter told of being bitten by a rattlesnake and of the depression that followed (Breintnall to Collinson, February 10, 17[45/]46, Philadelphia, in *Philosophical Transactions* 44 [March and April 1746]: 147–50). That depression may have led to Breintnall's suicide only a few months later (Frederick Tolles, "A Note on Joseph Breintnall, Franklin's Collaborator," *Philological Quarterly* 21, pt. 2 [April 1942]: 247–49). On Breintnall's meteorological records, see "Extract of a Letter from Mr. Joseph Breintnall to Mr. P. Collinson," Philadelphia, May 9, 1738, letterbook, 25:111–12, Royal Society of London Library; *Philosophical Transactions* 41 (January–June 1740): 59–60; and Peter Collinson Papers, 1:176b, Linnean Society of London. On Boerhaave's influence, see I. Bernard Cohen, "Franklin, Boerhaave, Newton, Boyle and the Absorption of Heat in Relation to Color," *Isis* 46, pt. 2 (June

1955): 99–104; and I. Bernard Cohen, "Franklin's Experiments on Heat Absorption as a Function of Color," *Isis* 34, pt. 4 (Spring 1943): 404–7.

[8] Hindle, *Pursuit of Science*, p. 22.

[9] John Fothergill, *Some Account of the Late Peter Collinson* (London, 1770), p. 11; Collinson to Charles Polhill, n.d., [London], Collinson Papers, 2:82, Linnean Society of London; Minutes Book, 1:178, LCP. Samuel Chew first mentioned Bartram to Collinson without result (Darlington, *Memorials*, pp. 166–67).

[10] Collinson to Bartram, January 20, 1734/35, London, as cited in Darlington, *Memorials*, pp. 59–62. Collinson had given both books he mentioned to Bartram to the Library Company. Bartram to Collinson, July 22, 1741, Bartram Papers, 1:21, Historical Society of Pennsylvania (hereafter cited as HSP). Minutes Book, 1:127 (December 13, 1742), LCP; Collinson to Breintnall, February 24, 1742/43, London, Gratz manuscripts, case 12, box 7, HSP; Bartram to Collinson, [1743], Bartram Papers, 1:29c, HSP; Bartram to Collinson, May 27, 1743, as cited in Darlington, *Memorials*, pp. 162–63.

[11] Breintnall to Collinson, [November 1737, postscript dated November 26, Philadelphia], Smith manuscripts, 1:164, LCP; Thomas Penn to John and Richard Penn, small letterbook, 1738–41, pp. 5–9, Penn Papers, HSP; Gray, *Franklin's Library*, p. 19.

[12] Minutes Book, 1:74, 125, LCP; Collinson to Thomas Penn, July 20, 1732, London, Jonah P. Thompson Collections, 2:113, HSP; Library Company to John Penn, [May 31, 1735], *Franklin Papers*, 2:34–35; Minutes Book, 1:74, 116, 124, 147–48, LCP.

[13] *Pennsylvania Gazette* (Philadelphia), June 5, 1740; Minutes Book, 1:102, LCP; Clifford K. Shipton, ed., *Sibley's Harvard Graduates*, vol. 6 (Cambridge: Harvard University Press, 1942), pp. 471–82.

[14] For accounts of attendees of Spencer's demonstrations, see R. A. Brock, ed., "The Journal of William Black," *Pennsylvania Magazine of History and Biography* 1, nos. 3, 4 (1877): 246, 413–14; and John Smith, notes, Smith MSS, 5:254–55, LCP. Both accounts are published in I. Bernard Cohen, "Benjamin Franklin and the Mysterious Dr. Spence," *Journal of the Franklin Institute* 235, no. 1 (January 1943): 1–25. N. H. de V. Heathcote, "Franklin's Introduction to Electricity," *Isis* 46, pt. 1 (March 1955): 29–35; J. L. Heilbron, "Franklin, Haller, and Franklinist History," *Isis* 68, no. 244 (December 1977): 540.

[15] *Pennsylvania Gazette*, December 6, 1750. The lectures were not, as has been said, given in the home of Jacob Duché. For Dove, see Carl Bridenbaugh and Jessica Bridenbaugh, *Rebels and Gentlemen: Philadelphia in the Age of Franklin* (New York: Reynal and Hitchcock, 1942), pp. 36–38, 49–50, 121–23, 331.

[16] *Pennsylvania Gazette*, April 11, 1751, September 14, 1752; J. A. Leo Lemay, *Ebenezer Kinnersley: Franklin's Friend* (Philadelphia: University of Pennsylvania Press, 1964).

[17] Collinson to Bartram, July 10, 1739, Bartram Papers, 3:9, HSP (also published in Darlington, *Memorials*, 131–33); Hindle, *Pursuit of Science*, pp. 68–73, 127–36.

[18] Minutes Book, 1:113, 131–32, 147–48, 156, LCP; *Charter and Laws and Catalogue of Books of the Library Company of Philadelphia* (Philadelphia: B. Franklin and D. Hall, 1757), pp. 22–23; *Pennsylvania Gazette*, December 20, 1748; Minutes Book, 1:147–48, LCP; I. Bernard Cohen, ed., *Benjamin Franklin's Experiments: A New Edition of Franklin's Experiments and Observation on Electricity* (Cambridge: Harvard University Press, 1941), p. 169; Franklin to Michael Collinson, [February 8, 1770], *Franklin Papers*, 17:34–35. Heilbron, "Franklin, Haller," pp. 540–45. The date of the tube gift has been in dispute, as Franklin remembered it as being both in 1745 and in

1746. Lemay, *Kinnersley*, pp. 54–58, first pointed to *Gentleman's Magazine* as the source of the Philadelphia experiments, and Lemay posited a specially annotated copy. The magazine was sent to Colden from London, March 30, 1745 (*Letters and Papers of Cadwallader Colden*, vol. 3 [New York: New-York Historical Society, 1920], pp. 109–11).

[19] Collinson to Colden, September 4, 1743, *Colden Letters*, 3:27–29; Cohen, *Franklin's Experiments*, p. 169; Minutes Book, 1:58, 134, LCP.

[20] Edward Potts Cheyney, *History of the University of Pennsylvania* (Philadelphia: University of Pennsylvania Press, 1940). Collinson, who also aided the academy and the college in their English purchases, on one occasion credited money for the college's apparatus to the Library Company; Minutes Book, 1:188, LCP. For the societies, see Hindle, *Pursuit of Science*, pp. 121–40. The Union Library in which the American Society met and which merged in 1769 with the Library Company seems to have shared the scientific inclinations of the company on which it was modeled.

[21] Minutes Book, 2:123, 3:37, 1:240, 3:55, 1:208, LCP.

[22] Minutes Book, 5:54–55 [Treasurer's Account], 223, 1:168–69, 186, 198, 199, 219, 223, LCP. See also I. Bernard Cohen, "Franklin and the Transit of Mercury in 1753," *Proceedings of the American Philosophical Society* 94, no. 3 (1950): 222–27.

[23] Minutes Book, 1:223, 2:5, 14–15, 54, 88, 100, LCP. Ewing served as one of the Pennsylvania commissioners for the survey; see Thomas D. Cope, "Some Local Scholars who Counseled the Proprietors and Their Commissioners during the Border Surveys of the 1760's," *Proceedings of the American Philosophical Society* 99, no. 4 (1955): 268–76.

[24] Minutes Book, 2:215ff., 3:187, LCP; Charles E. Peterson, "Library Hall: Home of the Library Company of Philadelphia," *Proceedings of the American Philosophical Society* 95, no. 3 (1951): 267.

[25] Adolph B. Benson, ed., *The America of 1750: Peter Kalm's Travels in North America*, 2 vols. (New York: Wilson-Erickson, 1937), 1:135; John Smith diary, November 7, 1749, John Smith manuscript, vol. 7, LCP; *Charter Laws and Catalogue*, pp. 22–23.

[26] Minutes Book, 1:193, 194, 209, LCP. See Atlanticus [Thomas Paine], "Useful and Entertaining Hints," *Pennsylvania Magazine; or, American Monthly Museum* 1, no. 2 (February 1775): 53–57.

[27] Minutes Book, 1:197, 208, 209, LCP; [Paine], "Useful Hints," pp. 53–57; Johann David Schōpf, *Travels in the Confederation*, trans. Alfred J. Morrison, 2 vols. (Philadelphia: W. J. Campbell, 1911), 1:86–87.

[28] Minutes Book, 2:70, 91, 101, 161, 3:6, 33, 39, 2:166, LCP; *Charter Laws and Catalogue*, pp. 22–23; N. Louise Bailey and Elizabeth Ivey Cooper, *Biographical Directory of the South Carolina House of Representatives*, vol. 3 (Columbia: University of South Carolina Press, 1981), pp. 515–17.

[29] Minutes Book, 2:198, LCP; Wolf and Korey, *Quarter of a Millenium*, p. 25. Peter Collinson, "An Account of Some Very Large Fossil Teeth Found in North America," *Philosophical Transactions* 57, pt. 2 (1767): 464–67; Whitfield J. Bell, "A Box of Old Bones: A Note on the Identification of the Mastodon, 1766–1806," *Proceedings of the American Philosophical Society* 93, no. 2 (May 1949): 169–77. Henry Bouquet to John Bartram, July 15, 1762, as cited in Darlington, *Memorials*, pp. 427–28; Minutes Book, 1:234, LCP. Jean-Pierre Brissot de Warville, *New Travels in the United States of America Performed in 1788* (Dublin: P. Byrne, A. Grueber, W. McKenzie, 1792), pp. 241–42; Minutes Book, 6:25, LCP.

[30] Minutes Book, 1:185, LCP. Only a few baskets now remain of the once-large collection of ethnological artifacts.

[31] *Charter Laws and Catalogue*, pp. 22–23.

[32] Minutes Book, 3:16, 21, LCP.

[33] Minutes Book, 1:253, 2:74 (June 29, 1772), LCP.

[34] Minutes Book, 2:174, LCP. See also *A Catalogue of the Books Belonging to the Library Company of Philadelphia* (Philadelphia: Zachariah Poulson, Jr., 1789), p. v.; and Joel J. Oroz, "Pierre Eugéne du Simitière: Museum Pioneer in America," *Museum Studies Journal* 1, no. 5 (Spring 1985): 7–18.

[35] Whitfield J. Bell, Jr., "The Cabinet of the American Philosophical Society," in Walter M. Whitehead, ed., *A Cabinet of Curiosities* . . . (Charlottesville: University Press of Virginia, 1967), pp. 1–34; Bridenbaugh and Bridenbaugh, *Rebels and Gentlemen*, pp. 273–74; William H. Williams, *America's First Hospital: The Pennsylvania Hospital, 1751–1841* (Wayne, Pa.: Haverford House, Publishers, 1976), p. 48. The hospital charged admission to view the collection. Charles Coleman Sellers, *Mr. Peale's Museum: Charles Willson Peale and the First Popular Museum of Natural Sciences* (New York: W. W. Norton, 1980), pp. 23, 76–80, 152–53.

[36] The "loan" of items to the Academy of Natural Science in 1832 has already been noted. In 1845 John Jay Smith recommended cutting through the ceiling to make gallery shelves above and in 1845 sold the remaining museum items for $50.72 (Minutes Book, 6:264–66, 269, LCP).

[37] Benjamin Franklin, *Autobiography*, ed. J. A. Leo Lemay and P. M. Zall (New York: W. W. Norton, 1986), p. 57; Margaret Barton Korty, *Benjamin Franklin and Eighteenth-Century American Libraries*, Transactions of the American Philosophical Society, ns., 55, pt. 9 (December 1965): 21–22; Hennig Cohen, *The South Carolina Gazette, 1732–1775* (Columbia: University of South Carolina Press, 1953), pp. 18, 23–24, 87, 88.

[38] Certainly the company's museum predated that of Charleston Museum or even Harvard's holdings in that area. The author disagrees with those who call it a mere private cabinet as distinguished from a public collection; for the opposite view, see Joel J. Oroz, "Curators and Culture: An Interpretive History of the Museum Movement in America, 1773–1870" (Ph.D. diss., Case Western Reserve University, 1986), pp. 1–42.

William Bartram
Sowing with the Harvest
Robert McCracken Peck

On Friday the 13th, July 1787, the United States Constitutional Convention appeared on the verge of collapse. After more than six weeks of rancorous debate and a month of sweltering, humid weather, the small and large states were bitterly divided on the issue of representation. Several delegates had already left in disgust, and others were threatening to follow. The convention, in the words of one participant, was being held together by "no more than a hair."[1] A change of scene was badly needed.

Someone suggested an excursion to the country to visit the house and garden of the Quaker naturalist William Bartram (1739–1823) in Kingsessing, just a few miles from town. The suggestion was greeted with enthusiasm—it was the first subject of general agreement in weeks. And so the next day the members of the Constitutional Convention boarded their carriages, crossed the Schuylkill River on the floating bridge at Gray's Ferry, and arrived en masse and unannounced at Bartram's garden.

The property, originally bought and developed by John Bartram (1699–1777) in 1728, consisted of a farmhouse, several out-buildings, and a botanical garden that had the reputation of being the first and finest in North America. Despite its importance, the garden's appearance was not up to everyone's expectations. Massachusetts delegate Manasseh Cutler (1742–1823) considered it "very badly arranged." The plants in the garden, he observed with disappointment, were "neither placed ornamentally nor botanically, but seem to be jumbled together in heaps."[2] The arrangement was revealing of John and William Bartram's practical approach to horticulture. Both were more interested in how plants grew and what agricultural or medicinal purposes they might serve than in their formal arrangement. The garden was primarily a scientific and commercial venture, not an aesthetic one.

Artistic arrangement aside, Bartram's garden and house (described by Cutler as "an ancient fabric built of stone and very large") were of considerable interest to the delegates, for they represented a center of American scientific activity that had captured attention around the world.[3]

John Bartram, who had died ten years before the delegates' visit, had been one of the country's most illustrious naturalists. A close friend of Benjamin Franklin and a founding member of the American Philosophical Society, he was a prominent and active member of Philadelphia's—and North America's—intellectual elite. His work was so highly regarded in England, that King George III appointed him Royal Botanist for North America in 1765. His steady correspondents constituted a who's who of British and European intellectuals including: Peter Collinson, a Quaker mercer in London who was also a benefactor of the Library Company of Philadelphia; Sir Hans Sloane, physician to King George II and president of the Royal Society; John Dillenius, director of the botanical garden at Oxford; and Philip Miller, director of the Chelsea Physic Garden and author of the influential *Gardener's Dictionary* (1731). Swedish naturalist Carl Linneaus, the father of modern scientific classification, reputedly called John Bartram "the greatest natural botanist in the world."[4]

William Bartram, the seventh of John's eleven children, inherited all of his father's intellectual curiosity. Unlike his father, however, William received a rigorous formal education. At the Academy of Philadelphia he studied history, Latin, French, and the classics. His early instruction in science—and his passion for botany—came directly from his father.

During William's formative years the two men traveled throughout the Middle Atlantic colonies and as far south as Florida collecting plants for propagation in their botanical garden. On John's death in 1777, William and his younger brother John, Jr. (1743–1812), took over the management of the garden, which had long since changed from a personal repository of unusual plants to a profitable commercial enterprise.

Seeds, bulbs, and live plants grown in the garden were sent from Philadelphia to horticulturists around the world.

William Bartram was, typically, at work with his plants when the constitutional delegation arrived in July 1787. "We found him with another man hoeing in his garden," wrote Manasseh Cutler. "[He was] in a short jacket and trowsers and without shoes or stockings. He at first stared at us and seemed to be somewhat embarrassed at seeing so large and gay a company so early in the morning."[5]

Shy and reclusive by nature, William Bartram (fig. 1) was more at home in the wilderness than surrounded by politicians. When the oc-

Figure 1. Charles Willson Peale, *William Bartram*, Philadelphia, 1808. Oil on canvas; H. 23″, W. 19″. (Independence National Historical Park.)

casion demanded, as it did this morning, however, he could be a gracious and instructive host. His brother John usually handled the business side of the enterprise, while William served as the family horticulturist. In 1787 he probably knew more than anyone else in North America about the plants and wildlife of the country. His was a knowledge based on first-hand observation as well as the best books available.

Following the extended apprenticeship with his father, William traveled alone more than 2,400 miles through southeastern North America to gather seeds and plant specimens for his English patron, Dr. John Fothergill, and others.[6] Like his father, he became something of an American institution through his writing, painting, correspondence, and exchange of plants.

The Bartrams, father and son, are credited with introducing literally hundreds of North American plant species to English and European gardens. Many of the dried specimens William collected are still preserved in the herbarium of the British Museum, along with paintings he made of American plants and animals during his most important expedition, a four-year collecting trip through the American Southeast (1773–77).[7]

William Bartram was a first-rate naturalist, but what set him apart from others of the period were his abilities to see beyond the narrow focus of his botanical inquiries and to share his unique vision of the world with others. Unfortunately, no records survive to reveal the nature of his conversations with the Constitutional Convention delegates that Saturday morning in July, but it is hard to imagine that they did not revolve in part around the extraordinary travels for which he was so well known.

Bartram had been working on a written account of his experiences ever since his return to Philadelphia a decade before. A public notice of his intention to publish a book of travels was issued by Philadelphia printer Enoch Story, Jr., in 1786. For whatever reason, this first attempt at publication was suspended for another five years. When Bartram's book finally did appear in print under the lengthy title *Travels through North and South Carolina, Georgia, East and West Florida, the Cherokee Country, the Extensive Territories of the Muscogulges, or Creek Confederacy, and the Country of the Chactaws*, it offered readers on both sides of the Atlantic a singular blend of scientific inquiry, matter-of-fact description, and a philosophy that blended traditional Quaker beliefs with Bartram's own form of pantheism. Bartram's *Travels* was without precedent in America. Far more than a travelogue or simple scientific treatise, this was a personal celebration of the wonder of wild nature. While others saw nothing (or worse) in the untamed world, Bartram saw "a glorious apartment of the boundless palace of the sovereign Creator." To him, every part of nature was wondrous and endlessly fascinating, each reflecting in its own way "the almighty power, wisdom, and beneficence of the Supreme Creator and Sovereign Lord of the Universe." Bartram believed that each living thing was designed by God for specific "purposes and use," and he devoted his life to trying to understand what some of these might be.[8]

Instead of looking at natural phenomena in isolation, as was the common practice of the period, Bartram found unity and purpose in the universe by observing its totality. A good example of this is his description of the struggle between a "bomble bee" and a garden spider in *Travels*. After a fifteen-minute battle, the bee "expired in the arms of the devouring spider, who, ascending the rope with his game, retired to feast on it under cover of leaves; and perhaps before night, became himself the delicious evening repast of a bird or lizard."[9] Here a traditional enlightenment view of natural hierarchy is reenforced by a first-hand account of ecology in action.

Bartram's book was generally praised for its many contributions to natural history. "The amateur of natural science cannot fail of being highly gratified by the perusal of this volume," wrote a reviewer. "Mr. Bartram has accurately described a variety of birds, fish, reptiles, hitherto but little known: His botanical researches are more copious than any other writers with whom we are acquainted."[10]

The unusual literary style was less highly regarded. Bartram's "rapturous effusions" were considered by some to be excessive and detrimental to the book. One reviewer considered the style "very incorrect and disgustingly pompous." Another found it "too luxuriant and florid to merit the palm of chastity and correctness." The flowery passages in *Travels* that attracted such criticism were quite atypical of scientific writing of the period. Bartram's descriptions of the setting sun, for example, parted conspicuously from the restrained, analytical style more often employed by scientists of his day: "How glorious the powerful sun, Minister of the Most High, in the rule and government of this earth, leaves our hemisphere, retiring from our sight beyond the western forests! I behold with gratitude his departing smiles, tugging the fleecy roseate clouds, now riding far away on the Eastern horizon; behold they vanish from sight in the azure skies! . . . The glorious sovereign of the day, calling in his bright beaming emanations, leaves us in his absence to the milder government and protection of the silver queen of night, attended by millions of bright luminaries."[11]

Bartram managed to balance such outbursts of poetic revelry with more objective observation, thus making his book as practical as it was inspiring. Although sensitive to the beauty of nature, Bartram was also capable of being extremely analytical: "The attention of a traveller should be particularly turned . . . to the various works of Nature to mark the distinctions of the climates he may explore and to offer such useful observations on the different productions as may occur," he explained in his introduction. "Observe the green meadows how they are decorated; they seem enamelled with beds of flowers. The blushing *Chironia* and *Rhexia*, the spiral *Ophrys* with immaculate white flowers, the *Limodorum, Arethusa pulcherima, Sarracenia purpurea, Saracenia galeata, Sarracenia lacunosa, Sarracenia flava*. Shall we analyze these beautiful plants, since they seem cheerfully to invite us?"[12]

The level of scientific detachment found in many parts of the book more than balanced the emotional outpourings that surprised so many of his contemporaries. While some were criticizing Bartram's writing style, others were stimulated by its refreshing novelty. This was particularly true overseas. European reviewers generally found Bartram's descriptions neither too dry nor too exaggerated, but "correct" and even "elegant."[13]

Its occasional lists of plants and animals notwithstanding, *Travels* was, along with Thomas Jefferson's *Notes on the State of Virginia* (1787), the most readable natural history to emerge from North America since the continent's first European settlement.[14] More personal and anecdotal than Jefferson's book, Bartram's *Travels* was also more self-consciously literate, written to entertain as well as to inform.

For whatever reasons, the first edition of *Travels* met with only limited sales in the United States and was not reprinted here until 1928. In Europe, however, the book met with a much more favorable reception. A 1792 London edition was quickly followed by a second edition there and by editions in Dublin (1793), Berlin (1793), Vienna (1793), Haarlem (1794–97), Amsterdam (1797), and Paris (1799 and 1801).

"Anthropology and ethnology have been considerably enriched by our author," enthused the editor of the Berlin edition: "But natural history proper receives the most important enrichment through this work. . . . He acquaints us with a considerable number of new plants. . . . The fauna has also gained much through him, both through the discovery of several hitherto unknown or doubtful species and reports on the migratory birds and on the life histories of large injurious animals, such as the Rattlesnake and the Alligator. . . . Especially he exhibits in the whole long journey fortitude, courage, and quiet endurance of all kinds of discomforts and dangers, whereby he is distinguished above many other travelers."[15]

For English romanticists, the fantastic world Bartram described was the Eden for which man had long been searching. The Native American, whose natural order he revealed, suggested pleasant images of man before the fall. Samuel Taylor Coleridge (1772–1834) considered the *Travels* "a work of high merit [in] every way" and copied sections of the book into his own notebook for further study.[16] He later adopted many of Bartram's images for use in such works as "The Rime of the Ancient Mariner," *Osorio*, "Kubla Khan," "Frost at Midnight," "This Lime-tree Bower, My Prison," "Christabel," "The Wanderings of Cain," and "Lewti." Similarly, William Wordsworth (1770–1850) drew ideas and images from Bartram's *Travels* for use in "Ruth," *The Prelude*; *The Excursion*; *The Recluse*; *A Guide through the District of the Lakes*; and the *Ecclesiastical Sonnets*.

What made Bartram so interesting to Coleridge, Wordsworth, and others, and what makes him such a pleasure to read today is his enthusiasm, even reverence, for nature. This attitude had as much affect on the scientific world as it had on the world's literary community. For almost fifty years after his return from the South in 1777, Bartram served as friend and mentor to a new generation of American naturalists, many of them living in and around Philadelphia. As the age of specialization in science began, each would-be specialist found in Bartram useful information about his or her field of interest in the natural world and inspiration for how to study it. According to his first biographer, George Ord (1781–1866), "there was scarcely an American or foreign writer who attempted the natural history of this country but applied to him for information on their relative treatises."[17]

Alexander Wilson (1766–1813), often called the "father of American ornithology," consulted with Bartram regularly and even lived in Bartram's house for periods during the writing of his pioneering book *American Ornithology* (1808–14).[18] Wilson's plates for the book, which stylistically resemble Bartram's own bird paintings, set a standard for scientific illustration in America until they were surpassed and overshadowed by the work of John James Audubon (1785–1851) in the middle of the nineteenth century. His precise verbal descriptions of bird behavior, also inspired by Bartram, are still consulted today.

An equally distinguished Bartram protegé was Benjamin Smith Barton (1766–1815), who would eventually inherit Bartram's mantle as the most knowledgeable botanist in North America. In 1803 he published the first American botanical textbook, *The Elements of Botany*. Much of the information included and most of the illustrations in the pioneering work were provided by William Bartram. Thomas Nuttall (1786–1859), another influential student of American botany, "had a room expressly reserved from him at [Bartram's Garden] called *Nuttall's room*," which he occupied for weeks at a time while writing his seminal *Genera of North American Plants* (1818).[19]

Nor was Bartram's influence limited to birds and plants. Thomas Say (1787–1834), a grandnephew of Bartram, born during the summer of the Constitutional Convention, was a frequent visitor to the garden during the final decades of Bartram's life. Say, who consciously retraced parts of Bartram's southern trip during winter 1817/18, is today recognized as the "father of American entomology and conchology" because of his pioneering work with insects and shells.[20] He was considered such an important figure in American science in the early nineteenth century that Charles Willson Peale (1741–1827) painted a portrait of him to hang near those of William Bartram and Alexander Wilson in his gallery of famous Americans.

In the decades following Bartram's death in 1823, as many Americans celebrated the taming of the American wilderness, others lamented its passing and looked on Bartram's descriptions of the virgin land with new appreciation. One of this new generation to take special note of Bartram's work was John James Audubon, who retraced much of Bartram's travel route and quoted him frequently in his journals. In his paintings, Audubon parted dramatically from Alexander Wilson's careful, neoclassical style to create the romantic life-size images for which he is so well known. By infusing his scientific work with emotion (at the risk of receiving criticism from some in the scientific community), Audubon did for wildlife painting what Bartram had done for literature three decades before.

Elsewhere in the country, far away from Bartram's moss-draped South, other distinctly American writers found universal truths in Bartram's sensitive descriptions of nature. Ralph Waldo Emerson (1803–82) and Henry David Thoreau (1817–62) were but two of the many New Englanders to read the *Travels* and be demonstrably affected by the images they contained.[21]

Bartram's original reason for traveling through the South was to collect living plants and seeds and other "rare and useful productions of nature" for his English patrons.[22] But William Bartram's influence went far beyond his activities as a collector. During his fruitful eighty-four years, with Philadelphia as his base, the quiet Quaker of Kingsessing sowed as many seeds as he harvested. Some are still bearing fruit today.

As for the Constitutional Convention, the delegates greatly enjoyed their visit to Bartram's garden and returned to the city refreshed. That afternoon the month-long hot spell gave way to cooler weather, and on the following Monday the convention broke its deadlock with the agreement since dubbed "the Great Compromise."

---

[1] Luther Martin, quoted in Jean Fritz, *Shh! We're Writing the Constitution* (New York: G. P. Putnam and Sons, 1987), p. 28.

[2] W. P. Cutler and J. P. Cutler, eds., *The Life, Journals, and Correspondence of Reverend Manasseh Cutler LL.D.*, 2 vols. (Cincinnati: R. Clarke, 1888), 1:258.

[3] Cutler and Cutler, *Life, Journals*, 1:258.

[4] Carl Bridenbaugh and Jessica Bridenbaugh, *Rebels and Gentlemen: Philadelphia in the Age of Franklin* (reprint, New York: Hesperides/Oxford University Press, 1962), p. 317; Emily Read Cheston, *John Bartram: His Garden and His House; William Bartram* (Philadelphia: John Bartram Association, 1938), p. 8; and D. Roger Mower, Jr.,"Bartram's Garden in Philadelphia," *Antiques* 125, no. 3 (March 1984): 631. The original source for this oft-quoted remark is unknown to the author. For more information on the life of John Bartram, see Edmund Berkeley and Dorothy Berkeley, *The Life and Travels of John Bartram: From Lake Ontario to the River John* (Tallahassee: University Presses of Florida, 1982).

[5] Cutler and Cutler, *Life, Journals*, 1:258.

[6] For information on Bartram's travels (including a state-by-state itinerary), see Robert M. Peck, ed., *Bartram Heritage Report* (Atlanta: United States Department of the Interior; Montgomery, Ala.: Bartram Trail Conference, 1978).

[7] For reproductions of the Bartram paintings now at the British Museum and a useful commentary, see William Bartram, *Botanical and Zoological Drawings, 1756–88*, ed. Joseph Ewan, Memoirs of the American Philosophical Society, vol. 74 (Philadelphia: By the society, 1968).

[8] William Bartram, *Travels through North and South Carolina, Georgia, East and West Florida* . . . (Philadelphia: James and Johnson, 1791), pp. xiv, xxiii, xiv. For a history of the publication of Bartram's *Travels*, see Robert McCracken Peck, "William Bartram and His Travels," *Contributions to the History of North American Natural History* . . . (London: Society for the Bibliography of Natural History, 1983), pp. 35–45.

[9] Bartram, *Travels*, p. xxxi.

[10] *Massachusetts Magazine; or, Monthly Museum* 4 (November 1792): 686–87. For sources of other contemporary reviews and reactions to Bartram's book, see Rose Marie Cutting, *John and William Bartram, William Byrd II, and St. John de Crevecoeur: A Reference Guide* (Boston: G. K. Hall, 1976), pp. 37–72.

[11] "Travels through North and South Carolina," *Universal Asylum and Columbian Magazine* 1 (March–April, 1792): 195–97, 255–67; *Massachusetts Magazine; or, Monthly Museum* 4 (November 1792): 686–87; and *Monthly Review; or, Literary Journal* 10 (January–April, 1794): 13–22, 130–38; Bartram, *Travels*, p. 158.

[12] Bartram, *Travels*, pp. xiii, xviii.

[13] "Voyage dans les Parties du Sud de l'Amérique Septentrionale," *La Clef du Cabinet des Souverains*, no. 733 (January–February 1799): 6267.

[14] William Byrd's *History of the Dividing Line Betwixt Virginia and North Carolina*, written in the 1720s but not published (even in abbreviated form) until 1841, might have ranked with Bartram and Jefferson had it been published earlier. By the time it was printed it was a historical footnote rather than a seminal work.

[15] Bartram, *Travels*, p. xiv.

[16] Samuel Taylor Coleridge, *Specimens of the Table Talk of Samuel Taylor Coleridge* (London: Samuel Murray, 1836), p. 33. For an extensive analysis of Bartram's influence on Coleridge, Wordsworth, and other romantic writers, see N. Bryllion Fagin, *William Bartram, Interpreter of the American Landscape* (Baltimore: Johns Hopkins Press, 1933); and John L. Lowes, *The Road to Xanadu* (Boston: Houghton Mifflin Co., 1927).

[17] [George Ord?], "Biographical Sketch of William Bartram," in *The Cabinet of Natural History and American Rural Sports*, vol. 2 (Philadelphia: J. and T. Doughty, 1832), p. vii.

[18] According to Ord, who knew both men, "it was through the encouragement and assistance rendered by Mr. Bartram that Wilson commenced and completed his splendid work on ornithology; and by his constant visits to the rural and delightful grounds of the botanic garden, he first conceived the plan of forming the work" (George Ord, "Biographical Sketch," p. v). For Wilson living with Bartram from 1811 to 1812, see Francis Harper, ed., *The Travels of William Bartram* (naturalist's ed.; New Haven: Yale University Press, 1958), p. xxxii. For Wilson and his relationship with Bartram, see Clark Hunter, *The Life and Letters of Alexander Wilson* (Philadelphia: American Philosophical Society, 1983).

[19] Elias Durand, "Biographical Notice of the Late Thomas Nuttall," *Proceedings of the American Philosophical Society* 7 (1860), p. 301. Joseph Ewan and Nesta Ewan of Missouri Botanical Garden are currently at work on a definitive biography of Benjamin Smith Barton. The author is indebted to them for information about Barton and for their encouragement and guidance since 1977.

[20] For this and other information about Bartram's relationship with Thomas Say, the author is indebted to Patricia Tyson Stroud and her book *Thomas Say: New World Naturalist* (Philadelphia: University of Pennsylvania Press, 1992).

[21] Thoreau quotes Bartram in *Walden* (1854), "The Succession of Forest Trees" (1860) and in several of his private notebooks, especially those on Indian customs.

[22] Bartram, *Travels*, p. 1.

The Enlightened City
Charles Willson Peale's Philadelphia Museum in Its Urban Setting

Sidney Hart

Charles Willson Peale (1741–1827) contributed in many diverse ways to the cultural life of Philadelphia and America. As an artist he helped to establish the Pennsylvania Academy of the Fine Arts, an institution that promoted and exhibited the work of American artists. As a naturalist and an inventor, he was an active member of the American Philosophical Society, helping to promote and disseminate scientific and technical information to Americans. Peale was active in contributing papers, drawings, and information and undertaking with the society's assistance a scientific expedition successfully exhuming the first complete skeleton of the American mastodon. As an artisan and a reformer, he developed and improved devices, machines, and patented inventions that would heat homes better and more economically, make kitchens safer and more efficient, enable people to bathe in their homes with less trouble, allow people to copy their letters and documents almost effortlessly, enable towns and cities to construct sturdy and lightweight bridges with less labor and expense, and provide American dentists with a method to

The author thanks Lillian B. Miller, editor of the Peale Family Papers, for providing the encouragement to do this paper and is indebted to David C. Ward, assistant editor of the Peale Papers, who read and commented on several drafts of this paper; the material on Peale's exhumation of the mastodon, in particular, benefited from Ward's work in *The Selected Papers of Charles Willson Peale and His Family*, vol. 2: *Charles Willson Peale: The Artist as Museum Keeper, 1791–1810*.

manufacture teeth out of porcelain, a material far superior to what dentists had been using at that time.

Overshadowing all these contributions—the activity in which Peale expended his greatest creative energies—was the establishment and operation of the Philadelphia Museum, Peale's most important contribution to Philadelphia's and America's culture. The museum, with a policy of open admission, was testimony to the vibrancy of America's democratic institutions; its didactic purpose of universal education and its amalgamation of virtue and wisdom, a reflection of America's republican ethos; and its orderliness and Linnaean classification, an actualization of the abstract laws and reason of the Enlightenment in the New World. A French philosophe who visited the museum in the 1790s grasped Peale's stunning achievement and exclaimed, "*This is the Temple of GOD! Here is nothing but TRUTH and REASON*."[1] Yet in many ways Peale's great achievement was dependent on the resources of Philadelphia—an environment that was severely tested in the early 1790s.

On Wednesday, August 21, 1793, at three o'clock in the afternoon, Peale, his wife, and their two youngest children boarded Captain West's packet at the Pine Street wharf. They took the packet to Cape Henlopen, Delaware, a rich source of waterfowl and other birds, and there spent several weeks shooting and preserving birds for the museum. The specimen collecting went well, but by the second week of September they began hearing of an alarming outbreak of sickness in Philadelphia and, fearing for the family members left in the city, made arrangements to return home.[2]

In Philadelphia, Benjamin Rush, the city's most influential physician, had identified the epidemic as yellow fever—a disease for which eighteenth-century physicians had no etiology and could not cure and that was often fatal. Rush had spent the summer in Philadelphia in a heroic struggle against the fever. He was convinced that a cure for this disease would be found only in a total understanding of the laws that underlay all disease. Such a discovery, Rush believed, would signify for medicine what Newton's laws did in celestial mechanics. In a symbolic sense Rush's struggle against the epidemic was a test of his Enlightenment faith—that nature was designed by a beneficent creator for the use of man and reality was based on simple and rational truths—and the outcome was a verdict of Philadelphia's status as an enlightened city. For

Peale even more was at stake; the health of his family and the success of his museum was dependent on Philadelphia's health.[3]

Notwithstanding Rush's heroic efforts, the epidemic raged on, and at its height, more than 100 Philadelphians were buried each day. By early September almost all business had ceased, and the normal operations of city, state, and federal governments had collapsed. Peale arrived back in the city on September 16 and found the conditions "shocking." Panic had set in, and people fearing contagion were fleeing the city, some in "shameful neglects of sacred duties," deserting even their spouses and children. Out of a population of 45,000, perhaps half fled the city and as many as 5,000 died. By the end of the decade coastal cities from Boston to Charleston had experienced five more yellow-fever epidemics. Peale feared that such epidemics might bring "a total decay of our large Cities." Unlike his friend Thomas Jefferson, who thought of urban areas as unhealthy places for both the human body and the body politic, Peale believed there was a close and symbiotic relationship between healthy populous cities and a flourishing national culture.[4]

Although lacking Rush's certainty, Peale just as fervently believed that nature provided remedies for all disease, if man was but "attentive" enough to perceive them. In 1799 he wrote to Gabriel Furman, who the previous year had been appointed by the New York City Council to investigate the causes of yellow fever, that the solution for such epidemics was reforms in the public-health programs as well as in the personal conduct of individuals. The yellow-fever epidemics would be "one of the greatest blessings that could happen," if people changed their harmful behavior. Reform would not only eliminate disease but also extend the life of man to its natural limit of "200 Years." Yet, a cure for the disease was not found in Peale's lifetime, his reforms for better and healthier regimens were not adopted, and even Peale did not live to be 200 years old. However, beginning in the 1790s numerous urban health measures (such as the creation of public health boards, improved sanitation measures, and more effective quarantine regulations) were enacted.[5]

Moreover, by 1793 Peale had committed himself and his museum to Philadelphia. This city was the capital of the American government, of American culture, and of the American Enlightenment. Philadelphia had the largest population of any American city, possessed an excellent press and prestigious legal profession, and in science and medicine ranked first in the nation. Cosmopolitan in religion, values, and population, the city was a primary attraction for foreign visitors and in the 1790s came as close as any American city ever would to being a London or a Paris.[6]

In 1792 Peale had invited a group of the city's political, cultural, and financial leaders, many of whom had national prominence, to become "Visitors," or trustees, of his museum. National politicians included Jefferson, Alexander Hamilton, and James Madison; Thomas Mifflin, Jonathan Bayard Smith, and Alexander James Dallas served in the state government. The educational and cultural community was represented by David Rittenhouse, who in 1791 succeeded the late Benjamin Franklin as president of the American Philosophical Society; Benjamin Smith Barton, perhaps the nation's most distinguished botanist and later a vice-president of the society; James Hutchinson, a professor of chemistry at the University of Pennsylvania; Robert Patterson, a professor of mathematics at the university and secretary of the society; John Beale Bordley, Peale's friend and patron and a noted agronomist and founder of the Philadelphia Society for Promoting Agriculture; Caspar Wistar, a leading physician and an authority on vertebrate paleontology and anatomy; Ebenezer Hazard, a historical editor and former postmaster general of the United States; and Samuel Powel Griffitts, founder of the Philadelphia Dispensary and a professor of *materia medica* at the University of Pennsylvania. From the religious community came Bishop William White, a leader in the reorganization of the Protestant Episcopal Church; Ashbel Green, chaplain of Congress and a professor of mathematics and natural philosophy at the College of New Jersey; and Nicholas Collin, pastor of the Swedish churches in Pennsylvania and the liaison between American scientists and the Royal Swedish Academy of Science in Stockholm. From the city's business and financial elite were John Vaughan, a merchant, treasurer of the American Philosophical Society, and local patron of the fine arts; and Robert Morris, John Francis Mifflin, Miers Fisher, and William Bingham. That the city had attracted so many of these powerful and influential men as residents and that these same men were eager to lend their support to the museum is indicative of the city's national preeminence.[7]

Along with their power and influence, these men possessed a common outlook derived from the Enlightenment. Whether liberal Christians or moderate deists, they viewed nature as benevolent and purpose-

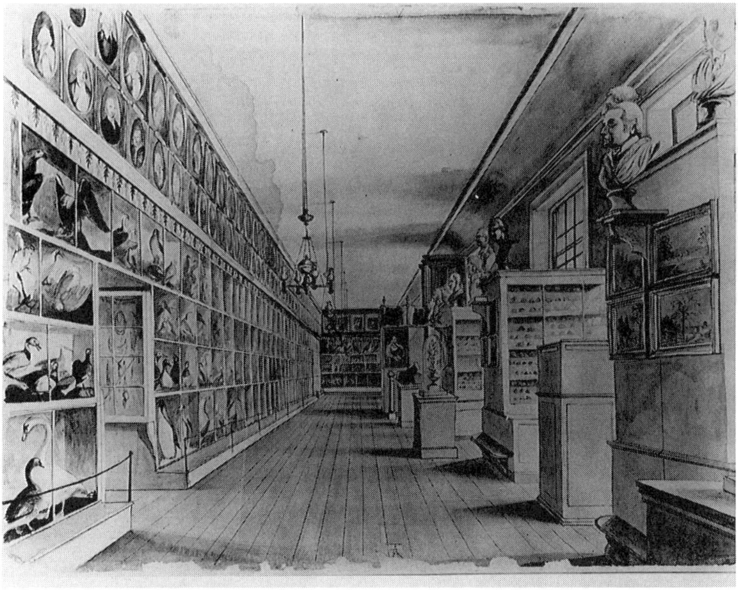

Figure 1. Charles Willson Peale and Titian Ramsay Peale II, Long Room, Philadelphia Museum, 1822. Ink and watercolor on paper; H. 14″, W. 20 3/4″. (Detroit Institute of Arts, Founders Society Purchase, Director's Discretionary Fund.)

ful. All forms of life had a specific place in a natural order that revealed the wisdom of the Creator. Since nature was designed by a wise creator for the use of man, science—the study of nature—would thus be useful to man. The museum was designed by Peale to represent these beliefs in a form intended for the education of large numbers of citizens in a republican society. Envisioned by Peale as a "world in miniature," the museum displayed the creations of nature and man in a rational and systematic order that conveyed the benevolent harmony of nature and the wisdom of the Creator (fig. 1). He arranged the specimens in Linnaean classification from the lowest to the highest order of life. Man and his creations were represented by portraits, models of machines and tools, and artifacts of different nations and cultures. Utilitarianism was the great attraction: farmers visited the museum to learn about soils and minerals, the benefits of snakes and insects, and new types of plows and threshers; artisans and mechanics viewed models of the latest tools and inventions. The proprietor's intention was clear: Americans would become more virtuous, more knowledgeable—better republicans—after having viewed the harmonies and purpose of God's creation in orderly display at Peale's museum.[8]

Peale's museum in one sense represented a step in the development of the culture and institutions of Philadelphia. A growing interest in collections, particularly of natural history, was evidenced by cabinets established at the University of Pennsylvania, the Library Company of Philadelphia, the Pennsylvania Hospital, the Carpenter's Company, and the American Philosophical Society. When Peale arrived in Philadelphia in 1776 there were two wax museums, one established by Rachel Wells had "subject pieces" in which figures enacted historical or biblical situations; the other, created by Abraham Chovet, contained anatomical figures of the human body, displaying its internal structure at different stages of development. In 1782 Pierre Eugène du Simitière, a Swiss miniaturist and collector of books, engravings, paintings, coins, Native American and African relics, and preserved animals and fossils, opened his cabinet to paying visitors. Peale began his museum almost by chance. In 1784 fossilized bones were brought to his portrait gallery so that he could make drawings for European scientists, and a friend bluntly remarked that the specimens attracted more public attention than portraits. Ultimately this prompted Peale to create a museum housing collections of science, natural history, and technology. Museum records in 1814 and 1819 indicate a collection of 269 portraits, 1,824 birds, 250 quadrupeds, 650 fish, more than 1,000 shells, and 313 books; the total number of objects has been estimated at 100,000. Museum revenue—derived solely from an admission price of 25¢ (fig. 2)—fluctuated from just under $1,200 to over $3,000 in the 1790s and was almost $12,000 in the peak year of 1816. Extrapolating from revenues, yearly attendance varied from 4,800 to 48,000.[9]

On July 7, 1786, the first public announcement for Peale's museum appeared in the *Pennsylvania Packet*. Two weeks later Peale was elected a member of the American Philosophical Society. The conjunction may have been adventitious, but the society was to play an active role in Peale's museum for many years. Peale both contributed much creative energy and drew on the rich network of scientific and technical expertise of the society. He became an energetic member and only a month after his election contributed a drawing of a fan chair invented by

Figure 2. Charles Willson Peale, admission ticket, Philadelphia Museum, 1788. (Elise Peale Patterson de Gelpi-Toro.)

Philadelphia instrument maker John Cram (fig. 3). The close relationship that developed between Peale and the society became evident some years later when he began to seek a new building for his museum. Peale's collection had quickly outgrown the space available in his home and gallery, and in 1794 he petitioned the state government for a loan that would enable him to build a large new building. When the loan was rejected, a suggestion was made that the society lease him space. Many of the museum's trustees were also members of the society, and it may have been one of them who initiated the arrangement. Peale accepted the offer and turned the actual move into a street parade, rounding up "all the boys of the neighborhood" and giving each of them one of the larger quadrupeds to carry. As part of a ten-year lease agreement, Peale was appointed assistant curator and librarian of the society and custodian of the meeting room. From the beginning the relationship between the society and its tenant was close, symbiotic, and almost always convivial. In 1796 Peale presented to the members his young son of four months and four days old, "being the first child born in the Philosophical Hall, and requested that the Society would give him a name." The members present "unanimously agreed" that the boy should be named Franklin, after the "founder and late President of the Society."[10]

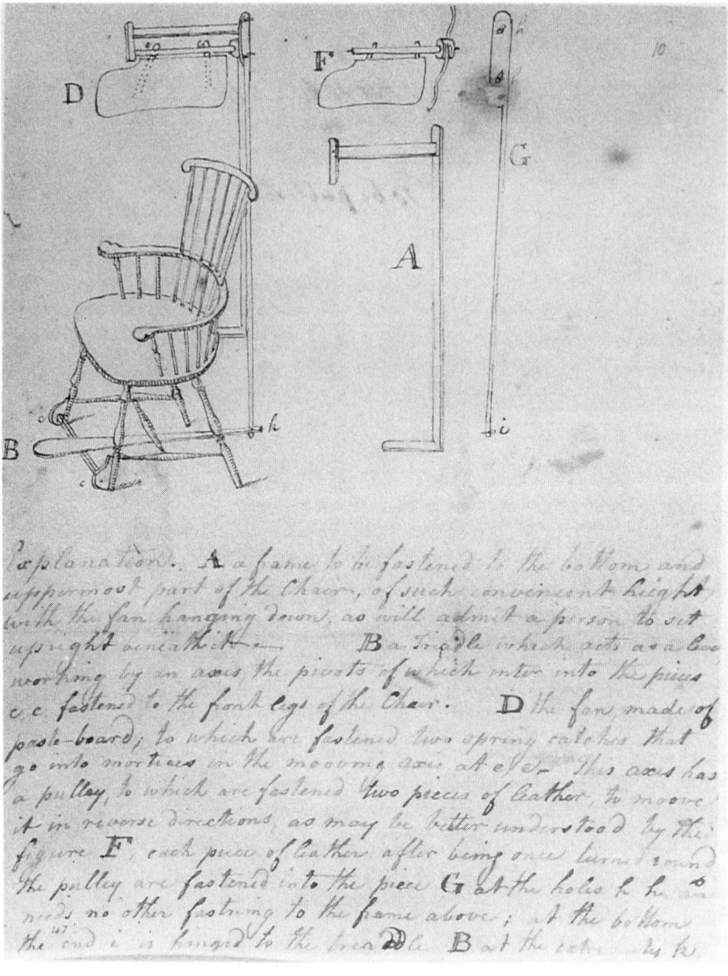

Figure 3. Charles Willson Peale, fan chair and explanation, Philadephia, 1786. India ink over pencil on paper; H. 9 13/16″, W. 8 1/8″. (Manuscript Communications, no. 10, American Philosophical Society, Philadelphia.)

The museum's presence in Philosophical Hall and the associations and friendships Peale was thereby able to form brought both the museum and its proprietor into the full mainstream of Philadelphia's cultural and intellectual life. Peale's fireplace and stove inventions illustrate the interaction. Since Franklin's invention of a stove in 1744, the society had been a center for discussion and investigation of more efficient interior heating, and in part due to the interest of society members, educated opinion in eighteenth-century America regarding standards of comfort was changing. The earlier belief that warm inside temperatures during the winter were unhealthy was giving way to the view that public buildings and even private homes should have efficient heating. Peale, on a more personal level, was interested in finding effective and efficient heating for his museum. He was one of twenty-one members present at the society's meeting on May 1, 1795, when fireplaces were discussed and a contest for the best fireplace design, with a $60 prize, was decided. He soon began experimenting with different stoves and with his son Raphaelle began working on fireplace designs. The father-and-son team came up with several improvements and innovations for fireplaces (fig. 4), including one marvel of ingenuity they called a "smoke-eater" in which smoke rose to the top of the stove, was sucked down a pipe, and then underwent further combustion (fig. 5). The society took several years evaluating the designs and in 1799 awarded the prize to the Peales (fig. 6).[11]

Another example of Peale–American Philosophical Society interaction concerns the exhumation and reconstruction of the mastodon skeleton. Although Peale received the public acclaim and profit from the venture, the society played a pivotal role in collecting information, coordinating scientific inquiry, and assisting Peale financially. Sometime in 1801 Peale read that a large number of bones belonging to an unclassified American mammoth had been discovered and partially exhumed from a marshy field in Ulster County, New York. The subject was of particular interest because late eighteenth-century scientists had begun to question the traditional belief that the natural world had remained unchanged since its creation. A skeleton of an extinct animal was crucial to those who were exploring theories of the evolution of species. In the mid 1780s Peale had contributed to the debate with drawings he made of another collection of bones, drawings that helped in the classification of the animal in the first decade of the nineteenth century. And in 1798 Peale, Jefferson, and Wistar were part of a society committee that was formed to collect information on archaeological artifacts of North America, singling out the mammoth as a specimen of special im-

Figure 4. Charles Willson Peale and Raphaelle Peale, models for improvements in fireplace design, Philadelphia, 1797. Painted wood and paper with brass and steel parts. (American Philosophical Society, Philadelphia.)

portance and establishing a goal of obtaining a complete skeleton of this animal. The opportunity offered by the New York discovery was too good to pass up, and Peale went quickly to the site and confirmed the existence of one and perhaps two complete skeletons. To conduct a scientific exhumation—an undertaking that would require considerable manpower and technical expertise—he requested a $500 interest-free loan from the society. On July 24, 1801, a special meeting was called by Patterson and Wistar (who also had been museum trustees), and the twenty-five members present unanimously voted to grant Peale the loan. Peale and his son Rembrandt recovered and assembled the two skeletons of the mammoth, only the second such reconstruction in the world (figs.

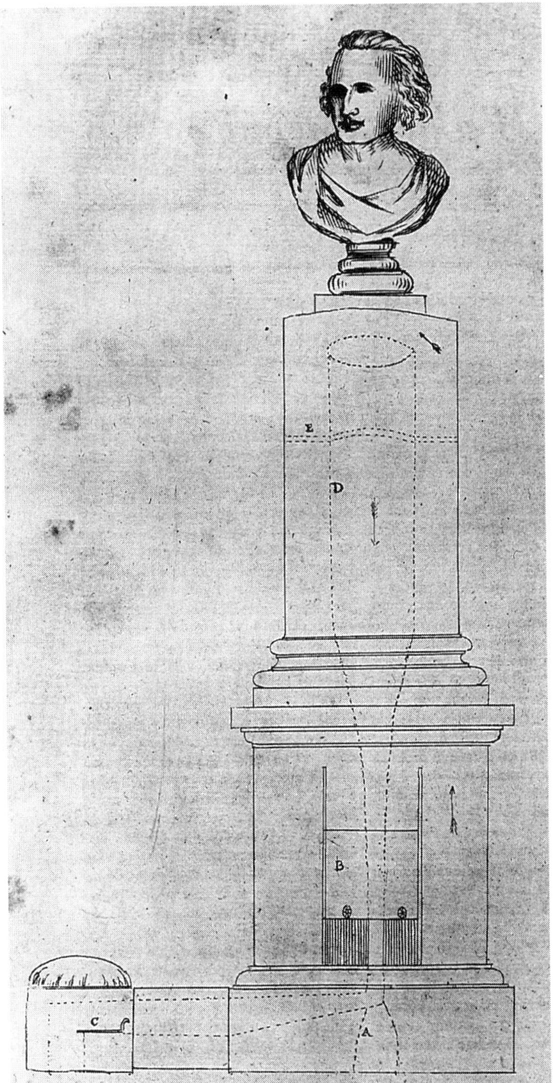

Figure 5. "Smoke-Eater," engraving after unlocated drawing by Charles Willson Peale. From *Weekly Magazine* 2, no. 25 (July 21, 1798): facing p. 353. (American Philosophical Society, Philadelphia.)

Figure 6. Charles Willson Peale and Raphaelle Peale, "Description of Some Improvements in the Common Fireplace," Philadelphia, 1797; design patented November 16, 1797. From *Transactions of American Philosophical Society* 5 (1802): 322 pl. 13.

7, 8). Their exhibition of one of the skeletons enormously increased the museum's profits, popularity, and reputation.[12]

A second institution of special value to Peale's museum was the Library Company of Philadelphia. Founded by Franklin in 1731, the Library Company had accumulated an extensive collection of books, pamphlets, and manuscripts by the late eighteenth century that were available to "civil gentlemen" in the library rooms and might be taken home by shareholders. For Peale the library made an exception. Although not a subscriber, he was given permission to borrow books for special projects. In 1788, as Peale collected specimens for his museum and transformed his portrait gallery into a museum of natural history, he borrowed Thomas Pennant's four-volume *British Zoology* and Richard Pultney's *General View of the Writings of Linnaeus* to teach himself natural history. In 1795 he borrowed volumes by Pennant, Mark Catesby, and John Latham to compare the plates with his animal specimens for

Figure 7. Charles Willson Peale, *The Exhumation of the Mastodon*, Philadelphia, 1806–8. Oil on canvas; H. 50″, W. 62 1/2″. (Peale Museum, Baltimore City Life Museums.)

the publication of his catalogue of the museum holdings. And in 1799 and 1800 when he prepared lecture courses on natural history, he was again allowed to borrow books from the Library Company. For many years Peale enjoyed an author's reciprocal relationship with the library, having the privilege of borrowing books in return for the donation of copies of his essays and publications on bridge design, health, and marriage.[13]

Peale also sought and achieved a close relationship with a third institution of local and national stature, the University of Pennsylvania. He often envisioned his museum becoming a state or national institution that was a part of a large university in which the faculty had direct access to the museum's collections and presented lectures, making the museum an integral part of the intellectual community of the university. Peale's associations with faculty members at the University of Pennsyl-

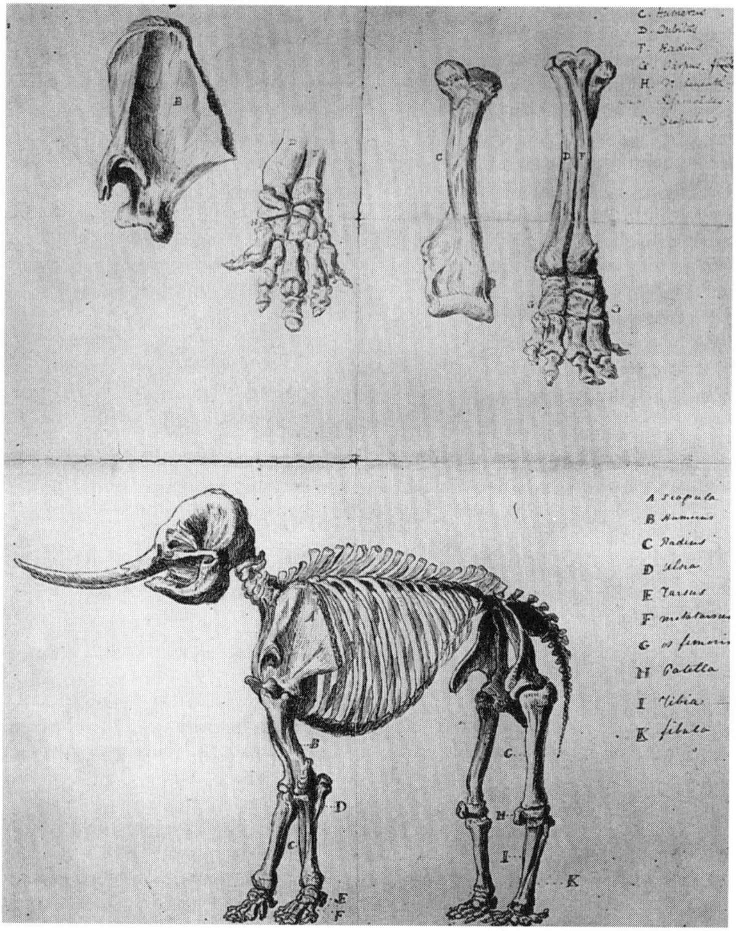

Figure 8. Rembrandt Peale, mastodon, 1801. Ink and watercolor on paper; H. 15 3/16", W. 12 3/4". (American Philosophical Society, Philadelphia.)

vania (several had been museum trustees) and the use of his museum by university medical students were early attempts to bring the museum within the university's orbit. In 1799 when Peale decided to give a course of lectures on natural history in his museum, he requested permission from university trustees to give the introductory lecture in their meeting hall. The university granted his request for both that year and the next.[14]

The reciprocity between the museum and the university is evident in Peale's aid to Wistar, professor at the university's medical school. Wistar was a pivotal figure in Peale's relationships with Philadelphia's institutions of culture and learning. He was a museum trustee, served with Peale on the American Philosophical Society's committee in charge of collecting information on the mammoth, assisted Peale in reconstructing the skeleton, and in 1808 turned to Peale when he thought of using models of human organs for his anatomy classes at the university. Peale, with the help of son Rembrandt and sculptor William Rush, made Wistar a wax and papier-mâché model of a human throat and windpipe and then a model of a human head in which the students could see the outline of the brain.[15]

Peale's interest in health and longevity contributed to a close relationship with the university's medical school and to many valuable friendships and associations with the city's physicians. In 1801 he patented a portable vapor bath for personal hygiene and as a cure for minor illness (fig. 9). As did most late eighteenth-century American physicians, Philadelphia's medical community believed that epidemics were transmitted by air, water, and food and stressed personal hygiene, including bathing, as a way of saving lives. Peale's vapor bath was noted with approval in a University of Pennsylvania medical school dissertation on bathing. He also received the gratitude of the city's medical community for his donations of the vapor baths to the City Hospital, the College of Physicians, and the Pennsylvania Hospital.[16]

The advantages of being in Philadelphia included the city's role as an important seaport and mercantile center. Interstate and international trade flowed through Philadelphia's harbor, and Peale enlisted the aid of many mariners in obtaining specimens from every continent for the museum. James Josiah, who in 1787 was appointed first officer of the *Asia*, a ship built especially for the China trade, and Richard Dale, who sailed with John Paul Jones during the Revolution and then later served on a merchant ship to Canton, donated exotic objects to the museum (fig. 10).[17]

Peale's background allowed him to work easily in Philadelphia's artisanal community. As a young man in Annapolis in the 1760s he was a saddlemaker, an upholsterer, a silversmith, and most significantly in

Figure 9. Charles Willson Peale, vapor bath, patented by Peale, 1801. From Henry Wilson Lockette, *An Inaugural Dissertation on the Warm Bath* (Philadelphia: Carr and Smith, 1801), n.p. (American Philosophical Society, Philadelphia.)

preindustrial mechanics, a clock and watch repairer. During the years he was a portrait painter and a museum keeper, and in retirement he continually was involved in mechanics and invention. Much of this centered in the workshop he established in his museum, and in turn, the museum provided an excellent location for Peale to display the inventions. The polygraph, a machine that copied letters, was developed in the workshop by English inventor John Isaac Hawkins with Peale often standing behind him offering "hints" or suggestions. Later, when Hawkins returned to England, Peale assumed control of the polygraph's development in America, hired and trained workers, established a small

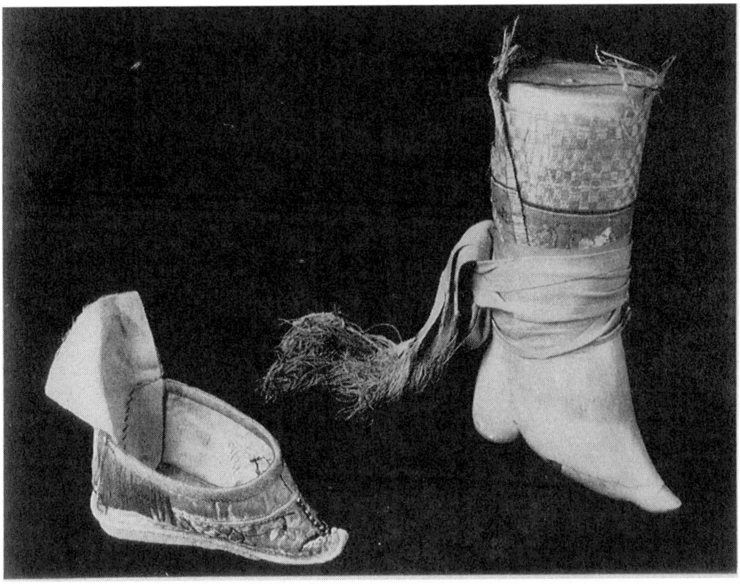

Figure 10. Model of a Chinese lady's foot and lower leg with silk shoe donated to Philadelphia Museum by Richard Dale, 1797. (Peabody Museum of Archaeology and Ethnology, Harvard University.)

manufacturing shop in the museum, and began marketing and selling the device (fig. 11). Peale also developed the idea of a lightweight, single-span arch bridge at the museum (figs. 12, 13). The original purpose of the design was to connect the walkways of the State House garden to a field across Walnut Street without interfering with city traffic. Peale, like other American bridge designers of his time, first built a model. The 20-foot model was placed in the museum, in the "passage of Philosophical Hall," and rigorously tested when "12 Indians and all stout men" stood on it at once.[18]

The artisans and mechanics who benefited from the museum and its proprietor were also an enormous resource to the museum. Hawkins, who used the museum's workshop and its proprietor's artisanal skills to develop the polygraph, provided Peale with a physiognotrace that attracted large numbers of visitors who paid to have their profiles traced; he also invented musical instruments that Peale used for concerts in the

Figure 11. Replica of polygraph manufactured by Charles Willson Peale and sold to Thomas Jefferson, ca. 1805. (University of Virginia Library, Special Collections Department.)

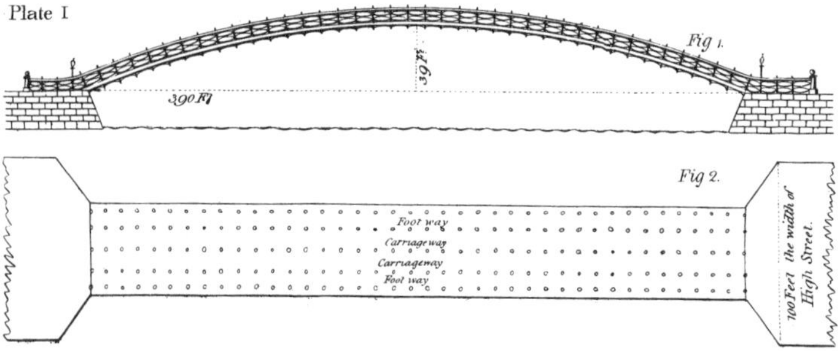

Figure 12. Charles Willson Peale, design for a bridge over the Schuylkill River, Philadelphia. From Charles Willson Peale, *An Essay on Building Wooden Bridges* (Philadelphia: Francis Bailey, 1797), pl. 1. (American Philosophical Society, Philadelphia.)

museum. Joshua Humphreys's shipyard, among the most innovative in the nation, provided Peale with techniques and ideas that he was able to adapt for his new bridge design. Peale's decision to design all his stoves

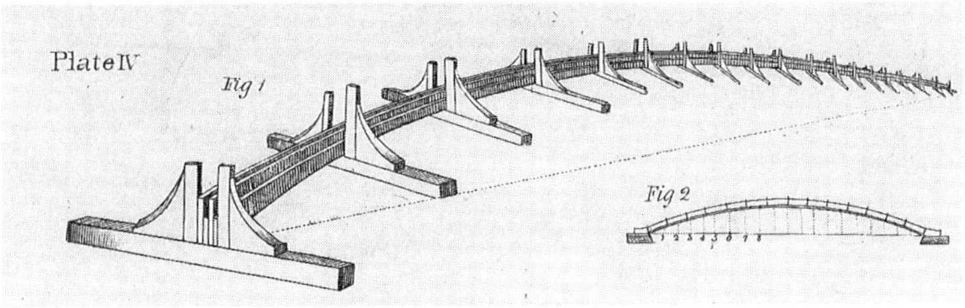

Figure 13. Charles Willson Peale, design for the bending of bridge ribs, Philadelphia. From Charles Willson Peale, *An Essay on Building Wooden Bridges* (Philadelphia: Francis Bailey, 1797), pl. 4. (American Philosophical Society, Philadelphia.)

and fireplaces in brick may have been influenced by the technology used in Philadelphia's excellent brick kilns.[19]

For many of his inventions and mechanical devices, Peale used, designed, or adapted specialized clock- and watchmaking tools: bow drills, spirit levels, rack quadrants, and collets—and used materials such as exotic, imported hardwoods and expensive brass for key parts of machinery. His watchmaker friends included Robert Leslie, who had assembled a collection of models and drawings of machines in foreign countries with which he had planned to open a museum of his own, and Jean Chaudron, who was also a silversmith, newspaper editor, and poet and shared Peale's interest in copying machines.[20]

The names of many of Philadelphia's artisans, mechanics, and inventors appear in Peale's correspondence and point to an extensive network of associations. James Traquair and his son Adam, owners of a marble yard at Tenth and Filbert streets, were knowledgeable about chimneypieces, and Adam Traquair also worked as a draftsman for Benjamin Henry Latrobe. The younger Traquair and Latrobe assisted Peale in transforming the temperamental polygraph prototype into a relatively sturdy machine capable of being commercially marketed. Thomas Gilpin, a paper manufacturer who was interested in draftsmanship and mechanical instruments, purchased a polygraph from Peale and suggested an improvement that Peale incorporated. Nathan Sellers, a skilled wireworker and designer of paper molds, sold Peale the fine wire needed for the springs of the polygraph. (With Sellers, the artisanal connection became personal; Nathan's son Coleman married Peale's daughter, Sophonisba.)[21]

The connections in the Philadelphia network of mechanics and artisans are often impossible to delineate because they were so commonplace and left no written record. For the historian, documentation of the associations and activities is difficult simply because these relationships were ubiquitous: these men knew each other and often communicated on a daily basis. Sometimes, however, a single document or an episode provides a freeze-frame, revealing a whole pattern of relationships and interconnections. A case in point was in 1806 when Peale added his name to those of the fourteen mechanics and artisans who joined with Oliver Evans in petitioning Congress to expand and extend patent rights. This joining together reflected wider involvements and partnerships in artisanal and mechanical activities and inventions. For example, Evans and another petitioner, Joseph Hawkins, were involved in the development of high-pressure steam engines, an idea later promoted by Newburyport, Massachusetts, mechanic Jacob Perkins, after he came to Philadelphia in 1814. Perkins frequently talked with Evans and Hawkins and formed a partnership with Peale's son-in-law Coleman Sellers for the manufacture of singe-chamber fire engines. Peale, who painted Perkins's portrait in 1816 (at the same time he painted one of respected mechanic Isaiah Lukens), visited the manufactory and was so impressed with a stove and central-heating system constructed by Perkins that he constructed a similar system in the museum to heat his painting room.[22]

In 1804 Peale wrote his friend Jefferson—who had been a museum trustee and even after becoming president of the United States retained a strong interest in the institution—that he had decided to use a part of his museum to "teach the mechanical arts" by exhibiting machines, models, and drawings "illustrative of various methods of workmanship." Such exhibits would demonstrate the rich artisanal and mechanical culture of the Philadelphia area. Perhaps influenced by Leslie's plan to establish a museum of technology, Peale was convinced that models of machines and inventions would be popular exhibits among Philadelphia's large artisan and mechanic population. This had been his experience with models of an iron bridge Peale kept in his museum that had been sent to him by his old friend and former political ally Thomas Paine. In formulating the use of his museum along these lines, Peale had arrived at a concept that was very much at the heart of the Enlightenment. He would use his museum in the same way as Denis Diderot and the philosophes used their encyclopedias: to demonstrate and classify the various branches of technology. His idea was to take the mystery out of technology so that "many trades which are thought difficult to those unacquainted with them, will here be found easey."[23]

In addition to its heuristic functions in technology, archaeology, and natural history, Peale envisioned an anthropological aspect to his museum. His portrait collection, initially a residue of his art gallery, quickly was made to represent man as the highest of the animal species. This is the reason that Peale in 1792 seriously proposed displaying the embalmed corpses of eminent men. Unable to make a convincing case for adding embalmed bodies to his museum, Peale pursued another direction in his study of man, the addition of Native American artifacts and portraits to his museum collection. To a great extent he moved in this direction because of Philadelphia's position as the nation's capital in the 1790s. As the seat of government, it was frequently visited by Native American delegations negotiating treaties with federal officials. In 1796 leaders of the major tribes of the southeastern United States arrived at the same time representatives of tribes in the Northwest Territory were in the city. During the visit both sets of tribes unexpectedly chose the same day to visit the museum. Peale later recounted that initially each side regarded the other with distrust, but in the museum, "surrounded by a scene calculated to inspire the most perfect harmony," they were able to form a treaty of peace. In short, in this event, the museum fulfilled all Peale's hopes as an embodiment of Enlightenment ideals of harmony and beneficence.[24]

There were also more tangible benefits to the museum. These visits provided Peale the opportunity to observe Native Americans, a scientific curiosity in the eighteenth century. The following year he painted the portrait of chief Joseph Brant and added it to the museum's portraits (fig. 14). In addition to this "specimen," Peale acquired tribal artifacts (fig. 15).[25]

By the end of the eighteenth century the very success of Peale's museum, which was so much the result of Philadelphia's contributions, had made it a national cultural institution as well as a local Philadelphia attraction. The mastodon skeleton had brought fame and increased revenues, allowing Peale to increase his collections. In 1802 the Pennsylvania legislature allowed him to move into the State House, which had

Figure 14. Charles Willson Peale, *Joseph Brant (Thayendanegea)*, Philadelphia, 1797. Oil on canvas; H. 25 1/2", W. 21 1/4". (Independence National Historical Park Collection.)

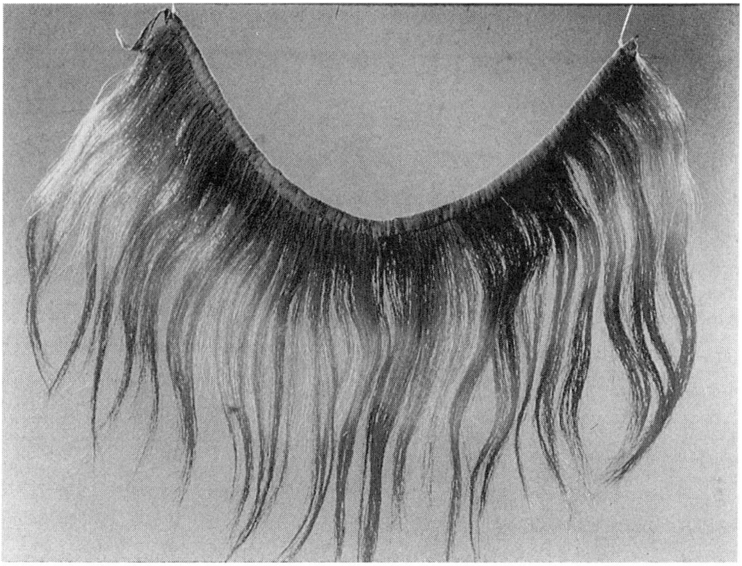

Figure 15. Choctaw necklace presented to the Philadelphia Museum, January 9, 1828. (Peabody Museum of Archaeology and Ethnology, Harvard University.)

much more room and served as official recognition of the museum's significance to the state and the nation. Jefferson, as president, continued his support, adding prestige to Peale's labors by contributing specimens himself and arranging that items from the Lewis and Clark and other scientific expeditions be sent to the museum (fig. 16). The museum's reputation, as both a popular cultural attraction and a serious educational institution, had spread beyond the nation's shores. Foreign scientists such as the comte de Volney, Alexander von Humboldt, Joseph Priestley, and François-André Michaux, aware of its extensive collections, expertly preserved and classically arranged, visited the museum to study or simply to observe what had been accomplished by the labors of one American. In Europe and in England the great collections were no longer in private hands but had been placed in state repositories. By the late eighteenth century Peale's proprietary status had become something of an anomaly and a testimony to the energy and creativity of a single individual, as well as an American landmark. Peale also placed his museum in the role of the nation's repository in his correspondence and

Figure 16. Hunting shirt, possibly worn by Meriwether Lewis or William Clark, from the Lewis and Clark expedition, donated through Thomas Jefferson to the Philadelphia Museum, 1809. (Peabody Museum of Archaeology and Ethnology, Harvard University.)

specimen exchanges with foreign scientists, such as Joseph Banks, Georges Cuvier, and Etienne Geoffroy Saint-Hilaire.[26]

It is tempting to conclude that Peale realized a good thing when he had it—that he was aware of how much his museum was a part of Philadelphia. But Peale's feelings were ambiguous. He viewed the museum as a product of his own private labors, usually making invidious comparisons with state-supported museums in England and on the Continent. Later in life when he felt an urgency to make his museum a permanent institution, either in some form of official association with a local or state government or affiliated with a state or national university, he had no disinclination against moving it to New York, or making it a part of the nascent University of Virginia, or even taking it to the sparsely settled District of Columbia. On the other hand, his involvement in Philadelphia is indicative of strong local feelings. He did a great deal for the city. His role in the formation of the Pennsylvania Academy of the Fine Arts testifies to his desire to enrich the cultural life of the city. He donated his time and inventions to such Philadelphia institutions as the City Hospital, the College of Physicians, and the Pennsylvania Hospital. He promoted Philadelphia artisans and mechanics, recommending them to friends and relatives in New York, Annapolis, and Virginia.[27] Peale settled in Philadelphia in 1776, and with the exception of a ten-year period in which he retired to his farm in Germantown (even then making repeated visits to the city and his museum), he remained in the city until his death in 1827. For Philadelphians of that time, it would have been hard to imagine Philadelphia without Charles Willson Peale, or Peale without Philadelphia.

For a brief period at the end of the eighteenth century Philadelphia had become America's capital in more than just a governmental sense, providing the unity and cohesiveness of politics, society, and culture that was a desideratum of the Enlightenment in Europe and America. It was a goal that received its most symbolic expression in the huge Fourth of July parade in 1790 in which Philadelphians celebrated the federal Constitution. In the parade, representatives from all over the city, organized by class, profession, trade, and social status, marched in order: laborers and sailors, merchants and clerics (including rabbis), the city's elite, and apprentices. It ended in a massive banquet with a final toast to "the Whole Family of Mankind."[28]

Peale's museum was predicated on this notion of unity. The museum educated Americans by demonstrating the unity of creation and knowledge, an Enlightenment concept pervasive in Philadelphia and America. The museum fit so well in Philadelphia because it so mirrored the city's function and ideals during this period. In a parallel sense also, the museum's decline by the end of the second decade of the nineteenth century followed closely that of the city. After 1802 Philadelphia had lost its role as capital of the nation and of the state of Pennsylvania. New York had begun to assume national leadership in commerce and finance and challenged Philadelphia in culture and the arts; Boston became dominant in literature. America's opportunity for a national capital such as London or Paris was lost. This centrifugal trend in American politics and society had its corollary in philosophy and the intellectual sphere and affected the museum. The Enlightenment's vision of the unity of knowledge had begun to unravel. In the late eighteenth and early nineteenth centuries there was a multiplication of organizations and societies directed to specific objectives, trades, and specialized branches of learning, which clearly indicated a breakdown of the Enlightenment's broad, universal approach to knowledge. The museum's rationale for a public role based on its public utility was undermined by this growing specialization. For both Peale's museum and Philadelphia there had been glory in a role of leadership and unity. Just as Peale drew on the city for its resources, and in turn served as a facilitator drawing together Philadelphia's people and institutions, the city served that role in the nation. In the nineteenth century there would be dispersal; for Philadelphia this meant relative decline and stagnation; for Peale's museum it would be worse, as there could be no public role in a society and culture unresponsive to his claim to serve the general good.[29]

---

[1] Constantin-François de Chasseboeuf, comte de Volney, who traveled in the U.S. from 1795 to 1798, as quoted in Lillian B. Miller, Sidney Hart, and David C. Ward, eds., *The Selected Papers of Charles Willson Peale and His Family*, vol. 2: *Charles Willson Peale: The Artist as Museum Keeper, 1791–1810* (New Haven: Yale University Press, 1988), pp. 137–38. For general information about Peale's life and museum, see Charles Coleman Sellers, *Charles Willson Peale* (New York: Scribner, 1969); and Charles Coleman Sellers, *Mr. Peale's Museum: Charles Willson Peale and the First Popular Museum of Natural Science and Art* (New York: W. W. Norton, 1980). Selected papers are in Lillian B. Miller, Sidney Hart, and Toby A. Appel, *The Selected Papers of Charles Willson Peale and His Family*, vol. 1: *Charles Willson Peale: Artist in Revolutionary America, 1735–1791* (New Haven: Yale University Press, 1983); and Miller, Hart, and Ward, *Peale: Artist as Museum Keeper*. The complete

family papers are on microfiche: see Lillian B. Miller, ed., *The Collected Papers of Charles Willson Peale and His Family* (Millwood, N.Y.: Kraus Microform, 1980) (references to the microfiche edition hereafter will be cited as F: followed by the alphanumeric code used to identify and locate documents in the edition and on the microfiche card).

[2] Charles Willson Peale, Diary 13, August 21–September 19, 1793, in Miller, Hart, and Ward, *Peale: Artist as Museum Keeper*, pp. 50–68.

[3] Benjamin Rush, *Letters*, ed. Lyman H. Butterfield, 2 vols., Memoirs of the American Philosophical Society, vol. 30, pts. 1, 2 (Princeton: Princeton University Press, 1951), pp. 637–38, 638n; John Harvey Powell, *Bring Out Your Dead: The Great Plague of Yellow Fever in Philadelphia in 1793* (Philadelphia: University of Pennsylvania Press, 1949), pp. 1–113; Chris Holmes, "Benjamin Rush and the Yellow Fever," *Bulletin of the History of Medicine* 40, no. 3 (May–June 1966): 246–63; Henry F. May, *The Enlightenment in America* (New York: Oxford University Press, 1976), pp. 208–11.

[4] Charles Willson Peale, "Autobiography," typescript, p. 216, F:IIC; Peale, Diary 13, in Miller, Hart, and Ward, *Peale: Artist as Museum Keeper*, pp. 64–65; Charles Willson Peale to Gabriel Furman, September 16, 1799, in Miller, Hart, and Ward, *Peale: Artist as Museum Keeper*, pp. 254–56; Powell, *Bring Out Your Dead*, pp. 1–113; John Duffy, *A History of Public Health in New York City, 1625–1866* (New York: Russell Sage Foundation, 1968), p. 135; J. Thomas Scharf and Thompson Westcott, *History of Philadelphia, 1609–1884*, 3 vols. (Philadelphia: L. H. Everts, 1884), 1:490–91, 495–96.

[5] Peale to Furman, in Miller, Hart, and Ward, *Peale: Artist as Museum Keeper*, pp. 254–56; A. C. Abbott, "The Development of Public Health Work in Philadelphia," in *Founders' Week Memorial Volume*, ed. Frederick P. Henry (Philadelphia, 1909), pp. 563–71; Duffy, *History of Health*, pp. 124–39.

[6] May, *Enlightenment*, p. 197.

[7] Charles Willson Peale, "My Design in Forming This Museum," broadside, Philadelphia, 1792, as reprinted in Miller, Hart, and Ward, *Peale: Artist as Museum Keeper*, pp. 12–19, 19–20n.

[8] Charles Willson Peale, *Introduction to a Course of Lectures on Natural History Delivered in the University of Pennsylvania*, November 16, 1799, as reprinted in Miller, Hart, and Ward, *Peale: Artist as Museum Keeper*, pp. 261–72; May, *Enlightenment*, pp. 197–222; John C. Greene, *American Science in the Age of Jefferson* (Ames: Iowa State University Press, 1984), pp. 4–26.

[9] Brooke Hindle, *The Pursuit of Science in Revolutionary America, 1735–1789* (Chapel Hill: University of North Carolina Press, 1956), pp. 260–61; *Peale: Artist in America*, p. 200; Sellers, *Mr. Peale's Museum*, p. 346; Sidney Hart and David C. Ward, "The Waning of an Enlightenment Ideal: Charles Willson Peale's Philadelphia Museum, 1790–1820," *Journal of the Early Republic* 8, no. 4 (Winter 1988): 401–4.

[10] Peale, "Autobiography," pp. 219–21, F:IIC; *Early Proceedings of the American Philosophical Society from the Manuscript Minutes of Its Meetings from 1744 to 1838* (Philadelphia, 1884), p. 239. *Pennsylvania Packet*, July 7, 1786, in *Peale: Artist in America*, p. 448; *Early Proceedings of the Society*, p. 144; Peale to Benjamin Rush, July 31, 1786, in *Peale: Artist in America*, pp. 450–51; for Cram, see *Peale: Artist in America*, p. 436n; Miller, Hart, and Ward, *Peale: Artist as Museum Keeper*, pp. 93–96.

[11] Charles Willson Peale and Raphaelle Peale, "Description of Some Improvements in the Common Fire-place," March 17, 1797, in Miller, Hart, and Ward, *Peale: Artist as Museum Keeper*, pp. 192–97; Peale, "A Letter from Mr. C. W. Peale

to the Editor of the Weekly Magazine," March 1798, in Miller, Hart, and Ward, *Peale: Artist as Museum Keeper*, pp. 209–15; Peale, "Description of the Stove Lately Built by Mr. Charles Willson Peale, in His Museum, and Which Burns the Smoke of Its Fuel," July 21, 1798, in Miller, Hart, and Ward, *Peale: Artist as Museum Keeper*, pp. 218–20; Sidney Hart, " 'To Encrease the Comforts of Life': Charles Willson Peale and the Mechanical Arts," *Pennsylvania Magazine of History and Biography* 110, no. 3 (July 1986): 335–41.

[12] "Editorial Note: The Mastodon," in Miller, Hart, and Ward, *Peale: Artist as Museum Keeper*, pp. 308–13; Peale to Patterson and Peale to Jefferson, July 24, 1801, in Miller, Hart, and Ward, *Peale: Artist as Museum Keeper*, pp. 346–47, 348–49; Gilbert Chinard, "Jefferson and the American Philosophical Society," *Proceedings of the American Philosophical Society* 87, no. 3 (July 1943): 269–70; Peale, Diary 18, June 5–July 2, 1801, Diary 19, July 29–September 25, 1801, and Peale to Jefferson, October 11, 1801, in Miller, Hart, and Ward, *Peale: Artist as Museum Keeper*, pp. 313–35, 340–42, 350–71, and 371–76.

[13] Peale, Diary 7, May 30–November 3, 1788, in *Peale: Artist in America*, pp. 525, 525n; Peale to the Directors, Library Company of Philadelphia, October 5, 1795, in Miller, Hart, and Ward, *Peale: Artist as Museum Keeper*, pp. 126–27.

[14] Charles Willson Peale, "Lectures on Natural History," *Claypoole's American Daily Advertiser*, September 26, 1799, as reprinted in Miller, Hart, and Ward, *Peale: Artist as Museum Keeper*, pp. 256–58; Peale to Honorable Trustees, University of Pennsylvania, October 28, 1799, in Miller, Hart, and Ward, *Peale: Artist as Museum Keeper*, pp. 258–59.

[15] Peale to Wistar, February, 9, 1808, in Miller, Hart, and Ward, *Peale: Artist as Museum Keeper*, pp. 1058–59.

[16] Peale to College of Physicians, April 7, 1801, F:IIA/24B3; Peale to Dr. Dorsey, October 6, 1803, F:IIA/28F11; Peale to Managers of the Pennsylvania Hospital, November 30, 1808, F:IIA/24B3; Peale, *An Epistle to a Friend on the Means of Preserving Health, Promoting Happiness, and Prolonging the Life of Man to the Natural Period*, March 1803, in Miller, Hart, and Ward, *Peale: Artist as Museum Keeper*, pp. 506–7; Hart, "To Encrease the Comforts," pp. 329–31.

[17] Peale's Museum, 1803–42 Records and Accessions, F:XIA/3–5.

[18] Hart, "To Encrease the Comforts," pp. 341–55; Charles Willson Peale, *An Essay on Building Wooden Bridges*, March 15, 1797, as reprinted in Miller, Hart, and Ward, *Peale: Artist as Museum Keeper*, pp. 181–91; Peale to Hawkins, February 14, 1802, and Peale to Jefferson, June 22, 1806, in Miller, Hart, and Ward, *Peale: Artist as Museum Keeper*, pp. 804–8, 970–72; Silvio A. Bedini, *Thomas Jefferson and His Copying Machines* (Charlottesville: University Press of Virginia, 1984).

[19] Charles Willson Peale, advertisement for physiognotrace, *Aurora*, December 28, 1802, as reprinted in Miller, Hart, and Ward, *Peale: Artist as Museum Keeper*, p. 478; Peale to Rembrandt and Rubens Peale, December 12, 1802, May 31, 1803, and Peale to John DePeyster, March 8, 1804, in Miller, Hart, and Ward, *Peale: Artist as Museum Keeper*, pp. 473, 530–31, and 643.

[20] Peale to Leslie, December 16–17, 1793, and Peale to Jefferson, January 28, 1803, March 13, 1804, in Miller, Hart, and Ward, *Peale: Artist as Museum Keeper*, pp. 76–78 and 484–85, 647; Hindle, *Pursuit of Science*, p. 260.

[21] Peale to Latrobe, November 6, 1803, Peale to DePeyster, March 8, 1804, Latrobe to Peale, March 9, 1804, Peale to Hawkins, October 7, 1804, December 28, 1806, and Peale to Jefferson, June 21, 1808, in Miller, Hart, and Ward, *Peale: Artist as Museum Keeper*, pp. 619–20, 643–44, 645–46, 772, 994–98, and 1091–92.

[22] "Petition of Sundry Patentees, Praying the Privilege of a Renewal of Their Patents for a Second Term Etc.," HR 9A–F7.2, December 11, 1806, National Archives, Washington, D.C.; Peale to Rembrandt Peale, January 8, 1818, F:IIA/60B12–14; Charles Coleman Sellers, *Portraits and Miniatures by Charles Willson Peale*, issued as *Transactions of the American Philosophical Society* 42, pt. 1 (1952): 170–71; Eugene S. Ferguson, ed., *Early Engineering Reminiscences (1815–40) of George Escol Sellers* (Washington, D.C.: Smithsonian Institution, 1965), pp. 12–15, 20, 26.

[23] Peale to Jefferson, February 26, 1804, and Peale to Paine, July 27, 1803, in Miller, Hart, and Ward, *Peale: Artist as Museum Keeper*, pp. 639–40 and 772, 994–98; Hart, "To Encrease the Comforts," pp. 355–56.

[24] Charles Willson Peale, *Discourse Introductory to a Course of Lectures on the Science of Nature* (Philadelphia, 1800), p. 40. Peale's proposal to display embalmed corpses is detailed in an untitled broadside, 1792, F:IID/1B8–11; "Indian Tribes Visit Peale's Museum," *Philadelphia Gazette*, December 6, 1796, in Miller, Hart, and Ward, *Peale: Artist as Museum Keeper*, pp. 160–64.

[25] Peale, "My Design," p. 14.

[26] Extract of "Minutes of the Senate of the Commonwealth of Pennsylvania," February 16, 1802, Peale to Timothy Matlack, March 15, 1802, extract of "Letter to Peale," *Aurora*, March 25, 1802, Peale to the Honorable Legislature of Pennsylvania, March 24, 1802, Jefferson to Peale, October 6, 1805, "Peale: Memorial to the Pennsylvania Legislature," *Dunlap and Claypoole's American Daily Advertiser*, December 26, 1795, Peale, Diary 20, pt. 1, May 29–June 21, 1804, Peale to Priestley, June 26, 1794, Peale to Rembrandt Peale, September 11, 1808, Banks to Peale, October 1, 1794, Peale to Banks, December 1800, Peale to Saint-Hilaire, July 13, 1802, Peale to Mrs. Rembrandt Peale, Rembrandt Peale, and Rubens Peale, August 30, 1802, in Miller, Hart, and Ward, *Peale: Artist as Museum Keeper*, pp. 400–401, 413–16, 417–18, 893–95, 136–38, 680, 96–97, 1133–44 and 1143n, 98–100, 297, 440–44, 449–53.

[27] Peale, *Introduction to a Course*, p. 269; Peale to Isaac Weaver, February 11, 1802, in Miller, Hart, and Ward, *Peale: Artist as Museum Keeper*, p. 398; Peale, *Discourse*, pp. 19–32; Peale to Jefferson, January 12, 1802, Jefferson to Peale, January 16, 1802, Peale to David Hosack, June 29, July 17, 1805, Peale to Jefferson, June 13, 1805, in Miller, Hart, and Ward, *Peale: Artist as Museum Keeper*, pp. 386–89, 389–90, 857–59, 865, 850–52; Peale, Diary 18, pt. 1, June 5–July 2, 1801, in Miller, Hart, and Ward, *Peale: Artist as Museum Keeper*, p. 315; Pennsylvania Hospital: Testimonial to Charles Willson Peale, November 23, 1805, in Miller, Hart, and Ward, *Peale: Artist as Museum Keeper*, p. 912; Peale to John Muir, January 22, 1804, Peale to DePeyster, March 8, 1804, Peale to Madison, January 9, 1803, Peale to Jefferson, January 10, 1803, in Miller, Hart, and Ward, *Peale: Artist as Museum Keeper*, pp. 631–33, 643–44, 479–80, 480–82.

[28] May, *Enlightenment*, p. 202.

[29] May, *Enlightenment*, pp. 309–10; Hart and Ward, "Waning of an Ideal," pp. 414–18.

An Identity Crisis

Philadelphia and Baltimore Furniture Styles of the Mid Eighteenth Century

Luke Beckerdite

More than any other American city, Philadelphia was responsible for shaping the culture of the southern backcountry and the colonies surrounding the upper Chesapeake Bay. As the Middle Atlantic region's largest port, Philadelphia was the point of entry for most of the Scots-Irish, German, and English settlers who populated the Delaware River valley and subsequently settled large areas of western Maryland, the Shenandoah valley, and piedmont North Carolina and South Carolina. Through these settlement patterns, the city's cultural identity was gradually extended over a broad geographic area.

In the upper Chesapeake Bay region, Philadelphia was also the dominant economic center. The phenomenal scope of her maritime trade and the short portage across the Head of Elk ensured commercial control of the grain-rich counties of southeastern Pennsylvania, southern Delaware, New Jersey, and Maryland until the rise of Baltimore in the mid 1760s. The grain trade, augmented by secondary exports such as lumber, cast iron, and manufactured goods, fostered the rise of a wealthy merchant class in Philadelphia. As Robert Morris wrote in 1776, "the

For assistance with this article, the author thanks William Voss Elder, III, Mr. and Mrs. Dudley Godfrey, Jr., Frank Horton, Mr. and Mrs. Robert Krikorian, the firm of Bernard and S. Dean Levy, Alan Miller, the National Park Service staff at Independence Hall, the firm of Israel Sack, Wes Stewart, and Gregory Weidman.

Spirit of Enterprise has seized most people & they are making or trying to make fortunes."[1]

Although most of this wealth was concentrated in the upper strata of society, the prosperity of Philadelphia's artisan community exceeded that of most colonial cities. Historian Gary Nash has concluded that between 1700 and 1745, one out of every six Philadelphia artisans attained a personal wealth in excess of £300 as compared with one out of twenty in Boston. Philadelphia tradesmen profited from the continual influx of people who had business in the colonial capital, and they actively marketed their goods in other cities. For example, carver Nicholas Bernard advertised his firm's services, stock carved work, and imported goods in Boston, New York, and Charleston; and Hercules Courtenay, another prominent Philadelphia carver, promoted his business in the *Maryland Gazette*.[2]

During the last quarter of the eighteenth century, Baltimore emerged as an important economic center, competing with Philadelphia for trade in the upper Chesapeake. From 250 inhabitants in 1752, Baltimore's population grew to more than 6,000 by 1776. According to British traveler William Eddis, by 1770 Baltimore's trade with the piedmont region was so lucrative that it "became an object of universal attention," attracting people of a "commercial and enterprising spirit." Virginia diarist Mary Ambler had "not heard of a single inhabitant who [did] not carry on a trade or follow some Business."[3]

The prospect of establishing an independent and lucrative business attracted two Philadelphia-trained cabinetmakers, Gerrard Hopkins in 1767 and Robert Moore in 1770. Hopkins (1742–1800) was a Maryland native and scion of a prosperous Quaker family. In 1754 he went to Philadelphia where he served an apprenticeship with cabinetmaker Jonathan Shoemaker. Assuming that Hopkins was bound until the age of twenty-one, he probably became a journeyman in 1764, and indeed, the receipt book of merchant Samuel Preston Moore documents transactions with Hopkins in September of that year. Hopkins also maintained an account with Quaker merchant Stephen Collins. On April 24, 1765, carver William Crisp charged twenty-five yards of linen to his account, possibly in exchange for furniture carving subcontracted by Hopkins. His account also shows a credit of £5.16.0 for "Two Chaimber Tables" in May 1766.[4] Although Hopkins reputedly worked as a journeyman for Robert Moore, his bartering and his involvement with tradesmen like Crisp suggest that he was working independently before moving to Baltimore. This conclusion is also supported by Hopkins's Philadelphia label, which was altered to read "Baltimore" and glued to the drawer of a high chest from his Maryland shop (figs. 1, 2).

In 1767 Hopkins moved to Baltimore and opened a shop at the "Sign of the Tea Table and Chair" on Gay Street. In his first advertisement on April 9, Hopkins announced that he was a "Cabinet and Chair-Maker, from Philadelphia . . . [who] Makes and Sells the following Goods . . . in Mahogany, Walnut, Cherry-Tree, and Maple, viz. Chests of Drawers . . . Desks, Scruitores, Cloth Presses . . . Bureaus, Card, Chamber, Parlor, and Tea-Tables . . . Easy, Arm, Parlour, Chamber and Corner Chairs, Settees, Clock-Cases, Couches, Candle-Stands, Decanter-Stands, Tea Kettle-Stands, Dumb-Waiters, Tea-Boards, Bottle-Boards, &c, &c. N.B. Any of the above articles to be done with or without carved Work."[5]

Although he plied his trade in the city for years, a high chest labeled by Hopkins is the only documented piece of Baltimore furniture made in the Philadelphia style. Hopkins's Philadelphia training is visible in the design, construction, and ornament of the chest. With its broken-scroll pediment, narrow fluted quarter-columns, and central shell drawer, the upper case is similar to that of a chest-on-chest signed by Hopkins's master, Shoemaker, and conforms roughly to sketches made by Samuel Mickle, another apprentice in Shoemaker's shop.[6] The drawers of the Hopkins chest have riven white-cedar bottoms with beveled edges that are dadoed to the sides and front and reinforced with segmented glue blocks. Like most Philadelphia pieces, the grain of the bottom boards is perpendicular to that of the drawer fronts. The use of shouldered drawer runners rather than dust boards in the upper case is the most significant departure from mainstream Philadelphia casework. The carving on the high chest is related to Philadelphia work of the late 1750s, a period when baroque designs were modified to conform to the lighter scale and openness of the emerging rococo styles (fig. 3).

The carved shells on the drawers and skirt of the Hopkins chest are virtually identical to that on the chimneypiece in the James Brice house in Annapolis (fig. 4). The construction of the house, which began in 1767 and continued through 1774, is thoroughly documented in Brice's ledger. In 1770 Brice paid William Bampton £40.0.1 for finishing the "Largest Room in [the] House . . . & carving [the] Chimneypiece."[7]

Figure 1. High chest with the label of Gerrard Hopkins, Baltimore, 1767–75. Mahogany with Atlantic coast white cedar and poplar; H. 89″, W. 44 3/8″, D. 24 5/8″. (Private collection: Photo, Breger and Associates, courtesy, Baltimore Museum of Art.)

Figure 2. Label pasted to lower drawer of upper case of high chest in figure 1. (Photo, Baltimore Museum of Art.)

In all likelihood, Hopkins employed Bampton either before or after Brice did.

Three armchairs and six side chairs can be attributed to Hopkins's shop based on the style and execution of their carving. Like the high chest and chimneypiece, they have relief-carved shells with undulating convex and concave segments (figs. 5, 6). The concave surfaces were sparsely veined with a small gouge, and the convex areas were decorated with lenticular chip cuts and circular gouge cuts. While the execution of the carving on these pieces is individualistic, the designs can generally be traced to Philadelphia. For example, the crest rails of the chairs have stylized shells, diaperwork, and flanking acanthus-leaf details that occur in similar configuration on many Philadelphia examples.[8]

With minor exceptions, Hopkins's chairs are also constructed like Philadelphia ones. Two-part, vertically grained glue blocks were used to reinforce the joints at the front corners of the frame, and single-piece

Figure 3. Lower shell drawer and skirt of high chest in figure 1. (Photo, Museum of Early Southern Decorative Arts.)

blocks, rabbeted to fit around the stiles, were used at the back. Although several of the mortise-and-tenon joints on the chairs are now pegged, it appears that they were originally secured with glue alone.

The furniture attributed to Hopkins's shop shows little evidence of a developing Baltimore style. The rather exaggerated curve of the high chest's legs and the bulbous arm supports of the armchairs are obvious departures from mainstream Philadelphia work; however, they represent individual conceits rather than regional details. Although such idiosyncrasies often form the basis for new regional styles, no other Baltimore artisans are known to have adopted these details.

The identification of Baltimore furniture made in the Philadelphia style has been a persistent problem for American furniture historians. Geographic proximity, intermarriage between families, and migration patterns of cabinetmakers contributed to the widespread dissemination of Philadelphia style. Since the 1940s scholars have attempted to overcome this problem by identifying regional characteristics of Maryland case construction and design.[9] Baltimore chairs are said to be lower and broader than their Philadelphia counterparts, and case pieces such as

Figure 4. Carved shell on central tablet of chimneypiece, parlor, James Brice house. (Photo, Museum of Early Southern Decorative Arts.)

cabriole-leg high chests are said to be distinguishable from Philadelphia ones by their fluted chamfers, lower drawers of approximately equal height, elaborately shaped skirts with applied carved shells, and closed ogee heads or "bonnet tops."

The only case piece with a firm Maryland history having several of these characteristics is a high chest that descended in the Ellicott family of Howard County, Maryland (fig. 7) and was reputedly owned by Thomas Ellicott (1777–1859).[10] Ellicott's father, Andrew, had moved from Bucks County, Pennsylvania, to the Elk Ridge area of Maryland in 1774. Although it has been assumed that Andrew Ellicott was the original owner and that the chest was made in Baltimore during the last quarter of the eighteenth century, the style of the case, brasses, brass placement, and carving suggest a date of 1740–50, a date far too early for construction in Baltimore (fig. 8). Furthermore, the chest can be tied to Philadelphia stylistically and constructionally as the following arguments show.

All the characteristics assigned to Baltimore "Chippendale" furniture are hallmarks of Philadelphia baroque style prevalent during the second quarter of the eighteenth century. In the last fifty years, several major Philadelphia case pieces have been attributed to Maryland, distorting Baltimore's role as a prerevolutionary style center and diverting

Figure 5. Armchair attributed to Gerrard Hopkins, Baltimore, 1767–75. Mahogany with yellow pine; H. 39 3/4", W. 25" (at knees). (Baltimore Museum of Art: Photo, Museum of Early Southern Decorative Arts.)

attention from Philadelphia. Included in this group are two cabriole-leg high chests whose Baltimore attribution was based on their closed ogee heads, fluted chamfers, and lower drawer arrangement (figs. 9, 10).

The construction of the high chests is typical in every way of Philadelphia work of the mid eighteenth century. The chest in figure 10 has lip-molded mahogany drawer fronts and riven white-cedar drawer

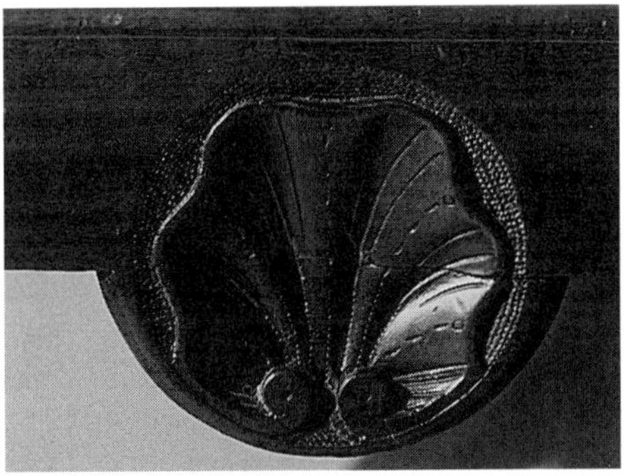

Figure 6. Relief-carved shell on front rail of armchair in figure 5.

bottoms that are beveled on all four edges, rabbeted to the sides and front, and covered with glue strips that are mitered at the front corners and sawn off at a 45 degree angle at the back. The chest in figure 9 differs in having lip-molded walnut drawer fronts with walnut veneer.[11] Both chests have full dust boards in the upper case and similar molding profiles and pediment construction. At the apex of the arch, the moldings are mitered and return on a board that is dovetailed to the tympanum and upper backboard of the pediment. The tympanum of the chest in figure 10 is cut from a solid mahogany board, and that in figure 9 is walnut veneered on yellow pine. The lower cases have similar skirts, lower drawers of equal height, and linen trays beneath the waist molding. The trays have lip-molded facings and wide battens with cock-beaded edges. Although the lower case construction of the chest in figure 9 was not recorded when it was photographed by the Museum of Early Southern Decorative Arts in 1972, given the other similarities, it is logical to assume that it is similar to the chest in figure 10: the large drawer is supported by a central runner dovetailed to the drawer blade and mortised into the back and two side runners tenoned into the drawer blade and nailed to the rear stiles; the small drawers are supported by outer runners nailed to the leg stiles and inner runners lapped onto the front rail and mortised into the back.

An early Philadelphia dressing table differs in drawer arrangement but is closely related in the shaping of the skirt, drawer, and case con-

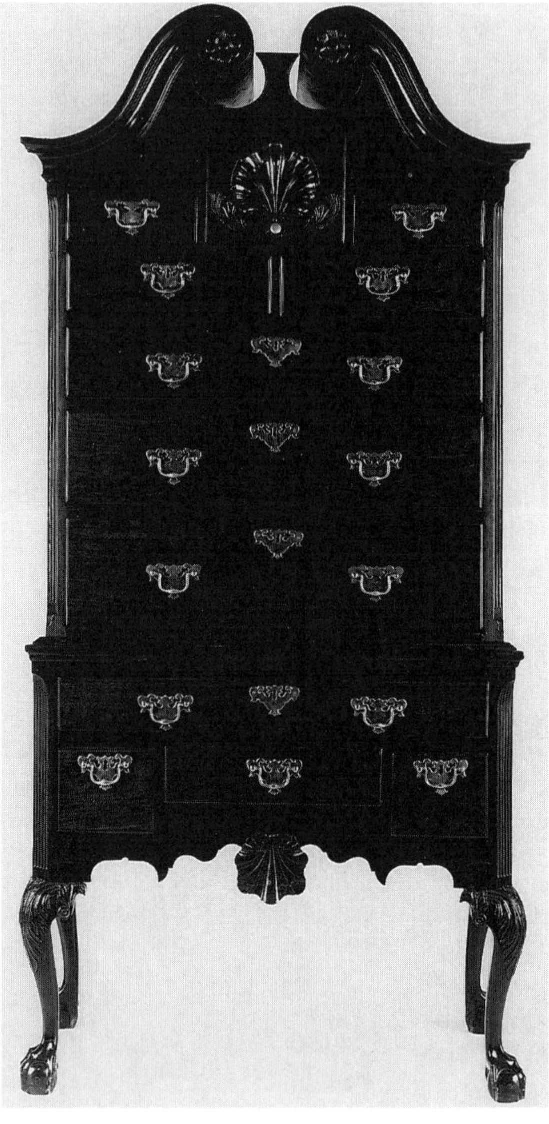

Figure 7. High chest, Philadelphia, 1745–55. Mahogany with Atlantic coast white cedar and tulip; H. 89 3/8″, W. 43″, D. 24 3/4″. (Baltimore Museum of Art, gift of Charles Ellis Ellicott, Jr., and Family.)

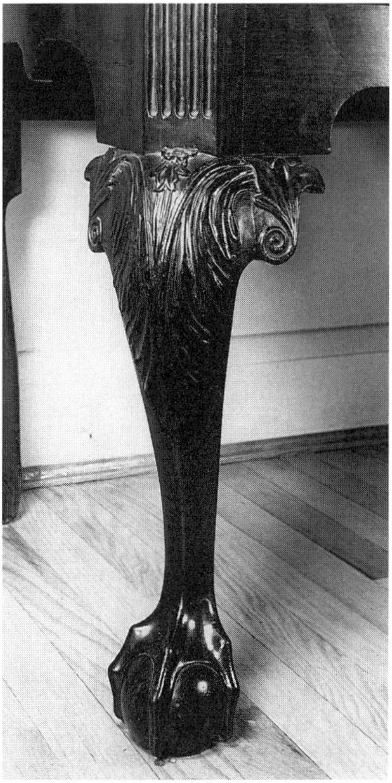

Figure 8. Leg of high chest in figure 7. (Photo, Museum of Early Southern Decorative Arts.)

struction (fig. 11). Although probably executed by two different hands, the carving on all three pieces was drawn and outlined in a similar manner (figs. 12, 13, 14). Bilaterally symmetrical carving was often laid out with half-patterns that were simply flopped to complete both sides of the design. The sizes of the gouges used in outlining the leaves vary from piece to piece; however, the radii of the tools and formula of cuts are closely related. The techniques used in modeling and veining the leaves are among the most distinctive aspects of this carving. The V-shaped area between the branches of acanthus was modeled with three deep flutes, the center of which was terminated with a vertical gouge cut. A small

Figure 9. High chest, Philadelphia, 1740–55. Walnut and walnut veneer with Atlantic coast white cedar, tulip, and yellow pine; H. 85 5/8", W. 43", D. 24". (Museum of Early Southern Decorative Arts.) The chest descended in the Skinner family of Perquimans County, N.C.

Figure 10. High chest, Philadelphia, 1740–55. Mahogany with Atlantic coast white cedar and tulip; H. 91½″, W. 43⅜″, D. 24″. (Maryland Historical Society: Photo, Museum of Early Southern Decorative Arts.)

Figure 11. Dressing table, attributed to the shop of Samuel Harding, Philadelphia, 1740–55. Mahogany with Atlantic coast white cedar, tulip, and yellow pine; H. 31″, W. 33″, D. 21″. (Private collection: Photo, Luke Beckerdite.)

gouge was used both for veining and for making shading cuts at the tips of the leaves. While shading cuts are normally made perpendicular to the flow of a design and are used to create shadow lines in a depression or simulate an overturned leaf, in this object short parallel flutes were used to highlight simple leaf ends—a technique that is more closely related to engraving than carving.

Similar techniques were used in carving the acanthus on two other dressing tables (figs. 15, 16), one of which has been attributed to Maryland on the basis of its case design and an inscription on the upper drawer. The appliqués on both shell drawers have broad leaves that were roughly modeled, then veined with a small gouge (figs. 17, 18). Although

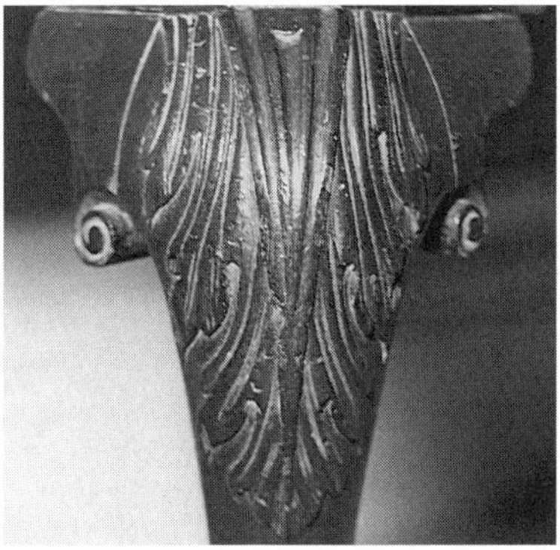

Figure 12. Knee of high chest in figure 9.

Figure 13. Knee of high chest in figure 10.

Figure 14. Knee of dressing table in figure 11.

Figure 15. Dressing table, Philadelphia, 1745–55. Mahogany with Atlantic coast white cedar, tulip, and yellow pine; H. 31", W. 33 1/2", D. 21 1/2". (Israel Sack.)

the veining flutes were executed with little regard to the natural flow of the design, the techniques used in shading the leaf ends conform to other carving in the group. The shells have broad convex and concave segments that emanate from retracted scroll volutes like those on the high chests, three side chairs from the collection of Howard Reifsnyder (fig. 19), and five side chairs from a set that descended in the Coates family of Philadelphia (fig. 20).[12]

Once referred to as "Hogarth" chairs because of their curvilinear design, the Reifsnyder and Coates chairs are unmistakably Philadelphian. They are distinguished by solid, crotch walnut splats, curved stiles, relief-carved crest rails, and blocked compass seats with two-piece

Figure 16. Dressing table, Philadelphia, 1740–55. Mahogany with unrecorded secondary woods; H. 29 3/4", W. 33 3/4", D. 21 1/4". (Israel Sack.)

shells. The upper section of each shell is carved from the solid, and the lower section is applied. In both design and execution, the knee carving (fig. 21) is a miniature version of that on the knees of the high chests and two of the dressing tables (see figs. 12, 13, 14). The chairs and the dressing tables in figures 15 and 16 also have nearly identical knee blocks.

Furniture historians traditionally have been overly conservative in dating Philadelphia casework in the late baroque style, and it is this tendency that has allowed numerous pieces to be misattributed to Baltimore. There is substantial evidence to support the mid eighteenth-century dates assigned to the preceding pieces. A high chest signed by Henry Clifton and Thomas Carteret is stylistically more advanced and is dated 1753. There are also early Philadelphia case pieces and chairs

Figure 17. Shell drawer of dressing table in figure 15.

Figure 18. Shell drawer of dressing table in figure 16.

with traditions of ownership by glasshouse owner Caspar Wistar (d. 1752) and Joseph Armitt (d. 1747). More important, the carving on the side chairs, dressing tables, and high chests is closely related to work documented abd attributed to Samuel Harding, a Philadelphia carver who died in 1758.[13]

The earliest work documented to Harding's shop is the carving in the Pennsylvania State House now known as Independence Hall. Between 1753 and 1757 his shop did the architectural carving for the steeple, stair tower, and first-floor hall. Harding's account, which totaled £195.13.11, includes more than 400 feet of molding, 146 banisters, 106

Figure 19. Side chair, Philadelphia, 1740–55. Walnut; H. 42 1/4". (Israel Sack.)

modillions, 76 floral appliqués, 58 stair brackets, 33 leaf appliqués that were described as "fishes," 32 trusses, 30 capitals, 29 garlands, 8 flame finials or "blases," 6 stair posts, 5 friezes, 4 angles, 2 tabernacle frames, 2 pediment frames, and 2 keystones with "faces."[14]

An elaborate frieze appliqué with a central shell and flanking acanthus leaves (figs. 22, 23) is among the original carving surviving in the State House; however, its precise architectural context is unknown. In

Figure 20. Side chair, Philadelphia, 1740–55. Walnut; H. 42½″. (Israel Sack.)

design and execution the acanthus is closely related to that on the furniture illustrated above. The outlining, application of veining flutes, and shading of the leaf ends show the same basic approach. The shell's folded segments, the strapwork stems of the acanthus, and the geometric composition of the appliqué are reminiscent of French baroque architectural designs of the late seventeenth and early eighteenth centuries. So is the design of the pediment frames in the first-floor hall, the earliest of which have mask keystones and bold scrollwork.

Figure 21. Detail of front rail and leg of side chair in figure 19.

A tea table with a history of ownership by physician Thomas Graeme (1688–1772) of Graeme Park in Horsham, Pennsylvania, supports this conclusion (fig. 24). The table was made in Philadelphia about 1750.[15] Its contoured rails, acanthus, husks, and shells are framed by scrolls and strapwork (fig. 25). The husks are similar to those in the garlands in the State House (fig. 26), and the shells are essentially scaled-down versions of the small overlapping shell on the frieze appliqué (see fig. 22). The leaves also compare favorably with those on the knees and drawers of the preceding case pieces and chairs.

Although technical parallels demonstrate that the furniture and architectural carving stem from the same shop tradition, minor variations in the work suggest that the shop was large enough to have had journeymen and apprentices. This is most noticeable in the modeling of ball-and-claw feet. Another instance of this are two rectangular tea tables

Figure 22. Detail of frieze appliqué, first-floor chamber, Pennsylvania State House, attributed to the shop of Samuel Harding, Philadelphia, 1753–58. (National Park Service.)

Figure 23. Detail of frieze appliqué, Pennsylvania State House. (National Park Service.)

Figure 24. Tea table attributed to the shop of Samuel Harding, Philadelphia, 1745–55. Mahogany with Atlantic coast white cedar and white pine; H. 27 1/2", W. 34 5/8", D. 21 1/8". (Winterthur.)

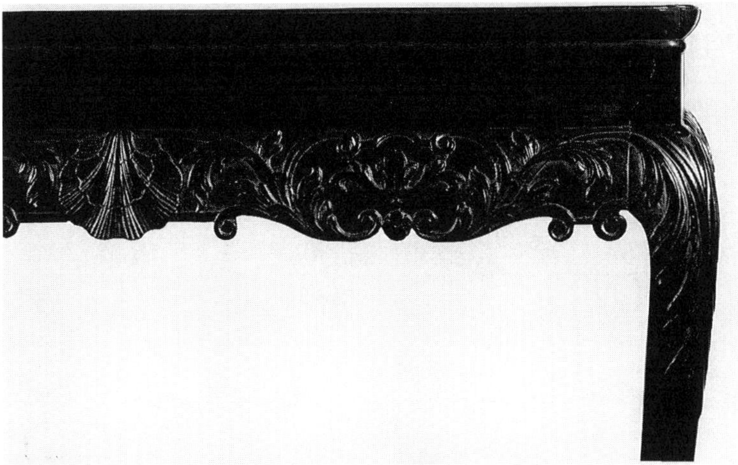

Figure 25. Detail of rail and knee of tea table in figure 24.

Figure 26. Detail of carved garland, second-floor stair tower, Pennsylvania State House. (National Park Service.)

with markedly different feet but similar knee carving (figs. 27, 28, 29, 30).[16] The shells on the knees have vertical veining flutes interrupted by irregular horizontal flutes like those on the State House frieze and a tea table (see figs. 22, 25).

A walnut tall-case clock has carved details that reflect the work of another artisan involved in the State House commission (figs. 31, 32). The shell on the tympanum has deep folds and segments that were modeled with crescent-shaped chip cuts and parallel gouge cuts like the shell on the frieze in the State House (see fig. 22); however, the acanthus leaves on the clock are more attenuated, and they have a spiny quality like those of an appliqué in the stair tower (fig. 33). Other than Harding, the only carver identified in the State House accounts was Brian Wilkinson, who presented a bill for unspecified carving valued at £85.8.10.[17] It is not known whether Wilkinson was an independent contractor associated with Harding or a journeyman in his shop.

The same carving techniques used on the clock appear in the appliqués on four early Philadelphia desk-and-bookcases, two of which are included in this study (figs. 34, 35). The leaves have curled lobes with sharp central ridges and trailing lobes that were modeled with a wide shallow flute and outlined primarily with quarter-round gouges (figs. 34,

Figure 27. Tea table attributed to the shop of Samuel Harding, Philadelphia, 1745–60. Mahogany with secondary woods (to be investigated); H. 29½″, W. 24½″, D. 19″. (Bernard and S. Dean Levy: Photo, Helga Photo Studio.)

36). Although the outlining and modeling techniques differ from those used on the frieze appliqué figures 22 and 23, Harding's influence is evident in the shading of the leaf ends and in the design and execution of the shell on the desk-and-bookcase illustrated in figure 34.

The appliqué on the bookcase in figures 35 and 36 provides a direct link to two dressing tables and a high chest that also have been misattributed to Maryland (figs. 37, 38, 39).[18] The acanthus appliqués on the first dressing table are related to those on the bookcase, having small clusters of leaves that descend from the scroll volutes of the shells (fig. 40). These leaves have sharp ridges, wide flutes, and parallel shading cuts on the ends. They are cut from the same board as the shell, conceal-

Figure 28. Knee of tea table in figure 27.

ing the joint of each of the flanking acanthus branches. This technique is consistent with the assembly of the appliqués on the other bookcase and the clock.

The appliqués on the dressing table are virtually identical to those on the lower shell drawer of a high chest in the Winterthur collection (fig. 41). The high chest and the dressing table illustrated in figure 38 have large oval shells with small shells inverted in the center, a detail that is stylistically related to the carving on three of the desk-and-bookcases (see fig. 34). When compared to the appliqué work, the acanthus carving on the legs of the high chest and the dressing table appears relatively coarse (fig. 42). The leaves have deep flutes separated by high ridges, sparse veining, rudimentary shading cuts, and background areas that were randomly stippled with a single-point tool rather than a gang punch. This probably represents the work of another artisan, who was at-

Figure 29. Tea table attributed to the shop of Samuel Harding, Philadelphia, 1745–55. (Historical Society of Pennsylvania.)

tempting to match his work to the appliqués. Philadelphia case pieces made during this period often show the work of more than one carver. In keeping with urban British practice, the better hand generally carved the most visible part.

The Philadelphia furniture examined in this paper spans a period of approximately twenty years and reflects the work of at least three cabinet shops and three carvers, yet there is an amazing degree of continuity in casework and carving. Philadelphia's own version of the late baroque style was well entrenched by the late 1730s and matured over the following two decades as the preceding objects suggest. That all the stylistic details traditionally associated with Baltimore "Chippendale" furniture are characteristics of Philadelphia attests to Philadelphia's dominance in the Middle Atlantic region before the Revolution.

Figure 30. Knee of tea table in figure 29.

Figure 31. Tall-case clock with movement by John Wood, Sr. (w. 1734–60), and carving attributed to the shop of Samuel Harding, Philadelphia, 1750–60. Walnut with tulip, red oak, and white oak; H. 107 1/2″, W. 23 1/2″, D. 11 3/8″. (Metropolitan Museum of Art: Photo, Richard Cheek.)

Figure 32. Tympanum of clock in figure 31.

Figure 33. Carved frieze, Pennsylvania State House. (National Park Service.)

Figure 34. Desk-and-bookcase with carving attributed to the shop of Samuel Harding, Philadelphia, 1750–60. (Kenmore.)

Figure 35. Desk-and-bookcase with carving attributed to the shop of Samuel Harding, Philadelphia, 1750–60. Mahogany with Atlantic coast white cedar and tulip; H. 103″, W. 41″, D. 23″. (Bernard and S. Dean Levy: Photo, Helga Photo Studio.)

Figure 36. Tympanum of desk-and-bookcase in figure 35. (Bernard and S. Dean Levy: Photo, Helga Photo Studio.)

Figure 37. Dressing table, Philadelphia, 1750–60. Walnut with Atlantic coast white cedar and tulip; H. $28\frac{5}{8}$″, W. $34\frac{3}{4}$″, D. $20\frac{1}{16}$″. (Winterthur.)

Figure 38. Dressing table, Philadelphia, 1750–65. Walnut with poplar, cedar, and yellow pine; H. 29″, W. 34″, D. 21 1/4″. (Photo, Museum of Early Southern Decorative Arts.)

Figure 39. High chest, Philadelphia, 1750–60. Walnut with Atlantic coast white cedar and tulip; H. 96¼", W. 43¾", D. 24½". (Winterthur.)

Figure 40. Shell drawer of dressing table in figure 37.

Figure 41. Shell drawer of high chest in figure 39.

Figure 42. Knee of dressing table in figure 39. (Photo, Museum of Early Southern Decorative Arts.)

[1] Morris to William Bingham, Philadelphia, October 20, 1776, as quoted in Wendell Garrett, "Editorial," *Antiques* 131, no. 5 (May 1987): 1043.

[2] Gary B. Nash, *The Urban Crucible: Social Change, Political Consciousness, and the Origins of the American Revolution* (Cambridge: Harvard University Press, 1979), p. 121; Luke Beckerdite, "Philadelphia Carving Shops, Part 2: Bernard and Jugiez," *Antiques* 128, no. 3 (September 1985): 510, 513; Courtenay ad as copied in Alfred Cox Prime Files, Decorative Arts Photographic Collection, Visual Resources Collection, Winterthur Library.

[3] Wilbur H. Hunter, "Baltimore in the Revolutionary Generation," in *Maryland Heritage: Five Baltimore Institutions Celebrate the American Bicentennial*, ed. John B. Boles (Baltimore: Maryland Historical Society, 1976), p. 189. In comparison, Philadelphia had more than 13,000 inhabitants in 1751 and more than 24,000 in 1775; Nash, *Urban Crucible*, p. 408. William Eddis, *Letters from America*, ed. Aubrey C. Land (Cambridge: Harvard University Press, Belknap Press, 1969), pp. 49–50; "Diary of M[ary] Ambler, 1770," *Virginia Magazine of History and Biography* 45, no. 2 (April 1937): 165–66.

[4] Accounts, January 1, 1765–December 31, 1766, cont. 73, Stephen Collins Papers, Library of Congress, as cited in Nancy Anne Goyne, "Furniture Craftsmen

in Philadelphia, 1760–1780: Their Role in a Mercantile Society" (Master's thesis, University of Delaware, 1963), pp. 22, 151 and 34, 80, 155, 168. Gregory R. Weidman, *Furniture in Maryland, 1740–1940: The Collection of the Maryland Historical Society* (Baltimore: By the society, 1984), p. 46; Samuel Preston Moore, receipt book, Library Company of Philadelphia.

[5] Hopkins advertisement, *Maryland Gazette* (Annapolis), April 9, 1767.

[6] Eleanor H. Gustafson, "Clues and Footnotes," *Antiques* 127, no. 5 (May 1985): 172–73.

[7] James Brice account book, pp. 29, 32, Hall of Records, Annapolis, Md.

[8] Two armchairs and one side chair are illustrated in Luke Beckerdite, "A Problem of Identification: Baltimore and Philadelphia Furniture Styles in the Eighteenth Century," *Journal of Early Southern Decorative Arts* 12, no. 1 (May 1986): 32–37. The third armchair is in a private collection. J. Michael Flanigan, *American Furniture from the Kaufman Collection* (Washington, D.C.: National Gallery of Art, 1986), pp. 30–31.

[9] The exhibition "Baltimore Furniture: The Work of Baltimore and Annapolis Cabinetmakers from 1760 to 1810," was a pioneer effort to "establish a local Chippendale style." Although the objects in the exhibition were recognized as resembling Philadelphia furniture of the period, specific stylistic details that appeared to be common to the group were used to separate them from Philadelphia work (Baltimore Museum of Art, *Baltimore Furniture: The Work of Baltimore and Annapolis Cabinetmakers from 1760 to 1810* [Baltimore: By the museum, 1947], p. 170). Subsequent publications and exhibitions have added to the list so that today there is a recognized Baltimore "Chippendale" style; *Maryland Queen Anne and Chippendale Furniture of the Eighteenth Century* (Baltimore: October House, 1968), pp. 5–128; and Weidman, *Furniture in Maryland*, pp. 42–68.

[10] *Maryland Furniture*, p. 84.

[11] Although veneered drawers often have cock-beaded edges during this period, there are other Philadelphia case pieces with drawer fronts like the Skinner family chest in figure 9; for a published example, see William Voss Elder III and Jayne E. Stokes, *American Furniture, 1680–1880, from the Collection of the Baltimore Museum of Art* (New York: By the museum, 1987), pp. 76–77.

[12] Israel Sack, *American Antiques from the Israel Sack Collection*, 9 vols. (Washington, D.C.: Highland House Publishers, 1969–89), 4:982, 5:1218–21; Flanigan, *American Furniture*, pp. 20–21. The other dressing table has a history of descent in the Bush Shayder family of Wilmington, Del. (Israel Sack, *American Antiques*, 6:1537).

[13] William Macpherson Hornor, Jr., *Blue Book, Philadelphia Furniture: William Penn to George Washington, with Special Reference to the Philadelphia-Chippendale School* (1935; reprint, Washington, D.C.: Highland House, 1977), pls. 23, 37, 39, 71, 303; *Philadelphia: Three Centuries of American Art* (Philadelphia: Philadelphia Museum of Art, 1976), p. 42.

[14] Samuel Harding bill for carving in the Pennsylvania State House, typescript, January 1, 1753–after January 7, 1757, card files, Pennsylvania State House, Philadelphia (original manuscript: General Loan Office Account Books, 1750–68 [bound, unpaged], Norris Papers, Historical Society of Pennsylvania).

[15] Winterthur, 53.93.1. For more on the history of the table, see Charles F. Hummel, "Queen Anne and Chippendale Furniture in the Henry Francis du Pont Winterthur Museum," pt. 3, *Antiques* 99, no. 1 (January 1971): 104–5.

[16] Horner, *Blue Book*, pl. 74. Although somewhat less exaggerated, the preceding high chests and dressing table with claw-and-ball feet have sharply sloping front talons with a low terminal joint like those of the tea tables.

[17] Morrison H. Heckscher, *American Furniture in the Metropolitan Museum of Art*, ed. Mary-Alice Rogers, 2 vols. (New York: By the museum and Random House, 1985), 2:306–7; *Philadelphia*, p. 42. Wilkinson bill, August 20, 1756, in *Pennsylvania Archives*, 8th ser., no. 7, 6429, Pennsylvania State House, Philadelphia.

[18] The dressing table in figure 38 descended in the Saunders family of Philadelphia. Among the first to question its Maryland attribution was Charles F. Hummel, *A Winterthur Guide to American Chippendale Furniture: Middle Atlantic and Southern Colonies* (New York: Crown Publishers, 1976), p. 117. The high chest, formerly attributed to Maryland, is illustrated in Joseph Downs, *American Furniture: Queen Anne and Chippendale Periods in the Henry Francis du Pont Winterthur Museum* (New York: Macmillan Co., 1952), fig. 199. The dressing table illustrated in figure 39 was attributed to Maryland in *Maryland Furniture*, pp. 72–73.

Politics and Style

An Analysis of the Patrons and Products of Jonathan Gostelowe and Thomas Affleck

Deborah Anne Federhen

The furniture produced in Philadelphia during the 1770s and 1780s by artisans like Jonathan Gostelowe and Thomas Affleck represents two very different schools of taste. While both are based on English models, one group perpetuates the ornately carved, curvilinear rococo style that had been popular in England in the middle of the eighteenth century; the other incorporates characteristics of the planar, architectonic neoclassical style that rose to prominence in England during the 1760s and 1770s. The coexistence of these two styles in Philadelphia during the turbulent political period leading up to and following the American Revolution is a significant indicator of the cultural atmosphere in Philadelphia. In "Style as Evidence," art historian Jules David Prown observed, "style is inescapably culturally expressive." Analysis of the patrons of Gostelowe and Affleck suggests a correlation between the political affiliations of the patrons and the furniture styles they favored.[1]

Jonathan Gostelowe was born in 1744, in Passyunk township, now part of Philadelphia. His father, George Gostelowe, emigrated from Sweden in 1729 to farm the rich Pennsylvania countryside; his mother, Lydia, came to the colonies from Northamptonshire, England. Gostelowe was baptized in Gloria Dei (Old Swedes) Church but became a member of Christ Church, possibly during his apprenticeship with Philadelphia cabinetmaker George Claypoole. Gostelowe's membership in the Anglican congregation was important to his career as a cabinetmaker, providing him with the social contacts necessary to acquire and maintain a wealthy, influential clientele. After 1750, "the Anglicans became definitely the congregation of wealth, fashion and position." Many members of prominent Quaker families attended the Anglican churches, including two William Penn descendants—son Richard Penn, who joined the Anglican congregation at an early age, and grandson John Penn, who was a pewholder at both Christ Church (1778–81) and St. Peter's (1782–92). Documents from Christ Church and St. Peter's record the marriages and baptisms of members of the Cadwalader, Chew, Fisher, Hollingsworth, Mifflin, Morris, Pemberton, Powel, and Wharton families.[2]

If Gostelowe followed the traditional pattern of a seven-year apprenticeship that began at age fourteen, he would have been fully trained by 1765. By the 1770s he had established his shop on Front Street, next to the London Coffee-house, near the heart of the city's social, commercial, and political life. The London Coffee-house, founded by printer William Bradford in 1754, was a lively meeting place for merchants, ship captains, statesmen, and tradesmen where "all manner of sales were conducted, [and] the newspapers of London and of other great cities were first to be seen." It served as a center for political discussion; the Committee of Safety, formed to govern the city during the early years of the Revolution, held meetings there, as did other public organizations. The courthouse, the post office, the college, academy and charity schools, the theater, the customhouse, the mason's lodge, the Presbyterian church, Christ Church, and Friends Meetinghouse were all within a few blocks.[3]

In 1768 Gostelowe was married to Mary Duffield at Christ Church, where both he and his father-in-law were vestrymen. Mary Duffield Gostelowe died two years later. Gostelowe abandoned his trade in 1776 to serve in the Continental army as a major in a corps of artillery artificers and as an assistant commissary general of military stores. He probably resumed his trade in 1781, when many of the men in Gostelowe's artillery company in Philadelphia were discharged. He had a label printed to announce the resumption of his cabinetmaking career: "Jonathan Gostelowe, Cabinet and Chairmaker, at his shop in Church

Alley, about midway between Second and Third Streets, Begs to inform his former Customers and the Public in general, That he hath again assumed his former occupation at the above mentioned place; A renewal of their favors will be thankfully received; and his best endeavors shall be used to give satisfaction to those who please to employ him." His relocation to Church Alley, on property inherited from his first wife, placed him close to St. Peter's, in the middle of Society Hill, where many of the city's prominent merchants resided. By 1783 Gostelowe's cabinetmaking business was productive and lucrative. An occupational tax levied in 1783 assessed Gostelowe £100, one of the highest assessments for a cabinetmaker, lower only than Benjamin Randolph and Thomas Affleck. Gostelowe's prominence among Philadelphia cabinetmakers is further substantiated by his selection in 1788 as chairman of the Gentlemen Cabinet and Chair Makers Society. Gostelowe was married on April 9, 1789, to Elizabeth Howell Towers, daughter of Robert Towers, commissary of military stores during the Revolution; the ceremony was performed at Christ Church. In 1793 Gostelowe sold the contents of his shop and retired to his farm in Northumberland County. He died two years later and was buried at Christ Church.[4]

Gostelowe's work as a cabinetmaker is exemplified by monumental chests of drawers and chest-on-chests and distinguished by his skillful use of dramatically grained mahogany, bold planar surfaces, canted corners, and distinctive ogee bracket feet. One of the earliest pieces of furniture that can be well documented to Gostelowe is a chest-on-chest that he may have made in 1768 as a wedding present for his first wife. This chest-on-chest (now in a private collection) displays bold ogee bracket feet, quarter columns set into the corners, a swan's neck pediment, and brasses that consist of a bail and elaborately pierced back plates. There is minimal use of carved decoration; the center drawer in the pediment has a recessed shell above a simple applied foliate swag, and applied rosettes and flame finials ornament the swan's-neck pediment. Two similar chest-on-chests (now in the Germantown Historical Society [fig. 1] and a private collection) were probably made between 1773 and 1776. They feature canted corners on the cases and ogee bracket feet, a rare feature on Philadelphia furniture that Gostelowe employed frequently throughout the 1770s and 1780s. The Germantown Historical Society chest-on-chest was commissioned by Judah Foulke (1722–76) for his

Figure 1. Chest-on-chest, attributed to Jonathan Gostelowe, Philadelphia, 1773–76. Mahogany, tulip poplar, yellow pine; H. 96″, W. 46″, D. 23″. (Germantown Historical Society: Photo, Winterthur.)

Figure 2. Jonathan Gostelowe, Chest of drawers, Philadelphia, 1772. Mahogany, tulip poplar, white cedar, yellow pine; H. 37¼″, W. 47¼″, D. 25½″. (Clivedon of the National Trust.)

house on Front Street. The other one was made for Richard Wistar (1727–81), who presented it to his daughter, Elizabeth Wyatt Wistar, at the time of her marriage to Richard Miller in 1788.[5]

In the 1770s Gostelowe also produced furniture for Benjamin Chew, a member of Christ Church; however, the receipt of February 12, 1772, for £6.13.9 "in full of all accounts & demands" does not indicate what had been commissioned from the cabinetmaker. Gostelowe's best known and best documented furniture examples are two labeled serpentine-front, canted-corner chests of drawers that he made for Chew between 1781 and 1789 (fig. 2). A third chest of drawers of this form, without Gostelowe's postrevolutionary label, has a history of ownership in the Chew family. A fourth, also unlabeled, was made for Bishop William White, and is visible in John Sartain's 1836 painting of White's study. These chests, with their bold interplay of sweeping planar surfaces, fluted corners, and richly grained mahogany, are close approximations

Figure 3. Jonathan Gostelowe, pembroke table, Philadelphia, 1781–89. Mahogany, tulip poplar, oak; H. 28 5/8″, W. 44″ (top open), D. 24″. (Bishop White House, Independence National Historic Park: Photo, Winterthur.)

of English prototypes. White also purchased a labeled Pembroke table from Gostelowe during the cabinetmaker's second period of shop operation (fig. 3). It is emphatically linear with unornamented straight legs and stretchers.[6]

Gostelowe's furniture exhibits an awareness and assimilation of current English styles. The chest-on-chest was au courant in England during the 1760s and 1770s while the chest-on-frame was a uniquely American form. Thomas Chippendale's pattern book, *The Gentleman*

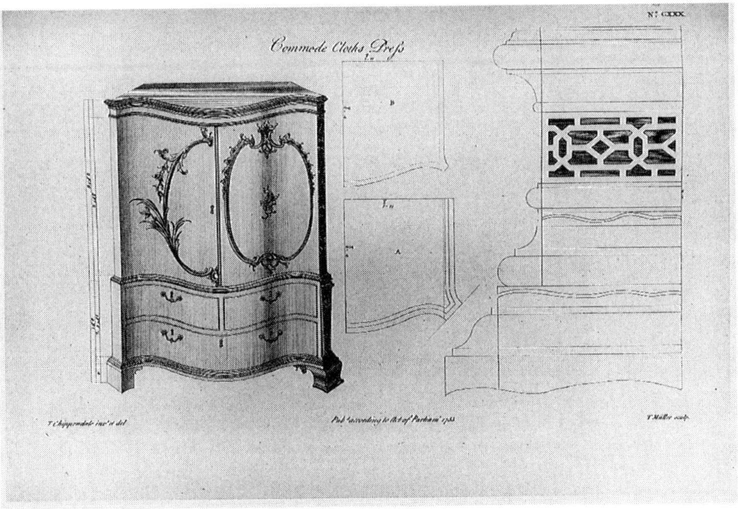

Figure 4. Thomas Chippendale, "Commode Cloths Press." From *The Gentleman and Cabinet Maker's Director* (3d ed.; London, 1762), pl. 130. (Photo, Winterthur.)

and Cabinet Maker's Director, published in 1754 and reissued in 1762, includes several designs for a serpentine-front chest and "Commode Cloths Press" with canted-corner ogee bracket feet (fig. 4). English chests of drawers made during the 1750s and early 1760s display the elaborate carving and robust curvilinear frame of the rococo style. During the 1760s and 1770s, however, the English turned from florid foliate-carved decoration to reeding, fluting, fretwork, or plain surfaces. The 1762 edition of *The Gentleman and Cabinet Maker's Director* illustrates many designs for case furniture and seating furniture that are asymmetrical or irregular in form and ornamented with elaborate naturalistic carving. In contrast, George Shearer's designs in *The Cabinet Maker's London Book of Prices* of 1788 feature sleek, smooth surfaces and self-contained forms that rely on exotic veneers for ornamentation. Although at least two copies of Chippendale's *Director* were present in Philadelphia before the Revolution, Gostelowe gained a direct link to English styles when he purchased the indenture of an English journeyman, Thomas Jones, on October 2, 1773. Jones was listed in the provincial tax

Figure 5. Thomas Jones, desk-and-bookcase, Philadelphia, 1775–85. Walnut, tulip poplar, yellow pine; W. 38″. (Private collection.)

of 1774 and the City of Philadelphia state tax of 1779. By 1797 Jones had acquired sufficient funds to establish his own shop, on Fifth Street, and he is listed in the Philadelphia directories until 1802. Furniture attributed to Jones exhibits the unadorned style prevalent in London at the time of his emigration and is made with characteristic English construction techniques (fig. 5).[7]

The canted-corner chest of drawers was a fairly common form in England, produced throughout the country in substantial quantities, but was uncommon in the colonies. Gostelowe appears to have been the primary American proponent of this form. His serpentine-front canted-corner chests of drawers stand out among the furniture produced in Philadelphia during the 1770s and 1780s as an exceptional manifestation of a distinctive and ubiquitous English furniture form. His decision to produce furniture that emulated the most current English styles, particularly during a period of strained political and economic relations with England, is a significant indicator of the character of his clientele. Prown maintains, "Through stylistic analysis of objects, we encounter the past at first hand. . . . This affective mode of apprehension through the senses that allows us to put ourselves, figuratively speaking, inside the skins of individuals who commissioned, made, used, or enjoyed these objects, to see with their eyes and touch with their hands, to identify with them empathetically, is clearly a different way of engaging the past than abstractly through the written word." An analysis of furniture style, therefore, should be an important index to the social milieu that promoted the object's creation. An assessment of Gostelowe's patrons suggests that the cabinetmaker adopted a distinctively English form in response to his customers' affinity for England during the Revolution.[8]

Gostelowe's patrons appear to have been predominantly Loyalists or neutral during the political struggles of the Revolution. In other aspects of their lives, his patrons are a heterogeneous group, displaying considerable variety in their native origin, education or training, religion, and occupation (tables 1, 2). The most notable common denominator among the group is their lack of active participation in the American struggle for independence from England. The only member of the group to serve in the military was John Henderson, named Warden of the Port of Philadelphia by Sir William Howe during the English occupation of the city. Henderson followed the British to New York and served on English ships until the end of the war. He received an annual allowance from the English government of £15 and was awarded £700 by Parliament in compensation for the losses he suffered for his loyalist stance. Benjamin Chew, attorney for the Penn family, supported the op-

Table 1. Jonathan Gostelowe Patrons: Biographical Data

Patron	Occupation	Birthplace	Place of Education
Michael Billmeyer (1752–1831)	printer[1]	York, Pa.	York, Pa.
Benjamin Chew (1722–1810)	lawyer, judge	Md.	Philadelphia London
Judah Foulke (1722–76)	merchant	Gwynedd, Pa.	Philadelphia
John Henderson	ship master	Scotland	—
Charles Swift	lawyer	—	—
William White (1748–1836)	Anglican bishop	Philadelphia	Philadelphia London
Richard Wistar (1727–1781)	glass manufacturer	Philadelphia	Philadelphia

[1] Billmeyer moved from York to Germantown, Pa., 1784.

position to the Stamp Act and signed the Nonimportation Agreement of 1765, "but holding a number of commissions under the Crown would not go to the length of counselling or aiding in armed resistance to the Crown." A biography of Chew published in the Philadelphia-based *Port Folio* in 1811, the year after his death, explained Chew's refusal to support the Revolution: "His views against the mother country were not pushed to the same extremity with those of many of his compatriots and friends. His object was of *reform* rather than *revolution–redress of grievances* rather than *independence*." In 1777 Chew was arrested for refusing to take the oath of allegiance and was held in Union Iron Works in New Jersey with John Penn for ten months.[9]

Patron Judah Foulke held a number of crown-appointed positions; collector of excise, 1745–50, sheriff of Philadelphia County, 1770–72, and keeper of brass for weights and measures, 1773. In addition, Foulke, the son of prominent Quaker minister Mary Evans Foulke, was a strict Quaker and supported the pacifist policies of the sect. The Reverend William White, another Gostelowe patron, maintained a policy of strict neutrality, balancing his devotion to the Church of England with the needs of his parishioners at Christ Church and St. Peter's. White had

Table 2. Jonathan Gostelow Patrons: Political and Religious Data

Patron	Military Service	Supported Nonimp. Agreement	Religious Affiliation[1] Quaker	Christ Church	Other
Michael Billmeyer	—	—	—	—	Lutheran
Benjamin Chew	—	X	—	X[2]	—
Judah Foulke	—	X	X	—	—
John Henderson[3]	British navy	—	—	X	—
Charles Swift[4]	—	—	—	—	—
William White	—	—	—	X	—
Richard Wistar	—	—	X	—	—

[1] Determined by church records for baptisms, marriages, and deaths. Some patrons appear in the records of more than one church.

[2] Also a member of St. Peter's Church.

[3] The extent of Henderson's dealings with Gostelowe is unknown. The only surviving documentation is a bill from Gostelow to Henderson for one quart of linseed oil, November 3, 1778 (Henderson-Wertmuller Papers, D-17, Historical Society of Pennsylvania).

[4] Charles Swift ordered a coffin for his wife, Mary, February 8, 1790 (Gratz Collection, Miscellanous Manuscripts, case 16, box 10, "Bills and Receipts, 1790–99," Historical Society of Pennsylvania). The bill is illustrated in Raymond B. Clark, "Jonathan Gostelowe (1744–1795), Philadelphia Cabinetmaker" (Master's thesis, University of Delaware, 1956), pl. 6.

been ordained deacon in the Royal Chapel, London, in 1770, and remained there as a divinity scholar until his ordination as priest in June 1772. He served as assistant minister of Christ Church from 1772 until 1779, when he was appointed rector of Christ Church and St. Peter's, positions he held until his death in 1836. Although he was selected as chaplain of the Continental Congress, and later of the Congress of the United States, White returned to London in 1787 to be consecrated Bishop of Pennsylvania in the Church of England. Biographers have noted that White "appeared to take little interest in politics and was loth to enter into public controversy." Elsewhere in this volume, Dee Andrews states that White was dedicated to preserving the established social, economic, and political order represented by the Church of England. Information on the remaining two documented Gostelowe patrons for whom furniture survives confirms that they did not sign the Nonimportation Agreement, serve in the military, or appear in the records for the oath of allegiance.[10]

Prown notes the correlation between decorative objects and political affiliations in his analysis of the patrons of John Singleton Copley: Of the 240 persons depicted in Copley's portraits, 55 percent were loyal to the Crown. Edgar deN. Mayhew and Minor Myers, Jr., cultural historians, explain: "Perhaps this is not surprising since many of those who followed the changing details of British decorative fashions might cling to the British model in their politics as well." Prown suggests that a stylistic analysis of decorative art objects as political indicators may offer a less biased historical interpretation than verbal accounts: "Although a society may prevaricate or intentionally distort in its utterances (journalism, propaganda, diplomatic communications, advertising) or in its pictorial statements (portraiture, mythology or religious art, socialist realism), a society does not bother to deceive itself or others in such mundane things as most buildings or the furniture or the pots that it makes for its own use." In their selection of furniture modeled after the most current London styles, Gostelowe's patrons affirmed their English affinities. Because the selection of furniture was not a conscious political statement, as Prown suggests, written corroboration of the association between political affiliation and furniture design during the American Revolution is predictably scant; however, Rebecca Shoemaker, wife of Loyalist Samuel Shoemaker, expressed the philosophy of many Loyalists and neutrals who patronized Gostelowe when she advised her daughter to avoid elaborate carved ornamentation on her furniture and to purchase furniture that was "all mahogany and the chairs plain, even if carved were the same price." The pattern of patronage and political affiliation suggested by the examination of Gostelowe's products and patrons is emphatically affirmed by analysis of the furniture and clientele of Gostelowe's contemporary, Thomas Affleck.[11]

Affleck produced two very different styles of furniture for two disparate groups of patrons—highly developed, ornately embellished rococo style furniture for the patrons who supported American independence from England and furniture in a planar style, with minimal carved decoration and marlboro legs for the clients who remained neutral or identified with the English cause. A birthright Quaker, Affleck was born in Aberdeen, Scotland. He received his training from Alex Rose of Ellen, Scotland, beginning in 1754. In 1760 he moved to London, possibly because of a familial tie with cabinetmaker James Affleck, who was working between 1744 and 1778 and an original subscriber to Chippendale's *Director*. Thomas Affleck was certainly familiar with Chippendale's designs and owned a copy of the 1762 edition of the *Director*. Arriving in Philadelphia in 1763, he opened a shop on Union Street. Five years later he moved to a more desirable location on Second Street in Society Hill. The provincial tax list for 1774 and the City of Philadelphia state tax of 1779 included Affleck in Dock Ward, along with many of the affluent merchants and professional men who became his patrons—John Cadwalader, John Dickinson, Miers Fisher, Thomas Fisher, Thomas Fitzsimons, Levi Hollingsworth, Joseph Pemberton, Thomas Shields, Charles Wharton, Thomas Wharton, and several members of the Morris and Mifflin families. Affleck, called a "joiner" by the assessor, was not charged a tax for 1774. In 1779 the "cabinetmaker" was taxed £2.5.0, only slightly less than the amount charged to lawyer Miers Fisher (1748–1819) and merchant Cadwalader Morris (1741–95), both relatively young men in the early stages of their careers. Affleck's occupation tax in 1783 was £250, two and a half times the amount levied on Gostelowe. The difference in their taxes may result from Gostelowe's closure of his shop for at least five years during the Revolution while Affleck remained open. Affleck was arrested in September 1777 when the military threat posed by the advance of General Howe on Philadelphia fostered official intolerance of Tories and pacifist Quakers in the city. Twenty-one Quakers and Tories who refused to take an oath of allegiance to the Commonwealth of Pennsylvania were imprisoned in the Mason's Lodge and subsequently exiled to Virginia for seven months. Patrons James Pemberton, Thomas Wharton, Thomas Fisher, and Miers Fisher shared this exile with Affleck. Affleck returned to Philadelphia and presumably worked until shortly before his death in March 1795.[12]

Affleck created furniture in an elaborate, curvilinear, heavily ornamented rococo style for eight patrons (Group A) during the 1760s, 1770s, and 1780s. One of the earliest groups of furniture was made for Thomas Mifflin circa 1768 and included a high chest and dressing table with intricately scalloped skirts and cabriole legs terminating in ball-and-claw feet (fig. 6). The edges of both cases feature inset quarter columns; the high chest has a swan's-neck pediment. Realistically carved foliage and shells ornament the knees, skirt, and center drawers in the base and pediment; rosettes, flame finials, and a central, lacy, openwork cartouche terminate the pediment. Between October 1770 and January 1771, Affleck produced a substantial amount of furniture for John Cadwalader's

Figure 6. High chest, attributed to Thomas Affleck, Philadelphia, ca. 1769. From William Macpherson Hornor, Jr., Blue Book, Philadelphia Furniture: William Penn to George Washington, with Special Reference to the Philadelphia-Chippendale School (1935; reprint, Washington, D.C.: Highland House, 1977), pl. 13". (Photo, Winterthur.)

Figure 7. Card table, attributed to Thomas Affleck, Philadelphia, 1770–71. Mahogany, white pine, tulip poplar; H. 28″, W. 39½″, D. 19¾″. (Philadelphia Museum of Art.)

Second Street house, newly purchased in 1769. A bill for part of this order lists beds, desks, commode sofas, an easy chair, a tea table, a breakfast table, a night stand, fire screens, a harpsichord frame, and a commode card table (fig. 7). Another card table and two sets of chairs were also produced by Affleck for this house, and portraits of the John Cadwalader family and of Lambert Cadwalader painted by Charles Willson Peale in 1771 include a card table and one chair (fig. 8). The Cadwalader furniture is a highly accomplished tour de force of the rococo style, a skillful juxtaposition of sinuous curves with a profusion of lush naturalistic carving, including the exotic addition of hairy-paw feet. Affleck's treatment of the commode card table contrasts dramatically with Gostelowe's handling of the serpentine form. Affleck employed trained carvers to render the rich ornamental schemes that are an essential part of his furniture designs. The Cadwalader bill of 1770–71

Figure 8. Charles Willson Peale, detail of Lambert Cadwalader, Philadelphia, 1771. Oil on canvas; H. 51″, W. 41″. (Private collection: Photo, Winterthur.)

charges the patron for the services of carvers James Reynolds and the firm of Barnard and Jugiez (fig. 9). The carved decoration is not, therefore, a manifestation of the cabinetmaker's skill as a sculptor but rather the result of a conscious design decision by a patron willing to pay for a desired effect.[13]

Michael Gratz purchased from Affleck an upholstered easy chair with elaborately carved cabriole legs with ball-and-claw feet. Three

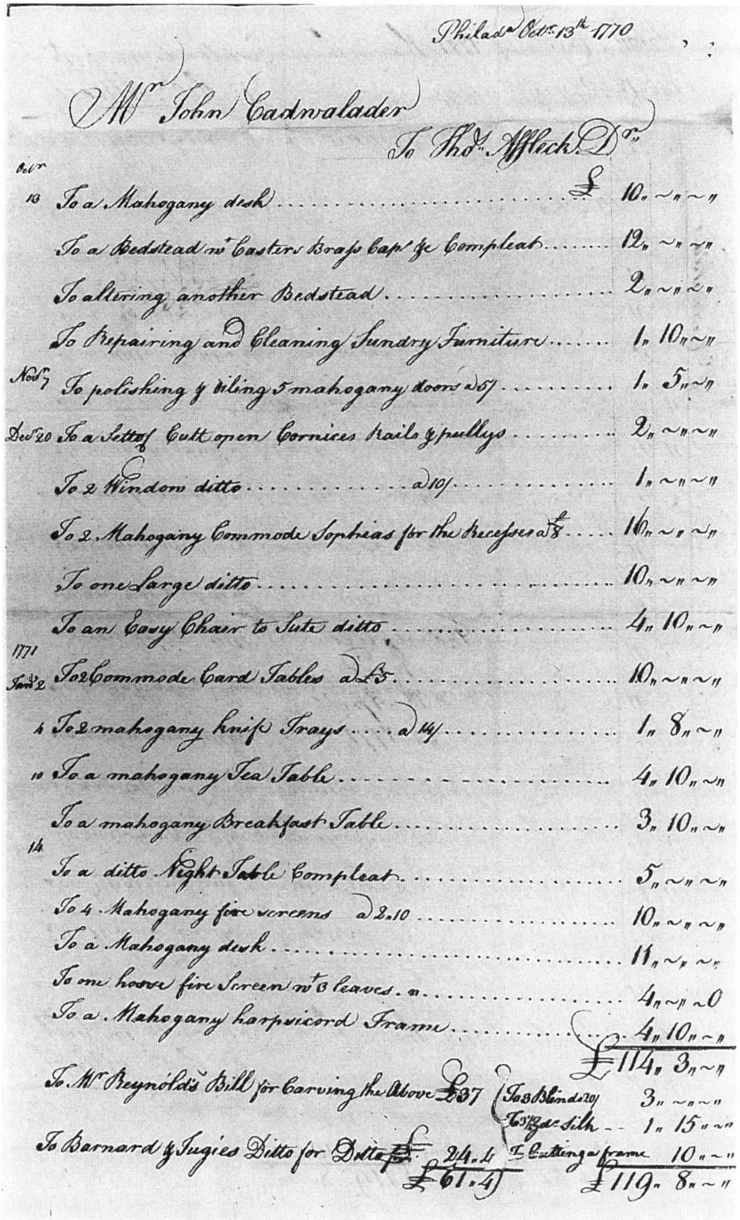

Philad^a Octr 13th 1770

Mr John Cadwalader

To Thos. Affleck Dr.

Octr 13	To a Mahogany desk	£ 10 ~ ~
	To a Bedstead w^t Casters Brass Cap^s & Compleat	12 ~ ~
	To altering another Bedstead	2 ~ ~
	To Repairing and Cleaning Sundry Furniture	1 10 ~
Novr 7	To polishing & oiling 5 mahogany doors a 5/	1 5 ~
Decr 20	To a Sett of Cutt open Cornices Rails & pulleys	2 ~ ~
	To 2 Window ditto a 10/	1 ~ ~
	To 2 Mahogany Commode Sophias for the Recesses a £8	16 ~ ~
	To one Large ditto	10 ~ ~
	To an Easy Chair to Sute ditto	4 10 ~
1771 Jany 2	To 2 Commode Card Tables a £5	10 ~ ~
4	To 2 mahogany knife Trays a 14/	1 8 ~
10	To a mahogany Tea Table	4 10 ~
	To a mahogany Breakfast Table	3 10 ~
14	To a ditto Night Table Compleat	5 ~ ~
	To 4 Mahogany fire screens a 2.10	10 ~ ~
	To a Mahogany desk	11 ~ ~
	To one horse fire Screen w^t 3 leaves	4 ~ 0
	To a Mahogany harpsicord Frame	4 10 ~
		£114 3 ~

To Mr Reynolds Bill for Carving the Above £37 — To 3 Blinds 20/ 3 ~ ~

To 3 yds silk 1 15 ~

To Barnard & Jugies Ditto for Ditto £24.4 — To Cutting a frame 10 ~

£61.4 — £119 8 ~

Figure 9. Bill, Thomas Affleck to John Cadwalader, October 13, 1770. (Historical Society of Pennsylvania, Cadwalader Collection.)

similar chest-on-chests were bought by Thomas Shields, Thomas Fitzsimons, and David Deshler. While employing the more modern chest-on-chest form, these chests display intricate openwork swan's-neck pediments with applied asymmetrical foliate terminals and a variety of prominently displayed central sculptural cartouches (fig. 10). In 1779 Levi and Hannah (Paschall) Hollingsworth commissioned Affleck for a double pair of high chests and dressing tables en suite with a set of eight mahogany chairs (fig. 11). Affleck also provided them with a tripod, tilt-top tea table with a pie-crust edge, foliate cabriole legs, and carved ball-and-claw feet, probably in 1783. The Hollingsworth furniture is a full-blown expression of the rococo style on a uniquely American form, crafted almost twenty years after the fashion for this style had begun to wane in London.[14]

A second group of patrons (Group B) commissioned Affleck to make furniture with more restrained carved decoration, planar surfaces, self-contained architectonic forms, and marlboro rather than cabriole legs. Furniture historian William Macpherson Hornor described the marlboro style as "a studied refinement of the earlier Chippendale [rococo] forms" inspired by an increasing familiarity among English designers with the "classic simplicity" of ancient architecture. When speaking of the marlboro furniture produced in Philadelphia, Hornor observed that "nearly all the productions bear close analogy to London originals." It is, therefore, not surprising that Gov. John Penn ordered several groups of furniture between 1763 and 1793 in this fashionable English style. Penn's marlboro furniture included side chairs, upholstered arm chairs, upholstered back stools, sofas, card tables, and marble-top serving tables, forms intended for parlors or other reception rooms where they served as a compelling manifestation of the governor's link with London (figs. 12, 13). The naturalistic carving that dominated the design of the Cadwalader and Hollingsworth furniture was reduced to a single flattened acanthus leaf along the arms of some of the armchairs. The rectilinear components of these objects were enhanced with architectural elements—geometric fretwork, fluting, and beading, the same decorative elements used by Gostelowe. Only the pierced brackets and gadrooned bands break the geometric purity of the forms.[15]

Affleck made similar furniture for other patrons who were opposed to the war. Thomas Wharton owned an upholstered armchair in the marlboro style that has descended in the Wharton family. Card tables

Figure 10. Thomas Affleck, chest-on-chest, Philadelphia, 1775. Mahogany, tulip poplar, white cedar; H. 97 1/2", W. 47 1/2". (Colonial Williamsburg Foundation.)

Figure 11. Thomas Affleck, high chest, Philadelphia, 1779. Walnut, poplar, pine, cedar; H. 94″, W. 42″, D. 20 3/4″. (Philadelphia Museum of Art, gift of Mrs. W. Logan MacCoy.)

made by Affleck for Sarah Redwood Fisher and James Pemberton are nearly identical. A table was one of forty objects commissioned by Pemberton from Affleck between February and June 1775 for the April 1775

Figure 12. Arm chair, attributed to Thomas Affleck, 1765–75. Mahogany, white oak; H. 40 5/8″, W. 28 1/8″, D. 28 5/8″. (Diplomatic Reception Rooms, Department of State.)

marriage of his daughter, Rachel. The turret-corner, serpentine form is similar to the canted-corner chests of drawers produced by Gostelowe, particularly a chest of drawers (Rockwood Museum, Wilmington, Delaware) with serpentine sides and a serpentine front. The card tables are ornamented only with a gadrooned band and fluted straight legs, relying on the graceful interplay of surfaces and reflections for visual impact. Another card table of similar form, with fluted marlboro legs and pierced brackets, is documented to Thomas Hockley. Affleck also made a sideboard table and side chair in this linear style for Pemberton.[16]

As with Gostelowe's patrons, the Philadelphians who patronized Affleck are characterized by diverse personal, professional, and religious backgrounds (tables 3, 4). However, they form two distinct groups with respect to their political ideology. Most of the men who purchased exuberant rococo furniture were actively dedicated to achieving American

Figure 13. Card table, attributed to Thomas Affleck, 1765–85. Mahogany, oak, tulip poplar; H. 28″, W. 35½″, D. 17¼″ (closed). (Bayou Bend Collection, Museum of Fine Arts, Houston, gift of Miss Ima Hogg.)

independence from England. John Cadwalader rose to the rank of brigadier general in the Pennsylvania militia; his brother Lambert was colonel of a New Jersey regiment; Thomas Fitzsimons raised and commanded a company of Philadelphia militia; Levi Hollingsworth was a member of the original troop of Philadelphia city cavalry; and Thomas Mifflin served as major of a volunteer company under General Cadwalader (aide-de-camp to General Washington), quartermaster general, and attained the rank of major general. Although Michael Gratz did not have a military career, he and his brother Barnard were staunch patriots who ran supplies through the British blockade. Several of these patrons held important political offices under the new state and national governments. John Cadwalader and Fitzsimons served on the Philadelphia Committee of Safety; Lambert Cadwalader, Fitzsimons, and Mifflin were elected to the Continental Congress and the United States Con-

Table 3. Thomas Affleck Patrons: Biographical Data

Patron	Occupation	Birthplace	Place of Education
Group A			
John Cadwalader (1742-86)	merchant	Philadelphia	Philadelphia
Lambert Cadwalader (1743-1823)	merchant	Trenton, N.J.	Philadelphia
David Deshler (1773-92)	merchant	Philadelphia	Unknown
Thomas Fitzsimmons (1741-1811)	merchant, statesman	Ireland	Ireland
Michael Gratz (1740-1811)	banker, merchant	Upper Silesia	London
Levi Hollingsworth (1739-1824)	merchant, ship owner	Elkton, Md.	Unknown
Thomas Mifflin (1744-1800)	merchant, statesman	Philadelphia	Philadelphia
Thomas Shields (1741-1819)	silversmith	Unknown	Unknown
Group B			
Sarah Redwood Fisher		Newport, R.I.	Unknown
(Miers Fisher)	(lawyer)	(Philadelphia)	(Philadelphia)
Thomas Hockley	merchant	Unknown	London
James Pemberton (1723-1809)	merchant	Philadelphia	Philadelphia
John Penn (1729-95)	proprietary governor	London	London, Geneva
Thomas Wharton (1730/1-82)	merchant	Philadelphia	Philadelphia

Note: Many patrons can be documented for Affleck due to the survival of an account book (cited in William Macpherson Hornor, Jr., *Blue Book, Philadelphia Furniture: William Penn to George Washington* [1935; reprint, Washington, D.C.: Highland House, 1977]) as well as receipts, bills, and other manuscripts. This table contains only those patrons who can be associated with surviving furniture.

gress. In addition, Fitzsimons was a signer of the Constitution, and Mifflin served nine years as governor of Pennsylvania. Although no military record has surfaced for David Deshler, a Germantown merchant, inscriptions on the chest-on-chest purchased by Deschler document its de-

Table 4. Thomas Affleck Patrons: Political and Religious Data

	Political Office/Revol. Gvt.	Military Service	Supported Nonimp. Agr.	Religious Affiliation Quaker	Anglican	Other
Group A						
John Cadwalader	X	X	X	X	X[1]	—
Lambert Cadwalader	X	X	X	X	X	—
David Deshler	—	—	X	X	—	—
Thomas Fitzsimmons	X	X	—	—	—	Catholic
Michael Gratz[2]	—	—	—	—	—	Jewish
Levi Hollingsworth	—	X	—	—	X	—
Thomas Mifflin	X	X	—	—	X	—
Group B						
Sarah Redwood Fisher (Miers Fisher)	—	—	—	X	—	—
Thomas Hockley	—	—	—	—	X	—
James Pemberton	—	—	X	X	X	—
John Penn	—	—	—	—	X[1]	—
Thomas Wharton	—	—	X	X	X	—

Note: Many patrons can be documented for Affleck due to the survival of an account book (cited in William Macpherson Hornor, Jr., *Blue Book, Philadelphia Furniture: William Penn to George Washington, with Special Reference to the Philadelphia-Chippendale School* [1935; reprint, Washington, D.C.: Highland House, 1977]) as well as receipts, bills, and other manuscript documentation. This table contains only those patrons who can be associated with surviving furniture.

[1] Also a member of St. Peter's Church.

[2] Gratz ran supplies for the troops through the British blockade. He also signed the oath of allegiance to the Commonwealth of Pennsylvania.

scent from Deshler's daughter, Catherine Deshler Roberts, whose husband Robert Roberts was active in First City Troop. The chest-on-chest was probably ordered specifically for Catherine Roberts by her father for her marriage in 1775. The fact that 75 percent of this group participated actively in the war, including members of the Anglican, Quaker, Jewish, and Catholic faiths, becomes an even more compelling and significant argument for the interrelationship of political affiliation and furniture style in Philadelphia during the revolutionary period. The complete lack of active participation demonstrated by the second group of patrons further substantiates this theory. None of these patrons were active in the military, and only one held a political office under the new government; Miers Fisher was a member of the Pennsylvania assembly in 1791 and 1792. Fisher, Pemberton, and Wharton were part of the group of Quakers and Tories exiled to Virginia for refusing to compromise their neutral pacifist stance. Thomas Hockley's position as the agent for Governor Penn, and the long history of association between the Hockley and Penn families allied him on the English side of the controversy.[17]

The nonimportation agreements of 1765 and 1769 placed a political significance on the ownership of certain types of goods by consumers in Philadelphia, a relationship that was still perceived into the 1770s. Capt. Samuel Morris wrote to his nephew Samuel Powell in London on May 18, 1765, "Household goods may be had here as cheap and as well made from English patterns. In the humour people are in here, a man is in danger of becoming Invidiously distinguished, who buys anything in England which our Tradesmen can furnish. I have heard the joiners here object this against Dr. Morgan & others who brought their furnishings with them." John Ewing, provost of the University of Pennsylvania, wrote from London on July 9, 1775, "I am getting a few things for you an ye children to bring over with me. They must not be talked of an account of ye new Importation Agreement, lest I should find difficulty in bringing them ashore." The lengthy ban on the ownership of English goods undoubtedly contributed to the stylistic preference of patriotic patrons for the familiar rococo style, which had developed a uniquely American vocabulary of forms and ornament by the 1760s.[18]

Prown concludes that "for the Post-Revolutionary mind, earlier rococo objects, with their exuberance and sensual appeal, represented indulgence in feelings and emotions; they aroused irrational responses; they embodied aspects of human nature that could imply social and political instability." The political passions of Mifflin, Hollingsworth, Gratz, Fitzsimons, and the Cadwaladers fostered social and political instability as a means of achieving greater personal freedom, are vividly and emphatically expressed in the unrestrained design of their furniture. In contrast, the desire for a peaceful, orderly perpetuation of English political and social systems shared by Chew, Hockley, Pemberton, Penn, Wharton, and White is manifested in their preference for furniture designed in the restrained, ordered, self-contained, architectonic style prevalent in England. For revolutionary Philadelphia, therefore, furniture style is a compelling statement of political affiliation.[19]

---

[1] Jules David Prown, "Style as Evidence," *Winterthur Portfolio* 15, no. 3 (Autumn 1980): 197.

[2] Clarence W. Brazer, "Jonathan Gostelowe, Philadelphia Cabinetmaker and Chair Maker," pts. 1, 2, *Antiques* 9, 10, nos. 6, 2 (June, August 1926): 386–93, 125–32; Raymond B. Clark, "Jonathan Gostelowe (1744–1795), Philadelphia Cabinetmaker" (Master's thesis, University of Delaware, 1956); Carl Bridenbaugh and Jessica Bridenbaugh, *Rebels and Gentlemen: Philadelphia in the Age of Franklin* (New York: Reynal and Hitchcock, 1942), p. 17; E. Digby Baltzell, *Philadelphia Gentlemen: The Making of a National Upper Class* (Glencoe, Ill.: Free Press, 1958), pp. 240, 244; "Christ Church, Philadelphia: Marriages, 1709–1800," "Christ Church, Philadelphia: Baptisms, 1769–1794," and "Christ Church, Philadelphia: Baptisms, 1769–1794," vols. 179, 167, Genealogical Society of Pennsylvania, Philadelphia. A second Anglican church, St. Peter's, was established in 1761 to relieve the overcrowded conditions at Christ Church.

[3] John William Wallace, *An Old Philadelphian: Colonel William Bradford, the Patriot Printer of* 1776 (Philadelphia: Sherman, 1884), pp. 54, 55. There were many variations possible in a contract of apprenticeship; however, when no specific information is known for a particular craftsman, the author assumes a traditional seven-year apprenticeship, allowing for an approximation of Gostelowe's initial working date as ca. 1765; see Ian M. G. Quimby, *Apprenticeship in Colonial Philadelphia* (New York: Garland Publishing, 1985), pp. 37–44. George Haughton, upholsterer, advertised that he had moved into the "house lately occupied by Jonathan Gostelowe, and next the London Coffee-house, in Front Street" (*Pennsylvania Evening Post*, May 18, 1776, as cited in Alfred Coxe Prime, comp., *The Arts and Crafts in Philadelphia, Maryland, and South Carolina, 1721–1785: Gleanings from Newspapers* [1929; reprint, New York: Da Capo Press, 1969], p. 204).

[4] Clark, "Jonathan Gostelowe," p. 3; Deed Book H, p. 583, Philadelphia County Recorder of Deeds; Baltzell, *Philadelphia Gentlemen*, pp. 241, 412; William Macpherson Hornor, Jr., *Blue Book, Philadelphia Furniture: William Penn to George Washington, with Special Reference to the Philadelphia-Chippendale School* (1935; reprint, Washington, D.C.: Highland House, 1977), p. 73; J. Thomas Scharf and Thompson Westcott, *History of Philadelphia, 1609–1884*, 3 vols. (Philadelphia: L. H. Everts, 1884), 1:449; *Pennsylvania Packet*, January 16, 1793, and the *Independent Gazetteer*, May 11, 1793, and May 18, 1793, cited in Prime, *Arts and Crafts*, pp. 179–80. Examples of his label survive on chests of drawers in Cliveden and Philadelphia Museum of Art; chairs in Yale University Art Gallery and Diplomatic Reception Rooms, Department of State; and a table in Bishop White House, Independence National Historic Park.

[5] Clark, "Jonathan Gostelowe," pp. 51–52; Richard Wistar Davids, *The Wistar Family: A Genealogy of the Descendants of Caspar Wistar* (Philadelphia: Privately printed, 1896), pp. 7–8; John W. Jordan, ed., *Colonial Families of Philadelphia*, 2 vols.

(New York: Lewis Publishing Co., 1911), 1:259. For the chest-on-chest probably made for Mary Gostelowe, see Brazer, "Gostelowe," pt. 2, pp. 125–27; Wallace Nutting, *Furniture Treasury* . . . , 3 vols. (Framingham, Mass.: Old America Co., 1928–33), 1: pl. 322; and "Jonathan Gostelowe," pp. 34–39. For the Wistar chest-on-chest, see Florence C. Maxwell, "Wistarberg, Yesterday and Today," *Antiques* 60, no. 3 (September 1951): 191. Gostelowe probably was introduced to the canted-corner form by his English journeyman, Thomas Jones, who joined his shop in October 1773. The style of brasses suggests that the chests were constructed before October 1776, when Gostelowe turned his attention to his military duties, rather than after 1781 when he resumed his cabinetmaking activities.

[6] Raymond V. Shepherd, Jr., "Cliveden and Its Philadelphia-Chippendale Furniture: A Documented History," *American Art Journal* 8, no. 2 (November 1976): 9. For the unlabeled Chew chest of drawers, see advertisement for David Stockwell, *Antiques* 60, no. 3 (September 1951): 177. For the Sartain painting, see Charles Dorman, "A Room with a View . . . the Bishop White Study," *The University Hospital Antiques Show* (Philadelphia: University of Pennsylvania Hospital, 1970), p. 97. Bishop's chest of drawers is still owned by a lineal descendant. The original ownership of this object also is documented by White's will, 1836-143, Philadelphia County Probate Records, Philadelphia. Gostelowe also made furniture for Philadelphia's Anglican churches between 1785 and 1793, communion tables and credence tables for Christ Church, St. Peter's, and St. Paul's.

[7] American Philosophical Society, "Record of Individuals Bound Out as Apprentices, Servants, Etc. and of German and Other Redemptioners in the Office of the Mayor of the City of Philadelphia, October 3, 1771, to October 5, 1773," (Philadelphia, microfilm, p. 823). William Henry Egle, ed., "Proprietary, Supply, and State Tax Lists of the City and County of Philadelphia for the Years 1769, 1774, and 1779," *Pennsylvania Archives*, 3d ser., 30 vols., 14 (1894–99): 14:64, 805. In 1797 Jones was listed on S. 5th St. between Market and Chestnut; in 1801 at 47 Arch St.; and in 1802 at 47 Mulberry St., *The Philadelphia Directory . . . 1797* (Philadelphia: W. W. Woodward, 1797); *The Philadelphia Directory . . . 1801* (Philadelphia: W. W. Woodward, 1801); *The Philadelphia Directory . . . 1802* (Philadelphia: W. W. Woodward, 1802). Thomas Affleck owned a copy of the *Director*, and there was a copy of the 1762 edition in the Library Company of Philadelphia by 1769. As a journeyman, Jones would have been a trained craftsman. For a discussion of the relationship of Gostelowe and Jones, see Deborah Anne Federhen, "The Serpentine-Front Chests of Drawers of Jonathan Gostelowe and Thomas Jones," *Antiques* 133, no. 5 (May 1988): 1174–84.

[8] Prown, "Style as Evidence," p. 208. There are scattered examples of the canted-corner cases by other makers: For William King (1754–1819) of Salem, Massachusetts, who produced a canted-corner chest of drawers ca. 1785, see "The Editor's Attic: Finding Feet for Serpentines," *Antiques* 12, no. 3 (September 1927): 201–3; for Joseph Armitt (d. 1747) of Philadelphia, who made a canted-corner chest-on-chest, see Hornor, *Blue Book*, pl. 37. Neither is likely to have influenced Gostelowe.

[9] Gregory Palmer, *Biographical Sketches of Loyalists of the American Revolution* (Westport, Conn.: Meckler Publishing, 1984), p. 377; Jordan, *Colonial Families*, 1:511; "Life of Benjamin Chew, Esq.," *Port Folio*, 3d ser., 5, no. 2 (February 1811): 97. Because no Gostelowe account book survives, the number of documentable patrons is small. While evidence of the composition of his clientele is not conclusive, analysis of the patrons of his contemporary, Thomas Affleck, strengthens the author's theory.

[10] Jordan, *Colonial Families*, 2:931–32, 1746; Edwin B. Bronner, "The Disgrace of John Kinsey, Quaker Politician, 1739–1750," *Pennsylvania Magazine of History and Biography* 75, no. 4 (October 1951): 414. Some biographers of White have cited the elimination from Anglican services at Christ Church and St. Peter's of prayers for the king after the signing of the Declaration of Independence as evidence for assigning White a patriotic position; however, White was only the assistant minister. The decision to eliminate the prayers was made by Jacob Duche, rector of Christ Church and St. Peter's. Duche, who had served as the official chaplain to the first and second Continental Congresses, chose the Tory position in October 1776, resigned his positions, and returned to England when the British occupation ended; see Baltzell, *Philadelphia Gentlemen*, p. 243; *Dictionary of American Biography . . .* , 11 vols. (New York: Charles Scribner's Sons, 1930), 4:122; Dee E. Andrews, "Religion and Social Change in Late Eighteenth-Century Philadelphia: The Rise of the Methodists," elsewhere in this volume.

[11] Edgar deN. Mayhew and Minor Myers, Jr., *A Documentary History of American Interiors from the Colonial Era to 1915* (New York: Charles Scribner's Sons, 1980), p. 54; Jules David Prown, *John Singleton Copley in America, Volume 1, 1738–1774* (Cambridge: Harvard University Press, 1966), pp. 125–26; Prown, "Style as Evidence," pp. 199–200; Shoemaker as quoted in David Lawrence Barquist, "The Meaning of Taste for Wealthy Philadelphians, 1750–1800" (Master's thesis, University of Delaware, 1981), p. 31.

[12] Hornor, *Blue Book*, p. 73 (Hornor owned many of the manuscript documents that are cited; these documents are still in a private collection and are unavailable for study); Morrison H. Heckscher, "Philadelphia Furniture, 1760–90: Native-Born and London-Trained Craftsmen," in *The American Craftsman and the European Tradition, 1620–1820*, ed. Francis J. Puig and Michael Conforti (Minneapolis: Minneapolis Institute of Arts, 1989), p. 95; Geoffrey Beard and Christopher Gilbert, eds., *Dictionary of English Furniture Makers, 1660–1840* (London: Furniture History Society, 1986), p. 5; Affleck advertisement, *Pennsylvania Chronicle*, December 12, 1768, as cited in Prime, *Arts and Crafts*, p. 158; Egle, "Proprietary, Supply, and State Tax Lists," pp. 24, 26, 27, 31–34, 36, 39, 59–63. Wallace (*Colonel William Bradford*, pp. 55, 139–52, 392–405) presents an extensive discussion of the arrests, including the complete text of the orders and the numerous appeals by the exiles for their release. Morrison H. Heckscher, *American Furniture in the Metropolitan Museum of Art*, ed. Mary-Alice Rogers (New York: By the museum and Random House, 1985), p. 25; Alfred Coxe Prime, comp., *The Arts and Crafts in Philadelphia, Maryland, and South Carolina, 1786–1800: Series Two, Gleanings from Newspapers* (Topsfield, Mass.: Wayside Press, 1932), p. 164.

[13] For the dressing table and a chair made for Mifflin, see Hornor, *Blue Book*, pls. 132, 133, and *Philadelphia: Three Centuries of American Art* (Philadelphia: Philadelphia Museum of Art, 1976), no. 109. For the provenance of the second card table and chairs, see Philip D. Zimmerman, "A Methodological Study in the Identification of Some Important Philadelphia Chippendale Furniture," in *American Furniture and Its Makers: Winterthur Portfolio 13*, ed. Ian M. G. Quimby (Chicago: University of Chicago Press, 1979), pp. 193–208.

[14] For the Gratz chair, see John S. Walton advertisement, *Antiques* 101, no. 4 (April 1972): 568. One pair of the Hollingsworth set is in the Philadelphia Museum of Art; the other is owned by the Chipstone Foundation, Milwaukee, which also owns a chair. The tea table is illustrated in Hornor, *Blue Book*, pl. 216, and the caption dates

it 1779, but the bills that Hornor reproduces (p. 87) include an entry for a tea table on July 16, 1783.

[15] Hornor, *Blue Book*, pp. 173, 182, 176. Affleck's perception of the marlboro style as appropriate for official commissions continued through the 1790s when he made chairs in this style for Congress Hall, the State House, the Supreme Court, and Pennsylvania Hospital. Two of the chairs used in the courthouse are in the collection of Independence Historic National Park. The Henry Ford Museum, Dearborn, Michigan, owns a chair that was made for the State House; all are illustrated in Hornor, *Blue Book*, pls. 263, 298, 299.

[16] Hornor, *Blue Book*, pls. 268, 266, 269, 255, 264, 265; Jordan, *Colonial Families*, 1:291; Affleck to Pemberton, invoice, Pemberton Papers, vol. 27, p. 175, Historical Society of Pennsylvania; Federhen, "Serpentine-Front Chests," pl. 11.

[17] Information on the military and political careers of these men was found in James Grant Wilson and John Fiske, eds., *Appleton's Cyclopedia of American Biography* (New York: D. Appleton, 1888); William H. Egle, ed., *Pennsylvania in the War of the Revolution: Associated Battalions and Militia, 1775–1783*, 2 vols. (Harrisburg: E. K. Meyers, 1892); Henry Flanders, "Thomas Fitzsimmons," *Pennsylvania Magazine of History and Biography* 2, no. 3 (1878): 306–14; Francis B. Heitman, *Historical Register of Officers of the Continental Army during the War of the Revolution, April 1775 to December 1783* (1914; reprint, Baltimore: Genealogical Publishing Co., 1967); *Dictionary of American Biography*; John W. Raimo, *Biographical Dictionary of American Colonial and Revolutionary Governors, 1607–1789* (Westport, Conn.: Meckler Books, 1980); and *Who Was Who during the American Revolution* (Indianapolis: Bobbs-Merrill Co., 1976). Thomas Shields has eluded documentation of any sort; his inclusion in this group of patrons is based on his marriage to Lydia Shields, a relative of active patriot Robert Morris.

[18] Morris to Powell, May 18, 1765, and Ewing to his wife, July 9, 1775, as quoted in Hornor, *Blue Book*, pp. 81, 82.

[19] Prown, "Style as Evidence," p. 208.

"The Honours of a Court" or "the Severity of Virtue"

Household Furnishings and Cultural Aspirations in Philadelphia

David L. Barquist

Studies of American decorative arts of the second half of the eighteenth century traditionally have interpreted the change from the rococo to the neoclassical styles—which coincided with the revolutionary war—as expressions of different pre- and postrevolutionary ideologies. Specifically, the rococo has been described as a style of worldly luxury based on foreign, aristocratic models (hence the name *Chippendale*), whereas neoclassicism has been viewed as a more intellectual style perfectly suited to a new nation seeking to model itself on Greek democracies and Roman republics (hence the name *federal*). That aristocratic patronage gave rise to neoclassicism in Europe just as it had to the rococo is glossed over by this explanation. More significantly, the explanation does not take into account the positive and negative rhetoric that accompanied the introduction of neoclassicism in late eighteenth-century America, none of which justified the style using the ideology employed by twentieth-century scholars.[1]

For their help in the preparation of this paper, the author thanks Carmen Bambach Cappel, William N. Hosley, Jr., Joshua W. Lane, Christine Meadows, Nancy E. Richards, Marion F. Sandquist, Kenneth C. Turino, Charles L. Venable, and Deborah D. Waters.

The household furnishings owned by Philadelphia's economic elite provide an important case study for a reexamination of this stylistic change. These furnishings were considered the finest in America and frequently discussed in contemporary letters, diaries, and even newspapers and magazines. Writers rarely referred to the rococo or neoclassical styles but focused instead on the furnishings' expense, national origin, and degrees of ornamentation. They drew distinctions between those owners whose cultural aspirations required an aesthetic of cosmopolitan display and those whose cultural aspirations rejected it. These distinctions existed before either the introduction of neoclassicism or the hostility with Great Britain and continued to exist well afterward.[2]

Beginning in the 1760s, some wealthy Philadelphians wanted their household furnishings to be visible signs of cosmopolitan sophistication that resulted from wealth and a familiarity with the standards that governed such productions in Europe. These cosmopolites believed that the prosperity of several generations of settlement had at last produced an era of refinement. Typical of this mind-set is the appeal for investors made by the Bonnin and Morris porcelain factory in 1771: "It will be recorded, to the Honour of *Pennsylvania*, that an infant Colony, scarcely risen One Hundred Years from the rude Vestiges of Nature, has produced Men who shine in the learned and polite Arts amongst the first Characters of the present Age." Cosmopolitan aspirations also had been shaped by theories of taste, theories that assumed considerable importance in England during the second half of the century. Many wealthy Philadelphians traveled extensively in Europe and while there moved in the intellectual and aristocratic circles where such topics were debated. Samuel Powel and John Morgan, for example, made a seven-year grand tour of Europe, during which they met Voltaire and traveled for a time in the suite of the duke of York.[3]

The Philadelphia cosmopolites viewed themselves as very different from most of their countrymen, and their shared preferences for household furnishings became an important means of maintaining this exclusivity. On a 1780 visit to the city house of former mayor Powel, the Marquis de Chastellux made note of its "handsome" furnishings "in the English manner" and the "fine prints and some very good copies of the best Italian paintings," a consequence of Powel's visits to "Rome and Naples, where he acquired a taste for the fine arts." The emphasis on the pleasure the marquis took in seeing Powel's painting collection

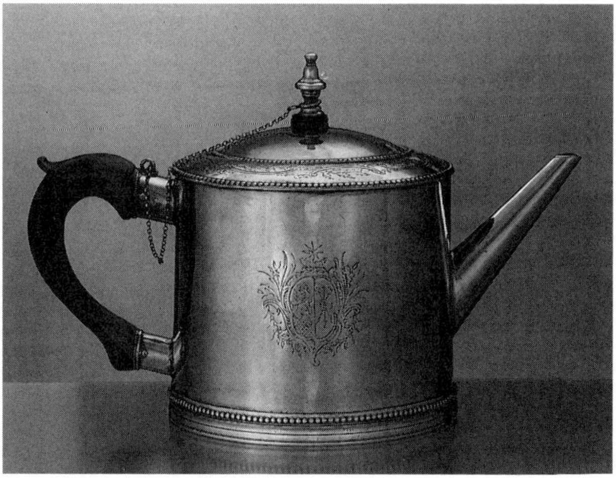

Figure 1. Joseph and Nathaniel Richardson, teapot, Philadelphia, 1775–85. Silver; H. 6 3/4″, W. 10 3/4″, Diam. 5 5/8″. (Yale University Art Gallery, Mabel Brady Garvan Collection.)

is significant, for it reveals how these particular men of taste viewed themselves as part of an intimate, cultivated circle in which sympathetic cultivation permitted enjoyable interaction. Art historian E. H. Gombrich has traced the origin of this concept to the medieval Courts of Love, in which an individual's *courtoisie* was his primary qualification. In eighteenth-century England, men of taste had adopted the name *dilettanti* to convey the delight they drew from their discussions of artistic matters. Thus household furnishings provided a normative system whereby those who shared taste could recognize their peers by their possessions. In this context, mimicry was not merely a convenient way of absorbing new fashions but also a requirement for inclusion in the group. According to historians, Powel gave his wife a silver teapot and commissioned a smaller but otherwise identical teapot for her niece, Ann Willing Morris (figs. 1, 2). If family tradition is correct, the similarity between the two teapots may have been intended to reinforce the young woman's connection to the exalted, intimate circle in which her aunt used and displayed her teapot. Ann's teapot, like her aunt's, was engraved with the Powel-Willing coat of arms.[4]

Figure 2. Joseph and Nathaniel Richardson, teapot, Philadelphia, 1775–85. Silver; H. 5 1/8″, W. 8 3/4″, Diam. 4 3/8″. (Yale University Art Gallery, gift of Margaret Littell: Photo, Joseph Szaszfai.)

Implicit in the assiduous cultivation of aristocratic European fashions was a strong element of noblesse oblige. Those who owned and appreciated current European furnishings considered themselves exemplars to individuals who were unable to travel to study the fashions firsthand. William Hamilton, a man whose inherited wealth enabled him to devote his attention to his estates and to art and science, returned from a two-year trip to England in 1786 and transformed his country estate, Woodlands, remodeling the house's interior and exterior in the Adam style and creating an emblematic garden on the pattern of Stowe and Stourhead. His goal was lofty: "I have the vanity to think I shall . . . introduce many conveniences & improvements that will be useful to my country as well as myself." Similarly, the collections of books, prints, and paintings that Morgan had acquired during his tour of Europe provided the introduction of European culture to other Americans, including Thomas Jefferson, who specifically sought out Morgan during a visit to Philadelphia in 1766. In 1788 George Washington asked Powel, who had a "taste for the fine arts," to select an armchair that could serve as a pattern for a set at Mount Vernon.[5]

An important interior created by a member of this cosmopolitan circle was the front parlor of John Cadwalader's house in the early 1770s. A master plan was devised for this room, perhaps by Cadwalader himself, and the furniture and paintings, although made by several Philadelphia craftsmen, functioned as a cohesive entity. The forms and ornament of the furnishings were unusually elaborate for Philadelphia and were conceived to rival the most elaborate English rococo models. Cadwalader's intentions in commissioning this group of furnishings, however, extended beyond ostentation. Although he never traveled to Europe, Cadwalader wanted subtle references to cosmopolitan sophistication in his parlor. With a mantelpiece tablet carved with the Choice of Hercules, an illustration that had been emblematic of aesthetic debate in both classical and contemporary treatises, Cadwalader signaled his intent to use his parlor as an arena for people of taste.[6]

Cadwalader also intended his parlor to symbolize an era of fulfillment. Between 1770 and 1772 he commissioned Charles Willson Peale to do five portraits for the room. Companion portraits depicting Cadwalader's parents, Hannah and Thomas, show the elder Cadwaladers dressed in simple clothing and seated in somewhat unostentatious chairs (fig. 3). The portrait of John Cadwalader with his wife and daughter (fig. 4) and those of his brother Lambert and sister Martha presented the rising generation attired in elegant costly fabrics (John and Lambert are posed next to the new, richly carved parlor furniture).[7] The portraits and the new furniture graced the same room, making the point that this sophisticated interior belonged specifically to the younger generation of Philadelphians who had fulfilled the expectations of their forebears and stood at the apogee of colonial refinement.

Many Philadelphians, some of them wealthy, stood outside this cosmopolitan circle and viewed costly, heavily elaborated, fashion-conscious furnishings with disapproval. William Penn's "holy experiment" in Pennsylvania had long attracted individuals who sought to establish and maintain a society free of the corruption and the excesses of European monarchies. These individuals and their descendants inter-

Figure 3. Charles Willson Peale, *Hannah Lambert Cawalader*, Philadelphia, 1772. Oil on canvas; H. 51", W. 41". (Philadelphia Museum of Art, Cadwalader Collection, purchased with funds contributed by the Pew Memorial Trust and an anonymous donor.)

preted the striving after aristocratic European models as evidence of moral decline. In 1772 Quaker John Woolman observed:

Friends in early times refused on a religious principle to make or trade in superfluities, of which we have many large testimonies on record, but for want of faithfulness, some gave way, even some whose examples were of note in Society, and from thence others took more liberty. Members of our Society worked in superfluities and bought and sold them, and thus dimness of sight came over many. At length Friends got into the use of some superfluities in dress and in the fur-

Figure 4. Charles Willson Peale, *The John Cadwalader Family*, Philadelphia, 1772. Oil on canvas; H. $51^{1}/_{8}''$, W. $41^{1}/_{4}''$. (Philadelphia Museum of Art, Cadwalader Collection, purchased with funds contributed by the Pew Memorial Trust and an anonymous donor.)

niture of their houses, and this hath spread from less to more, till superfluity of some kinds is common amongst us.

In this declining state many look at the example one of another and too much neglect the pure feeling of Truth.

In his autobiography, non-Quaker Benjamin Franklin recalled:

We kept no idle Servants, our Table was plain and simple, our Furniture of the cheapest. For instance my Breakfast was a long time Bread and Milk (no Tea) and I ate it out of a twopenny earthen Porringer with a Pewter Spoon. But mark how Luxury will enter Families, and make a Progress, in Spite of Principle. Being call'd one Morning to Breakfast, I found it in a China Bowl with a Spoon of Silver. They had been bought for me without my Knowledge by my Wife, and had cost her the enormous Sum of three and twenty Shillings, for which she had no other Excuse or Apology to make, but that she thought *her* Husband deserv'd a Silver Spoon and China Bowl as well as any of his Neighbours.[8]

Like Woolman and Franklin, many well-to-do Philadelphians were convinced that only restrained furnishings allowed them to remain faithful to their beliefs and principles. They defined restraint as the virtuous avoidance of expense and superfluity. An absence of costly, ornamented furniture was a sign of moral purity. Ann Warder, English-born wife of a prominent Philadelphia Quaker merchant, was enthusiastic about a Moravian farmhouse, in which the master's room "reminded [her] of a Hermits cell & convinced [her] of his being a truly good Man or in this World of Splendour and Ellagence he could not find contentment with so little."[9]

The advocates of restraint preferred furnishings of high quality and fashionability that nevertheless were simple and lacking in unnecessary enrichment. In 1765 Deborah Franklin wrote to her husband, describing their new house: "[I]n the [dining] rom down stairs is the sid bord that you be spoke which is verey hansum and plain with two tabels maid to sute it and a Doz of Chairs allso. . . . [T]he potterns of the Chairs air a plain Horshair and look as well as a Paddozway everey bodey admiers them." When ordering urns for the roof of Cliveden in 1766, jurist Benjamin Chew cautioned his English agent that they should have "little or no carve work as most suitable to the plainness of [his] building." Rebecca Rawle Shoemaker, widow of Francis Rawle and second wife of merchant Samuel Shoemaker, advised her daughter Anna Rawle in 1783 to purchase furniture that was "all mahogany and the chairs plain, even if carved were the same price."[10] A drawing done in 1766 by Samuel Mickle, apprentice to cabinetmaker Jonathan Shoemaker (who probably was unrelated to Samuel Shoemaker), indicates that a rococo-style chair was considered "plain" when it lacked an openwork splat, carved feet, or shaped seat rails (fig. 5). The similarity in these last three examples is the individual's exercise of restraint, of deliberately choosing less than elaboration. The issue is not the acceptance or rejection of a specific style.

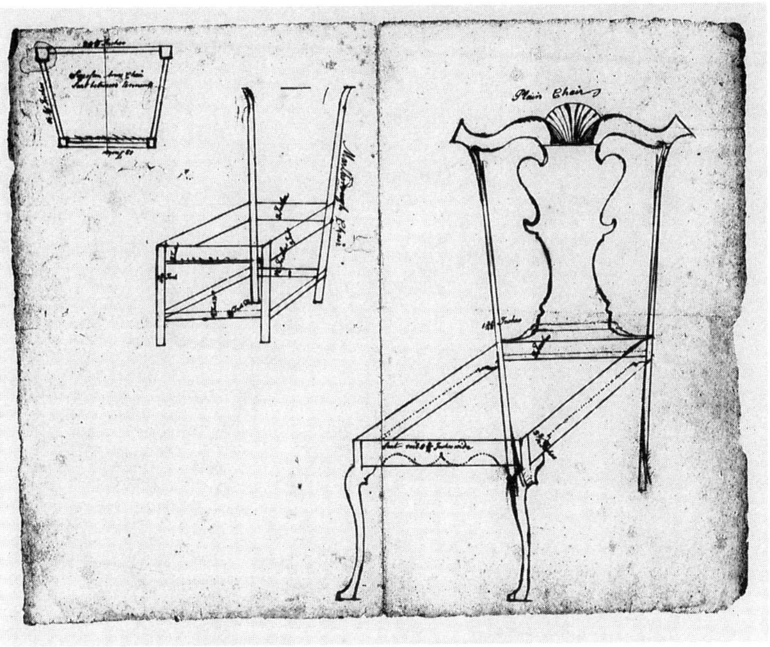

Figure 5. Samuel Mickle, marlboro and plain chairs, Philadelphia, 1765. Ink on paper; H. 13″, W. 16¾″. The dotted lines indicate possible shaping of seat rails. (Philadelphia Museum of Art, gift of Walter M. Jeffords.)

Thomas Mifflin belonged to the group that favored simplicity in choosing stylistic attributes. Although he lacked the extraordinary wealth of the Powels and the Cadwaladers, Mifflin's career as a representative to the Continental Congress, general in the Continental army, and later governor of Pennsylvania made him their social equal. Like both Powel and Cadwalader, he frequently entertained visiting dignitaries, including Washington and John Adams. As a Quaker, Mifflin belonged to a group that traditionally favored simplicity in dress and homes. A comparison of the Cadwaladers' portrait with one commissioned in the following year by the Mifflins from John Singleton Copley when Mifflin was twenty-nine years old, one year younger than Cadwalader was at the time his portrait was painted, provides insights into the group of wealthy Philadelphians who preferred a less ostentatious self-image (fig. 6).

Figure 6. John Singleton Copley, *Mr. and Mrs. Thomas Mifflin*, Boston, 1773. Oil on canvas; H. 61 1/2", W. 48". (Historical Society of Pennsylvania.)

Mifflin wore a drab-colored suit with fabric-covered buttons rather than a bright-colored suit and a vest adorned with gold buttons and gold trim; Sarah Mifflin covered her head and bosom with a linen cap and fichu instead of lace and jewels; and both Mifflins pursued worthwhile endeavors as they sat for their portrait. Their self-conscious restraint was also applied to their choice of household furnishings, as their high-post bed with carving only on the feet indicates.[11]

As noted above, art historians have interpreted the revolutionary war as the watershed between the taste of the colonial period and the

New Republic, inspiring Americans to reject the worldly charms of the rococo for the republican virtue of neoclassicism. Evidence in letters, diaries, and objects, however, suggests that the political separation of America from England and the rejection of both a monarchy and an aristocracy did not diminish the passion for extravagant, aristocratic furnishings among the cosmopolites. They continued to identify with the European upper class. They were convinced that the leaders of American society had to follow foreign models to demonstrate that the new nation rivaled older nations in sophistication. When criticized for having spent so much time in France, young Ann Willing Bingham, wife of financier William Bingham and another niece of Samuel and Elizabeth Powel's, retorted: "The agreeable resources of Paris must certainly please and instruct every Class of Characters. The Arts of Elegance are there considered essential, and are carried to a state of Perfection; the Mind is continually gratified with the admiration of Works of Taste."[12]

The only impact the Revolution seems to have had on the taste of cosmopolites was in heightening their interest in the fashions of France. France had been America's ally during the war, and although its monarchy was much more despotic than England's, several of America's political leaders became enthusiastic Francophiles. Robert Morris, financier of the Revolution and one of the wealthiest men in the country, almost exclusively patronized the large community of French émigré merchants and craftsmen in Philadelphia and imported many other furnishings from France. Jefferson returned to Philadelphia in 1790 with 86 crates of French furnishings, including 59 chairs and 145 rolls of wallpaper.[13]

Ann and William Bingham had spent several years traveling in Europe, and upon their return their European experiences gave them considerable influence over the other members of the cosmopolitan circle. The house they had built was based on architectural drawings by London architect John Plaw. It was among the few freestanding homes in the city and had carved reliefs on the facade and a formal garden complete with statuary. The furnishings, like the architecture, were self-consciously lavish and cosmopolitan. They were in the avant-garde of the neoclassical style, yet visitors emphasized their costliness and European origin. Rufus Griswold focused first on the "self-supporting broad stairway of fine white marble—the first of that description, probably, ever known in America—leading to the second story, which gave a truly Roman elegance to the passage. . . . Much of the furniture, including the carpets, which were remarkable for their elegant richness, had been made in France. The halls were hung with pictures, of which the greater number had been selected in Italy; and the library was well filled with the best authors of the day." Englishman Henry Wansey's description of the Bingham house might well be a bill of lading for a cosmopolite: "I found a magnificent house and gardens in the best English style, with elegant and even superb furniture: the chairs of the drawing room were from Seddons's in London, of the newest taste; the back in the form of a lyre, adorned with festoons of crimson and yellow silk, the curtains of the room a festoon of the same: the carpet one of Moore's most expensive patterns: the room was papered in the French taste, after the style of the Vatican at Rome."[14]

Postrevolutionary cosmopolites also maintained an aristocratic tone in their discussions of proper furnishings. Approval and mimicry were permissible only within their limited, exalted circle. After describing what table decorations he wished diplomat Gouverneur Morris to purchase in France, President Washington added a general directive: "If I am defective recur to what you have seen on Mr. Robert Morris's table for my ideas *generally*." It might be argued that Washington was selecting a convenient reference, but the tone in all the correspondence from this circle is one of exclusion. Commenting on the order for a plateau, Washington's secretary noted the rarity of this form in Philadelphia: "Mr. [Robert] Morris & Mr. Bingham have them, and the French & Spanish Ministers [both titled noblemen] . . . but I know of no one else who has." Bingham used a similar context and tone, requesting from Paris "24 small coffee cups, with a design similar to those used by the Queen & the Duke d'Angoulême."[15]

The quasi-aristocratic role of the cosmopolites took on a larger dimension with the transfer of the national capital to Philadelphia in 1790. Most cosmopolites were Federalists, members of the party in power during this decade, and this political hegemony supported their efforts to style themselves as arbiters of taste for the new nation. Morris explained to Washington that the table decorations he purchased in France cost more than the president had authorized him to pay and then added, "I think it of very great important to fix the taste of our country properly, and I think your example will go very far in that respect." The Louis XVI-style furniture that the president had purchased in 1790 from the Comte de Moustier, French minister to the United States, apparently inspired

Figure 7. Adam Hains, armchair, Philadelphia, 1793–97. Mahogany and ash; H. 33 3/4", W. 23 1/4", D. 19 1/4". (Society for the Preservation of New England Antiquities, gift of the children of Arthur and Susan Cabot Lyman: Photo, J. David Bohl.)

the American-made copies owned by status-conscious wealthy Federalist politicians. By 1794 Philadelphia cabinetmaker Adam Hains had made several nearly identical sets of ornate Louis XVI-style chairs. Orders were placed by treasury secretary Alexander Hamilton of New York and financier Andrew Craigie, governor Christopher Gore, and merchant Theodore Lyman of Massachusetts (fig. 7).[16]

The Bingham house and its furnishings had a significant impact on new mansions built elsewhere by ambitious Federalist merchants. John

Brown of Providence was greatly influenced by the reports sent back by his son James, who wrote: "I had not seen the Drawing Room since the Furniture was put up. It altogether is most superb, I can scarce form an idea of superior Taste, neatness, Propriety, & Splendor." The wallpaper in that drawing room—described by Wansey as like "the Vatican at Rome"—had Roman-style grotesques similar to the Loggia of Raphael at the Vatican. Brown subsequently decided to paper his drawing room with neoclassical grotesques. Boston's Harrison Gray Otis knew the Binghams and visited their home often. His architect, Charles Bulfinch, saw the Bingham residence in 1789, described it as "in a stile which would be esteemed splendid even in the most luxurious parts of Europe," and then copied several architectural features into his 1795–96 designs for Otis.[17]

Outsiders who imitated the cosmopolites of Philadelphia were sometimes not fully convinced of the appropriateness of these models. Oliver Ellsworth acquired fine fabrics and a porcelain tea set for his Connecticut home but also commented that his daughter Abigail was "dressed up like the rest of the Philadelphia ladies, almost too fine for Windsor." Bulfinch decided that the "Elegance of construction, white marble staircase, valuable paintings, the richest furniture and the utmost magnificence of decoration make [the Bingham house] a palace . . . far too rich for any man in this country." Even Otis, who visted with many cosmopolites, had reservations:

> Those who constitute the fashionable world [of Philadelphia] are at best a mere oligarchy, composed of a few natives and as many foreigners. Having none to rival or eclipse them; or contend with them for the right of entertaining strangers, they pursue their own course without interruption. . . . My experience is yet to inform me wherein consists the pleasure, elegance & taste of these Parties. . . . I fancy they are often very formal, unenlivened by general conversation and that the food for the mind contains as little nourishment as the cold tea which is applied to the dilution of the grosser part of the system.[18]

Philadelphians who advocated self-conscious restraint were even more concerned. The uncertainties that they saw in the new nation's political and economic future convinced many in this group that the highly visible cosmopolites posed a real moral and political threat to Philadelphia society in particular and American society in general. This view was reinforced by the strong anti-European sentiments that had emerged among the populace at large in the postwar period. *Columbian Magazine*, published in Philadelphia between 1786 and 1792, became a spokespiece for such ideas:

> The manners of an absolute government, and those of a republic, where the system of each is strictly preserved, are very opposite to each other. The honours of a court . . . [form] the manners of a kingdom; the severity of virtue, those of a republic. Luxury, therefore, may be permitted in an absolute monarchy, without injury, whilst the introduction of it into a commonwealth will terminate in its destruction. The effect which it produces in a free state is to alienate the people from the love of their country, directing their views solely to their own particular interests and pleasures.

These Philadelphians also viewed the obsession with European goods as harmful to the economic development of the nation. Jefferson "consider[ed] the extravagance which has seized them as a more baneful evil than toryism was during the war," especially since "the example is set by the best and most amiable characters among us."[19]

The avid importation and imitation of European goods and fashions also sent political signals: "Amongst the uppermost circles in Philadelphia, pride, haughtiness, and ostentation are conspicuous," wrote Englishman Isaac Weld. "It seems as if nothing could make them happier than that an order of nobility should be established, by which they might be exalted above their fellow citizens as much as they are in their own conceit." Most cosmopolites were also involved in Federalist intrigues that depended on a strong central government, and from this a few critics inferred a larger scheme was afoot: "They [the cosmopolites] are indebted to the French for many parts of their luxuries. Simplicity of manners in the American republics neither suited the disposition of that nation, nor afforded them the probability of preserving so powerful an influence over these new states. . . . By means of dress, equipage, and the pleasures of the table, temptations which are sure to captivate young men, [the French] endeavored to attach the rising generation to the interest of France. There was great policy in this conduct."[20]

The highly visible ostentation of the Binghams quickly made them a target in public and in private. Poet Peter Markoe accused Bingham of using cultivation to mask his corrupt political and financial dealings:

> What tho' the pomp of wealth, the pride of power
> Swell thy mean heart, and gild thy present hour;

Tho' *Luxury* attract the worldly wife,
Who, when they most caress thee most despise,
Tho' to thy mansion wits and fops repair,
To game, to feast, to saunter and to stare,
Thine eyes amid the crowd who fawn and bend,
View many a parasite, but not one friend.
Virtue and sense indignant stand aloof,
Whilst each knave's *friendship* is a keen reproof.

Abigail Adams described Ann Willing Bingham and her elder daughter, Ann Louisa, as "fine women and in the first Rank, [who] are leaders of the fashion," then added disapprovingly "they show more of the [bosom] than the decent Matron, or the modest woman." Ann Warder "walked to looked at Binghams new house which cause much talk here being quite upon a new plan—but very ungenteel I thinks much resembling some of our [English] heavy public Buildings—bow windows in back & the Front very paltry with figures in Stocoa." Samuel Breck opined that Binghams had consciously chosen exclusionary furnishings: "The forms at his house were not suited to our manners. . . . In this drawing-room the furniture was superb Gobelin, and the folding doors were covered with mirrors, which reflected the figures of the company, so as to deceive an untraveled countryman, who, having been paraded up the marble stairway amid the echoes of his name—ofttimes made very ridiculous by the queer manner in which the servants pronounced it—would enter the brilliant apartment and salute the looking-glasses instead of the master and mistress of the house and their guests."[21]

Regrettably for historians, descriptions of the homes and furnishings of Philadelphians who preferred restrained embellishments are less vivid. When she recorded her first impressions of the city, Warder focused on what was absent as much as what was present: "the regularity of the streets and Buildings with there intire plainness I much admire. . . . there Furniture is neat but mostly in Friends houses consistent to the rest of there appearance[.] Brother Jerrys resemble Bury Street for size has no superfluitys or extravagance to complain off." Nonetheless, Warder is one of the few to have left a detailed description of her "best parlor," a room she proudly furnished with restraint:

It really is a more comfortable Room take it altogether than I was ever mistress off[.] with some alteration the Carpet that was at Peckham does nicely for it filling up the part cut out for the fire place which is here at one end—& a pleasant

Figure 8. Tray, probably English, 1780–87. Painted and tinned sheet iron; W. 36″, D. 30″. (Lynn Historical Society.)

> Window close by the side of it with three other in the room so that for light we do not want[.] it takes nine of our Blue Chairs the Sopha & three Tables two of which that stand between the Windows we have borrowed of Sister Emlen & a pembroke one at bottom of the room on which stands our new Urn.

Although less wealthy than the Robert Morrises and William Binghams, Ann and John Warder belonged to the economic elite of Philadelphia. Their parlor was still an upper-class room with a suite of imported upholstered furniture and a room-size carpet. A rare visual image of a comparable parlor is on a tray once owned by Ebenezer Breed, who lived in Philadelphia between 1786 and 1800 (fig. 8).[22] It depicts a space with a room-size carpet, a sofa, and an urn on a pembroke table at one end of the room.

The eighteenth-century equation of restraint and patriotism, however, should not be taken at face value. Those Philadelphians who used such terms had borrowed them from English authors who also were extolling simplicity over extravagance, a long-popular theme in English letters. Yet American advocates of restraint were convinced of its importance to the citizens of the young Republic. Both Franklin and Warder viewed themselves as arbiters of taste, albeit for very different groups of people and furnishings; the furniture they held up to be imitated were largely imports. Ann Warder spoke of "our new Urn a piece of Furniture much admired & for this Country particularly Convenient Coffee being mostly used," and added, "Uncle Head have requested us to order one for each of his Daughters exact like it." While in London Franklin mused about building a house that would be "a kind of Pattern House by future Builders, within the Power of Tradesmen and People of moderate Circumstances to imitate and follow."[23]

Thus the debate in Philadelphia over appropriate household furnishings raged. On one side were wealthy men and women who sought to rival the Old World on its own terms; on the other side were wealthy men and women who believed that the new nation should set a new example for the Old World to follow. Never, before or after the Revolution, did either group champion a particular formal style. They instead couched their arguments in appropriateness of display or restraint and applied the dicta to objects decorated in both the rococo and the neoclassical styles. Style was not a major issue; the manner in which it was expressed was. Those who sought to rival the furnishings of European nobility chose furnishings as highly embellished as those made for European artistocracy. Those who preferred to express benefits of republican virtue chose furnishings embellished with restraint.

---

[1] R. T. H. Halsey and Elizabeth Tower, *The Homes of Our Ancestors* (New York: Doubleday, Page, 1925), pp. 147–48, 168–69; Alan Gowans, *Images of American Living: Four Centuries of Architecture and Furniture as Cultural Expression* (Philadelphia: J. B. Lippincott Co., 1964), pp. 164–66, 256; Jules David Prown, "Style in American Art: 1750–1800," in *American Art, 1750–1800: Towards Independence*, ed. Charles F. Montgomery and Patricia E. Kane (Boston: New York Graphic Society, 1976), pp. 32–39.

[2] Thomas Jefferson noted in 1786, "[In] buildings and furniture Philadelphia takes the lead, without doubt" (*Thomas Jefferson Papers*, ed. Julian P. Boyd, 23 vols. to date [Princeton: Princeton University Press, 1950–], 10:36).

[3] "To the Public," *Pennsylvania Gazette*, August 1, 1771. For the importance of taste in eighteenth-century Anglo-American thought, see Lawrence Lipking, *The Ordering of the Arts in Eighteenth-Century England* (Princeton: Princeton University Press, 1970), pp. 3–20; and David L. Barquist, "The Meaning of Taste for Wealthy Philadelphians, 1750–1800" (Master's thesis, University of Delaware, 1981), pp. 1–11. For references to the grand tour, see *The Journal of Dr. John Morgan of Philadelphia* (Philadelphia: J. B. Lippincott Co., 1907), pp. 25–27, 216–29.

[4] François-Jean, Marquis de Chastellux, *Travels in North America in the Years 1780, 1781, and 1782*, trans. Howard C. Rice, Jr., 2 vols. (Chapel Hill: University of North Carolina Press, 1963), 1:302; E. H. Gombrich, "Visual Metaphors of Value in Art," in *Meditations on a Hobby Horse and Other Essays on the Theory of Art* (London: Phaidon, 1963), pp. 27–28. For a discussion of *dilettanti* in eighteenth-century England, see Mark Girouard, *Life in the English Country House: A Social and Architectural History* (New Haven: Yale University Press, 1978), pp. 176–78. Research and analysis conducted after delivery of this present paper indicate that the two Richardson pots were made for Samuel and Elizabeth Powel and that Ann Willing Morris received the smaller teapot at a later date; see David L. Barquist, "'Well Made from English Patterns': Richardson Silver for the Powel Family," *Yale University Art Gallery Bulletin* (1993): 76–85.

[5] Sophia Cadwalader, ed., *Recollections of Joshua Francis Fisher Written in 1864*, as cited in Patricia L. Heintzelman, "Elysium on the Schuylkill: William Hamilton's Woodlands" (Master's thesis, University of Delaware, 1972), p. 14; Richard J. Betts, "The Woodlands," *Winterthur Portfolio* 14, no. 3 (Autumn 1979): 224–25; William Howard Adams, ed., *The Eye of Tho. Jefferson* (Washington, D.C.: National Gallery of Art, 1976), pp. 96–97; Helen Maggs Fede, *Washington Furniture at Mount Vernon* (Mount Vernon, Va.: Mount Vernon Ladies' Assn., 1966), p. 34.

[6] *Philadelphia: Three Centuries of American Art* (Philadelphia: Philadelphia Museum of Art, 1976), pp. 114–18; Nicholas B. Wainwright, *Colonial Grandeur in Philadelphia: The House and Furniture of General John Cadwalader* (Philadelphia: Historical Society of Pennsylvania, 1964), pp. 22–23.

[7] Thomas, Lambert, and Martha Cadwalader's portraits, part of the Cadwalader Family Collection, Philadelphia Museum of Art, are illustrated in Charles Coleman Sellers, *Portraits and Miniatures by Charles Willson Peale*, Transactions of the American Philosophical Society 42, nos. 97, 98, 181 (1952).

[8] *The Journal and Major Essays of John Woolman*, ed. Phillips P. Moulton (New York: Oxford University Press, 1971), p. 184; *The Autobiography of Benjamin Franklin*, ed. Leonard W. Labaree et al. (New Haven: Yale University Press, 1964), p. 145.

[9] Ann Warder, journals, 15 vols., 1786–89, vol. 3, August 19, 1786, Historical Society of Pennsylvania, Philadelphia. As Gombrich has observed, the equation of morality with good taste depends on the notion that restraint is the ideal operative in both spheres (Gombrich, "Visual Metaphors," p. 22).

[10] Deborah Franklin to Benjamin Franklin, October [6–13?], 1765, *The Papers of Benjamin Franklin*, ed. Leonard W. Labaree, William B. Willcox, and Claude A. Lopez, 27 vols. to date (New Haven: Yale University Press, 1959–), 12:296. "Paddozway," or paduasoy, is a heavy silk tabby with a self-colored pattern that is usually brocaded. Raymond V. Shepherd, Jr., "Cliveden and Its Philadelphia-Chippendale Furniture: A Documented History," *American Art Journal* 8, no. 2 (November 1976): 2; Rebecca Rawle Shoemaker to Anna Rawle, June 4, 1783, as cited by Robert James Gough, "Towards a Theory of Class and Social Conflict: A Social History of Wealthy Philadelphians, 1775 and 1800" (Ph.D. diss., University of Pennsylvania, 1977), p. 391.

[11] Charles L. Venable, *American Furniture in the Bybee Collection* (Austin: University of Texas Press, 1989), no. 25.

[12] Ann Willing Bingham to Thomas Jefferson, June 1, 1787, Boyd, *Jefferson*, 11:393. For discussions of the Revolution as a catalyst for the adoption of neoclassicism, see Halsey and Tower, *Homes of Our Ancestors*, pp. 147, 168–69; Gowans,

Images of American Living, pp. 164–66, 256; and Prown, "Style in American Art," pp. 32–39.

[13] Beatrice B. Garvan, *Federal Philadelphia, 1785–1825: The Athens of the Western World* (Philadelphia: Philadelphia Museum of Art, 1987), pp. 57–58. Francis J. B. Watson, "The Eye of Thomas Jefferson: Americans and French Eighteenth-Century Furniture in the Age of Jefferson," *Antiques* 110, no. 1 (July 1976): 120.

[14] Rufus Wilmot Griswold, *The Republican Court; or, American Society in the Days of Washington* (rev. ed.; New York: D. Appleton, 1855), p. 262; Henry Wansey, *The Journal of an Excursion to the United States of North America in the Summer of 1794* (2d ed.; Salisbury, Eng.: J. Easton, 1798), p. 123; Garvan, *Federal Philadelphia*, p. 37.

[15] George Washington to Gouverneur Morris, October 1789, letterbook, p. 43, Washington Papers, Library of Congress, Washington, D.C.; Tobias Lear to Clement Biddle, June 1789, as cited in Kathryn C. Buhler, *Mount Vernon Silver* (Mount Vernon, Va.: Mount Vernon Ladies' Assn., 1957), p. 49; William Bingham to Pierre Richard, November 20, 1791, as cited in Margaret L. Brown, "Mr. and Mrs. William Bingham of Philadelphia: Rulers of the Republican Court," *Pennsylvania Magazine of History and Biography* 61, no. 3 (July 1937): 309.

[16] Morris to Washington, January 14, 1790, *The Diary and Letters of Gouverneur Morris . . .*, ed. Anne Cary Morris, 2 vols. (New York: Charles Scribner's Sons, 1888), 1:270–71. For a discussion of the aristocratic pretensions of this group, see Gough, "Towards a Theory," pp. 403–8; and Ethel E. Rasmusson, "Democratic Environment—Aristrocratic Aspiration," *Pennsylvania Magazine of History and Biography* 90, no. 2 (April 1966): 155–82; Fede, *Washington Furniture*, pp. 34–40; Kathleen Catalano and Richard C. Nylander, "New Attributions to Adam Hains, Philadelphia Furniture Maker," *Antiques* 117, no. 5 (May 1980): 1112–16; Charles A. Hammond and Stephen A. Wilbur, *"Gay and Graceful Style": A Catalogue of Objects Associated with Christopher and Rebecca Gore* (Waltham, Mass.: Gore Place Society, 1982), pp. 47–48. Four chairs and a sofa from the Hamilton set are now in the Museum of the City of New York.

[17] James Brown to Abigail Francis, January 22, 1791, as cited in Wendy A. Cooper, "The Purchase of Furniture and Furnishings by John Brown, Providence Merchant," *Antiques* 103, no. 4 (April 1973): 734, 741–42; unidentified letter by Charles Bulfinch, 1789, as cited in Charles A. Place, *Charles Bulfinch: Architect and Citizen* (Boston: Houghton Mifflin Co., 1925), p. 27; Harold Kirker, *The Architecture of Charles Bulfinch* (Cambridge: Harvard University Press, 1969), pp. 118–23.

[18] Oliver Ellsworth to Oliver Ellsworth, Jr., January 18, 1791, Ellsworth Papers, Connecticut Historical Society, Hartford; Place, *Bulfinch*, p. 27; Harrison Gray Otis to Sally Otis, November 20, 1797, as cited in Samuel Eliot Morison, *Harrison Gray Otis, 1765–1848: The Urbane Federalist* (Boston: Houghton Mifflin Co., 1969), pp. 125–26.

[19] "Thoughts on Emigration, Particularly to America, from a Late Publication," *Columbian Magazine; or, Monthly Miscellany* 1, no. 15 (November 1787): 762; Thomas Jefferson to John Page, May 4, 1786, Boyd, *Jefferson*, 9:445.

[20] Isaac Weld, Jr., *Travels through the States of North America and the Provinces of Upper and Lower Canada during the Years 1795, 1796, and 1797*, 2 vols. (3d ed.; London: J. Stockdale, 1800), 1:21; "Thoughts on Emigration," p. 762.

[21] Peter Markoe, *The Times: A Poem* (Philadelphia: William Spotswood, 1788), pp. 12–13; Abigail Smith Adams to Mary Smith Cranch, March 15–18, 1800, *New Letters of Abigail Adams, 1788–1801*, ed. Stewart Mitchell (Boston: Houghton Mifflin

Co., 1947), p. 242; Warder, September 26, 1786, Journals, vol. 4; Samuel Breck, *Recollections . . . with Passages from His Note-Books*, ed. H. E. Scudder (Philadelphia: Porter and Coates, 1877), pp. 201–2.

[22] Warder, June 12, 1786, October 20, 16, 1788, Journals, vols. 2, 13; Isabel Morgan Breed, "Ebenezer Breed," *Register of the Lynn Historical Society* 15 (1911): 69–78.

[23] Warder, October 20, 1788, Journals, vol. 13; Benjamin Franklin, undated [1757–75] specifications, in *Franklin Papers*, 7:321; Barquist, "Meaning of Taste," pp. 28–33.

The Philadelphia Windsor Chair
A Commercial and Design Success Story

Nancy Goyne Evans

When Moreau de St. Méry, a temporary resident of Philadelphia in the mid 1790s, commented on the popularity of "wooden chairs painted green like garden furniture" of Europe, these chairs, which we now routinely call windsor chairs but were in the late eighteenth century frequently denominated by the color of their paint, had been used in Philadelphia for more than fifty years and had come to dominate the American market. The style had probably been introduced to the colonial capital by Lt. Gov. Patrick Gordon, who arrived from England in 1726. At his death ten years later he owned what the estate appraisers identified as five "Windsor Chairs," a form absent from colonial records before this date. The 1736 name association of Gordon's chairs with Windsor, the site of a royal castle where this type furniture was first used as out-of-doors rural seats, implies they were imported. London, the logical point of origin for the chairs, was the chairmaking center in which the style was refined during the 1710s and 1720s, and it was the place of Gordon's residence before 1726. During these same years the turners and chairmakers of London became leading consumers of the enormous beechwood growth in nearby Buckinghamshire. This inexpensive material was used principally for turned and shaved parts.[1]

The fashion for English windsors spread rapidly among prosperous Philadelphians. By the mid 1740s mention of windsors appears in the estate records of a merchant, a gentleman, a shopkeeper, a house carpenter, a former city mayor, and a well-to-do widow. Local chairmakers recognized the potential market for this new type of furniture, which was produced with relative ease from turned, shaved, and bent parts. In 1748 David Chambers announced that he was making and selling "Windsor Chairs" at his Society Hill shop in Philadelphia. By 1752 the chairs were being made in sufficient quantities to export them to Caribbean ports.[2]

These early Philadelphia windsors were blatantly patterned on their English antecedent. Unmistakably similar are the large size, high back, saddled seat, bent arm rail, and slat-style arm posts (figs. 1, 2). Innovative Pennsylvania chairmakers adapted the undercarriage, using local patterns with which they were most familiar—the turned front posts in the Delaware River valley slat-back chairs (fig. 3). Thus, the first Philadelphia windsor chairs had refined leg turnings instead of shaved or simply modeled sticks. A stretcher system strengthened the undercarriage. The same craftsmen introduced other progressive refinements by the mid 1750s: carved terminals in the crest reflecting the Queen Anne style in formal seating (fig. 4), turned arm posts resembling the elements of the upper legs, and arm rails with decorative flat-scrolled terminals (fig. 5). They also introduced a companion low-back chair that substituted a heavy, three-piece sawed rail for a bent arm to provide structural strength (fig. 6). The model for the low chair, which was heavily influenced by English work, was the cabinetmaker's framed roundabout, or corner, chair.

In the quarter century following its introduction, the American windsor gained substantial status and by 1775 had effectively replaced the slat-back chair as the most popular vernacular seating form in Philadelphia. The furnituremakers achieved success with their new chair because its canted back and contoured wooden seat provided considerably more comfort than the ramrod-straight rush-bottom chair, and its seat was permanent, not requiring frequent rerushing or repair. Like the slat-back, rush-bottom chair, scuffed surfaces could be renewed easily with a coat of paint.

Probate documents and furniture accounts demonstrate the windsor's rising acceptance in Philadelphia during the early years of production from the 1750s to the early 1780s. Within a broad sample containing

Figure 1. High-back windsor armchair, Thames valley, England, 1740–55. Ash, elm, oak; H. 42½″, W. 27½″, D. 16½″. (Victoria and Albert Museum, London.)

more than 300 probated estates, 80 documents list "Windsor" seating. Occupations are unknown for 9 percent of the decedents. Members of the professions, merchants, and gentlemen constituted 29 percent of the owners. Tradesmen, the largest group, accounted for 45 percent; however, some were individuals of more than merely moderate means whose estates equaled, if not exceeded in value, those of some members of the previous group. At least 5 men—a mariner, a cooper, a printer, a baker, and an innkeeper—possessed estates valued in excess of £1,000; 5 others were worth more than £500. This was when a horse and riding chair, the eighteenth-century equivalent of the modern economy-model automo-

Figure 2. High-back windsor armchair, Philadelphia, 1748–54. Yellow poplar, maple, oak. (Photo, George Schoellkopf.)

bile, was valued in estate records at £32; few owned such conveyances. Of particular interest is the sizable group of 11 innkeepers (comprising 14 percent of the total decedents) represented among the tradesmen-owners of windsor furniture. Their use of windsors provides an index of this sturdy seat's public function, although such use constitutes only a prelude to the later wholesale acceptance of windsor furniture in the daily life of federal America. Single women and widows, who represented another 9 percent of the windsor owners, also constituted half the group of 8 individuals who used cushions, which were valued possessions, with their windsor seating. (Of the 4 male owners of cushions, 3 can be iden-

Figure 3. Slat-back armchair, Philadelphia, 1740–60. Maple, rush; H. 43″, W. 24 7/8″, D. 20 1/2″. (Winterthur.)

tified as gentlemen.) Among the small group of farmers, or "yeomen," who accounted for 5 percent of the users, 2 possessed substantial estates valued at about £500. Two other men (3 percent of the owners) were identified by the title "Captain." Thus, while windsor use broadened considerably in this quarter century, the new furniture form retained a strong identity with the prosperous element of society. The windsor's role as a seating form for the masses came in ensuing decades.[3]

Substantiating the information drawn from probate records are accounts documenting windsor furniture sales to Philadelphia area residents between 1750 and 1775. The principal customers were merchants,

Figure 4. High-back windsor armchair, Philadelphia, 1760–68. Maple, ash, hickory; H. 43 3/8″, W. 24 5/8″, D. 15 1/16″. (Winterthur.)

who bought the furniture for their own use and for exportation. Chairs sold for between 10*s*. and 18*s*. each, about double or triple the price of slat-back, rush-bottom chairs. (During the early 1770s the average craftsman's daily wage was about 5*s*.)[4]

Windsor seating was becoming fashionable outside Philadelphia when the revolutionary war temporarily halted exports. Chairmaker

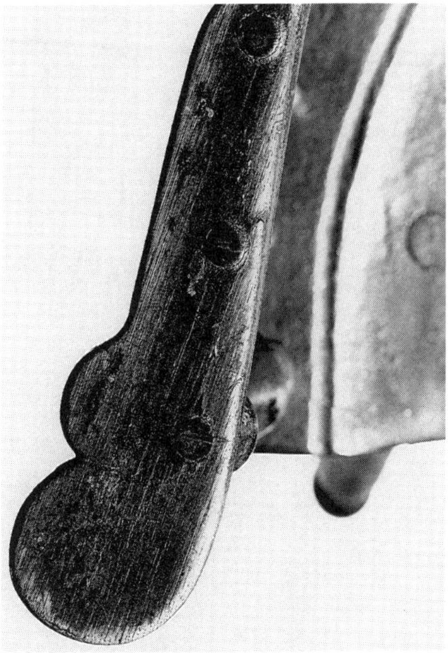

Figure 5. Top of arm of chair in figure 4.

Francis Trumble's December 1775 advertisement of a stock of 1,200 windsor chairs speaks to the rising dimension of the trade and Philadelphia's role in the distribution of this commodity. The Delaware River facilitated regional trade and encouraged householders from neighboring New Jersey to more distant Baltimore County, Maryland, to furnish their homes with windsor seating. Overland routes permitted the distribution of windsor seating to the interior counties surrounding Philadelphia.[5]

The upper Chesapeake Bay was served by two freight routes from Philadelphia—the one downriver to New Castle or Christiana Bridge, Delaware, and overland by wagons to the bay; the other south through Delaware Bay and around the Delmarva Peninsula into the lower Chesapeake. Several commercial accounts provide a composite picture of this trade. Between 1764 and 1766 merchant Zebulon Rudolph acquired windsor chairs from Trumble, shipped them by river vessel to Christiana Bridge, then freighted them overland to Head of Elk (Elkton) on the upper Chesapeake Bay to his merchant kinsman Tobias Rudolph

Figure 6. Low-back windsor armchair, Philadelphia, 1758–65. Yellow poplar, maple, oak; H. 27 3/4″, W. 24 5/8″, D. 17″. (Winterthur.)

for distribution. Other Philadelphia merchants sent windsors to Baltimore, Annapolis, Georgetown, Upper Marlboro, Oxford, Hampton, York River, and James River in the middle of the lower bay. Clement Biddle and Company shipped their merchandise for the bay entirely via the water route, which although longer in distance proved no more expensive.[6]

In the deep South, Charleston constituted an early and enduring market for the windsor. Notices reading "IMPORTED IN THE LAST VESSEL FROM PHILADELPHIA . . . a parcel of neat Windsor Chairs" are not uncommon in the late 1760s and 1770s. The sloop *Henry* deposited 150 chairs in the southern city in a single voyage in 1762. Occasional minor prewar southern outlets for the Philadelphia windsor were Savannah, Georgia, and St. Augustine in East Florida, the latter then under British control.[7]

Northward in New York, where local production probably did not commence until the early 1770s, various shops offered Philadelphia windsor seating during the previous decade. In contrast, the contemporary trade in Philadelphia windsors to New England was small, partly because local rush-bottom chairs of several styles retained their commercial stature into the federal period. Also, windsor production was inaugurated in Rhode Island during the late 1750s, and distribution, albeit limited, occurred throughout the region.[8]

Philadelphia records and other documents describe the styles and forms of windsor seating distributed in the coastal trade during the 1760s and 1770s. Zebulon Rudolph shipped high-back chairs and at least one child's windsor to Head of Elk. His Maryland exports probably also included an occasional settee. One dating from the late 1760s or early 1770s is a central feature of a family group painted some years later (fig. 7). The Ramsey-Polk garden overlooked the family's commercial landing where hogsheads of shad and herring lined the shore. Well before Levi Hollingsworth shipped "Round top" windsors to Chesapeake in 1772, he and other Philadelphia merchants had introduced this new arched-top armchair, also called a "sack-back" windsor, to the regional market (fig. 8).[9]

Charleston newspapers recorded another style change when William Sykes announced his receipt of "Windsor Chairs of a new fashion" in 1770, a date too early for the commercial introduction of a windsor side chair. The notice probably identifies a change in windsor leg design. The modification is best described visually in two high-back chairs of medium size introduced in the 1760s (figs. 9, 10). One chair is supported on ball-foot legs of the "old" style, the other on legs of the new, tapered form. While the original impetus for the change may lie in the structural weakness of the narrow neck that joins the ball foot and cylinder of the early leg, the alteration cut construction time by simplifying the turning and paved the way for increased production, a condition critical for mass marketing. Philadelphia craftsmen were at the forefront of American windsor design, although their principal role was that of entrepreneurs rather than arbiters of style. However, a successful enterprise dictated product refinement and change to keep the market stimulated.[10]

Figure 7. James Peale, *The Ramsey-Polk Family*, Charlestown, Md., 1793. Oil on canvas; H. 49¼", W. 39". (Collection of Mrs. Lammot Copeland: Photo, Winterthur.)

Chairmakers John Kelso and Adam Galer carried the Philadelphia windsor style to New York City, where they illustrated pictorial advertisements of 1774 with a high-back and a sack-back chair respectively. New York born and trained Thomas Ash, whose early products also appear to have been close copies of their Philadelphia models, already practiced his trade in the city. Within a decade, a distinctive New York windsor style evolved, likely spearheaded by Ash and his brother William. Their new sack-back chair (fig. 11), while still imitative of

Figure 8. Joseph Henzey, sack-back windsor armchair, Philadelphia, 1770–85. Yellow poplar, maple, oak; H. 39 1/16", W. 25 1/4", D. 16 1/8". (Winterthur.)

Philadelphia work in breadth and firm stance (see fig. 8), has the fuller, more robust turnings that were a hallmark of New York windsors through the end of the century.[11]

As stated, the Philadelphia windsor was not commercially prominent in New England in the late colonial period. The novelty of such construction even in the early 1770s is well demonstrated in correspondence between Quaker merchants William Barrell of Philadelphia and John Andrews of Boston, his brother-in-law. Excerpts from Andrews's letters illuminate his interest: February 26, 1773, "I forgot . . . to desire you to send me as soon as convenient another Chair for a particular friend

Figure 9. High-back windsor armchair, Philadelphia, 1764–70. Yellow poplar, maple, hickory, oak; H. 39 3/16″, W. 19″, D. 17 3/16″. (Winterthur.)

of ye same kind of pattern you sent me last with two of ye same sort for Doct'r Loring." An asterisk within the body of the letter refers to a page-bottom sketch showing a Philadelphia sack-back chair. On September 2 Andrews had a further request: "My principal motive in writing this is to oblige Mr Breck who is about moving . . . and wants six chairs of the same kind as you sent me last with two high back'd ones, which should

Figure 10. High-back windsor armchair, Philadelphia, 1768–76. Yellow poplar, maple, hickory, oak; H. $40^{11}/_{16}$″, W. $20^{1}/_{2}$″, D. $14^{3}/_{8}$″. (Winterthur.)

be glad you'd send me as soon as possible, as one of his rooms must remain unfurnish'd till they come." This prudent businessman would hardly have paid freight and risked damage to the merchandise had similar furniture been available locally. During the next few years the "Philadelphia chair" rose in standing among eastern Massachusetts affluent residents. For example, Samuel Barrett, who asked his brother-

Figure 11. Sack-back windsor armchair, possibly by Thomas and William Ash, New York, 1783–90. Yellow poplar, maple, oak; H. 34″, W. 21 3/8″, D. 16 1/4″. (Private collection: Photo, Winterthur.)

in-law Stephen Salisbury (I) of Worcester to purchase "6 Green Chairs" at auction in 1779, qualified his request by adding, "if made at Philadelphia." When Boston chairmakers began windsor-chair production, they copied the high-back and sack-back Philadelphia patterns of the 1770s. Characteristic of their early production is Samuel Jones Tuck's sack-back windsor (fig. 12). The Philadelphia style is reflected in the chair's broad seat and stance; innovation occurs in the bulge of the tapered feet.[12]

Philadelphia continued as the leading producer and distributor of windsor furniture during the early federal period. Supplementing the

Figure 12. Samuel Jones Tuck, sack-back windsor armchair, Boston, 1791–98. Pine, oak; H. 37 1/4", W. 21 3/16", D. 15 7/8". (Collection of Thomas B. Rentschler: Photo, Winterthur.)

adult chairs were windsor seating for children and a benchlike seat, called a settee, accommodating two or more persons. Craftsmen introduced the fan-back chair, the first windsor side chair, in the late 1770s (fig. 13), and the sack-back armchair continued to be commercially viable for a few years longer. At the height of his career, Daniel Rose, a clockmaker and musician of Reading, Pennsylvania, posed confidently while resting his left hand on the bow of a sack-back chair whose elongated turnings suggest that it came from the Philadelphia shop of Joseph Henzey (fig. 14).[13] German American chairmakers in the counties of

Figure 13. Francis Trumble, fan-back windsor side chair, Philadelphia, 1778–85. Yellow poplar, maple, black walnut, oak, and hickory; H. 35 3/4", W. 18 1/4", D. 19 1/4". (Winterthur.)

Berks, Lancaster, and York, who first created their regional market for windsor seating in the federal period, produced mannered versions of the Philadelphia sack-back chair (fig. 15) about ten years after its introduction in the city (see fig. 8). Long arm extensions and thick, stiffly

Figure 14. *Daniel Rose*, attributed to William Witman, Reading, Pa., 1795–1800. Oil on canvas; H. 62 1/8″, W. 39″. (Historical Society of Berks County, Reading, Pa.)

Figure 15. Sack-back windsor armchair, probably Lancaster County, Pa., 1780–90. Yellow poplar, maple, hickory; H. 37 7/16", W. 21 3/16", D. 15 13/16". (Winterthur.)

modeled planks are marks of a provincial origin, although such features were not unique to rural Pennsylvania shops. On the other hand, the dual leg system—ball feet at the front and tapered toes at the back—was purely regional in concept.

While the sack-back windsor was a major vehicle in disseminating the early Philadelphia style, in the postwar period the bow-back chair inaugurated an era of mass-produced windsor seating (fig. 16). Philadelphia chairmakers introduced the bow-back windsor during the mid 1780s, basing their design, like others, on English chairs. The loop pat-

Figure 16. Gilbert Gaw, bow-back windsor side chair, Philadelphia, 1798–1802. Yellow poplar, maple, hickory, oak; H. 37 9/16″, W. 17 1/4″, D. 16″. (Winterthur.)

tern was easily imitated and invited experimentation. From the start the Philadelphia chair was fitted with simple turnings of a new style that closely imitated bamboo work, then in considerable vogue in English furniture construction. For a time the saddled seat remained, but increasing demands in domestic and oversees markets, as indicated by the sharp rise in chair sales, dictated even greater production economies, and a seat saucered on the top surface and flat at the edges soon replaced the contoured one. These production shortcuts coincided with the introduction of a broad palette of surface color in supplement to the stan-

Figure 17. Bow-back windsor armchair, Philadelphia, 1796–1802. Yellow poplar, maple, hickory, mahogany; H. 37″, W. 20½″, D. 15⅞″. (Winterthur.)

dard windsor green and the use of painted ornament. The latter took the form of penciling, or narrow striping, as an accent for grooves in bamboo-simulated turnings, on bow faces, and on seat edges.[14]

Hand in glove with changes wrought by paint and mass production was the introduction of design variants—the work of imaginative craftsmen, both metropolitan and rural. One was a back panel featuring pierced and curved slats in imitation of high-style joined seating (figs. 17,

Figure 18. Armchair, Philadelphia, 1785–95. Mahogany; H. 38 1/4", W. 28 5/8", D. 24 5/8". (Winterthur.)

18). Natural finished mahogany arms, contrasting strikingly with the painted surfaces, provided another option in the best work. Generally, the arms curved in an undulating forward scroll imitative of their high-style prototypes (rotated a quarter turn).

German craftsmen of rural Pennsylvania continued to produce seating modeled after Philadelphia work but interpreted in their characteristic manner. Side chairs usually had broad, shallow seats, producing backs of comparable form. The southern coastal trade accelerated in

Figure 19. Bow-back windsor side chair, Rhode Island, 1790–95. Pine, maple, oak; H. 37 1/8", W. 16 1/8", D. 19 1/4". (Private collection: Photo, Winterthur.)

the federal period: old markets expanded, particularly in the lower Chesapeake; new strong ones were created, among them fast-rising Savannah; and well-established centers like Charleston became veritable entrepôts for the distribution of windsors, especially to the byways and small landings of the region.

New England and New York craftsmen strove to compete with Philadelphia imports in the bow-back style. In producing the new pattern, they retained the old-style baluster leg for several years before adopting the bamboo-turned support. New York and Rhode Island chairmakers introduced a braced back, in which a pair of extra sticks were anchored in a rear seat extension. Figure 19 pictures a braced, bow-back Rhode Island chair whose excellent proportions, turned work, and sculpted seat mark it as a regional chair of the first rank.

Boston chairmakers, who were particularly mindful of Philadelphia competition in the local market, also succeeded in making some individual statements. In the earliest Boston published notices, which began in 1786, Ebenezer Stone emphasized that he made green chairs (the color common to Philadelphia production until about 1790) "equal to any imported from Philadelphia." Tuck and others added their voices of protest in the 1790s. By then the bow-back windsor was well established in the local market. In general, Boston chairs can be distinguished from their Philadelphia and Rhode Island counterparts by the central channel that marks the bow faces (as opposed to the crowned Philadelphia bow and the Rhode Island flat, beaded surface). Other Boston features are the projecting front corners of the well-saddled seats and the full, long oval profile of the baluster turnings (fig. 20). Some windsor chairs of both Boston and Rhode Island origin have swelled, tapered feet. Bamboo-turned windsors were first produced in Boston about 1800 (fig. 21). The illustrated chair is marked by two distinctive, although occasional, Boston features: a stylish extra swell in the spindles at midpoint and an unusual curved stretcher punctuated by medallions. Originally these oval surfaces served to introduce bits of leafy or floral accent decoration.[15]

The competition of Philadelphia imports remained strong in New England through the turn of the century. In Salem, Massachusetts, chairmaker James C. Tuttle informed customers in 1796 that he was at last "able to answer their demands with all kinds of Philadelphia or windsor, Chairs and Settees made in the newest style." About that date Daniel Lawrence of Providence advertised fashionable windsors "beautifully painted after the Philadelphia Mode." Oliver Pomeroy of Northampton, Massachusetts, announced that he had acquired his experience in making fashionable windsor chairs by having previously "worked two or three years in the city of Philadelphia."[16]

Postwar windsor production in the United States achieved considerable dimension by the 1790s, equaling, if not exceeding, that of all

Figure 20. William Seaver, bow-back windsor side chair, Boston, 1795–1800. Pine, birch, oak; H. 37 7/8", W. 17 1/2", D. 16 1/8". (Private collection: Photo, Winterthur.)

other seating combined. The windsor furnished household and public spaces both grand and modest. In 1796 a young Philadelphia bride from a prosperous Quaker family placed eight green windsors in her "back parlour" as an accompaniment to two large armchairs, a small dining table, and a tea table standing beneath a looking glass. George Washington acquired two dozen chairs in Philadelphia for the "New Room" (a large dining room) at Mount Vernon, while Thomas Jefferson bought

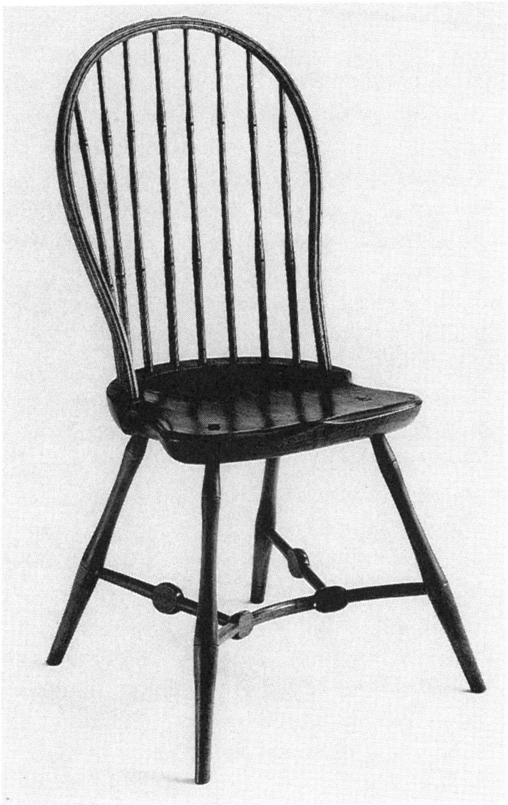

Figure 21. Bow-back windsor side chair, attributed to William Seaver and James Frost, Boston, 1800–1802. Pine, maple, birch, oak; H. 36 5/8", W. 17 7/16", D. 15 5/8". (Winterthur.)

windsors for Monticello and his country home, Poplar Forest (Lynchburg). Seating in the small 25-by-15-foot, two-story New York house occupied in 1794 by John Cooper, a laborer and cartman, consisted of eight windsors and six rush-bottom chairs "half worn." A few years later the $3 valuation of four windsors owned by housewright Somerby Chase was nearly twice that of the remaining nine miscellaneous chairs in his Newburyport, Massachusetts, home. Trustees of the First Federal Street

Theatre in neighboring Boston furnished several secondary rooms surrounding the auditorium with windsor seating. Inns and places of public accommodation made frequent use of windsors. The quality range was broad, from the Golden Tun run by Samuel Fraunces of Philadelphia to the lowly country ordinaries, dubbed by one traveler "extra-ordinaries." Several first-floor rooms in the Golden Tun contained mahogany furniture, gilded looking glasses, and silver-plated lighting fixtures besides windsor seating, while the frontier inns usually had only a table and a few chairs.[17]

Diffusion of the windsor chair was complete in the 1790s, and the influence of the Philadelphia windsor chairmakers was all pervasive. Indeed, Philadelphia shippers sent windsor seating to forty-six coastal ports of record from Maine to Louisiana. The number of windsors exported annually from Philadelphia in 1786 exceeded 5,100, and figures for a five-month period of 1789 suggest a 22 percent annual increase, to an estimated 6,240 items. As the city's population hovered at 45,000 in the 1790s, Philadelphia chairmakers played an aggressive role in securing a greater share of the monetary rewards of the export trade. At least 10 of them conducted business directly with retailers in other coastal communities, retaining the middleman profit for themselves. Chairmaker Lawrence Allwine ventured a single consignment of 480 chairs to Charleston in 1798. The average consignment, however, numbered about 60 chairs, which represented an $80 venture on a chairmaker's part. The economic risk also must be gauged in terms of average shop profits, which were about $9 to $12 for a six-day workweek in the 1790s. Occasionally armchairs and a few settees were part of the shipments and, rarely, children's seating and stools. The bread and butter of the trade was the side chair. As a leading Philadelphia merchant house succinctly informed a client for whom they had purchased bow-back seating, "The Windsor chairs are of the cheapest kind, yet neat and fashionable." Thus, within half a century of its introduction, the "Philadelphia Chair" had become a cultural and economic force unlike any other in the ranks of American furniture production to that time.[18]

---

[1] *Moreau de St. Méry's American Journey, 1793–1798*, trans. and ed. Kenneth Roberts and Anna M. Roberts (Garden City, N.Y.: Doubleday, 1947), p. 264; Patrick

Gordon, inventory, 1736, Register of Wills, Philadelphia; Edward Hazen, *Popular Technology; or, Professions and Trades*, vol. 2 (1846; reprint, Albany: Early American Industries Assn., 1981), p. 150; Daniel Defoe, *A Tour through England and Wales*, vol. 1 (1724–26; reprint, London: J. M. Dent and Sons, 1959), p. 299; Nancy Goyne Evans, "A History and Background of English Windsor Furniture," *Furniture History* 15 (1979): 27–35.

[2] Windsor chairs are listed in the following estate inventories: Hannah Hodge, 1736; Owen Owen, 1741; Amos Lewis, 1744; William Bell, 1745; David Evans, 1745 (some references courtesy of Wendy Kaplan); and William Fishbourn, 1742, Register of Wills, Philadelphia (hereafter cited as RW); Chambers advertisement, *Pennsylvania Gazette* (Philadelphia), August 23, 1748, as quoted in Arthur W. Leibundguth, "The Furniture-Making Crafts in Philadelphia, c. 1730–c. 1760" (Master's thesis, University of Delaware, 1964), p. 43; snows *Charming Polly*, October 4, 1752, and *Hannah*, December 20, 1752, Shipping Returns, Barbados, 1728–53, Colonial Office, Public Record Office, London (hereafter cited as PRO).

[3] Probate information drawn from estate inventories, 1750–88, RW, and Philadelphia city and county inventories, microfilm, Joseph Downs Collection of Manuscripts and Printed Ephemera (hereafter cited as Downs Collection), Winterthur Library; the complete body of Philadelphia "Forfeited Estates: Inventories and Sales" in Thomas Lynch Montgomery, ed., *Pennsylvania Archives*, 6th ser., 15 vols. (Harrisburg, Pa.: Harrisburg Publishing Co., 1906–), 13:496–912; Alice Hanson Jones, *American Colonial Wealth: Documents and Methods*, 3 vols. (New York: Arno Press, 1977), 1:126–325. Cushions, whether used with windsor or other seating, were usually considered luxury items and valued as such.

[4] Nancy A. Goyne, "Francis Trumble of Philadelphia, Windsor Chair and Cabinetmaker," in *Winterthur Portfolio 1*, ed. Milo M. Naeve (Winterthur, Del.: Henry Francis du Pont Winterthur Museum, 1964), pp. 228–30, 235; William Macpherson Hornor, Jr., *Blue Book, Philadelphia Furniture: William Penn to George Washington, with Special Reference to the Philadelphia-Chippendale School* (1935; reprint, Washington, D.C.: Highland House, 1977), p. 295.

[5] Trumble advertisement, *Pennsylvania Gazette*, December 27, 1775; John Coxe, Esq., inventory, Trenton, 1753, and Joseph James, inventory, Woodstown, N.J., 1767, Downs Collection; Mary Richards, James Lownes, and James Bailey, estate inventories, Baltimore Co., Md., 1773–74, Downs Collection.

[6] Zebulon Rudolph, Levi Hollingsworth, and miscellaneous accounts, Hollingsworth Manuscripts, Business Papers, and Society Collection, Levi Hollingsworth Papers, Historical Society of Pennsylvania, Philadelphia (hereafter cited as HSP); Thomas A. Biddle Co. business books, Clement Biddle letterbook, vol. 2 (1771–74), HSP; inward entries, schooners *Betsey* (November 22, 1768, and December 2, 1769) and *Industry* (November 20, 1770), Oxford Port of Entry account books, 1759–73, Maryland Historical Society, Baltimore; sloop *John* and schooner *Peggy*, *Virginia Gazette* (Williamsburg), March 31, 1768, February 3, 1774, and sloop *Success*, *Virginia Gazette, or Norfolk Intelligencer*, June 23, 1774, as recorded in Research Files, Museum of Early Southern Decorative Arts (hereafter cited as MESDA files), Winston-Salem, N.C.

[7] Edward Lightwood import notice, *South Carolina Gazette* (Charleston), June 27, 1761, MESDA files; sloop *Henry*, July 30, 1762, South Carolina Naval Office Lists, PRO; schooners *Ogeeche*, June 19, 1766, and *Mary*, June 1 and August 20, 1767, Shipping Returns, Georgia, 1764–67, and East Florida, 1765–69, PRO.

[8] Thomas and James Franklin advertisement and Andrew Gautier advertisement, *New-York Mercury*, January 4, 1762, and April 18, 1765; Jonathan Hampton

advertisement, *New-York Journal*, May 19, 1768, as quoted in [Rita Susswein Gottesman], *The Arts and Crafts in New York, 1726–1776: Advertisements and News Items from New York City Newspapers* (New York: New-York Historical Society, 1938), pp. 112–14, 123; Perry, Hayes, and Sherbrooke advertisement, *New-York Mercury*, December 2, 1762 (reference courtesy of Susan B. Swan).

[9] Charles Coleman Sellers, *The Artist of the Revolution: The Early Life of Charles Willson Peale* (Hebron, Conn.: Feather and Good, 1939), p. 267; Francis Trumble bill to Levi Hollingsworth, Hollingsworth Papers.

[10] Sykes notice, *South Carolina Gazette*, May 1, 1770, MESDA files.

[11] Kelso advertisement, *New York Gazette and Weekly Mercury*, September 5, 1774, supplement; Galer and Thomas Ash advertisements, *Rivington's New York Gazetteer*, September 2, and February 24, 1774.

[12] Andrews to Barrell, February 26, September 2, 1773, Andrews-Eliot Papers, Massachusetts Historical Society, Boston; Barrett to Salisbury, April 1, 1779, Salisbury Papers, American Antiquarian Society, Worcester, Mass.

[13] A few fan-back side chairs were produced in Philadelphia from the 1750s to the early 1770s, but the chair was not a commercial success until the late 1770s.

[14] Few surfaces remain intact on early federal windsor seating. Our knowledge of their appearance is dependent largely on images in folk paintings.

[15] Stone advertisements, *Independent Chronicle* (Boston), April 13, 1786, June 21, 1787; Tuck advertisement, *Columbian Centinel* (Boston), October 3, 1795.

[16] Tuttle advertisement, *Salem Gazette*, August 19, 1796, as quoted in Mabel M. Swan, *Samuel McIntire, Carver, and the Sandersons, Early Salem Cabinet Makers* (Salem: Essex Institute, 1934), pp. 29–30; Lawrence advertisement, *United States Chronicle* (Providence), July 19, 1787, as quoted in Irving Whitall Lyon, *The Colonial Furniture of New England: A Study of the Domestic Furniture in Use in the Seventeenth and Eighteenth Centuries* (1891; 3d ed., Boston: Houghton Mifflin Co., 1924), pp. 180–81; Pomeroy advertisement, *Hampshire Gazette* (Northampton, Mass.), April 8, 1795 (reference courtesy of Susan B. Swan).

[17] Susanna Dillwyn Emlen to William Dillwyn, January 11, 1796, Dillwyn-Emlen Correspondence, 1770–1818, Library Company of Philadelphia; Helen Maggs Fede, *Washington Furniture at Mount Vernon* (Mount Vernon, Va.: Mount Vernon Ladies Assn., 1966), pp. 58–59; Charles L. Granquist, "Thomas Jefferson's 'Whirligig' Chairs," *Antiques* 109, no. 5 (May 1976): 1056–60; Fiske Kimball, "Thomas Jefferson's Windsor Chairs," *Pennsylvania Museum Bulletin* 21, no. 98 (December 1925): 58–60; Jefferson expense account books, 1791–1803, New York Public Library; John Cooper, inventory, microfilm, 1794, Downs Collection; Somerby Chase, inventory, 1803, Registry of Probate, Essex County, Mass., vol. 371, p. 285; Lyon, *Colonial Furniture*, pp. 180–81; William Seaver bills to Joseph Russell, January 21, October 18, 1794, Boston Theatre Papers, Boston Public Library; Samuel Fraunces, inventory, 1795, RW; John Bernard, *Retrospections of America, 1797–1811* (New York: Harper and Brothers, 1887) as quoted in "Clues and Footnotes," *Antiques* 117, no. 4 (April 1980): 806.

[18] Philadelphia Coastwise Manifests, 1790–1800, U.S. Customhouse Records, National Archives, Washington, D.C.; "Port of Philada. Exports 1786," photostat, Downs Collection; exports from Philadelphia, August 1 to December 31, 1789, in *American Museum; or, Universal Magazine* 8 (1790): 115 (reference courtesy of Arlene Palmer); Stephen Collins and Son to Samuel Cheesman, October 27, 1792, Stephen Collins Papers, Library of Congress.

Can Words Speak to Things?

An Inconclusive Conclusion

Michael Zuckerman

In their various ways, the papers in this collection do discuss the Philadelphia experience in the shaping of a national culture. But they were meant to do much more.

The contributors to the collection were deliberately drawn from two distinct disciplines, American material culture studies and early American social history. These two fields may seem, in abstract logic, inherently inseparable. They are, in fact, almost utterly isolated from each other. Specialists in one scarcely speak to specialists in the other, let alone read the works requisite to sophisticated scholarship in the alien area.

The shapers of *Shaping a National Culture* hoped to stimulate collaboration between these uncommunicative communities of scholars, or at least to test the possibilities of such collaboration. At the same time, the organizers of the collection also meant this auspicious opening of discourse to be their own distinctive offering to the celebration of the miracle at Philadelphia whose bicentennial America marked in 1987.

Yet the difficulties of dialogue and the distance between the disciplines are evident in the unmistakable disparities between the two camps in their disposition to participate in such celebration. The students of material culture are generally quite comfortable in assuming that the Quaker capital at the confluence of the Schuylkill and the Delaware rivers was indeed the cultural center of the rebellious colonies and the new nation. The social historians are far more skeptical, and their tone more elegiac than enthusiastic.

Virtually every paper in the first half of this book dwells on prefigurations of Philadelphia's decline more than on the manifestations of its golden moment. Beth Twiss-Garrity shows that the city's planned form, and especially its geometrical regularity, had fallen from favor as an ideal of cityscape by 1800, even as political primacy was passing to Washington and economic ascendancy to New York. Robert Gough argues that Philadelphia's splintered elites could not lead the constitutional convention of 1787, although it was held in their own backyard, and that their fragmentation foretold future failures. Steve Rosswurm similarly suggests that the city's leadership in the last decade of the eighteenth century foreshadowed the insular, inept gentlemen who would prove incompetent to keep abreast of developments in the succeeding century. Mary Schweitzer proposes that the hinterland that gave Philadelphia its glory in the eighteenth century was insufficient to sustain such prepotence in the nineteenth, that the geography that favored the Quaker City in the colonial period proved far less favorable in the era of the new nation, and that the collapse of the second Bank of the United States assured the city's decline. Jean Soderlund wryly observes that, by the time the city's Quakers consolidated their reformist convictions, they had lost the power to enact them into law across the Commonwealth.

Like Mark Twain complaining that the reports of his death were greatly exaggerated, I find these lamentations for Philadelphia's demise a little loony.

Take Twiss-Garrity's treatment of the changing aesthetics of the cityscape. The French visitors she studies did, no doubt, find the City of Brotherly Love deficient by their new romantic standards. But they elaborated their indictment in such detail because they studied the city so carefully. It was the essential stop on their New World tour, the place their readers at home wanted most to know about. And more than a few French visitors were so effectually undeterred by the city's austere geometry that they took up temporary or even permanent residence in its red brick houses on its rectilinear streets. Several successive cohorts of Napoleonic refugees, including consequential courtiers and the very family of the emperor himself, chose Philadelphia rather than picturesque New York or L'Enfantine Washington when they sought sanctuary in America in the nineteenth century. They regretted, perhaps, the repetitive regularity of William Penn's plan; they recognized, quite certainly, the new nation's most cosmopolitan center of culture. And Americans themselves did not even cease to admire Philadelphia aesthetically or to follow its urban form. As Richard Wade demonstrated decades ago, Philadelphia rather than its older neighbors to the north was the model for city builders and boomers in every one of the primate metropolises of the new West in the first half of the nineteenth century. All the early Western centers were self-consciously styled on the Enlightened plan of the Quaker capital rather than on the romantic examples of New York or Boston.[1]

Or take Soderlund's ironic conception of the Quakers and their relation to larger currents of reform. In the colonial years, almost the only Quaker movement for reform that was not totally tribal was the campaign against slavery, and that struggle was still essentially insular, an episode within a single denomination in a single colony and adjacent areas of a couple of others. In the era of the early Republic, Philadelphia Quakers played prominent roles—generally, preeminent roles—in an extensive array of national reforms. As they seized moral initiative in meliorative as well as radical efforts to assert the rights of Native Americans, African Americans, women, prisoners, mad people, and paupers, Friends in the Delaware River valley grew immeasurably more influential in a continental perspective after 1800 than they had ever been before.[2]

Or take Gough's, Rosswurm's, and Schweitzer's insistence on Philadelphia's failures of leadership, emergent insularity, and incipient economic and cultural decline by the end of the eighteenth century. None of these scholars offers the slightest intimation that the city's population would grow faster from 1800 to 1850 than it had from 1750 to 1800. None of them sees—or, at any rate, says—that at the turn of the century the city was barely beginning its career as the country's premier industrial city. None of them appears to appreciate that Philadelphia would be more nearly the cultural capital of America in the first half of the nineteenth century than it ever was in the second half of the eighteenth. As Richard Shryock pointed out in a landmark article that is now more than fifty years old, Philadelphia surpassed the soi-disant Athens of America in painting, sculpture, music, architecture, publishing, journalism, medicine, science, engineering, and virtually every other realm of culture but literature. Boston made that one peculiar corner of culture definitive of culture, at least to its own provincial satisfaction, and historians since have foolishly taken that city at its own outlandishly inflated estimate.[3]

I am wary, then, of the portions of these papers predicated on a presumption of the nineteenth-century decline of Philadelphia. I am skeptical, indeed, of the aspect of this collection in which such a presumption of decline is implicit. But beyond declaring my doubts about the way that *Shaping a National Culture* suggests that the City of Brotherly Love once did shape that culture and then ceased to do so, I must also register my reservations about another premise on which many of the essays in this volume are conceived. I am not avid to embrace the assumption that there *was* a national culture to shape in the latter half of the eighteenth century, or indeed for several generations after that.

Let me put my misgivings as baldly as possible. Philadelphia did not surrender its place as the national political capital after 1800 because it never had any such place to lose before that point. It did not lose its position as the national economic capital to New York because it did not have such a position to begin with.

In advancing such assertions, I do not deny that, at a number of moments of revolutionary and counterrevolutionary crisis, Philadelphia was the city where American leaders came together to resolve and promulgate policy. I do not even doubt that, when a site for the standing government of the new national enterprise had to be settled, Philadelphia was a more plausible choice than any other town, or that it was the seat of the Continental, Confederate, and Constitutional congresses for more time than all their other residences put together. I simply say what any number of scholars have said before me, that the national government that convened in Philadelphia until 1800 did not really govern the nation. Central authority laid lightly, if at all, on most Americans when it was ensconced in Philadelphia in the eighteenth century, and it laid almost as lightly on most Americans when it was transferred to Washington in the nineteenth. A national government that actually impinged persistently and powerfully on the mass of the people awaited the New Deal and its cold war aftermath.

Similarly, I do not deny that Philadelphia was the largest city in English America in the eighteenth century. I do not even doubt that it was in certain ways the richest; for all that Charleston was, in certain others, much richer. I simply say that there was no national economy in the eighteenth century for Philadelphia, Charleston, or any other place to shape. Indeed, for some fair way into the nineteenth century, there was no national economy for New York to shape either.

The very premise of a national polity or economy or culture to be shaped by a single dominant center is problematic at best in a heterogeneous society rife with regional folkways and parochial peculiarities. Even the notorious diversity of the Delaware valley paled before the vaster multiplicities of the American colonies and the new American nation in the eighteenth century, and those multiplicities surely multiplied many times over after 1800.

Before we rush to prepare our rabbit stew, we must first have our rabbit. Before we hasten to hail Philadelphia or any other place in the shaping of our national culture, we must first ask about the place of national activity itself in a decentered society that was, apart from ideology, scarcely a nation at all. We must first seek the significance of cosmopolitan elites in a culture whose commonalities, such as they were, came at least as much from the bottom as from any shaping influence at the top. But such inquiries would constitute a different collection than this one.

For me, the most intriguing issues that these essays, taken together, set simmering are issues of the conditions of creativity—political creativity, economic creativity, and especially cultural creativity—in the eighteenth-century city. Why was Philadelphia so substantially the most prolific of American places in inventions of so many sorts? Why did it draw the men who made the museums and scientific societies and constitutions of the new nation? Why did it attract the men who set and satisfied the young country's highest standards of taste?

Some part of the answer to such questions is surely a simple application of the golden rule—not the real golden rule but its American variant: those who have the gold make the rules. Philadelphia had the wheat the world wanted, so Philadelphia could call some of the cultural tunes.

But cultural creativity is never so simple. For one thing, the wheat that Philadelphia had did not grow itself, or transport itself to the mills, or grind itself, or ship itself. A rising generation of scholars is now elucidating the ingenuity and innovation and enterprise, in technology and in marketing, that made possible the Quaker City's dominance of the grain trade. Geography is only opportunity, not destiny.[4]

For another thing, cultural leadership does not necessarily or automatically attend economic ascendancy. In the nineteenth century, New York was notoriously indifferent to artists and intellectuals for decades after its rise to commercial power, and conversely in the early twentieth century Los Angeles legislated culturally for the country—through movies made in Hollywood—long before it rose to its current economic and demographic consequence. Similarly in our own time, Miami exerts no notable cultural force although it has the narcotics the nation wants, and conversely Nashville supplies the country cultural cues out of all proportion to its population and economic position.

So Philadelphia's dominance of the grain trade does not and cannot, in and of itself, explain the cultural creativity of the city in the era often taken for its golden age. Perhaps no single element, or even any concatenation of elements, does or can. Perhaps cultural creativity will always elude our explanations. But perhaps we can pick up some clues from the pieces in this collection.

Twiss-Garrity, for example, reminds us of the confinement of the city to a rather narrow band of building along the west bank of the Delaware River, almost to the end of the eighteenth century. She specifies effectively the elaboration of subdivisions and alleys that defeated Penn's plan for a green country town and even Thomas Holme's plan for half-acre lots, and she establishes suggestively the ways in which such infilling allowed an immense increase in population to be contained within the same few blocks that the city already occupied fifty years before. Gough, similarly, reminds us that in the revolutionary city rich and poor lived in the same residential neighborhoods and indeed on the same densely settled streets. And Billy Smith shows how very differently the rich and poor did live, and how differently even the black poor and the white poor lived, on the streets they all shared. A place as compact as Philadelphia simply could not shield men and women of separate social strata from recurrent encounters with one another.

Just as Twiss-Garrity, Gough, and Smith detail developments that made citizens of many classes familiar if not intimate with one another, so several other contributors to this collection delineate the evolution and ideals of crucial cultural institutions that precluded any radical isolation of the arts and sciences—or of artists, scientists, technicians, and tradesmen—from one another. George Frick's analysis of the intellectual density of the Library Company of Philadelphia captures the easy fusion of literary, artistic, scientific, and ethnological studies which that pioneering association fostered. Sidney Hart's treatment of Charles Willson Peale's museum presents an even more incessant intersection of trades, crafts, art, science, and technology and insists brilliantly besides on the ingenious impresario's adamant rejection of every pretension to monopolies and mysteries in knowledge.

It is entirely possible that this demographic density made a milieu much more favorable to creativity than, say, the suburban seclusion in which we now live. It is quite likely that this cultural density encouraged a casual commingling of artistic, scientific, and technological pursuits and their practitioners across domains, which we in our present pride take to be deeply disparate. And it is in any case unbecoming in us to pronounce judgments of insularity on a community that promoted the fertile interaction of 50,000 people and more in a few square blocks, when it is we who live on the very half-acre lots that they disdained. It is bizarre for us to condescend to a scientific and literary culture that produced Benjamin Franklin.

Gough and others also emphasize the diversity within the influential elite of late eighteenth-century Philadelphia. Gough finds fascinating disjunctions between the city's leaders in economic, social, religious, and political life, and he traces these fissures as far back as the birth and education of the men who ultimately made their way into the upper echelons. Rosswurm is not keen to concede that the elite was never cohesive, but he is eager to aver that it was never cohesive for long. On his account, the successive ruling classes of the city were so far from perpetuating their power over the generations that none of them managed more than a decade of dominance. In the event, then—whether we follow Gough or Rosswurm—the urban gentry failed utterly to consolidate a corporate concern for its own welfare or its city's. It never achieved an assured hereditary hegemony in its own right, and it never defined a distinctive Philadelphian interest for which it presumed to speak.

Gough and Rosswurm set forth these findings as though they are exposing the defects of the eighteenth-century elite. I read the same findings rather differently. They seem to me susceptible of some striking inversions that might also furnish clues illuminating the enigmas of creativity.

Compare Philadelphia with Boston in these years. Boston was a city that still clung to a vestigial concern for cohesion. Its ideal image if not its actual experience of itself was still framed in social solidarity. Perhaps on that account it did not proliferate in this period the voluntary associations that were so clearly the carriers of cultural creativity in Franklin's Philadelphia. Such associations were predicated on pluralism. They conceded the impossibility of achieving communal unity, and they implicitly asserted the unnecessariness even of aspiring to it. Boston, a much more homogeneous city than Philadelphia in spite of its earlier origin and more extended evolution, did not develop the virtuosity in associational strategies that its younger rival did. Boston, a city managed by elites that more nearly maintained the cohesion that Gough and Rosswurm claim Philadelphia could not sustain, lacked the cultural, economic, and political vitality that its upstart adversary on the Delaware had.

Such comparisons surely suggest that an unsettled society and an incoherent elite—or, at any rate, a heterogeneous society and an incompletely consolidated elite—may provide a more propitious and energizing environment for achievement than a solidary state. Certainly Philadelphia outstripped Boston in the later eighteenth century and into the nineteenth. Certainly New York, with an even more pushing, pummeling, pluralistic culture, far outstripped both Philadelphia and Boston in the later nineteenth century and into the twentieth.

Indeed, I suspect that the very fragility and instability of the elite in eighteenth-century Philadelphia might have been a condition of its accomplishments. Gough, Rosswurm, and others stress the vulnerability of the city's leading men: their exposure to credit contractions, speculative manias, overextendedness, and the like. Might it be that this risk-driven, go-for-broke milieu made good ground for great achievement? After all, the heroic endeavors of the revolutionary generation were extravagantly audacious and altogether susceptible to ruination: in 1776 a rebellion against the mightiest military power on the face of the earth, in 1787 a veritable coup d'état against the very regime established by that rebellion. And in realms beyond politics, an identical daring appeared. Some of the great gamblers—Robert Morris, John Nicholson, John Fitch—went bust, but others—William Bartram, Oliver Evans, and Peale, to take just a few of whom we read in these essays—did not.

Environments marked by fleeting fortunes and sudden surges of wealth have often been supportive of cultural innovation. Think of the extraordinary architecture of Mobile, Natchez, and other boom towns of the cotton South in their brief moment in the nineteenth-century sun. Think of the entire panoply of cultural institutions endowed by the Gilded Age plutocrats and parvenus of New York, as they strove to signal their new social stature by their unprecedented patronage.[5]

Communities characterized by failure itself—at least by certain sorts of failure, beyond mere instability—may also be propitious for cultural creativity. Indeed, that possibility is for me the truly tantalizing one posed by the disjunction between the pieces presented by the social historians and those offered by the interpreters of artifacts in this collection.

The analysts of material culture do not doubt for a moment that Philadelphia in the age of Franklin was a focal point for all America, a center of influence and often of leadership in the arts as well as the crafts. Nancy Evans speaks explicitly of its saga as a "success story," and most of the others imply as much or take the city's preeminence as axiomatic. But such assumptions seem almost inexplicable in light of the treatment of the city's social history as it is charted here. The historians are so far from tracing a tale of triumph that their accounts may be taken as a kind of collaborative exposition of the second law of thermodynamics. In them everything falls apart. Everything tends to dissipation and dissolution. Nothing works, nothing lasts.

Yeats worried that the center could not hold. In the late eighteenth-century city that these social historians set forth, the peripheries do not hold either. The loftiest and the lowliest, the genteel and the slaves, the Quakers, the Methodists, and even the Jews, all experience decomposition, fission, fragmentation, and decline.

It is not easy to square such studies with the economic and demographic data, which show Philadelphia steadily the premier city in America in this period. It is not easy to reconcile them with other evidence in this collection of essays: on the one hand, the palpable ineptitude of the affluent to rule and the patent incompetence of the denominations even to keep themselves together; on the other, all those museums, scientific societies, and windsor chairs, all that botanic brilliance and domestic elegance.

One resolution would posit the very failures of the affluent and of all the forces of effective organization as contributing conditions of cultural efflorescence, insofar as they stimulated innovative performance and challenged innovating performers. On such a speculation, it would be only as Philadelphia came to have an authentic upper class, at the end of the nineteenth century—the Protestant establishment that Digby Baltzell discovered, congealing in its country clubs, lunching at its Union League, living off trust funds, perpetuating itself hereditarily in its Social Register, ensconced in its elite business sanctuaries, riding to hounds and running with beagles—that Philadelphia culture would become for the first time truly insular and truly torpid.[6]

Another resolution, and a rather more radical one, would simply deny any systematic relationship at all between culture and society or between culture and economy. It would warn that, if we expect steady and straightforward connections between the findings of the social historians and those of the students of culture, we are nurturing an inappropriate expectation. Cultural performances may be directly expressive of their society, but they may also be oblique to it. They may manifest social reality, but they may also mask it. To take but a single example of the way in which cultural forms can be facades for far different social formations, consider once more the nineteenth-century notion of New England as the intellectual hub of the nation if not the universe. This myth of New England was essentially invented in the years after the accession of Thomas Jefferson to the presidency; it was invented as a veneer to compensate the region for its socioeconomic decline and for the passage of power from the Federalists to the Republicans. Philadelphia endured no comparable decline in the decades after 1800—as Gough says, the new nation was going the acquisitive, pluralistic way in which Philadelphia had gone from the first—so Philadelphia never needed such a myth as cultural compensation.[7]

Yet another resolution, and probably at once the most conservative and the most demanding, would scorn both iconoclasm and nihilism. It would anticipate neither an inverse relationship nor a whimsical one between culture and society. Instead, it would postulate a multitude of microcosmic or partial relationships and seek to specify them in something of their fullness and interconnectedness. It would cease to speak of culture as an encompassing entity—and cease to suppose society utterly integrated as well—and would attempt to establish affinities between component cultures and constituent sectors of the society. It would abandon conventional conceptions of culture as unitary and attend more closely to the complex tensions and uneasy balances among ideals and interests in the community.

In truth, most of the essays in this volume do attend to such strains. There is more implicit accord between the disciplines on the desirability of disentangling the diverse strands and supports of new national culture than on anything else. And there is more substantive convergence too.

Schweitzer and Luke Beckerdite alike remind us that the economy of the Philadelphia region was marked by middling prosperity as much as by mercantile affluence and that the culture of the yeomen and artisans was therefore as consequential as that of the gentry. Dee Andrews and David Barquist both discover a culture contested by Americans who aspired to the most elevated standards of European sophistication and by other Americans who rhapsodized republican simplicity. In paper after paper, the social historians and the students of culture discern the same claimants on the conscience of the young Republic that Carl and Jessica Bridenbaugh did so many decades ago: one contingent unabashedly anglophilic, the other stridently chauvinistic; one cherishing urbanity and hierarchical authority, the other idealizing an egalitarian plainness and practicality.[8]

But several of these essays also go far beyond the Bridenbaughs, revealing arresting complexities and intricate ironies as they do. Evans traces the diffusion of elite taste into middle-class consumption and mass production and marketing, and she thereby undoes the very dichotomy of high and common culture on which her analysis depends. Rosswurm observes the attachment of the postrevolutionary leadership to notions of authority it identified with England, and he therein finds the source of that elite's undoing. Deborah Federhen studies producers and consumers of high-style furniture in the incendiary days of the Revolution, and she therewith uncovers a contradiction as fascinating as it is bewildering: ardent patriot Jonathan Gostelowe designed and executed his pieces primarily for Loyalists and others committed to maintaining the traditional social order, while Tory Thomas Affleck turned out his chests and cabinets for patrons who were partisans of the insurrection. Barquist develops his argument in the disputed ethical and aesthetic terrain between genteel extravagance and republican plainness—between desire to rival the Old World and determination to evolve an indigenous American outlook—and unveils a delicate dialectic in which both camps took their cues from British rather than from American thinkers and both camps betrayed their elitism in their expectation of instructing their inferiors in appropriate values. Robert Peck depicts Bartram as the quintessential child of New World nature, the epitome of the American, and he shows that the botanist's remarkable writings were much better appreciated in Europe than they were in his native land.

These paradoxes and conundrums beg further investigation and explication, not least because they cut across the cleavages between the historians and the scholars of culture. And the cleavages themselves equally beg elucidation because the discrepancies between the accounts they yield are so acute and so intriguing. These discrepancies will not be dissolved by pronouncing one side right and the other wrong. Both sides are surely right, at least in some degree. The question is, how?

All the contributors to this collection embraced the occasion for conversation between their own discipline and the other which had always seemed so near yet stood so far away. Yet the exciting thing about this collection is not that the conversation occurs, because it never quite does. The exciting thing is that the discrepancies intimated in these essays disclose a whole new range of questions that neither discipline is now asking and that nonetheless need to be asked. The exciting thing is that these discrepancies reveal some real reasons for the conversation to begin, and some real issues for it to begin about.

---

[1] Roger G. Kennedy, *Orders from France: The Americans and the French in a Revolutionary World, 1789–1820* (New York: Alfred A. Knopf, 1989); Richard C. Wade, *The Urban Frontier: The Rise of Western Cities, 1790–1830* (Cambridge: Harvard University Press, 1959).

[2] Jack D. Marietta, *The Reformation of American Quakerism, 1748–1783* (Philadelphia: University of Pennsylvania Press, 1984); Sydney V. James, *A People among Peoples: Quaker Benevolence in Eighteenth-Century America* (Cambridge: Harvard University Press, 1963).

[3] Thomas C. Cochran, *Frontiers of Change: Early Industrialism in America* (New York: Oxford University Press, 1981); Philip B. Scranton, *Proprietary Capitalism: The Textile Manufacture at Philadelphia, 1800–1885* (Cambridge, Eng., and New York: Cambridge University Press, 1983); Richard H. Shryock, "Philadelphia and the Flowering of New England: An Editorial," *Pennsylvania Magazine of History and Biography* 64, no. 3 (July 1940): 305–13.

[4] Thomas M. Doerflinger, *A Vigorous Spirit of Enterprise: Merchants and Economic Development in Revolutionary Philadelphia* (Chapel Hill: University of North Carolina Press, 1986); David Dauer, "Colonial Philadelphia's Intraregional Transportation System: An Overview," *Working Papers from the Regional Economic His-*

tory Research Center 2, no. 3 (1979): 1–16; Linda K. Salvucci, "Development and Decline: The Port of Philadelphia and Spanish Imperial Markets, 1783–1823" (Ph.D. diss., Princeton University, 1985).

[5] Roger G. Kennedy, *Architecture, Men, Women, and Money in America, 1600–1860* (New York: Random House, 1985); Neil Harris, *The Artist in American Society: The Formative Years, 1790–1860* (New York: George Braziller, 1966); Lillian B. Miller, *Patrons and Patriotism: The Encouragement of the Fine Arts in the United States, 1790–1860* (Chicago: University of Chicago Press, 1966).

[6] E. Digby Baltzell, *Philadelphia Gentlemen: The Making of a National Upper Class* (Glencoe, Ill.: Free Press, 1958); E. Digby Baltzell, *The Protestant Establishment: Aristocracy and Caste in America* (New York: Random House, 1964); but see John Lukacs, *Philadelphia, Patricians and Philistines, 1900–1950* (New York: Farrar, Straus, and Giroux, 1981).

[7] Michael Zuckerman, "Puritans, Cavaliers, and the Motley Middle," in *Friends and Neighbors: Group Life in America's First Plural Society*, ed. Michael Zuckerman (Philadelphia: Temple University Press, 1982), pp. 3–25.

[8] Carl Bridenbaugh and Jessica Bridenbaugh, *Rebels and Gentlemen: Philadelphia in the Age of Franklin* (New York: Reynal and Hitchcock, 1942).